WOMEN, PROPERTY, AND THE LETTERS OF THE LAW IN
EARLY MODERN ENGLAND

Women, Property, and the Letters of the Law in Early Modern England

EDITED BY

Nancy E. Wright
Margaret W. Ferguson
A.R. Buck

UNIVERSITY OF TORONTO PRESS
Toronto Buffalo London

© University of Toronto Press Incorporated 2004
Toronto Buffalo London
Printed in Canada

ISBN 0-8020-8757-4

Printed on acid-free paper

National Library of Canada Cataloguing in Publication

Women, property, and the letters of the law in early modern
England / edited by Nancy E. Wright, Margaret W. Ferguson,
A.R. Buck.

Includes bibliographical references and index.
ISBN 0-8020-8757-4

1. Women – Legal status, laws, etc. – England – History.   2. Right of
property – England – History.   3. Women – England – History – Modern
period, 1600–   4. Women – Legal status, laws, etc. – England – History –
Sources.   5. Right of property – England – History – Sources.
6. Women – England – History – Modern period, 1600– – Sources.
I. Wright, Nancy E.   II. Ferguson, Margaret W., 1948–   III. Buck, A.R.

KD811.W64 2004   305.42′0942′0903   C2003-907354-8

University of Toronto Press acknowledges the financial assistance to its
publishing program of the Canada Council for the Arts and the
Ontario Arts Council.

University of Toronto Press acknowledges the financial support for its
publishing activities of the Government of Canada through the
Book Publishing Industry Development Program (BPIDP).

Contents

Acknowledgments

This collection of essays, *Women, Property, and the Letters of the Law in Early Modern England,* unravels a number of common modern ideas about intellectual property, including the central notion of single authorial ownership of a certain textual object. It is therefore appropriate that the book itself is a collective production supported by several institutions and reflecting the labour of many individuals. The editors are grateful for the substantial material and intellectual help we have received from various sources.

The Australian Academy of the Humanities and the Law Foundation of New South Wales, through its Legal Scholarship Support Fund, generously provided funding for the publication of this book. So did Elizabeth Langland, Dean of the Humanities, Arts and Cultural Studies at the University of California, Davis, and the Centre for the Interdisciplinary Study of Property Rights at The University of Newcastle. Many of the chapters that follow originated in papers presented at the research colloquium 'Women and Property in Early Modern England' hosted by the Humanities Research Centre at the Australian National University and organized by Nancy Wright. We thank not only all those who participated in that colloquium but also Professor Iain McCalman, Director, Dr Caroline Turner, Deputy Director, and Leena Messina, Programs Manager, of the Humanities Research Centre for their support. We thank Professor Rosalind Atherton, Dean of the Division of Law at Macquarie University, for her support. We also wish to thank David Simpson for giving Margaret Ferguson time to travel to Australia and, subsequently, to participate in the shaping of this volume. We thank the writers of each of the following essays for their initial work of composition and research; their patience with a long process; and their willingness to revise for the common good. We thank Kathleen Haushalter and Anette Bremer for their research assistance. We also thank the scholars who read our manuscript for the University of Toronto Press; their suggestions enriched and refined our book. Finally, we thank Suzanne Rancourt, our editor at the University of Toronto Press. Barb Porter, our production editor, oversaw the book's transformation into a printed object with intelligence and tact; and James Leahy, our copy editor, contributed to the long labour of making individual essays into a unified book.

Chapter 6 originally appeared in *Shakespeare's Domestic Economies: Gender and Property in Early Modern England* by Natasha Korda © 2002 University of Pennsylvania Press. It is reprinted here by permission of the University of Pennsylvania Press.

WOMEN, PROPERTY, AND THE LETTERS OF THE LAW IN
EARLY MODERN ENGLAND

Introduction

NANCY E. WRIGHT WITH MARGARET W. FERGUSON

In 1766 William Blackstone advised his contemporaries: 'There is nothing which so generally strikes the imagination, and engages the affections of mankind, as the right of property; or that sole and despotic dominion which one man claims and exercises over the external things of the world, in total exclusion of the right of any other individual in the universe. And yet there are very few, that will give themselves the trouble to consider the original and foundation of this right' (1979, 2: 2). This is the beginning of a fascinating turn in Blackstone's discussion of the institution of property – a turn from analytical theory to narrative. Carol Rose argues that this turn to storytelling characterizes the work of many early modern theorists of property, including political theorists, such as Locke, and legal theorists, such as Blackstone. Both men begin their narratives by unfolding a story that begins with plenitude. In the *Second Treatise of Government* (1689/90), Locke traces a story 'beginning in a plenteous state of nature, carrying through the growing individual appropriation of goods, then proceeding to the development of a trading money economy, and culminating in the creation of government to safeguard property' (Rose 1994, 26). Blackstone in Book 2 of his *Commentaries on the Laws of England* describes human beings 'beginning in a state of plenty, gradually accumulating personal and landed property, and finally creating government and laws to protect property' (Rose 1994, 26). Both Locke and Blackstone, Rose emphasizes, were indifferent to the issue that these narratives were not accurate, factual histories. Instead they used narrative to provide a persuasive *post hoc* explanation for the peculiarities of the property regimes of their times and to valorize the ownership of individual private property, which bestowed legal agency and political subjectivity upon a minority of the population of England.

Theories that specifically address gender and women's property rights use narrative in a similar manner. A lesser-known treatise on early modern law and property, *The Lawes Resolutions of Womens Rights: or, The Lawes Provisions for Women* (1632), returns to the biblical accounts of the creation and the fall in Genesis in order to link present custom with an origin. This narrative about the origin of women's property rights begins not in a state of plenty but instead with a story of loss; in the third chapter of Genesis

> is declared our first parents transgression in eating the forbidden fruit: for which Adam, Eve, the serpent first, and lastly, the earth itselfe is cursed: and besides, the participation of Adams punishment, which was subjection to mortality, exiled from the garden of Eden, injoyned to labor, Eve because shee had helped to seduce her husband hath inflicted on her, an especiall bane; In sorrow shalt thou bring forth thy children thy desires shall bee subject to thy husband, and he shall rule over thee.
>
> See here the reason ... that Women have no voyse in Parliament, They make no Lawes, they consent to none, they abrogate none. All of them are understood either married or to bee married and their desires [are] subject to their husband. (1632, 6)

The integration of church and government in seventeenth-century England made this a persuasive narrative about the origins of women's legal disabilities within the property regime.[1] The property relationship that defined 'Baron and Feme' in common law was one for which the anonymous author of *The Lawes Resolutions* admitted, 'I know no remedy though some women can shift it well enough' (1632, 6). That acknowledgment, however, should direct our attention to alternatives to the well-known narrative about women's legal disabilities in the common law property regime of early modern England. Narratives about resourceful women who managed to 'shift' the boundaries placed upon them by legal disabilities indicate that the letter of the law was neither definitive nor irremediable. Factual narratives about their lived experiences as businesswomen and heiresses, for example, as well as their own and their contemporaries' writings tell different stories about their relationship to property. Attention has been turned to these narratives in the chapters that follow in *Women, Property, and the Letters of the Law in Early Modern England*.

Our project extends the important line of inquiry defined by Donna Dickenson in *Property, Women and Politics: Subjects or Objects?* (1997). Her political analysis outlines a narrative of property that constructs women as subjects of property and as political agents, a narrative through which women, now, can intervene to change the property regimes in which they live. We approach this timely concern by studying different competing narratives of property told by and about women as subjects and agents in commercial and domestic economies, and as objects shaped by a network of social and jural relationships based upon property in early modern England. These narratives confirm the contention of Carol Rose in *Property and Persuasion* (1994) that narratives produce societal constructions of property and rights. Rose argues that feminists must challenge dominant narratives in order to revise existing theorizations of individual, private property as the kind of tenure that most effectively maximizes productivity and satisfaction. The chapters that follow show how women and men in the early modern period undertook a similar task. Both women and men produced a variety of societal constructions that analysed different roles for women and constituted diverse models of property and ownership. Both their lived experience and writings provide answers to such questions as: What were the competing narratives of property circulating in early modern England? How did women contribute in their households, in courts, and in their writings to the cultural production of narratives about property? How do texts written by women, including business, familiar, and household letters, as much as works by noted authors, such as Shakespeare, position women as subjects and objects of property?

Scholars are most familiar with narratives about privileged married women, such as Elizabeth Cary. In 1602 her marriage to Sir Henry Cary, later viscount of Falkland, changed not only her social status but that of her father, a wealthy lawyer, and her husband; as Nancy Pearse comments, Elizabeth's marriage raised her father, Lawrence Tanfield, from middling status to the gentry just as her marriage portion 'raised Henry Cary from the gentry into the peerage' (1977, 602). Under the common law doctrine of coverture, Elizabeth Cary was a feme covert; her legal personality was merged with that of her husband, who held the use rights to her real property and the ownership of her personal property. She lost access to her future use rights of property specified in her marriage settlement when she agreed, in 1622, to allow fines to be passed on her jointure in order to obtain funds necessary for her husband to secure the position of Lord Deputy of Ireland. Subsequently, in 1626, when they became estranged, Henry stopped her allowance, removed their children and all but one servant from her, and demanded she return to her mother's home. Elizabeth's position within this network of property relationships exemplifies the concept of a woman as an object of property, a person whose legal disabilities deprive her of the legal agency and political subjectivity that property ownership conferred in early modern England.

The narrative of these events from Elizabeth's marriage and their similarity to those of other women of her time, such as Anne Clifford (and those of much later date, such as Caroline Norton) may too readily direct our attention away from the occasions when she and other women acted as a subject of property. It should be recognized that Elizabeth Cary did take a part that the law allowed her in mortgaging her jointure properties. Her signature indicating her consent to this transaction was necessary as jointure was a legal device intended to secure a married woman's legal and moral right to provision during her widowhood. Although we cannot ascertain whether she consented to this transaction freely or was coerced, Elizabeth, after her estrangement from Sir Henry, stated to Charles I in a letter dated 18 May 1626, 'Upon my lords goinge into Ireland, I was drawne, by seeinge his occasions, to offer my joynter into his handes, that he might sell, or mortgage it, for his supply' (*SP* 16 [Charles I] 63/89, 18 May 1627; cited from Lewalski 1993, 188). Elizabeth's explanation of her consent to the mortgage demonstrates the argument of Carol Rose that property and property rights 'are the means through which one may make choices about one's interactions with the world' (1994, 254). In this instance, it may seem that Elizabeth exercised her limited legal agency foolishly by choosing to 'sign away' her future property rights. Another understanding of her decision is one that she offers to the king; she acted in accordance with the duties and office of a wife by supplying her husband with the necessary means to fulfil an important public office.[2] That interaction, when narrated to the king, clearly constituted an understandable and acceptable role for Elizabeth – a role that, despite a married woman's legal disabilities, enabled her to exercise agency that secured a decree requiring her husband to provide for her maintenance. Her letter, quoted above, continued by explaining that the jointure

> beinge gone from mee, I have nothinge to trust to, hereafter, but my mothers bounty, at her death, for my father disinherited mee, onely, for resigninge my joynter ... I desire nothynge but a quiet life, and to reobtaine

my lords favour, which I have done nothynge to loose ... I beseech your majesty, to comand one of your secretarys, to send for [my lord's] agent, and to comand him ... [to] supply me weekely with [what is] ... necessary to support mee for victualls, houserent, and apparell. (*SP* 16 [Charles I] 63/ 89, 18 May 1627; cited from Lewalski 1993, 188)

The letter explains that, having cooperated to provide the means to 'supply' her husband with the requirements of a public office, he should reciprocate and 'supply' her with a home and funds for her maintenance not only in the present but also in the future. In this and other letters petitioning the king, Sir Edward Coke, and Sir Edward Conway, she used narrative and its potential to explain and persuade as a means to constitute for herself the role of a married woman with specific entitlements based upon the real and chattel property that her marriage brought to her husband. Her letters, as Lewalski explains, secured a Privy Council decision that she reside in a house provided by her mother, receive £500 a year from her husband's estate, and immediately receive from him funds for her needs (1993, 187–8). Elizabeth's composition of a narrative about her role as a wife whose 'proper' conduct entitled her to specific property rights persuaded the king and his councillors that her claim was relevant and should be taken seriously.

This narrative that she wrote about her relationship to property was, of course, possible because of her exceptional literacy skills – skills that not all women in early modern England commanded. But her very different use of those skills to 'sign away' her jointure rights, to compose and sign persuasive letters, and to write translations and original works of drama and historiography indicate why scholars investigating women's property relationships must extend their field of study beyond the evidence provided by common law rules, legal doctrines, case law, and well-known narratives about women's legal disabilities. Elizabeth Cary's representation of coverture within *The Tragedy of Mariam, The Fair Queen of Jewry* illustrates not only her knowledge of property law (Travitsky 1987) but more importantly, we argue, her ability to constitute new narratives that problematized women's roles within a property regime. It is upon narratives about property rights and ownership written by women in a variety of genres including letters, chronicles, and wills that many chapters in this book base their studies of women and property in early modern England.

Historical narratives about women's relationships to property often have 'origins' quite unlike those told by the anonymous author of *The*

Lawes Resolutions of Womens Rights. In the years surrounding the English civil war, for example, the property relationships of wealthy married women on occasion changed although their legal standing did not. Memoirs and letters record narratives about the roles played by wives when their husbands' estates had been sequestered by Parliament. Sir Roger Twysden of Roydon, whose estates were sequestered in the early 1640s, relied upon Lady Isabella, his wife, whom he described as 'a wise and temperate solicitrix' (Twysden 1861, 4: 147), to recover the family property. As Christopher Durston has documented, she successfully argued their case and engaged in jurisdictional disputes between the parliamentary composition committee at the Goldsmiths' Hall and the local sequestration committee in order to secure the family's estate (1989, 104). Similarly, Lady Ann, wife to Sir Richard Fanshawe, travelled to England from the Channel Islands alone in 1646 to initiate composition proceedings and secured money needed for their maintenance (Halkett and Fanshawe 1981, 119). In a letter to her son, Lady Ann confided that 'this was the first time that I had taken any journey without your father, and the first manage of business hee ever put into my hand' (Halkett and Fanshawe 1981, 119). The role of 'solicitrix' was a novel experience that she shared with other married women, like Margaret Cavendish, the Duchess of Newcastle, who witnessed women effectively performing as 'pleaders, attornies, petitioners and the like' (1886, 304), when their Royalist husbands incurred political and legal disabilities because they had been dispossessed of property.[3] The agency that women exercised in such roles, in relation to both law and property, was limited and temporary but nonetheless requires analysis and explanation if we are to understand the diverse consequences of property law for women in early modern England.

Indeed the role of the 'solicitrix' performed by women with the consent of their husbands around the time of the English civil war invites comparison with Tim Stretton's detailed account of 'women waging law' throughout the sixteenth century in England. According to the letter of the law, a feme sole or singlewoman, either never married or widowed,[4] had access to the law as a 'forum of action' in a manner denied a married woman, who, because of the common law doctrine of coverture, was dissociated from ownership of property and agency derived from litigation in courts of law.[5] Stretton draws our attention to the fact that according to the letter of the law, coverture

> made it impossible for married women, *femes covert*, to enter contracts or to assert or defend their rights in court, except with the consent and assis-

tance of their husbands. A woman who married lost her surname, her right to choose where she lived, her right to legal protection against her husband (except in the most extreme cases) and her ability to own property ... A married woman could not independently inherit legacies, nor could she accept gifts, even from her husband. She could not make a will without her husband's agreement, and any existing will and testament became invalid on the day of her marriage. (1998, 22–3)

Stretton's study of litigation in the Court of Requests, however, indicates many married women 'waged law' with the assistance and support of their husbands, brothers, and fathers. Although they could not act independently of their male relatives, married women with assistance and cooperation of men in their families did obtain access to the courts and the law.[6]

Women pursued litigation using various laws that regulated property ownership – common law, customary law, ecclesiastical law, and equity. Requests was a conciliar court that heard petitions from the poor and offered redress for causes concerning property. It dealt primarily with civil cases concerning property issues, such as enclosure, rack rents, and tenants' rights. The Court of Requests offered a venue for litigating cases involving the rights of tenants who held their land by the custom of the manor. Such cases were often heard not only in the Court of Requests but also in a manorial court or customary court run by the lord of the manor or his bailiff (Hand and Bentley 1977, 21–3). The customary law administered by manorial courts varied from locality to locality (Staves 1990, 20) but could be challenged in King's Bench and the Court of Common Pleas, two of the common law courts that dealt with actions over property (Baker 1979, 34–48; Holdsworth 1923, 1: 35, 195; Kenyon 1966, 149–50). King's Bench and Common Pleas 'handled a wide variety of litigation based on claims of legal estates or interests in both real and personal property, claims including trespass, ejectment, widows' claims of dower in their husbands' lands, debt and conversion' (Staves 1990, 21). Chancery, known by the Tudor period as a 'court of conscience,' corrected the extremity or 'rigour' of the law (Baker 1979, 83–100; Cioni 1985; Holdsworth 1923, 1: 319; Kenyon 1966, 151). As Staves has explained, Chancery during the eighteenth century played an important role in litigation of property cases involving trusts in the development of married women's separate property or separate maintenance contracts (Staves 1990, 175–6). Church courts, such as the bishop of London's Consistory Court, were an ecclesiastical jurisdiction that dealt with many matters, including probate as well as correction of the morals of the laity.

As Ingram (1987) and Gowing (1996) have shown, in the sixteenth and seventeenth centuries women litigants found the consistory courts an accessible arena for litigation that indirectly affected their property relationships.

The chapters that follow construct narratives about women and property in early modern England that challenge the assumption that canonical legal theory or rules of property law adequately describe women's lived experience within a property regime. By constructing conversations across the disciplinary boundaries of legal theory, legal and social history, sociology, and literary criticism, this book explores a diverse range of women's property relationships. Our research has been informed by recent, innovative legal and economic histories. Studies contained in *Early Modern Conceptions of Property* (Brewer and Staves 1995) direct attention to the social, legal, economic, and political contexts that produced various forms of individual, private property – not only real property in freehold land but also property in persons and property in literary texts. Using different disciplinary perspectives, studies in *Early Modern Conceptions of Property* perceptively address the question 'To what extent, and in what contexts, did ownership of private property confer personal autonomy and liberty?' Answers to this question note that jural relationships between people constituted by private property have multiple and conflicting consequences. Liberal capitalist theory, which posits that private property endows an individual with the means to exercise will or liberty, does not adequately theorize the consequences of property. Another result of absolute private property is that 'one person's property rights ... impose burdens on another person, and so invariably restrict freedom for some while creating it for others' (Gordon 1995, 95–110), an apt description, many legal historians and feminists have argued, of the consequences not only of primogeniture, which ensured the transfer of property between eldest males of each generation, but also of the common law doctrine of coverture.

In *Law, Land and Family: Aristocratic Inheritance in England, 1300 to 1800* (1993), Eileen Spring studies the consequences for women of the transmission of property between generations by means of primogeniture and marriage settlements. Spring's legal history about inheritance practices answers the question 'How did the common law rules of inheritance, which recognized the rights of a female heir-general before those of a collateral male, fall into abeyance?' Spring's study of social elites, that is, the landed aristocracy and gentry, traces not only changes in inheritance practices but also the rise of legal devices – the entail, the use, and the strict settlement – that eroded women's common law property right of dower. The narrative that she constructs traces the decline of women's common law property rights effected by means of landowners' practices in the early modern period.

Spring's narrative, as some scholars have argued, is controversial. A different perspective is offered by Susan Staves (1995, 194–218), who places the story of female heirs in the context of other family members, particularly younger male siblings whose lives and life stories were also shaped by landholders' inheritance practices. In eighteenth-century England, the period studied by Staves, the eldest male child's inheritance of real property, she explains, did not entirely deprive female children or younger males of the means to access liberty and agency that liberal theory associates with private property. Instead their parents' marriage settlement made provisions for female and younger male siblings not to 'own' but instead to 'share' in the benefits of family property. Legal devices within a marriage settlement, made prior to a marriage, determined future provisions, not only maintenance for a wife but also portions for then unborn female and younger male children. Both women and men, Staves reminds us, experienced inequalities within the distribution of family property. Indeed, inequalities based on criteria other than gender, Staves emphasizes, were fostered by the English state, which placed peculiar limitations on the testamentary freedom of Catholic and Jewish fathers by enabling a sibling who converted to Protestantism to displace claims of an elder male sibling who did not. Taking a cue from Staves's perception, the chapters that follow within *Women, Property, and the Letters of the Law* examine how daughters' and widows' tactics for responding to landholders' inheritance practices intervened in the decline of women's property rights described by Spring.

Barbara J. Harris, in *English Aristocratic Women, 1450–1550: Marriage and Family, Property and Careers* (2002), also evaluates how marriage settlements complement primogeniture within a series of related social systems that ensured patriarchal 'institutions and expectations remained securely intact throughout the Yorkist and early Tudor periods' (Harris 2002, 8). Both dower and jointure assigned a widow life rights in her husband's land rather than title to or inheritance rights in it. During their widowhood, however, women wielded significant control over their husbands' lands. Most widows, Harris documents, competently administered huge amounts of real and personal property as their husbands' executors and their children's guardians because as wives they had participated in managing family estates. Harris's study addresses the question 'Is there a disjunction between aristocratic women's apparent power, authority and control of resources, particularly property, and the patriarchal institutions that framed their lives?' She concludes, 'the contradiction between aristocratic women's interests as members of the ruling elite and a subordinated gender' encouraged them to develop 'networks centred on their mothers, daughters, sisters, aunts, and nieces' (Harris 2002, 9). Evidence of these networks can be found in the wills of widows, who distributed property among female relatives from their 'multiple' families. Rather than dissociating women from control of real and chattel property, Harris argues, their 'careers' as wives prepared aristocratic widows to administer property and benefit their families, meaning both their natal family and the multiple families into which they were integrated by marriage and remarriage.

In *Married Women's Separate Property in England, 1660–1833* (1990), Staves examines the consequences of different, competing legal rules – rules of common law and equity – upon women's entitlements. When examining the question 'What relation did ideology have to changes in the law of property?' Staves directs our attention to the practices not only of property owners but also of the judiciary and conveyancers, who limited contract law and theory that, in the mid-eighteenth century, secured specific property rights for married women. Evidence drawn from equity cases enables Staves to demonstrate how judges exercised discretion and applied legal principles selectively in order to ensure, despite contract law entitling married women to pin money, jointure, and separate maintenance, that property continued to be transmitted between men in order to secure patriarchal social structures. New legal rules, like the old, she argues, facilitated 'the transmission of significant property from male to male' while ensuring 'a level of basic protection for women and young children' (1990, 221). Within such a property regime, women did not exercise agency as theorized by liberals; women, in Staves's words, enjoyed 'entitlement to profit from capital, but not control over capital itself or the power to alienate capital' (1990, 222). Married women's experiences, however, did vary within the property regime of early modern England. In contrast to women of elite landed status (discussed by Staves and Harris), married women of middling sort in some regions were admitted to a customary estate as the tenants or as joint tenants with their husbands. This practice, as the chapter by Christine Churches explains, secured to a wife 'a capital asset which would yield an income after her husband's death.'

Amy Louise Erickson's economic history *Women and Property in Early*

Modern England (1993) answers the question 'What is the relationship between law and practice?' by constructing from probate documents and legal records of suits about marriage settlements patterns of property ownership and property transfer between 'ordinary men and women.' Erickson explains that the narrative about property relationships among the social elites who owned landed property on a large scale differed from the narrative of the lives of 'ordinary people.' She shows that among the majority of the population primogeniture was not the customary practice of inheritance. Instead, she argues, 'When it came to distributing the patrimony, fathers normally gave their daughters shares comparable in value with those of their brothers, although girls usually inherited personal property and boys more often real property' (1993, 19). When evaluating the consequences of coverture, Erickson notes the 'ingenuity of many ordinary women in working within a massively restrictive system. Individually, they registered their collective disagreement with the principles of inheritance and marital property laws' (1993, 19). It is through study of women not only of the social elites, that is, the landed aristocracy and gentry, but also of 'ordinary' women, members of the commons or the lower sort, that Erickson contributes greatly to our understanding of the range of narratives about women's property relationships.

Recent research has revealed fissures in our knowledge about women's property relationships within a regime characterized by competing jurisdictions, diverse systems of tenure, and multiple concepts of property. *Women, Property, and the Letters of the Law* turns to these points of departure for the study of women's legal status and property relationships in the early modern period. Part One, 'Credit, Commerce, and Women's Property Relationships,' examines the roles of women within property relationships forged not simply by legal rules but also by discourses of commerce, contract, and credit. Patricia Parker examines the extensive lexicon of commerce and contract law in the late Shakespearean play *The Winter's Tale*. Metaphors of gestation, pregnancy, and the delivery of 'issue' are part of the commercial language of the play that relates usury as an economic practice 'of growth and increase' to lending on the basis of 'credit,' meaning belief and trust in one's neighbours. The relation of women and gestation to the discourses of commerce and contract in the play provides insight into what Craig Muldrew calls 'the culture of credit and social relations in early modern England' (1998).

Women's vital roles in the commercial life of the port of Whitehaven during the seventeenth century are revealed in the chapter by Christine

Churches. She draws upon an archive of letters about the estate of Sir John and James Lowther to show how single and married women within this local economy figured in colliery and harbour management and family businesses. Extensive documentation is available for the study of women's property ownership within the locality of Whitehaven because, within that fast-growing port in the seventeenth century, property was often held by customary tenure, which enabled a married woman to inherit. In such cases a woman became the tenant, not her husband. Churches's chapter, like those that follow in this section, turns our attention to the plurality of laws and jurisdictions that, in the early modern period, could potentially come to bear in disputes about property. Tenants – both women and men – resorted to not only manorial courts but also Common Pleas and King's Bench when disputes about customary tenures arose. David Lemmings's research on the consistory courts, in which women of middling and lower sorts could defend their sexual reputation or 'propriety' in order to secure their marital or marriageable status, evaluates the reasons for the decline of these ecclesiastical courts during the period 1689 to 1791, despite the legal redress these courts offered to 'ordinary' women who could not afford to pursue suits in equity. He provides insight into changes within the legal system that affected women's access to courts.

Property and 'propriety' had resonance not only for women who wished to defend their sexual honour, but also for prostitutes, who are the subject of Laura Rosenthal's chapter. It is from Roman law that early modern England derived 'language in which "property" – that which you owned – and "propriety" – that which pertained or was proper to a person or situation – were interchangeable terms' (Pocock 1985, 104). The term propriety is a measure of the subtle difference of two concepts of property: the first, a political concept that related civic virtue to landed estates, a form of property that secured an individual's autonomy, which was assumed to be necessary for virtuous political activity; and the second, a jurisprudential concept that defined relationships between people and things as rights, such as ownership, that facilitated exchange and transfer of property that could change one's 'propriety' or status (Pocock 1985, 104). Rosenthal analyses popular biographies of the notorious prostitute Sally Salisbury; these challenge any easy differentiation of the two theories of property and the social values that rest upon them. The discourses of property, commerce, and contract, Rosenthal contends, enabled Sally Salisbury to articulate ideas of ownership of, and property in, the body, and to defy gendered concepts of honour and credit.

Mary Murray introduces Part Two, 'Women, Social Reproduction, and Patrilineal Inheritance,' by arguing that a new theorization may assist in conceptualizing social practices of inheritance in medieval and early modern England. Inheritance and marriage, as anthropologist Jack Goody (1976) has explained, are usually analysed as the mechanisms by which society reproduces itself by transmitting property from generation to generation. Murray posits that changing attitudes to death are a factor to be considered when analysing changes in inheritance practices, such as the ascendancy of primogeniture, which, in the Middle Ages, had been only one custom among many. She argues that we may more fully understand the symbolic significance of primogeniture, an inheritance practice of the landed elites, if we theorize it as a resurrective practice that emphasized patrilineage in order to confer immortality upon a community and its members.

How changing concepts of property and practices of inheritance affected the relationship of members of a community – not only fathers, sons, and daughters but also 'the poor' and the parish – are the subject of subsequent chapters in this section. Natasha Korda analyses the pre-Reformation setting of Shakespeare's *Measure for Measure* as an indication of his society's perception of placeless singlewomen as a threat to an economy burdened with responsibility for provisioning the poor. With the Reformation, monastic 'charity' was secularized at the moment that female religious found themselves not only displaced from cloisters but often without opportunity to marry. Particular 'cultural anxieties associated with the figure of the propertyless and propertied singlewoman,' a category that includes both never-married women and widows, differed by degrees. Both, Korda argues, were perceived as threats to the patrilineal property regime of early modern England. Her argument is borne out by case studies of two wealthy heiresses, Elizabeth Wiseman and Lady Anne Clifford, in a chapter by Mary Chan and Nancy E. Wright. Elizabeth Wiseman, a widow with an inheritance of £20,000, did not have a simple understanding of her inheritance; she assumed that it did not endow her with property rights or wealth to exercise simply on her own behalf but instead on behalf of her family and its honour. At the heart of this family conflict, like that involving Anne Clifford, was the heiress's assumption that neither her inheritance nor her property rights should be reduced simply to a commodified asset.

Commodified understandings of real and personal property during the seventeenth century were of consequence to the reproduction of the social system. The discourses of commerce and contract, discussed in

Part One, had impact upon understandings of real property and the rights it bestowed upon owners. The great landowners of early modern England, such as the Cliffords, like their medieval forebears, held an understanding of real or landed property based on its 'value' as a means to secure their status. Legal devices, such as the entail and the strict settlement, impeded the alienation of land in order to secure the land–family nexus. Although in the later seventeenth century land continued to be the primary source of status for social elites, during this period they pursued new methods of agriculture that required capital in order to improve and more fully exploit land. Legal developments after the Restoration, as A.R. Buck explains, protected aristocratic estates by preventing fraudulent transactions and preserving legitimate titles. These ideas about aristocratic property and their consequences for women, he argues, circulate within Nahum Tate's *King Lear*, in which Cordelia lives not to inherit her family's estate in her own right but instead to serve as the conduit to transmit a legitimate title to lands from her father to her husband.

The chapters in Part Three, 'Women's Authorship and Ownership: Matrices for Emergent Ideas of Intellectual Property,' undertake reevaluation of selfhood conceived of as the 'property' of an autonomous individual. Modern discourses of autonomy and individual private property stand in an uneasy relationship to texts written by women during the sixteenth, seventeenth, and early eighteenth centuries, before the historical emergence (in the nineteenth century) of a coherent or consistent law defining and regulating intellectual (including literary) property. Prior to 1710, indeed, a written work in manuscript or print was not, under English law, property owned by an author – and this fact should inform our approach to women's writings of the period. Jennifer Summit argues, for instance, that when 'read within the communal structures of the early modern household, women's letters do not offer autobiographies of individual selves so much as they do maps of relationships that extend outward into broader social and textual networks.' And yet, as Summit also shows, women's letter writing emerges as a female 'accomplishment,' subject to artifice and tightly bound up with women's perception of their 'selves' as subjects and objects of property.

Lloyd Davis studies how wills, an important genre in which early modern women wrote or dictated, were shaped by and, in turn, shaped interpersonal, familial, and social relationships. Wills, he argues, provide an important means to study both 'elite and ordinary women's involvement in producing texts, entering discourse, and representing themselves.' As a genre, the will obliges historians and literary critics to appreciate the complex relation of written words to concepts such as authorial intention and the individual voice because, of course, the genre contains formulaic phrases and a will was usually written and transcribed by a clerk rather than the testator. The female testator's voice and identity 'do not exist separately from a network of relationships between people, objects and entitlements.' Nonetheless, Davis proposes that we measure women's wills as evidence of their 'social identity in action.' Bequests given to daughters and friends by other women indicate that they did associate ideas of identity not only with small items of personal property but also with the activity of producing a text such as a will.

And as other essays in this section demonstrate, many early modern women of middling and elite backgrounds, even those occupying such a rigorously 'self-less' place as the Benedictine convent at Cambrai, did articulate complex ideas about ownership in relation to texts – their own and others. The community of nuns discussed by Claire Walker renounced all right to inherit the property of their secular kin or to own property individually; but when a dispute over a set of manuscripts by their spiritual leader Augustine Baker arose in 1655, these nuns asserted a right to 'spiritual property' in the manuscripts that in some ways resembles later concepts of rights to 'intellectual property.' Religious communities of seventeenth-century women, such as the Benedictines, had sophisticated understandings of their shared use rights in communal property. Walker studies female religious, who willingly embraced vows of poverty that, she explains, must be understood as part of a communal property regime. That regime provided members of the community with use rights in diverse properties, which included 'personal' letters as well as books and convent buildings. Their complex theorization of 'property rights' emerges most forcefully from the community's adamant claim to be the owners of manuscripts about their method of spiritual meditation – a claim to ownership based on ideas of their part in its collaborative or communal authorship. Some years before and after the legal appearance of the first copyright statute in 1710, then, literate women were actively participating in cultural disputes about what property was and in whose name it could be secured, alienated, and/or transmitted to posterity.

The asymmetries of gender in relation to property are the subject of chapters by Eleanor Shevlin and Paul Salzman. In her study of female surnames in the titles of eighteenth-century fiction, Shevlin notes that in this period personal names became 'increasingly important as signs of the personal property one has in one's self' while at the same time names retained their traditional significance 'as signs of status and markers of landed property.' Shevlin studies some of the ways in which naming practices in novels illuminate changing social, economic, and political connections among gender, marriage, and property. Paul Salzman analyses the ways in which two wealthy women writers, Margaret Cavendish and Lady Anne Clifford, evince an idea of ownership of their material texts through their habits of overseeing the production of, and personally annotating, copies of their writing. They do not regard their books simply as commodities, Salzman shows, but they certainly attempt to control their books' reception at the hands of future readers, including, in Clifford's case, her female heirs stretching across generations. And when Cavendish deploys the old metaphor of the book as a child, it acquires new meanings, as a matrix for modern ideas about intellectual property – property of the mind – because Cavendish is highly aware of the tensions that exist between her status as the (childless) second wife of a gentleman and her status as a writer who sought to control her texts' reception by 'embodying' her readers in her books. The tension between a woman's role as wife under the doctrine of coverture and her roles – actual or imagined – as a subject of property informs the (quite different) practices of Cavendish and Clifford. Read as a whole, this section dramatizes Raymond Williams's argument that cultural critics need to attend to both 'emergent' and 'residual' strands in a society's ideas about a key concept such as property; the essays in this section also suggest, however, that gender matters, perhaps more than has been generally allowed, in the critical determining of what is 'emergent' and what is not.

Research in the fields of English property law and property theory has produced a vast scholarship, from medieval treatises by Glanvill and Bracton to polemics of the late twentieth century by specialists in law and economics. Much of the scholarship that pertains to the early modern period, however, assumes that women cannot be theorized as subjects of property and, as a result, are not subjects for research. As notable and perceptive a scholar as J.G.A. Pocock dismisses women as subjects of early modern political and legal theories of property with the comment 'not until Mary Wollstonecraft do we encounter a thinker systematically interested in adding "she" to this context' (1985, 103). His firm assumption is confirmed by works and authors of canonical legal theory but called into question by important but neglected texts such as the 1735 treatise *The Hardships of the English Laws in Relation to Wives ... in a Humble address to the Legislature.*[7] This is only one of many neglected sources that belong to the field of 'legal literature' about women's property relationships. The chapters that follow employ not only legal treatises and case law that conform with the modern disciplinary definition of legal literature but also extralegal materials including works of literature and familiar letters. This variety of genres provides new insight into narratives concerning property relationships told by and about women of different social statuses in early modern England. These draw to our attention the meaning of Blackstone's words 'There is nothing which so generally strikes the *imagination,* and engages the *affections* of mankind, as the right of property' ([1766] 1979, 2: 2; emphasis added). Like case studies of women's lived experience, well-known plays by Shakespeare and familiar letters written by women reveal a variety of roles that women performed in what Donna Dickenson describes as the 'theatre of property' (1997, 30).

Notes

1 Almond (1999, 104–7) notes that Sir Robert Filmer's *Patriarcha: or, The Natural Right of Kings* (written c. 1630, printed 1680) also makes use of the narrative of the fall in order to explain the social and political order as well as property relationships.

2 On the early modern concept of an office and its relation to duty and rights see Condren (1997).

3 Blackstone explains: 'A woman indeed may be attorney for her husband; for that implies no separation from, but is rather a representation of, her lord' (1979, 1: 430).

4 Bennett and Froide (1999) use the compound term 'singlewomen' to describe both women who never married and widows.

5 Dickenson explains that coverture was not typical of Continental civil law jurisdictions: 'In contrast to coverture, the Continental doctrine of community of property in civil law jurisdictions recognizes the wife's economic contribution to the marriage. There is some implication under community of property that marriage is an equal partnership. Each spouse retains all property acquired before marriage, and any property inherited during marriage; but the earnings of each spouse, plus all other non-inherited property acquired during marriage, become the couple's "community" or joint property. However, under community of property, the husband has the

right to control and manage such joint ownings' (1997, 84–5). For discussion of different customs affecting marital property on the Continent see Howell (1998, 29–34).

6 Compare the analysis of coverture and its consequences in Mendelson and Crawford (1998, 38–42) and Korda (2001). Other studies of courts to which women had access include Cioni (1985), Gowing (1996), and Ingram (1987).

7 See Todd (1998) on this treatise and other chapters in Smith (1998).

Works Cited

Almond, Philip C. 1999. *Adam and Eve in Seventeenth-Century Thought.* Cambridge: Cambridge University Press.

Baker, J.H. 1979. *An Introduction to English Legal History.* 2nd ed. London: Butterworths.

Bennett, Judith M., and Amy M. Froide, eds. 1999. *Singlewomen in the European Past, 1250–1800.* Philadelphia: University of Pennsylvania Press.

Blackstone, William. [1765–9] 1979. *Commentaries on the Laws of England,* ed. A.W.B. Simpson. 4 vols. Facsimile ed. Chicago: University of Chicago Press.

Brewer, John, and Susan Staves, eds. 1995. *Early Modern Conceptions of Property.* London: Routledge.

Cary, Elizabeth. 1994. *The Tragedy of Mariam, The Fair Queen of Jewry, with The Lady Falkland Her Life By One of Her Daughters,* ed. Barry Weller and Margaret W. Ferguson. Berkeley: University of California Press.

Cavendish, Margaret. 1886. *The Life of William Cavendish, Duke of Newcastle,* ed. C.H. Firth. London: J.C. Nimmo.

Cioni, Maria. 1985. *Women and Law in Elizabethan England with Particular Reference to the Court of Chancery.* New York: Garland.

Condren, Conal. 1997. Liberty of Office and Its Defence in Seventeenth-Century Political Argument. *History of Political Thought* 18.3: 460–82.

Dickenson, Donna. 1997. *Property, Women and Politics: Subjects or Objects?* Cambridge: Polity Press.

Durston, Christopher. 1989. *The Family in the English Revolution.* Oxford: Basil Blackwell.

Erickson, Amy Louise. 1993. *Women and Property in Early Modern England.* London: Routledge.

Goody, Jack. 1976. Introduction to *Family and Inheritance: Rural Society in Western Europe, 1200–1800,* ed. Jack Goody, Joan Thirsk, and E.P. Thompson, 1–9. Cambridge: Cambridge University Press.

Gordon, Robert W. 1995. Paradoxical Property. In *Early Modern Conceptions of Property*, ed. John Brewer and Susan Staves, 95–110. London: Routledge.

Gowing, Laura. 1996. *Domestic Dangers: Women, Words and Sex in Early Modern London*. Oxford: Clarendon Press.

Halkett, Lady Anne, and Lady Ann Fanshawe. 1979. *The Memoirs of Anne, Lady Halkett and Ann, Lady Fanshawe*, ed. J. Loftis. Oxford: Clarendon Press.

Hand, G.J., and D.J. Bentley, eds. 1977. *Radcliffe and Cross The English Legal System*. 6th ed. London: Butterworths.

Harris, Barbara J. 2002. *English Aristocratic Women, 1450–1550: Marriage and Family, Property and Careers*. Oxford: Oxford University Press.

Holdsworth, W.S. 1923. *A History of English Law*. 3rd ed. 17 vols. London: Methuen.

Howell, Martha C. 1998. *The Marriage Exchange: Property, Social Place, and Gender in Cities of the Low Countries, 1300–1550*. Chicago: University of Chicago Press.

Ingram, Martin. 1987. *Church Courts, Sex and Marriage in England, 1570–1640*. Cambridge: Cambridge University Press.

Kenyon, J.P. 1996. *The Stuart Constitution 1603–1688*. Cambridge: Cambridge University Press.

Korda, Natasha. 2001. 'Judicious Oeillades': Supervising Marital Property in *The Merry Wives of Windsor*. In *Marxist Shakespeares*, ed. Jean Howard and S. Shershow, 82–103. Routledge: London.

The Lawes Resolutions of Womens Rights: or, The Lawes Provisions for Women. 1632.

Lewalski, Barbara Keifer. 1993. *Writing Women in Jacobean England*. Cambridge: Harvard University Press.

Mendelson, Sara, and Patricia Crawford. 1998. *Women in Early Modern England 1550–1720*. Oxford: Clarendon Press.

Muldrew, Craig. 1998. *The Economy of Obligation: The Culture of Credit and Social Relations in Early Modern England*. London: Macmillan.

Pearse, Nancy Cotton. 1977. Elizabeth Cary, Renaissance Playwright. *Texas Studies in Literature and Language* 18: 601–8.

Pocock, J.G.A. 1985. *Virtue, Commerce and History*. Cambridge: Cambridge University Press.

Rose, Carol. 1994. *Property and Persuasion: Essays on the History, Theory, and Rhetoric of Ownership*. Boulder: Westview Press.

Smith, Hilda L., ed. 1998. *Women Writers and the Early Modern British Political Tradition*. Cambridge: Cambridge University Press.

SP State Papers.

Spring, Eileen. 1993. *Law, Land and Family: Aristocratic Inheritance in England, 1300 to 1800*. Chapel Hill: University of North Carolina Press.

Staves, Susan. 1990. *Married Women's Separate Property in England, 1660–1833.* Cambridge: Harvard University Press.

– 1995. Resentment or Resignation? Dividing the Spoils among Daughters and Younger Sons. In *Early Modern Conceptions of Property,* ed. John Brewer and Susan Staves, 194–218. London: Routledge.

Stretton, Tim. 1998. *Women Waging Law in Elizabethan England.* Cambridge: Cambridge University Press.

Todd, Barbara. 1998. 'To Be Some Body': Married Women and *The Hardships of the English Laws.* In *Women Writers and the Early Modern British Political Tradition,* ed. Hilda L. Smith, 343–61. Cambridge: Cambridge University Press.

Travitsky, Betty. 1987. The *Feme Covert* in Elizabeth Cary's *Mariam.* In *Ambiguous Realities: Women in the Middle Ages and Renaissance,* ed. Carole Levin and Jeanie Watson, 184–96. Detroit: Wayne State University Press.

Twysden, Sir Roger. 1861. Sir Roger Twysden's Journal. *Archaeologia Cantiana.* 4: 131–202.

Williams, Raymond. 1977. *Marxism and Literature.* Oxford: Oxford University Press.

Part One

Credit, Commerce, and Women's Property Relationships

1

Temporal Gestation, Legal Contracts, and the Promissory Economies of *The Winter's Tale*

PATRICIA PARKER

The Winter's Tale, like other Shakespeare plays, exploits an extraordinary number of contractual, commercial, and legal terms. This is not surprising, given the interrelation of market and theatre in early modern England (see Bruster 1992; Dillon 2000). Jean-Christophe Agnew has argued that the problem of credibility, 'representation and misrepresentation' (1986, 11) foregrounded by the public theatre in the period was shared by the market economy. According to Craig Muldrew, rapid economic change, the expansion of consumption, and the increasing complexity of marketing structures contributed to a culture of credit, which redefined community as 'a conglomeration of competing but interdependent households which had to trust one another.' Both individuals and households were linked 'through trust in the credit of others in the face of increased competition and disputes' (1998, 4). The word 'credit' itself, as explained by Muldrew and by Lorna Hutson (1994), was becoming part of a new economy of promises and representations, even as it retained the older social and ethical dimension derived from Latin *credo*, related to belief or trust. This chapter will consider the late Shakespeare play *The Winter's Tale* (as well as the role of female figures within it) in relation to what Muldrew (1998) calls 'the culture of credit and social relations in early modern England' and the temporal trajectory that combines gestation or pregnancy with a series of contractual, commercial, and legal terms. This chapter thus shares with others in this section an interest in understanding the concept of credit in early modern England.

The Winter's Tale, I will argue, explores the multiple dimensions of 'credit' and credibility, grafting a new lexicon of commercial and legal terms onto its romance plot of separation and 'return.' In the opening or 'winter' half of the play, Leontes (king of Sicilia), convinced even against the oracle of Delphi that his pregnant wife has committed adultery with his boyhood friend Polixenes (king of Bohemia), consequently loses his son Mamillius to death and his wife Hermione to apparent death. Wrongly assuming that his newborn daughter Perdita is a 'bastard' (2.3.76), he orders that she 'instantly' be killed (2.3.134). But then – urged by his Lords to give them 'better credit' when he calls them 'liars all' (2.3.146–7) and told by Antigonus that he will 'pawn the little blood which I have left / To save the innocent' (2.3.167) – he swears Antigonus to promise to 'perform' his bidding, to 'carry / This female bastard hence' and 'bear it / To some remote and desert place' (2.3.169–76). In the final 'winter' scene, Antigonus abandons the newborn Perdita in Bohemia and is killed there by a suddenly appearing 'bear,' after the most notorious stage direction in all of Shakespeare: 'Exit pursued by a bear' (3.3.58). An impoverished Bohemian shepherd and his son find the abandoned child or 'barne' and rejoice that the 'gold' and treasure found with her will make them 'rich' (3.3.117). At this pivotal juncture – between 'things dying' and 'things new-born' (3.3.114) – the Chorus of 'Time' appears, to announce the 'wide gap' or interim of 'growing' between the play's two halves, through which Perdita, as an adopted 'shepherd's daughter,' has 'grown in grace' by sixteen years. The play's second half opens not in Sicilia (where Leontes was left 'grieving') but in Bohemia, where the shepherds, who sixteen years before had found 'gold' with the abandoned babe, have thereby 'grown' in wealth 'from very nothing' to an 'unspeakable estate' (4.1.39–40). In this second half – while Leontes submits to the counsel of Antigonus's widow Paulina not to remarry out of an anxious concern for 'issue' but patiently to forbear until the lost is returned – Polixenes' son Florizel (in love with the apparent shepherd's daughter) returns with Perdita to the Sicilian court. The offstage reunion of Leontes and Perdita is described by narrators who remark that its incredibility or lack of 'credit' is like an 'old tale' (5.2.61). The Bohemian shepherd and his son are raised to the status of 'gentlemen born' (5.2.127), and the awakening to life of the statue of the 'dead' Hermione in the final scene (5.3) is presided over by Paulina, the woman who has already been called a 'midwife' (2.3.160), who makes possible this plot of patient travail.

Onto this trajectory of forbearance and the gestational passage of 'Time,' *The Winter's Tale* grafts a host of commercial and legal terms that invoke the temporal gap between 'promise' and 'performance,' as part of what might be called the promissory economy of the play itself.[1] Its second half introduces the new character of Autolycus (preying on 'Honesty' and 'Trust' [4.4.595]), who becomes (paradoxically) responsible for much of the romance plot's 'return.' Described as 'litter'd under Mercury' (4.3.25), this peddler-thief is linked in multiple ways with Mercury or Hermes, god of the marketplace as well as of lying, stealing, and tale-telling, whose thefts included stealing or bearing back from death.[2] The wares peddled by Autolycus, at the Bohemian sheep-shearing festival, include the ballad of a 'usurer's wife ... brought to bed of twenty money-bags at a burthen' (4.4.263–4). Autolycus's claim that this ballad was vouched for as 'true' by the midwife 'Mistress Tale-porter' (4.4.267–70) directly assimilates the credibility of tale-bearing to the question of 'credit.' Its highlighting of usury simultaneously calls attention to yet another form of gestation through time and the increase made possible by a delayed return.

What I want to do, therefore, in the detailed examination of the play that follows, is to suggest ways in which the promissory language of contract and 'credit,' as well as of quittance, payment, or 'redemption,' is crucial not only to its explicitly merchandising second half but also to its overarching plot, from its opening focus on 'debt' to the statue that beguiles 'Nature' of her 'custom' in its final scene. In the process, I want to foreground the connections the play itself forges between its dramatic emphasis on pregnancy, gestation, or bearing (including the prodigious increase of the 'usurer's wife') and the new economy of contractual relations that depended on the gestational passage of time. My reading of *The Winter's Tale* thus seeks to bridge a gap of its own – between criticism that has emphasized the centrality in this play of pregnancy, bearing, and generational 'issue' and analyses like those of Stanley Cavell (1987), Michael Bristol (1991), and Sandra K. Fischer (1985) which stress its strikingly economic and legal terms.

Critics of *The Winter's Tale* have frequently noted the importance within it of pregnancy and issue. As Carol Thomas Neely has observed, 'childbirth is the literal and symbolic centre of the play,' transforming 'many actions and scenes into analogues of birth' (1985, 101). The first half of the play presents a barren masculine world, threatened by female sexuality and what Gail Kern Paster has called 'the specter of birth' and generation (1993). Its nostalgic boyhood brotherhood of 'twinned lambs' and what Janet Adelman (1992, 224–8) describes as its fantasy of male parthenogenesis is disrupted by the presence on stage of Hermione's pregnant body, emblem of increase but also of what Polixenes calls 'Temptations [that] have since then been born [Folio 'borne'] to us' (1.2.77). The play is rescued from barrenness or lack of issue (caused when Leontes banishes both female generativity and his newborn female heir) by the gestational patience and 'forbearance' of the intervening 'Time' and the delayed return of the daughter found by the shepherds in the pivotal scene of the 'bear.'

Stephen Booth and Margreta de Grazia have explored the connection between this pivotal 'bear' and the emphasis on bearing and breeding more generally within the play, including the upward mobility that ultimately transports these shepherds to the status of 'gentlemen borne' (the Folio spelling of both 'born' and 'borne' allows for the generative complexity of such terms). De Grazia (1990, 148) calls attention to the rich homophonic network that connects 'born' in this play with 'carried' or 'borne' (a connection exploited further in the association of 'Mistress Tale-porter' with various forms of bearing or delivery) and to the homophonic reminders of both kinds of 'bearing' in the scene of the 'bear' itself, where as soon as Antigonus exits pursued by a 'bear' the Bohemian shepherds find a 'bearing-cloth' with the 'new-born(e)' bairn or 'barne' (3.3.70–115). Antigonus – killed by the 'bear' after Hermione warns that for the 'ungentle business' of exposing the newborn child, he will see his wife no more (3.3.34–6) – combines 'Anti' in his name with the Greek root *gone* of generation or birth. In de Grazia's rich analysis, which observes that Antigonus had already threatened to 'geld' his daughters and himself (2.1.140–50) if Hermione proved to be an adulteress (as, in abandoning the babe, he believes her to have been), the play's preoccupation with bearing further extends to the multiple senses within it of *breeding*, a term that simultaneously suggests comportment (or gentle breeding) and generational increase. The 'gentleman' Antigonus (killed by a 'bear') is recalled as the figure who bore or 'carried hence' the child (5.2.60) in the later Recognition Scene, which refers to the uncertain 'credit' of the 'tale' it delivers (5.2.60–1) and then foregrounds the transporting of the low-born shepherds to the status of 'gentlemen born' (5.2.127) or (as the Folio has it) 'gentlemen borne.' Bearing as carrying, transporting, delivering, and birthing (combined in the name of 'Mistress Tale-porter,' in lines where Autolycus goes on to ask 'Why should I carry lies abroad?' [4.4.271]) thus becomes part of an associational network that connects bearing tales (and the attendant problem of credibility or 'credit') with other kinds of credit and bearing.

The exploitation, in the play's final act, of the paradox of 'gentlemen borne' (when the 'gentlemen' in question are not 'born' but made or artificially raised to that estate) gives to its meditation on the multiple forms of bearing and breeding unmistakable reminders of the social mobility of the period itself. The social trajectories of *The Winter's Tale* include not only the downward mobility of Autolycus (the vagabond who boasts that he was once servant to the Prince) but the upward mobility of the originally poor shepherds, who are raised first 'from very nothing' to 'unspeakable' wealth (4.2.39–40), after they find the gold, and then to the status of 'gentlemen born(e)' (5.2.127), a status frequently achieved in the period by wealth (or merit) rather than birth.

The Winter's Tale features several instances of such upward mobility. Camillo (the servant of Leontes who escapes Sicilia with Polixenes and returns only after the sixteen years have elapsed) is reminded by both of his masters that he himself was raised from 'meaner form' (1.2.314–15) to the status of 'a gentleman, thereto / Clerk-like experienc'd, which no less adorns / Our gentry than our parents' noble names, / In whose success we are gentle' (1.2.391–4). In a play that moves between older aristocratic models of social place and reminders of the new economy of contract and credit, the Folio's 'borne' foregrounds the passage from an identity based on fixed 'estate' or birth to the mobility of such new social forms (which included the proliferation in England of 'gentlemen made' rather than 'born,' noted by Sir Thomas Smith in *De Republica Anglorum* ([1583] 1982, 71–2). The difference within the homophones of 'born' and 'borne' thus calls attention to yet another aspect of the tension between 'nature' and 'art' featured in the sheep-shearing scene, which mingles kings and clowns and raises the question of a hybrid 'breeding' (4.4.85–103). In this regard, 'bearing' (like gentle 'breeding' or 'carriage') is both natural and potentially mimicked or credibly performed, a mobility that allows Autolycus (whose placelessness and malleable role-playing evoke the new market economy) to perform the role of a gentle 'courtier' once he has aquired the right clothes (4.4.729–830).

Bearing and breeding become at the same time part of the commercial language of the play, combining its emphasis on gestation through 'Time' with economic forms of growth and increase. The 'gold' left to 'breed' the abandoned Perdita (a breeding whose double sense is underscored in Antigonus's 'both breed thee, pretty, / And still rest thine' [3.3.48–9]) enables both her bringing up by the foster shepherds and a surplus, remainder, or 'rest,' part of what enables the shepherds to have 'grown' from 'nothing' to a prosperous estate by the time the second half begins. These Bohemian shepherds thus recall not only the shepherds of the biblical Nativity scene but also the more mercenary shepherd of Greene's *Pandosto*, Shakespeare's source, who with the newfound 'gold' both fosters the child and uses 'the sum to relieve his want' (Orgel 1995, 249–50). The prodigious wealth or increase made possible by the growth or 'breeding' through 'Time' of gold itself is then comically iterated in Autolycus's ballad of the 'usurer's wife ... brought to bed of twenty money-bags at a burthen' (4.4.263), in the marketing atmosphere of the play's second half.

The play's own gestational emphasis on bearing and issue is mirrored in this prodigious delivery, since usury (as another form of 'bearing' and 'breeding') depended both on forbearance and on gestation through time. 'Delivery' – which already connects birthing with the delivering of tales through the designation of 'Mistress Tale-porter' as the midwife to this usurious birth (Bicks 2003, chap. 1) – was simultaneously the term for the lending of money in the period, while usurers were known as 'deliverers' (Rollison 1992, 52). Opponents of usury routinely describe its 'increase and multiply' as an unnatural breeding or monstrous birth (Fischer 1985, 138; Shell 1982, 47–83). The Doctor of Thomas Wilson's *A Discourse Upon Usury* remarks that 'Usurie ... is called in greeke a byrthe, because that moneye bringeth moneye' ([1572] 1925, 275). Wilson's *Discourse* cites Aristotle and other authorities ([1572] 1925, 286) on the unnaturalness and monstrosity of usury's form of bearing or breeding, even as its comparison of usurers to 'vile artificers' makes clear the relation of usury's mimickry of 'natural' birthing to the problem of 'nature' and 'art' (see also Wilson 2000, 331). Roger Fenton's *A Treatise of Usury* (1612, 6–7, 51), comparing its continual bearing to 'an unnatural and monstrous brood' (1612, 6–7), notes that the ancients called usury 'birth, because it brings the pangs of travell [i.e., travail] upon the soule of the debtor' ('A woman in travel ... doth not sweate and labour to bring foorth with greater anguish of minde, then a debtor compelled to bring home the principall with increase'). In ways suggestive for the plot of *The Winter's Tale* – in which the issue of the pregnant Hermione is condemned as a 'bastard' birth and the ballad of the usurer's wife so pointedly evokes the gestational metaphorics of pregnancy and delivery – the issue or increase of usury itself was routinely described in the period as a 'bastard' birth (Shell 1982, 51).

Given the ease with which sexual and monetary 'usury' were combined, including in the 'two usuries' of *Measure for Measure* (3.2.5), it is not surprising that a ballad of a 'usurer's wife' is the first to be retailed by Autolycus, the pedlar whose 'traffic' in 'sheets' (4.3.23) recalls Leontes' earlier anxiety about the purity of his 'sheets' (1.2.327). In a canon in which usury or 'use' is compared to the 'generation' of 'ewes' or 'sheep' in *The Merchant of Venice* (1.3.76–96), it is also not surprising that Autolycus's reminder of usury and its monetary increase occurs in the sheep-shearing scene of *The Winter's Tale*. As both Cavell (1987, 214) and Bristol (1991, 164) have argued, the sheep shearing itself is explicitly foregrounded as a commercial enterprise, introduced when the Shepherd Son enters trying to calculate the yield on 'fifteen hundred shorn' (4.3.34). R.H. Tawney observes that credit and usury were crucial 'at every point' in the burgeoning wool trade, 'from the breeding of sheep to the sale of cloth,' while the 'primary dealers in money and economic matters' in England were 'wool broggers,' who provided loans to wool producers at one end and sold wool to cloth-makers at the other (1925, 46–9). 'Sheep' were not only part of the contemporary network of exchange and 'use' but were routinely invoked in the discourses of 'credit' and credibility on which the new market economy depended (Tawney 1925, 49). 'Sheep-shearing' and 'fleecing' were simultaneously part of the lexicon of usury, equated with both theft and the proverbial wolf among sheep. In the sheep-shearing scene of *The Winter's Tale*, Autolycus (whose name means 'the wolf [by] himself') determines to make the 'shearers prove sheep' (4.3.121), providing an ironic fulfilment of the Shepherd's worry, in the scene of the devouring 'bear,' that the 'wolf' will sooner find his 'sheep' than he will (3.3.66).[3]

Usury was linked not only with 'bearing' and 'breeding' but also with gestational 'forbearance' through time. The ballad of the usurer's wife thus evokes not only Hermione's pregnancy and the play's gestational plot of loss and return but also one of the multiple economic and commercial counterparts of Leontes' patient forbearing (or going without 'issue') in the 'wide gap' of 'Time' before Perdita returns, in contrast to his initial assumption that his losses can be quickly recovered (3.2.150–6). The passage of 'Time' that is so important to the play was central to usury, which was understood as 'the price of tyme, or the delaying or forbearing of moneye,' as well as a 'gayne takyng for tyme' by 'merchauntes of tyme,' condemned by Wilson and others as merchandizing or 'sellynge tyme' itself (Wilson [1572] 1925, 276, 266, 309, 355). 'Forbearance' was a keyword in the lexicon of usury as well as of patience, or waiting patiently for a delayed return. The 1571 Act of Elizabeth allowing usury (while restricting the taking of interest to 10 per cent) speaks of 'Money so to be lent or for-born' and of lenders as 'Forbearers' as well as 'Deliverers.'[4] Usury is that which 'in processe of time bringeth forth

Money' (1578, 11), pronounces the Treatise annexed to Philippus Caesar's
A General Discourse Against the Damnable Sect of Usurers (translated 1578),
invoking 'processe' in the gestational sense that is also used for the 'law
and processe' of 'great Nature' when Perdita herself is 'deliver'd' (2.2.23–
59). A text of 1590 (cited by the *OED* in its definition of 'forbearance')
treats of 'what is wonne or lost in the 100 pound forbearance for 12
moneths,'[5] stressing the greater issue or increase of such delayed returns. Wilson's *Discourse* is literally filled with examples of *forbearance* in
this sense, observing that 'when anye overplus or excesse is taken over
and above the pryncipal that was lent ... in consideration of forbearing
money for time,' it is 'usury,' the generation of a greater return or
increase through 'tarying and forbearinge,' or 'the delaye of tyme'
([1572] 1925, 304–8). Well before *The Winter's Tale*, Shakespeare exploited the double meaning of 'forbearance' in 'lend me patience to
forbear a while' (*Two Gentlemen of Verona* 5.4.27), in a context whose
reference to lending invokes the usurious as well as the spiritual sense of
going without.[6] The conclusion of such patient 'forbearing' was the
'quit' or 'quittance' that designated the end of the period of gestation or
travail: this is the term exploited by Shakespeare in its gestational and
usurious senses in 'God safely quit her of her burthen' in *Henry VIII*
(5.1.70); in the 'quit' of *The Merchant of Venice* (4.1.381); and the 'quittance' juxtaposed in *Timon of Athens* (1.1.280) with both 'breeds' and
'use' (1.1.279–80). 'Forbear' or 'quit' – terms from the final scene of *The
Winter's Tale* (5.3.85–6), where Paulina pronounces 'Dear life redeems
you' (5.3.103) – was therefore already an integral part of the simultaneously economic and spiritual lexicon of 'redemption.'

Contemporary commentaries on usury explicitly drew the temporal
analogy with what Wilson and others called 'spiritual usury,' defined as
'the right usurie in dede ... the multiplicacion of the giftes and graces of
God' (Wilson [1572] 1925, 19). 'Increase and multiply' – the gestational
'issue' artificially mimicked by the increase of the usurer's wife – thus
also applied to the multiplication of 'graces' and 'gifts.' As Lorna Hutson
observes, 'Dialogic texts which debated the question of usury, such as
Thomas Wilson's *Discourse uppon usurye* (1572), William Harrys' *The
market or fayre of Vsurers* (1550) and Thomas Lupton's *Siuqila* (1580)'
urged the 'return of credit extension to its traditional status as a sign of
friendship' or 'an emplacement of trust in the debtor,' since 'if lending
for gain were utterly abolished, the meaning of trust, they argued, would
be restored' (1994, 144). Such texts hearken back to an older sense of
'credit' (trust and the reliability of one's word as the basis of credibility)

and 'conjure up an idealistic or nostalgic vision in which promissory discourse is binding at the level of conscience' (Hutson 1994, 144). Spiritual usury was a 'spiritual investment' (Fischer 1985, 147), a different form of surplus or 'increase,' as well as a compensation for loss and patient 'forbearance.'

The 'usury' or 'use' that depends on the passage of 'Time' is foregrounded repeatedly in *The Winter's Tale*. The Chorus of Time itself – which is filled with legal and commercial terms ('try,' 'untried,' 'witness,' 'law,' 'spent,' and 'stale') as well as references to the gestational time of pregnancy before ultimate delivery ('let Time's news / Be known when 'tis brought forth' [4.1.25–6]) – entreats the audience's own patience for the temporal 'growing' of its 'scene,' in a speech whose 'in the name of Time, [I] *use* my wings. Impute it not a crime' (4.1.3–4) exploits the contemporary sense of 'use' both as 'employ' and as putting out to usury or 'use.' 'Use' in this doubled sense appears even earlier in the play, not only in the hope of the messengers to Delphi that the 'issue' of their 'business' will be 'gracious' and that the 'time' they have spent will be 'worth the use on't' (3.1.14, 22) but also in the promise of penitence and patient forbearance by Leontes at the end of the play's winter half ('So long as nature / Will bear up with this exercise, so long / I daily vow to use it' [3.2.240–2]), a bearing and 'use' that, through time, ultimately yields an unexpectedly rich return.

Within the promissory economy of this late Shakespearean romance, the temporal gestation crucial to usury and to patient forbearance of all kinds is simultaneously foregrounded by the play's highlighting of commercial and contractual concepts and terms that similarly depended on the passage of time. These include not just 'issue,' 'charge,' 'discharge,' and the host of other terms studied by Cavell, Bristol, and Fischer, but also the dramatization of the multiple meanings of terms such as 'consideration,' 'pawn,' 'earnest,' and 'note' in relation to the temporal interval between 'promise' and 'performance.' Luke Wilson has argued that a contract economy involves a system of promises and considerations affecting participants in an environment in which 'social actors can make tactical use of time' (1994, 86). The market and the law in the long sixteenth century (1550–1650), he observes, were forging new concepts and relations bound by time, including the relation between 'promise' and 'performance.' As Agnew makes clear, the word 'performance' itself was acquiring 'new connotations of illusion and imposture, connotations that complemented and, at the same time, subverted the word's earlier meaning as the ceremonial execution or discharge of a command or obligation' (1986, 83). Performance was just beginning to acquire, according to Wilson, its now-familiar theatrical sense (1994, 69). The theatrical connotations of performance merge with its contractual senses right from the beginning of *The Winter's Tale* – when Camillo defends himself from the implication of 'non-performance' for failing to obey Leontes' command to kill Polixenes (1.2.261), when Hermione says, 'The King's will be perform'd' (2.1.115), and when Leontes commands Antigonus to 'perform [his] bidding' (2.3.169). Here, the king's repeated 'Mark and perform it' (2.3.170), swearing Antigonus to keep his promise to 'carry' or 'bear' this 'female bastard' hence, prepares for the appearance of the onstage 'bear,' in the scene that actualizes Antigonus's performance in both senses.

'Performance' in these multiple senses sounds throughout the opening half of *The Winter's Tale*, from Leontes' charge against Hermione (after Polixenes and Camillo have fled) that the plot 'of the two fled hence / Be left her to perform' (2.1.196) to his arraignment of Hermione at her public trial ('I ne'er heard yet / That any of these bolder vices wanted / Less impudence to gainsay what they did / Than to perform it first' [3.2.54–7]). In the marketing atmosphere of the play's second half, performance is underlined in its contractual sense when Autolycus is told that he will be paid in full only after he has done what he has 'promis'd' and 'the business is perform'd' (4.4.810–22). Performance through time, in several of its overdetermined senses, is echoed in Cleomenes' 'Sir, you have done enough, and have perform'd / A saint-like sorrow' (5.1.1–2), after the interim of 'Time' that has included the performance of Leontes' promised penance. As the play draws to its end, the multiple meanings of performance sound once again in Leontes' remark to Florizel that he so reminds him of his father that 'I should call you brother, / As I did him, and speak of something wildly / By us perform'd before' (5.1.128–30); in the description of the statue of Hermione as 'many years in doing and now newly perform'd by that rare Italian master, Julio Romano' (5.2.96–7); and ultimately in the concluding words of the play itself – 'Good Paulina, / Lead us from hence, where we may leisurely / Each one demand, and answer to his part / Perform'd in this wide gap of time, since first / We were dissever'd' (5.3.153–5). Here, artistic or theatrical performance is conflated with the sense of a task performed or carried out, even as these lines suggest something in the future, still to be 'performed.'

The contractual and legal sense of 'non-performance' (the term introduced into the play explicitly by Camillo) is likewise part of its recurring reminders of broken, breached, or unrealized 'promises,' highlighted in the sheep-shearing scene in Mopsa's reminder to the Shepherd Son of what she was 'promised ... against the feast,' in Dorcas's 'he hath promised you more than that,' and Mopsa's rejoinder 'He hath paid you all he promis'd you. May be he has paid you more' (4.4.235–40). The language of contract is iterated in relation to marriage in Florizel's acknowledgment that he and Perdita have not 'our contract celebrated' (5.1.204). 'Non-performance' or failure to carry out a promise was part of the legal action of *assumpsit*, defined as follows in Minsheu's *Ductor in Linguas*: 'Assumpsit (a terme of Law) is a voluntarie promise made by word, whereby a man affirmeth, or taketh upon him to performe, or pay anything unto another (It holds good in Law where there is something laid downe in consideration.) The civilians expresse it by divers words, according to the nature of the promise' ([1617] 1978, 21). *Assumpsit*, as Muldrew explains, became more common as a plea for broken contractual arrangements from the end of the sixteenth century. In contrast to suits for debt, actions of *assumpsit* (formally entered as 'trespass on the case')

> concentrated on what would now be considered the 'contractual' nature of agreements. Actions on the case were based on the concept of harm done to the plaintiff by the defendant's breaking of their promise. The wrong arose not directly out of the failure of the defendant to make good the *quid pro quo* by giving to the plaintiff something equivalent to the property they had received, as was the case in a plea of debt, but rather from the potential suffering incurred by the plaintiff because of the defendant's failure to honour his bargain, and the plaintiff sued for damages based on breach of trust. In addition, such agreements did not need to have been written down, as trespass on the case dealt with 'parol' (oral) agreements. The promise, however, had to be linked to an actual exchange, which became known as the doctrine of 'consideration,' because the plaintiff's sale or delivery of goods, loan of money or promise to undertake a service was said to have been made 'in consideration' of the defendant's promise of payment. (Muldrew 1998, 207)[7]

'Consideration' in this promissory or contractual sense is defined in Rastell's *Termes de La Ley* as 'the material cause of a contract, without the which no contract can binde the party' (1624, 91). The influential *Doctor and Student* explains that 'yf the promyse be so naked that there ys noo maner of consyderacyon why yt sholde be made, then I thynke hym not bounde to performe yt' (St German 1530, fol. xviiiv). Rastell similarly renders Latin *nudus* or French *nude* (for 'nude contracte') into English as naked or 'bare' (1624, 198), a terminology that may have made material 'consideration' available for connections with other kinds of clothing and exchange.

In *The Winter's Tale*, Autolycus receives 'boot' in his exchange of clothing with Florizel in Act 4 (4.4.637). 'Boot' here is simultaneously the term for the surplus, overplus, or profit that he receives in this exchange and the punning 'boot' or article of clothing that transforms him from vagabond into an apparent courtier, able with these new garments to fool the Shepherd and his son into adopting him as their 'advocate' to the 'court' (4.4.726–842).[8] Autolycus's proposed role as go-between or 'advocate' in this scene is that of the middleman who agrees for a 'consideration' to reestablish the reputation, credibility, or 'credit' of the shepherds as honest men: 'Tell me ... what you will have to the king: being something gently considered, I'll bring you where he is aboard, tender your persons to his presence, whisper him in your behalfs' (4.4.792–7).

'Consideration' – like 'promise' and 'performance' – is evoked repeatedly in *The Winter's Tale*, both in its older and in its newer contractual senses. Polixenes – concerned that Camillo wants to return to Sicily – asks him if he has not been 'enough consider'd' (4.2.17), in lines that exploit both the older sense of well regarded and the new material sense of adequately compensated for the managing of his 'businesses,' which none but he can adequately 'execute' (4.2.14–15). In the scene in which Autolycus hints that if he is 'gently consider'd' (4.4.795), he will 'undertake the business' he is asked to 'perform' (4.4.796–823), the material sense of 'consideration' takes the form of the shepherds' available 'gold' (4.4.807), a 'moity' to be paid at the time of their contracting and the rest after the 'business' is 'perform'd' (4.4.822). As part of this transaction, the Shepherd's son is left as a 'pawn' to be later redeemed (*Shep.* 'And't please you, sir, to undertake the business for us, here is that gold I have. I'll make it as much more, and leave this young man in pawn till I bring it you' [4.4.806–9]). As a pledge or security for a loan to be repaid in time or for the performance of some action, 'pawn' is already introduced in this temporal sense when Antigonus pledges to 'pawn the little blood which I have left' (2.3.166) in order to save Perdita's life and Camillo figures his own 'honesty' as 'impawned,' secured by the double-meaning 'trunk' that Polixenes will 'bear' away (1.2.435–6). Pawning also involved risking or staking in the hope of future profit, as in *Timon of Athens*: 'I'll pawn my victories / ... upon his good returns' (3.5.80–1).

'Earnest' is yet another of the terms exploited in *The Winter's Tale* in both its older and its newer contractual and legal registers. *Econolingua* defines an 'earnest' as 'a sum of money paid down on conclusion of a bargain as a security for its due performance,' a 'material representation of a promise' that was part of the promissory economy directed towards future fulfilment in time (Fischer 1985, 70). Elsewhere within the Shakespeare canon, *1 Henry VI* refers to an 'earnest of a further benefit' (5.3.16), *Macbeth* to 'an earnest of a greater honor' (1.3.104), and *Cymbeline* to 'an earnest of a farther good' (1.5.65). In *The Winter's Tale*, 'earnest' appears first in Leontes' 'No, in good earnest,' in response to Hermione's, 'Are you mov'd, my lord' (1.2.149–50). 'Earnest' here (underscoring the repeated 'verily' of this scene) becomes part of the protestation of sincerity, truth-telling, or 'credit,' in a context in which such reliability is increasingly called into question. In the play's second half, 'earnest' is iterated in the midst of an 'exchange' (4.4.633) that simultaneously foregrounds its contractual and material meaning – in Autolycus's 'Are you in earnest, sir?' (after Camillo has offered him 'some boot') and in his feigning 'Indeed I have had earnest, but I cannot with conscience take it' (4.4.642–6). The Chorus of Time evokes its temporal along with its other senses ('of this allow, / If ever you have spent time worse ere now: / If never, yet that Time himself doth say, / He wishes earnestly, you never may' [4.1.30–2]). In a speech that asks the audience to believe, trust, or credit him, 'earnestly' both underlines the sense of sincerity and underwrites what 'Time' himself promises to perform.

In relation to the temporal and promissory trajectory of the play as a whole, perhaps the most intriguing term from this lexicon of promise and performance is the 'note' with which it begins. Even though this term is familiar from *The Merchant of Venice* or *Much Ado about Nothing*, it is rarely noticed in its commercial, prosecutory, and promissory senses in *The Winter's Tale*. Critics of *Much Ado* have long observed the exploitation in its title of the homophones of 'nothing' and 'noting,' as well as the importance within it of noting or observing, of external signs or 'notes,' and of noting as accusing, staining, or branding with disgrace (a sense it shares with the lines on those 'condemn'd and noted' in *Julius Caesar* [4.3.2]). The 'nothing' of *Much Ado* (whose plot turns on the accusation of adultery against Hero) simultaneously evokes what Hamlet calls the 'nothing' that lies 'between maids' legs' (*Hamlet* 3.2.119–21), the place of female sexuality and of generational bearing or increase. This 'noth-

ing,' 'nought,' or 'O' is part of a rich Shakespearean network, linking
the generative female 'O' to the zero, cipher, or 'O' of a different kind of
increase and multiplication (capable of expanding '1,' for example, into
'1, 000, 000') – invoked in the prologue to *Henry V,* where 'O' may 'Attest
in little place a million' (Prol. 12–16).[9]

'Note' in the sense of 'promissory note,' or a 'written promise to pay a
certain sum at a specified time,' was not, according to the *OED,* in
standard use until the later seventeenth century. But 'note' as a 'bond
for debt' in the context of usury or commerce appears in several
Shakespeare plays, including in the commercial 'note' or 'bill of account' presented for the 'chain' in *The Comedy of Errors* (4.1.27); in the
'note of certain dues' in *Timon of Athens* (2.2.16), where 'forfeiture'
makes clear its relation to 'non-payment on the due date'; and in
Bassanio's announcement in *The Merchant of Venice,* 'I come by note, to
give, and to receive' (3.2.140), a 'note' glossed as 'a bill, or note, of
dues,' or 'IOU,' in a play that involves a debt or 'bond' whose payment
comes due.

The Winter's Tale exploits all of these senses of 'nothing' and 'note,'
including the 'note' that provides a merely outward sign – with no
guarantee of its credibility or 'credit' – in the report of the offstage
Recognition Scene of father and daughter in Act 5. There, the Gentle-
man-narrator who reports that 'the changes I perceived in the King, and
Camillo, were the very notes of admiration' (5.2.12) admits that his
narrative can make only 'a broken delivery of the business' (5.2.9), in a
scene whose multiple reports of offstage events explicitly beg the question of 'credit' in relation to a story that is 'like an old tale still' (5.2.61–
2). 'Note' in its promissory as well as its other senses is introduced in the
play's opening scene, in the description of Leontes' son Mamillius as a
'gentleman of the greatest promise that ever came into my note' (1.1.35–
6). The description combines notice or observation with the temporal
sense of a 'promise' to be fulfilled, in an exchange that simultaneously
recalls the biblical figures of Simeon's waiting until old age to see the
'promised one' and the 'Promise' to Abraham regarding *his* issue, a
promise fulfilled only after the long passage of time and in a different
sense from what might have been expected. In an opening scene that
repeatedly stresses 'means to pay' and what is owed in contrast to what is
'freely given' (1.1.6–18), 'promise' and 'note' at the same time turn the
play as a whole into a delayed as well as an altered or different kind of
fulfilment, realized through the detour of a daughter (rather than a son)
who finally returns.

'Note' in its multiple senses appears again in the first scene to bring Hermione's pregnant body on stage, in the speech of Polixenes, whose reference to 'Nine changes of the watery star' or moon (1.2.1) already evokes the gestational time of pregnancy. Here – in an exchange concerned with what might be 'breed(ing)' in his 'absence' and the owing of a 'debt' to Leontes that will continue 'in perpetuity' (1.2.1–9) – Polixenes' further reference to the 'shepherd's note' evokes the 'note' (or 'notice') of shepherds long before the Bohemian shepherd and his son appear, in the scenes in which they find the gold left to 'breed' Perdita, and grow (in time) from 'nothing' to the wealth of an 'unspeakable estate' (3.3.48; 4.2.39–40). Polixenes' opening speech moves from 'shepherd's note' and the 'nine' evocative of gestation or pregnancy to the nothing, 'cipher,' or 'O' – 'therefore, like a cipher / (Yet standing in rich place), I multiply / With one "We thank you" many thousands moe / That go before it' (1.2.6–9) – in lines whose 'standing in rich place' simultaneously evokes the female 'O' of Hermione's pregnant increase. As the scene proceeds, the compound implications of such terms manage to suggest not only 'anxieties about indebtedness and separation' between the two men, but also the potentially uncontrollable 'nothing' or 'O' of female sexuality and 'anxiety about the male role in' (or lack of control over) procreation itself (Adelman 1992, 220–2).[10]

'Noting' in the sense of 'nothing,' following Polixenes' concern for what might 'breed' in his absence, itself begins to multiply or breed out of control in these opening scenes, as Leontes' conviction mounts (from the external signs or 'notes' of Hermione's bearing with Polixenes) that he has been cuckolded ('Many thousand on's / have the disease and feel it not' [1.2.206–7]). It pervades his anxious questioning of Camillo ('Didst note it? ... Not noted is't' [1.2. 214–25]) and finally explodes into the paranoid notings and nothings of his frenzied speech on 'a note infallible / Of breaking honesty' ('Is whispering nothing ... / Is this nothing? / Why then the world and all that's in't is nothing, / The covering sky is nothing, Bohemia nothing, / My wife is nothing, nor nothing have these nothings / If this be nothing,' [1.2.284–96]). Within the play's barren winter half, 'nothing' or 'O' multiplies by a kind of negative increase, like the tragic 'nothing will come of nothing' in *King Lear* (1.1.90).

The scene of Hermione's public arraignment as 'an adult'ress' situates her in relation to the accumulating language of property and credit, as well as the compounding of 'notes' as both circumstantial evidence and condemning blots, marks, or stains. Adultery is described by Leontes even before this trial in terms of a trespass upon his property caused by 'one that fixes / No bourn [or boundary] betwixt his and mine' (1.2.133–4). In the scene of Hermione's public branding, the king's 'mark her well' (2.1.65) turns on the double sense of noting or remarking and the stigmatizing mark, note, or stain with which she (like Hero) is slandered. At the same time, this first half of *The Winter's Tale* repeatedly evokes the language of credit and the repayment of a debt or 'note.' Implications of a 'bastard' sexual usury surround the accusation against Hermione, in Leontes' reference to her 'vild principal' (2.1.92), the term exploited in *All's Well That Ends Well* in relation to both sexual and usurious increase ('Within [t'one] year it will make itself two, which is a goodly increase, and the principal itself not much the worse' [1.1.147–9]). The Sicilian Lords beseech Leontes to give them 'better credit' (2.3.147), while Leontes invokes his own credit-worthiness ('What? lack I credit?' [2.1.157]), as the mounting series of his 'trespasses' compounds what will become an increasing debt by the time Paulina enters to reckon what its homophone 'death' has done (3.2.175–202).

   In the scene of her trial, Hermione's 'it shall scarce boot me / To say "Not guilty"' when her 'integrity' is 'counted falsehood' (3.2.25–7) evokes the 'boot' or profit that will be later underscored in its material sense, in the 'boot' of Autolycus's exchange of clothing with Florizel in the play's second half. 'Boot' as overplus or profit is already identified with a different kind of surplus or increase in the 'Grace to boot' (1.2.80) of Hermione's first appearance on stage. It continues in its multiple appearances in *The Winter's Tale* to suggest the tensions as well as complex negotiations in this play between various forms of profiting (including from the passage of time) and attempts to reckon or tell what is beyond recounting or accounts. 'Counted' in Hermione's speech combines the sense of counting, tallying, or reckoning with rendering an account, report, or tale, in a trial in which she is condemned by the notes or 'circumstances' (3.2.18) of purely circumstantial evidence and a case of adultery whose ultimate truth or credit is beyond the reach of ocular proof. In her trial, Hermione's 'To me can life be no commodity' (3.2.93), when Leontes threatens her with death, similarly participates in the language of commerce, usury, and debt. 'Commodity' evokes both the sense of something that can be used or put out for sale (as the market-place of *The Comedy of Errors* features 'commodities to buy' [4.3.6]) and yet another term central to the discourse of usury or 'use,' for goods sold on credit by a usurer at a higher price than the person could resell them, explicitly evoked in the 'commodity of brown paper' owed by 'young

Master Rash' in *Measure for Measure* (4.3.5).[11] Hermione recounts in this scene (3.2.94–106) the losses she has already sustained ('the crown and comfort of my life, your favor'; 'My second joy / And first-fruits of my body'; 'my third comfort ... / Hal'd out to murther'; 'myself on every post / Proclaim'd a strumpet'; 'child-bed privilege denied, which 'longs / To women of all fashion'; 'lastly, hurried / Here to this place, i' th' open air, before / I have got strength of limit'). 'To me can life be no commodity' suggests an ability to do without 'life' itself, in the face of the losses she has already sustained. But in a scene in which she says to Leontes 'You speak a language that I understand not' (3.2.80), it simultaneously suggests the impossibility of speaking (or accepting) the terms of the transaction in which she has been (involuntarily) involved.

In this sense, Hermione's ambiguous words join the language of unutterability or unspeakability within the play as a whole. 'Utterance' itself appears in *The Winter's Tale* in the compounded senses of something spoken or expressed and something available for sale – the merchandising sense foregrounded by Autolycus's 'utter'd' wares ('Come to the pedlar, / Money's a meddler, / That doth utter all men's ware-a' [4.4.321–3]). The praise of Autolycus's ability to 'utter' his 'tunes' combines these double senses of expressing and selling, in lines that simultaneously draw attention to the multiple meanings of 'telling' as counting or tallying as well as recounting or providing a verbal account ('He sings several tunes faster than you'll tell money; he utters them as he had eaten ballads' [4.4.190]).[12] The connection between telling and tallying or counting has been brilliantly charted for this play by Stanley Cavell (1987, 193–221). Counting is evoked throughout *The Winter's Tale*. It appears not only in the attempt to reckon or tally breeding or increase – when the shepherd's son, for example, attempts to calculate the profit on the sheep-shearing, a computational problem he cannot solve 'without compters' (4.3.32–6) – but also in the repeated combination of accounting, reckoning, or tallying with tale-telling or recounting. The contrasting sense of what is 'beyond accompt' (both counting and telling) – the term used for the 'speed' of Cleomines' and Dion's return from Delphi, which Leontes immediately insists on counting ('Twenty-three days / They have been absent; 'tis good speed' [2.3.198–9]) – is joined in the final scenes by what may be finally unutterable in every sense.

The play's final act begins (back in Sicilia) with Cleomines' assurance to Leontes: 'Sir, you have done enough, and have perform'd /A saint-like sorrow. No fault could you make / Which you have not redeem'd;

indeed paid down / More penitence than done trespass' (5.1.1–4). The explicitly commercial language of the preceding Bohemian scenes, including Autolycus's contracting on a promise to 'perform' a 'business,' is here both echoed and transformed, in the reminder of the 'penitence' that Leontes has 'perform'd' offstage for sixteen years. Leontes' own remembrance in this scene – of Hermione as 'the sweet'st companion that e'er man / Bred his hopes out of' (5.1.11–12) – continues the play's repeated emphasis on breeding, in a scene in which his male counsellors express their anxious concern for 'issue' (5.1.27), for 'royalty's repair' (5.1.31), and for 'future good' (5.1.32), as well as the 'dangers' that might breed from 'fail of issue' (5.1.26–8). Through the contrasting counsel of Paulina – who responds to Leontes' memory of the 'treasure' of Hermione's 'lips' by reminding him that he 'left them / More rich for what they yielded' (5.1.49–54) – anxiety for immediate 'issue' is converted into continuing patience and forbearance, as the king agrees to 'swear' to keep his promise to do without both wife and issue until his 'first queen's again in breath' and 'Never till then' (5.1.69–84).

The offstage (and hence merely reported) Recognition Scene brings together all of the terms that have up to this point aligned the uttering of a tale with other kinds of outering or 'delivery,' in the 'broken delivery of the business' (5.2.9) by three gentlemen who take turns recounting it on stage. The language of gain and 'loss' – as of 'credit,' currency, and 'thrift' – continues as the verbal currency of this description, from Leontes caught between 'joy' and 'loss' and 'clipping' his daughter (5.2.50–4) to the Third Gentleman's 'like an old tale still, which will have matter to rehearse, though credit be asleep' (5.2.60–1). The 'tale' these reporters tell, described as so full of 'wonder' that 'ballad-makers cannot be able to express it' (5.2.24–5), recalls the ballads uttered by Autolycus and the testimony of 'Mistress Tale-porter' to the truth of the ballad of the usurer's wife, even as it suggests something both incredible and beyond utterance. 'Circumstance' (in 'Most true, if ever truth were pregnant by circumstance' [5.2.30–1]) invokes the term already used in Hermione's trial for circumstantial evidence or judicial 'proofs' in the absence of ocular proof or eyewitnessing, here for the uncertain 'credit' of a reported reunion of father and daughter that takes place entirely off-stage.[13] 'Performance' – in the multiple senses it has accrued throughout the play – sounds here in the simultaneously theatrical and performative senses of an 'act' that 'was worth the audience of kings and princes, for by such was it acted' (5.2.79–81) as well as explicitly in the first mention of the 'mother's statue,' as a 'piece many years in doing, and now newly perform'd, by that rare Italian master Julio Romano' (5.1.94–7).

Even the introduction of this statue is surrounded by commercial terms, of 'traffic' and trade as well as 'performance.' The 'custom' of the statue's description – as the product of the 'Italian master' who '(had he himself eternity, and could put breath into his work) would beguile Nature of her custom' (5.1.97–9) – combines the sense of 'custom' as the traditional or customary with its meaning as a tribute, toll, or duty levied on commodities on their way to market or on exports or imports borne across boundaries, what Marbeck's *Book of Notes* called the 'customes ... paide of merchaundises, and of those things which are either carried out or brought in' (1581, 271). The commercial lexicon it invokes is underscored by the editorial glossing of the line as 'drive Nature out of business' (Shakespeare 1974, 1601) or 'deprive Nature of her trade – do Nature's work for her in peopling the earth with creatures of his manufacture' (Shakespeare 1963, 150). This language continues when the First Gentleman concurs with the Second Gentleman's urging to be present at the statue's unveiling ('Every wink of an eye, some new grace will be born – our absence makes us unthrifty to our knowledge' [5.2.110–12]), an 'unthrifty' glossed as 'wasting opportunity to increase' (Shakespeare 1963, 151).

The final scene of the statue's unveiling (and the return of Hermione to 'life') opens with Paulina's assurances to Leontes about what he has fully repaid, with a 'surplus' explicitly linked with 'grace' ('all my services / You have paid home; but that you have vouchsaf'd, / With your crown'd brother and these your contracted / Heirs of your kingdoms, my poor house to visit, / It is a surplus of your grace, which never / My life may last to answer' [5.3.3–8]). 'Grace' – the richly suggestive but simultaneously undetermined term already introduced in Hermione's 'Grace to boot!' and her remarking of the fictive 'elder sister' to her 'last good deed,' 'O, would her name were Grace!' (1.2.80, 98–9) – is sounded throughout this scene of the play's own final issue. In this sense, it recalls Dion's 'gracious be the issue!' (3.1.22), from the scene of the messengers to Delphi, who note the temple's 'surpassing / The common praise it bears' (3.1.2–3), the insufficiency (as well as the responsibility) of 'report' (3.1.3), and their hope that 'the time is worth the use on't' (3.1.14), in yet another reminder of the potentially profitable 'use' of time itself. Paulina's 'It is a surplus of your grace' – echoing even more immediately the First Gentleman's 'Every wink of an eye some new grace will be born' (5.2.110–11) – is joined in the play's final scene by Leontes' 'she was as tender / As infancy and grace' (5.3.26–7), as the curtain is drawn and the 'stone' of the statue is discovered. The aging performed by the sculptor makes Hermione herself an 'elder' version of the figure who had appeared in the opening scenes. The statue's 'wrinkled' form, described as the product of 'our carver's excellence, / Which lets go by some sixteen years, and makes her / As she liv'd now' (5.3.30–1), lends to its dramatic and artistic performance the accompanying sense of a 'performance' realized through the passage of time. The scene itself conflates Leontes' own performance of 'sixteen winters' of 'sorrow' with the artistic image of drying paint ('My lord, your sorrow was too sore laid on, / Which sixteen winters cannot blow away, / So many summers dry' [5.3.49–51]).

The problem of credibility is once again foregrounded in Paulina's 'It is requir'd / You do awake your faith' (5.3.94–5), as the counsel of a woman whose name recalls the Pauline definition of faith itself as the evidence of things unseen. In this final scene, where the lexicon of 'credit' (and the redeeming of a debt) is infused with reminders of Christian as well as other forms of 'grace' and redemption (in Paulina's 'Dear life redeems you' spoken to the statue of Hermione in 5.3.103), the play's multiple promissory trajectories are underscored and combined. Michael Bristol argues that the extended time of the play's sixteen-year plot means that Leontes' 'initial sacrifice takes on the surprising character of a successful long-term investment' (1991, 166). Leontes, who loses 'everything that has value for him' in the first or winter half of the play, here, 'in the fulness of time,' has at least some of these losses made good (Bristol 1991, 166). *The Winter's Tale* simultaneously recalls the promissory language of spiritual redemption that, according to Muldrew, informed the conceptualizations of interpersonal relationships based on commerce and credit. But the play's temporal, gestational, and promissory trajectory – combined with its striking performance of terms drawn from the lexicon of contract and credit – makes it impossible to say, finally, whether it ever completely uncouples the commercial or utterable from its adumbrations of something beyond utterance or ocular proof. It is likewise impossible to reduce its evocations of spiritual usury, surplus, or 'boot' to any identifiable contemporary theology or 'faith,' including versions of covenant theology whose emphasis on contract and trust 'paralleled some ... changes in descriptions of economic exchanges' (Muldrew 1998, 141). In its own final lines, the play looks forward to yet more 'performance,' both the recounting offstage, beyond the notice of eyewitness or reporter, of what has been 'perform'd in this wide gap of time' (5.3.154), and the iterated performance of shows yet to come.

Notes

1 I am indebted to Lorna Hutson (1994) and Luke Wilson (1994 and 2000), who treat of promissory plots apart from *The Winter's Tale*. Wilson explores 'promise' and 'performance' in *The Tempest, Hamlet,* and other plays (including *Timon of Athens* in relation to 'timing'). Unless otherwise noted, all quotations from *The Winter's Tale* and other Shakespeare plays are cited in my analyses from Shakespeare (1974).

2 In the final scene of *The Winter's Tale*, Hermione herself (whose name recalls Hermes) is spoken of as 'stol'n from the dead' (in Polixenes' 'make it manifest where she has liv'd, / Or how stol'n from the dead' [5.3.113–14]). Porter (1988) discusses the linking of Autolycus and Hermione to Mercury/ Hermes and the historical connection between Mercury and marketing (reflected in the description of Mercutio as a 'saucy merchant' in *Romeo and Juliet* and in the name of the 'rich Mercatio' of *Two Gentlemen of Verona*), together with the association of Mercury/Hermes with theft, lying, taletelling, rhetoric, boundaries or bourns, interpretation, going between, and bearing back (or stealing) from the dead. Agnew (1986, 20) also notes that Hermes 'was god of the boundary stone, who became the Greek patron of trade.'

3 Usurers themselves were routinely compared to wolves (or wolves in sheep's clothing). Thomas Wilson's preface to the *Discourse* cites King Edgar's proclamation to rid England and Wales of wolves and then proceeds to describe usurers as wolves the realm needs to be rid of ('these bee the greedie cormoraunte wolfes in deede that ravyn up both beaste and man, who whyles they walke in sheepeskynnes, doe covertlye devoure the flocke of England') (Wilson 1925, 182). Rogers's English Epistle Dedicatorie to Caesar's *Discourse* (trans. 1578) calls 'an Usurer' a 'Wolfe in a Lambes skinne,' citing the desire of 'the honourable Maister Secretarie Wilson' to 'see as faire a riddaunce of them out of England and the Queenes dominions, as, God bee thanked, there is of Wolves by the meanes of King Edgar.'

4 See *OED*, 'forbear,' citing 1570 *Act 13 Eliz.* c. 8 par. 5: 'Any Money so to be lent or for-born'; and *OED*, 'forbearer' and 'forbearing,' with 1570 *Act 13 Eliz.* c. 8 par. 5. On the usury statute of 1571, see Jones (1989, 47–65).

5 *OED*, 'forbearance' #3, citing 1590 RECORDE etc. *Gr. Arts* (1640) 495: 'What is wonne or lost in the 100 pound forbearance for 12 moneths.'

6 Hutson (1994, 95) cites William Painter's use of the language of debt and
  forbearance in his dedication to Sir George Howard of the second volume
  of his *Palace of Pleasure*: 'The same I offre now, not with such usurie and
  gaine as your benevolence and singular bountie, by long forbearing hath
  deserved.'

7 Discussions of *assumpsit* in relation to Slade's Case and early modern
  English drama are also included in: Wayne (1982, 118–20); Wilson (1994,
  289–96); Ibbetson (1982 and 1984); Simpson (1975, esp. 199–315); Levine
  (2000, 421–4). Part 2 of Simpson (1975, esp. 316–488), devoted to 'The
  Action for Breach of Promise,' has an extensive discussion of the doctrine
  of 'Consideration.' See also Hutson (1994), esp. 146–9; and Levine
  (2000).

8 The etymology of 'investment' itself, Agnew explains, is an important
  example of a shift in meaning from its older sense of an outward 'garment,
  insignia, or office into which one was installed by ritual or communal fiat'
  to its newer one of 'a commercial asset that, properly deployed, might yield
  more than a small profit' (1986, 85).

9 'Note' is capable of an extraordinary range of meanings, exploited in the
  network of 'nothing' and 'note' that pervades the Shakespearean canon. In
  an older sense (from northern dialect rather than Latin *nota*), it can mean
  'use, usefulness, profit, advantage' and 'a matter, affair, or circumstance,'
  as well as 'office, employment, occupation or work.' In the senses derived
  from Latin *nota* (or 'mark'), it can designate a 'written character or sign,
  expressing the pitch and duration of a musical sound' (as well as a single
  musical tone of definite pitch); a 'mark of interrogation' as well as a 'sign
  or character (other than a letter) used in writing or printing.' This is the
  meaning for which *OED* cites *The Winter's Tale*: 'the changes I perceived in
  the King, and Camillo, were the very notes of admiration' (5.2.12). The
  noun also meant 'a brief record or abstract of facts'; 'a short letter or
  written communication'; 'a mark, sign, token, or indication of some quality,
  condition, or fact; from which something may be inferred'; 'an observation
  deserving of notice or remembrance,' and 'an interesting or noteworthy
  remark.' It can also involve, as it clearly does in *Much Ado About Not[h]ing*, a
  'stigma,' 'reproach,' accusation, or stain to one's repute. The *OED* records
  the latter sense being 'in common use from c. 1570 to 1650' as when
  Cooper's *Thesaurus* cites 'To be in suspicion, and noted with infamy.' It
  could also, finally, figure in the context of commercial exchange as the
  marking of a debt, bond, or charge – as in the 'note' in the sense of 'a bill
  or account' presented to Antipholus in *The Comedy of Errors* (4.1.27); or
  'notes' in the context of debt elsewhere in Shakespeare.

10 See also Cavell (1987, 109 ff.) on the computational inferences in this speech, and the anxieties in these opening scenes not only about debt but about a breeding out of control.

11 For 'commodity' in its simultaneously economic and sexual senses in early modern writing, see Williams (1994), vol. I, under 'commodity' and Fischer (1985, 57).

12 The close relation between 'utterance' and 'outering' (or the 'outward') is made clear by the *OED* entries on 'utter' and 'utterance,' which include citation of Nashe's *Christ's Tears* R4b on the 'utter show of things'; Tyndale (1526, John vii.24) on 'the utter aperaunce'; 1581 Mulcaster, *Positions* xxxix.210 ('some gainefull commoditie verie utterable abroade'); 1611 Cotgrave 'Marchandise Latine ... the best, or most utterable commodities'; and Shakespeare's *Love's Labour's Lost* (2.1.15–16: 'Beauty is bought by judgment of the eye, / Not utt'red by base sale of chapmen's tongues'). In the sense of 'the action of giving out of a store' or 'stock,' *OED* records that *utterance* also had a usurious sense (as when Breton observes that 'Usurers are halfe made, for lack of utterance of their money'). The anonymous pamphlet entitled *The Death of Usury, or the Disgrace of Usurers* (1594) observes that 'he that puts forth money' dares 'not exceed the rate of ten in the hundred; but he that uttereth wares doth make the rate at his own contentment' (see Tawney 1925, 24). The delivery of money is linked to birthing and the utterance of speech, both forms of outering, in *Two Gentlemen of Verona*, where Proteus's 'open the matter in brief' prompts Speed's 'Open your purse, that the money and the matter may be both at once deliver'd' (1.1.127–30).

13 Editors of *The Winter's Tale* frequently assume that 'circumstance' here means 'evidence.' But 'circumstances' were part of the *rhetorical* construction of substitutes for ocular proof, and hence subject to all of the scepticism due to 'telling' of various kinds. On 'circumstances' in the legal as well as rhetorical senses, see Parker (1996, 354–5).

Works Cited

Adelman, Janet. 1992. *Suffocating Mothers: Fantasies of Maternal Origin in Shakespeare's Plays, Hamlet to The Tempest.* New York: Routledge.

Agnew, Jean-Christophe. 1986. *Worlds Apart: The Market and the Theater in Anglo-American Thought, 1550–1750.* Cambridge: Cambridge University Press.

Bicks, Caroline. 2003. *Midwiving Subjects in Shakespeare's England.* Aldershot: Ashgate Publishers.

Booth, Stephen. 1981. Exit, Pursued by a Gentleman Born. In *Shakespeare's Art from a Comparative Perspective*, ed. Wendell M. Aycock, 51–60. Proceedings of Comparative Literature Symposium, vol. 12. Texas: Texas Tech Press.

Bristol, Michael. 1991. In Search of the Bear: Spatiotemporal Form and the Heterogeneity of Economies in *The Winter's Tale*. *Shakespeare Quarterly* 42.2: 145–67.

Bruster, Douglas. 1992. *Drama and the Market in the Age of Shakespeare*. Cambridge: Cambridge University Press.

Caesar, Philippus. 1578. *A General Discourse Against the Damnable Sect of Usurers whereunto is annexed another Godlie treatise Concerning the Lawfull use of ritches*. Trans. Thomas Rogers. London.

Cavell, Stanley. 1987. *Disowning Knowledge in Six Plays of Shakespeare*. Cambridge: Cambridge University Press.

de Grazia, Margreta. 1990. Homonyms before and after Lexical Standardization. *Jahrbuch der Deutschen Shakespeare-Gesellschaft West*. 143–56.

Dillon, Janette. 2000. *Theatre, Court and City, 1595–1610: Drama and Social Space in London*. Cambridge: Cambridge University Press.

Fenton, Roger. 1612. *A Treatise of Usury*. London.

Fischer, Sandra K. 1985. *Econolingua: A Glossary of Coins and Economic Language in Renaissance Drama*. Newark: University of Delaware Press.

Harrys, William. 1550. *The market or fayre of Vsurers*. London.

Hutson, Lorna. 1994. *The Usurer's Daughter*. London: Routledge.

Ibbetson, David. 1982. Assumpsit and Debt in the Early Sixteenth Century: The Origins of the Indebitatus Count. *Cambridge Law Journal* 41: 142–61.

– 1984. Sixteenth-Century Contract Law: Slade's Case in Context. *Oxford Journal of Legal Studies* 4: 295–317.

Jones, Norman. 1989. *God and the Moneylenders: Usury and Law in Early Modern England*. London: Basil Blackwell.

Levine, Nina. 2000. Extending Credit in the *Henry IV* Plays. *Shakespeare Quarterly* 51.4: 403–31.

Marbeck, John. 1581. *A Booke of Notes and Commonplaces*. London.

Minsheu, John. [1617] 1978. *Ductor in Linguas: (Guide to the Tongues) and Vocabularium Hispanicolatinum (A Most Copious Spanish Dictionary)*. Facsimile ed. Intro. Jürgen Schäfer. Delmar, NY: Scholars' Facsimiles and Reprints.

Muldrew, Craig. 1998. *The Economy of Obligation: The Culture of Credit and Social Relations in Early Modern England*. London: Macmillan.

Neely, Carol Thomas. 1985. *Broken Nuptials in Shakespeare's Plays*. New Haven: Yale University Press.

Parker, Patricia. 1996. *Shakespeare from the Margins*. Chicago: University of Chicago Press.

Paster, Gail Kern. 1993. *The Body Embarrassed: Drama and the Disciplines of Shame in Early Modern England.* Ithaca: Cornell University Press.

Porter, Joseph. 1988. *Shakespeare's Mercutio.* Chapel Hill: University of North Carolina Press.

Rastell, John. 1624. *Les Termes de La Ley; or, Certaine difficult and obscure Words and Termes of the Common Lawes of this Realm Expounded.* London.

Rollison, David. 1995. *The Local Origins of Modern Society: Gloucestershire 1500–1800.* London: Routledge.

St German, Christopher. 1530. *A Dyalogue in Englysshe bytwyxt a Doctoure of Dyuynyte and a Student in the Lawes of Englande.*

Shakespeare, William. 1974. *The Riverside Shakespeare,* ed. G. Blakemore Evans. Boston: Houghton Mifflin Company.

– 1963. *The Winter's Tale,* ed. J.H. Pafford. London: Routledge.

– 1995. *The Winter's Tale,* ed. Stephen Orgel. New York: Clarendon Press.

Shell, Marc. 1982. *Money, Language and Thought: Literary and Philosophical Economies from the Medieval to the Modern Era.* Berkeley: University of California Press.

Simpson, A.W.B. 1958. The Place of Slade's Case in the History of Contract. *Law Quarterly Review* 74: 381–96.

– 1975. *A History of the Common Law of Contract: The Rise of the Action of Assumpsit.* Oxford: Clarendon Press.

Smith, Sir Thomas. [1583] 1982. *De Republica Anglorum,* ed. Mary Dewar. Cambridge: Cambridge University Press.

Tawney, R.H. 1925. Introduction to *A Discourse Upon Usury by Thomas Wilson,* 1–172. London: G. Bell & Sons.

Wayne, Don. 1982. Drama and Society in the Age of Jonson: An Alternative View. *Renaissance Drama.* New ser. 13: 103–29.

Williams, Gordon. 1994. *A Dictionary of Sexual Language and Imagery in Shakespearean and Stuart Literature.* 3 vols. London: Athlone Press.

Wilson, Luke. 1994. Promissory Performances. *Renaissance Drama.* New ser. 25: 59–87.

– 2000. *Theaters of Intention: Drama and the Law in Early Modern England.* Stanford: Stanford University Press.

Wilson, Thomas. [1572] 1925. *A Discourse Uppon Usurye.* In *A Discourse Upon Usury by Thomas Wilson,* ed. R.H. Tawney, 173–384. London: G. Bell & Sons.

2

Putting Women in Their Place: Female Litigants at Whitehaven, 1660–1760

CHRISTINE CHURCHES

Scholars studying early modern England are largely dependent on the legal records of courts for our understanding of how the majority of women, especially those below the gentry class, used and experienced the legal system when asserting or defending their property rights. The survival of personal letters, a diary, or a journal in which a Lady Anne Clifford or a Mistress Alice Thornton recorded her legal battle for land or possessions is rare. The bibliographical index provided by Amanda Vickery in her book *The Gentleman's Daughter* (1998) indicates that for the majority of women a 'Single letter' is all that is extant. Consequently we must be circumspect when evaluating the evidence provided by personal and business letters, such as that written by the newly widowed Dorothy Lamplugh to James Lowther, in 1725, concerning his mortgage interest in her late husband's estate as it affected her right of dower. 'I return to you my thanks,' she wrote,

> especially as you are willing to adjust the difference betwixt us, and let me into my right without making any abatement other than what you say the law entitles you to, as the case is thus I hope there are not great difficulties but what may easily be determined by the learned in the law where persons are disposed to peace, which for my part can truly say I am and as you are so too. I shall beg leave to propose the adjusting of any differences between us to be referred to two eminent counsel, the one to be named by yourself, and the other on my behalf.[1]

What does this letter alone reveal of her knowledge of legal procedure and property law? Although it may seem that of an individual with an impressive knowledge of the law, the letter may not have been composed by Dorothy Lamplugh but instead may have been dictated to her by her lawyer, Nicholas Hall. It is this kind of uncertainty that imposes upon scholars who study the property relationships of women and their experiences as litigants in early modern England the need to devise methodologies to evaluate the evidence found in extralegal documentation, such as personal and business letters, as well as court records.

In this chapter, I trace litigants in any jurisdiction with the common background of living or having dealings between 1660 and 1760 in Whitehaven, a town and port on the coast of Cumberland. This focus on litigants from a specific locality serves an important purpose: it reconnects litigants to the society in which they lived and worked, and reminds us, particularly if we are concentrating on the problems and disabilities specific to gender, that most women lived and worked as part of a family unit and did not perceive themselves as autonomous individuals. The methodology that I have used differs from that of several recent studies of women's experiences as litigants. Amy Erickson in her important study of *Women and Property in Early Modern England* (1993) samples selected localities to plot the experience of women in each of the separate jurisdictions – common law, customary law, ecclesiastical law and equity – which regulated property ownership. In contrast, the recent work by Tim Stretton (1998) and Laura Gowing (1996) focuses on women litigants before one institution. Stretton estimates that up to one-third of all plaintiffs in the Elizabethan Court of Requests were female, while Gowing testifies to a predominance of female suitors appearing in the London consistory court. The restriction of their studies to one institution by no means indicates a narrowness of purpose but instead enables Stretton to provide finely detailed pictures of differences made by marital status, age, and place of residence to women litigants in the Court of Requests, and Gowing to reveal how women responded to accusations of slander and defamation. Yet even in courts which followed civil or equity procedures that encouraged more circumstantial tale-telling, each case remains an isolated fragment of the litigant's experience, a vignette of a part of a life, while the records of the central courts of common law and of most local borough and manorial courts furnish scant evidence, and that in highly stylized and often misleading form, of the matter in dispute which brought about the litigation. The different methodology used in this chapter contextualizes the experiences of women litigants affected by the particular property regime customary in the locality of Whitehaven.

Whitehaven owed its rapid expansion from the 1660s firstly to the

investment of the Lowther family, who began to exploit the coal seams
which underlay their manorial lands and who built a small pier from
which to ship that coal to Dublin; and secondly to the merchants and
masters of ships who engaged in that trade, who developed a transatlan-
tic tobacco trade on the back of it, and who shared the costs of extending
and maintaining the harbour. The given occupations of litigants reflect
the mixed economy of the town and its hinterland: merchants and
masters of ships, shipowners (where we find people of very modest
means owning a part share of a ship), customs officers, yeoman farmers,
artisans, servants, colliery supervisers, coal miners, and those who carted
the coal to the harbour. Most property in the town was held by a form of
customary tenure or tenant right widespread throughout the north
country and assimilated by southern-bred lawyers to the copyhold tenures of the south. During the period 1660 to 1760 such property could
be freely transferred by sale or gift, though the transaction was still
authenticated by a surrender and new admittance (which could not be
refused) in the customary court. The procedure was frequently used to
secure mortgages and to effect family settlements of customary estates,
the tenant surrendering and immediately taking a new admittance to
himself and his wife (or herself and her husband) jointly, with remain-
ders to heirs, or the tenant or joint tenants surrendering to the use of
one of their children, reserving a life occupancy to themselves and the
survivor of them. Unlike a freehold, a customary tenement could not be
devised by will, for the court jury would find a deceased tenant's next
heir according to the custom regardless of any testamentary bequest. In
particular, if a married woman was found heir to an estate by the custom,
she became the tenant, not her husband. By an agreement with the lord
of the manor in 1680, customary tenants were given an option to purchase a freehold title: most of them saw no advantage in taking it
(Churches 1998, 165–80). Although the standard common law disabilities applied to a married woman who was joint or sole owner of a house
in that the income was at her husband's disposal while he lived, such
arrangements secured to the wife a capital asset which would yield an
income after her husband's death. The value of the property lay in the
houses or shops built, rather than the land itself, and wives or widows
could rent out house-room or shops or themselves work from their own
premises to generate an income.

Hence, among litigants residing in Whitehaven were women suing as
landowners – against neighbours' trespassing livestock, the breaking
down or the planting of hedges, the blocking of an ancient right of way,

the diversion of a watercourse. They sued as part owners of ships. Female servants sued for their wages. Women sued for debts owed them on money lent, and for goods or services provided: for food and lodging, taking in laundry, selling malt, hiring out horses to cart coal and stone. Children claimed their mothers were attempting to dispossess them; family members of either sex chased one another for their portions or legacies. An action in ejectment where the plaintiff alleged that the defendant had dispossessed him of premises 'which A and B his wife demised to him for a term not yet expired' may really have served the purpose of establishing the joint title of A and B in the premises, perhaps pursuant to a marriage settlement, plaintiff and defendant being their collaborators or even fictitious persons.[2] Women defended themselves against defamatory allegations made by either sex, not just in the ecclesiastical courts discussed by David Lemmings in the next chapter in this book, but also in manorial courts and at common law. The latter enabled women to claim damages for loss of reputation.

Two areas of litigation exhibit a higher proportion of female litigants: widows were often obliged to sue for maintenance, and women, whatever their marital status, were caught up in litigation over deceased estates more often than men. Both men and women clearly recognized the capabilities of their wives, daughters, or sisters as they chose them almost routinely to be executors of their wills.[3] In the Common Pleas and King's Bench records I have examined only one in nine of the parties to suits were women, and over half of them were exercising administration of the effects of deceased husbands or brothers.

Proceedings to recover small debts in the manor court were routinely instituted by or against women, either on their own or in conjunction with husbands. Some suits suggest at the very least the active involvement of the wife, if not her sole management of some aspect of a family enterprise. Thomas Pow and his wife Elizabeth sued for debts owed on tailoring work, though he was a sailor. Robert and Jane Beeby, besides running an inn, also supplied horses and carts for leading coal to the harbour: Jane, 'the wife of Robert Beeby,' was sued on her own for debts she owed on malt; they were sued together for various other debts and for the grazing they rented for their horses; and they in turn combined to sue for money owed them. Why else should the merchant Isaac Milner's wife be so frequently conjoined with him in suits for shop debts and money owed for malt, if not because she managed the Whitehaven branch of their business while he was absent attending to the other branch in Dublin?[4] Often this is the real situation behind proceedings at

common law, as when a husband and wife jointly take out a writ but make
it apparent in the declaration that the wife had lent the money, or that
the goods provided were properly hers; or, if the defendants in a suit are
man and wife, that she had incurred the debt, that the trespassing cattle
were hers, or that she had uttered the words of slander.

Of the 118 suits in Chancery and Exchequer between 1660 and 1760
that I have examined, 43 have women as principals.[5] In thirty of these a
woman is named as defendant, but we should not cast her as a passive
victim. Many bills were exhibited for the sole purpose of staving off
proceedings at common law, or to stay execution of a judgment already
given, for either of these courts had the power to halt proceedings at
common law pending its own determination if there appeared to be
matter of equity in the case. In fifteen instances where a woman is the
defendant, the plaintiffs were suing her because she had first sued them.

Stretton, in his study of the Court of Requests, concludes that in that
particular jurisdiction women pleaded poverty and weakness more often
than men, while men on the whole preferred to focus attention on the
strength of their opponents rather than exaggerate their own weakness
(1998, 178–87). Requests, of course, was specifically a court to provide
remedy for poor and helpless suitors, so it is no great surprise to find this
style of pleading common there. Only one woman among my sample of
Whitehaven litigants chose to represent herself as weak and helpless:
Jane Ashburne recounts a harrowing tale of a threatening creditor bully-
ing her mother, the mother in turn harassing her daughter until, 'sick,'
'ill,' 'not knowing her right,' and 'not having anything to subsist on,' she
agreed to an assignment of a mortgage.[6] The depositions collected on
her behalf suggested to those qualified to know that she had a good case,
but she let it lapse because her lawyer would not proceed further without
payment.[7] We do not find such pleas of helplessness even where we
might expect it, in those disputes over a deceased estate where a woman
could credibly plead ignorance of accounts, or of the nature and conduct of the business. Instead, Mabel Scott detailed the trading accounts
she managed for her son, while carefully segregating business she conducted on her own account. (She also appeared in both the manor court
and at Common Pleas, suing for debts owed to herself.) Eleanor Beck
admitted the book debts for her late husband's ropery were 'very intri-
cate and obscure,' but instead of pleading her own incapacity to deal
with them, she reprobated her late husband's unskilfulness in keeping
books and added that he wrote in 'but a very bad hand.' She sturdily
repudiated the accusations of trickery and deceit brought by her

husband's family, and resisted their attempts to force revaluations, as that would be a reflection on the integrity of the appraisers.[8] In the answers of twenty women in suits concerning administration of deceased estates one widow alone pleaded ignorance, and she, I think, was devious rather than helpless, as she continued to run their haberdashery business.[9]

The confident handling of legal terms and procedures by Mrs Lamplugh, as I suggested earlier, raises another problem. Did she actually compose the letter herself or was it at the dictation of her lawyer, Nicholas Hall? James Lowther describes the protracted negotiations 'for a great many weeks together,' but he describes them in terms of Hall bringing proposals from the widow, rather than dealing with the attorney alone.[10] How much input a client of either sex had is well-nigh impossible to judge from the legal record by itself and for this we must turn to private records, in this instance, business letters concerning the Lowther estate. Here the conduct of women is observed largely through male eyes, for all but a handful of the letters surviving from Whitehaven were written by men. Between 1666 and 1750 successive stewards at Whitehaven exchanged letters at least twice a week with their employers, Sir John and Sir James Lowther, both of whom resided in London. Women do figure in this masculine world of colliery and harbour management, town planning and government, but if their activities elicit comment, it is by and large because they are up to something troublesome in the eyes of the stewards. Nonetheless, the stewards' reports leave us in no doubt that such women were handling money, controlling assets, running small businesses, and helping in the management of their absent husband's affairs, a situation common in any seaport.[11]

Mrs Thomas Lutwidge remains invisible in the legal record, yet was involved in day-to-day manoeuvres to salvage her husband's fortune from the impending lawsuits of his clamorous creditors. The assets were diversified among his trade in tobacco, real estate in the town, ship shares, a bottle-making enterprise, and a lease of a lighthouse. She had brought a sizeable portion to the marriage and Lowther's steward, John Spedding, reports his discussions with her alone as often as those with the couple together. He had had 'a good deal of talk with him and Mrs Lutwidge' and again, 'Mrs Lutwidge sent for me this evening and they are now in the greatest consternation that can be imagined' while it was Mrs Lutwidge who was writing letters to her brother begging for his assistance in the matter.[12] When her husband retreated to Ireland to escape his creditors, she stayed in Whitehaven to manage the property that had been secured to her through her marriage articles. The steward reported, 'His wife is a very prudent frugal manager of the rents of his houses in town' and that by some judicious selling off of goods which remained in the warehouse, 'she makes a shift to support her family without pressing her neighbours to send her money.' Spedding was so convinced of her capacity to manage that he himself lent her money, which was duly repaid.

Elizabeth Lowes, wife of the master of the ship *Centurion*, had letters of commission from him empowering her to act as his factor while he was overseas. She joined with her husband and successfully sued two Glasgow merchants in the Scottish Admiralty Court for breaking a charter party agreement. The other partners in the ship concurred in her management, and she was sole signatory of a commission empowering an agent to travel to Glasgow and collect the money awarded to them. When he was fobbed off by the defendants, the owners sent a fresh commission appointing as their factor the Scotsman John Binning, who was retained by several Whitehaven merchants and also by the English Treasury. The defendants were still disposed to quibble because not all the owners had joined in signing, but Binning had no doubt that 'it would have been sufficient if only Mrs Lowes had signed.'[13] Casual remarks in John Spedding's letters reveal that other merchants and mariners absent overseas had left their wives letters of attorney to conduct business on their behalf.[14]

Exploring the records of one particular court as Gowing has done makes it the more likely that we will uncover a complex of cases generated by the same or a related dispute, and she has been able to show that 30 per cent of defamation cases in the London consistory court had some connection to others at the same court (1996, 133). Extending the search across a variety of jurisdictions gives some idea of individual engagement in both local and national courts, and a greater chance of uncovering links and connections between what might otherwise read as isolated incidents of litigation. This methodology provides important insights into the experiences of widows such as Mary Addison, whose husband had died in 1690, leaving her with two very young children, shares in a ropery, and a life interest in a large house. Over the next decade she set about improving and extending the property, some of which she let out for shops and accommodation. These extensions to her empire engaged her in disputes with her neighbour, Anthony Whiteside, who sued her at common law in 1700 for assaulting his workmen as they tried to lay paving stones in front of his house.[15] The following year the two prepared to try their respective titles to the disputed ground, each putting up a fictitious lessee to complain of forcible eviction by the other.[16] Though all three suits reached the stage of being dispatched for trial at the assizes, no outcome there is recorded in any of them. Whiteside was still pursuing the matter in the manor court held in October, two months after the assizes, alleging encroachment on his ground as his opponent extended her house still further. Three deponents declared her new building was blocking a passageway which formerly ran between the two houses, and that the stairs she had built intruded into Whiteside's ground.[17] Two years later and still building, she faced a more formidable foe, as Sir John Lowther sued her in the same court for extending onto the manorial waste and for ignoring building regulations spelled out in the tenants' admittances to town property. 'Less than this was not to be expected when her father is her adviser,' commented Lowther, recollecting that father's ingenious sapping and undermining of his seigneurial authority over the previous forty years. He wrote to her brother-in-law Thomas Addison, hoping to raise up some countervailing voice within her family, but Addison replied that Mary scorned advice as much as her father 'and had rather spend £100 in law than be determined by the best and wisest of their neighbours.'[18] He had a Chancery bill drafted in which the Addison property was described as 'a line of mean, low and contemptible buildings ... to the great deforming of that part of town,' but finally came to a compromise whereby the offending structure remained intact, on condition to be demolished if he or his heirs should ever demand it.[19] Ten years later, when James Lowther sued her in the Exchequer for refusing his demands that she pay him rectorial tithes on her freehold land, she at once addressed herself to the Duke of Somerset, in whose lordship the freehold lay, soliciting his support.[20]

In a dispute with Sir John Lowther over the boundaries of Bransty colliery, Katherine widow of Mr George Johnson was able to recruit five neighbouring gentlemen as her arbitrators, including two currently serving JPs and one professional lawyer, three of whom had the additional qualification of being themselves colliery owners, eager to limit Lowther's expansion in any direction by this as by any other means. They 'all made noise sufficient and would understand no reason but palpable injuries to the widow,' wrote Lowther's steward, Thomas Tickell. He protested in vain that Mrs Johnson's level was in fact a tunnel planned to undermine Lowther's workings, and letter by letter recorded the ensuing subterranean warfare. Mrs Johnson's miners reached the coal seam first. Lowther's men sank another pit to it. Their rivals extracted the coal from under it, but could not continue working without the benefit of Lowther's pit for air, so Tickell had it closed and sealed up further air vents which they bored. He triumphantly reported that although her miners possessed the coal face they could no longer work it. His forecast that she and her referees would keep inventing delays to prevent a more orderly settlement was thoroughly vindicated as meetings arranged in 1671, 1672, and 1673 all proved inconclusive.[21] In 1670 she was being sued in the manor court for not paying tithes, arguing that the land in question was tithe-free because it had never been ploughed. The jury found otherwise, but when the bailiffs seized corn to the value, she was prepared to sue for damages at common law, and only active conciliation by Sir John persuaded her to desist.[22]

There is no doubt that Mary Wybergh was closely involved in the management of her Chancery suit in 1672 against Sir John Lowther as he attempted to foreclose a mortgage on the Wybergh portion of the manor of St Bees.[23] Her obduracy at the door of her house had dissuaded the sheriff from taking possession at a first attempt, and her steadfast refusal to join with her husband in signing an agreement meant, upon his death, that effective settlement was delayed twelve years more until her son came of age. Meanwhile she continued to battle for her rights and her son's at two consecutive assizes. She pursued the judges to Appleby, the next stage of the circuit, and 'so importuned them' that they asked Lowther's kinsman, Sir John Lowther of Lowther Hall, to intercede to obtain her some maintenance.[24] She turned next to Chancery, sued out subpoenas against both Lowthers, and served one of them in person. And though poverty constrained her to let the suits lapse, she pressed her claims by other methods: urging her neighbours to withold their tithes from Lowther and encouraging her stock to stray into neighbouring fields to disrupt his farmers. When her son reached his majority, she joined with him in a new bill in Chancery. Lowther's sour remark is a monument to her capacity: 'To have to deal with an obstinate pauper is no small matter.'[25]

Widows' knowledge of property law and business strongly suggests their active participation in these areas of social life before their widowhood, though much clearly depended on individual personality and competence. In Thomas Tickell's opinion, Mrs William Fletcher of Moresby Hall preferred her husband to remain in gaol for debt, as it left her free to manage the estate.[26] Before his empire crumbled, Thomas Lutwidge had directed in his will that his wife be given the 'power to carry on the trade and business what I am at present concerned in and have agreed to carry, as she shall think proper.'[27] James Lowther clearly expected her to be more capable in managing affairs than her husband could ever again be. Widowed Elizabeth Williamson complained in the manor court that she had contracted with Richard Wilkinson and Richard Brownrigg to build her new house, but they had built so poorly that she had to engage others to make good the work. The manorial jury found in her favour, and the bailiff Jonathan Branthwaite distrained four rugs and a counterpane to cover the costs and damages awarded. Wilkinson in turn sued the bailiff at common law for entering his house with force and seizing goods illegally. We have to piece together from other records that as early as 1695 she had mortgaged the tenement for £30 to none other than Richard Wilkinson, and that six months after signing the contract to build, she and Wilkinson had remortgaged the property to a third party for £500, presumably to pay Wilkinson for building what must have been an imposing house. The tenurial history of this property demonstrates the way widows could capitalize on their assets and redirect property among family members. Elizabeth had entered as joint tenant with her first husband, becoming the surviving tenant after his death. When she married John Williamson, she remained sole tenant, surrendering it to their daughter only after his death. Even then, she retained a life occupancy and rented out rooms to provide an income. The mortgage was cleared and the granddaughter to whom it eventually passed purchased the freehold. Two other properties, which Elizabeth held as surviving joint tenant with her second husband, passed at her death according to the custom of the manor to their son.[28] We can also note in passing that Elizabeth Williamson's experience of litigation begins earlier, when, as Elizabeth Pow, she and her husband sued Andrew Herbert and his wife for debts owed for tailoring, and the Herberts in turn sued the Pows for unpaid lodging bills.

Most suits, both in law and in equity, never progressed beyond the initial complaint, as the threat of litigation was of itself enough to bring the parties to settle through private agreement or court-sponsored arbitration. Even when a suit was pursued to judgment the real purpose might be to gain leverage in negotiating a final compromise settlement. Dorothy Lamplugh's problem was how to salvage anything for herself from the wreckage of her late husband's fortunes, given that he had not redeemed the real estate from the mortgage to Lowther, and that the money he owed to others almost equalled his personal estate. Her best hope was to get Lowther to buy her off so that he could sell or let the land freely, and she and her solicitor tried to strengthen her position by bringing an action of dower even while negotiating with him, and by surprise obtained judgment in her favour. But as the estate had already been heavily encumbered before her marriage, it was clear that dower could not ultimately defeat the claims of creditors. On Lowther's application the judgment was set aside, and while proceedings impended on a second writ Dorothy offered to settle for a thousand guineas. He expected to beat her down but did not achieve very much. A few days later he paid her a thousand pounds and she executed a release of all her claims of dower. 'I think I have done what is handsome,' he maintained, 'and she might have fared as well long since without either trouble or expence.'[29] (But that is what both Lowthers invariably protested after the event.) It is from an exchange between Lowther and his steward that we learn of Lamplugh's attempt shortly before he died to make new arrangements for his property, so as 'to screen him from his wife's demands.'[30] By 1727 she was embroiled in an Exchequer suit when Sir Christopher Musgrave sued her and her father, John Brisco, in part over a bond owed to Dorothy by Musgrave. The lawyer who had earlier acted on her behalf in the suit with Lowther transformed into the solicitor for her opponent.[31] The Exchequer court defined an issue to be tried between the parties at the next assizes, in which Dorothy, now remarried, was to be plaintiff. The verdict going against her, she took it on appeal to the House of Lords, where Musgrave was finally ordered to repay the bond money, but it had by then emerged in depositions that she had borne his child while a widow, so that if her finances were restored, her reputation was 'entirely ruined.'[32]

Shortly before his death in 1726, William Feryes, another of Whitehaven's wealthy merchants, bequeathed to his wife all his household goods and £600 to be raised out of his real and personal estate, in full discharge of her dower. Six years after his death, when she and her second husband filed a bill against the executors in Exchequer, she had received only one year's interest and had been sued by Feryes's younger brother as heir at law claiming the personal estate. The course of her litigation is muddied by suits and counter-suits between the heir and the executors, in common law, Chancery, Exchequer, and an appeal to the House of Lords, a sequence which ends only with the death of the heir. In 1735, the surviving executor was ordered to account with the Deputy Remembrancer touching the payment of the dower, but the Exchequer records show no final resolution of the case, while Lowther's steward describes the estate as 'a good deal of it torn to pieces in law.'[33] Frances Addison, whose husband Thomas had prefaced his bequest to her with the words, 'Now my will and desire is that my said affectionate and dearly beloved wife may live as much as is possible free from trouble and disturbance and spend her time suitable to her birth and quality in peace, security and piety,' faced two separate Chancery suits in the last two years of her life, one brought by her step-daughter and her husband, the other by her deceased daughter's husband, who had recently married his third wife. In the meantime she had to sue her farmers for their rent and petition the Treasury for arrears owed to her husband.[34]

To conclude with the somewhat obvious remark that the behaviour of these women demonstrates the gap which existed between their use of litigation on the one hand and the legal doctrine of coverture, notions of patriarchy, and expectations of seemly behaviour on the other seems drab recognition of the complexities and ambiguities of that experience and how we might interpret it. Thomas Tickell once described Mrs Johnson as a woman ready to 'burst with her own venom.' If just this single letter had survived from him, we could dismiss his outburst as just another specimen of misogyny. However, his correspondence spans twenty-six years, all meticulously kept, and containing a multitude of choleric expression about any tenant, male or female, deemed to be obstructing Lowther's interests. Tickell in fact was generally on good terms with Mrs Johnson, and helpful in her affairs after her husband's death, and that gave rise to this particular outburst: he was defending himself, not very gallantly perhaps, against the accusation of being overzealous in her concerns to the detriment of his employer's. When it suited Lowther to resume friendly relations with her, we find Tickell smoothly assuring him that he had 'held her very good friendship this long time and shall still do.'[35]

Women, according to Christopher Brooks's impressive quantitative study of litigants in late sixteenth- and early seventeenth-century society, comprised 5 to 13 per cent of all litigants (1998, 111). The number of women litigants may seem surprising in light of a married woman's lack of legal standing. A married woman could not sue at common law, nor write a will, obtain credit, or enter into a contract without her husband's consent. At her marriage she surrendered to him all personal estate and control of any real estate unless specifically exempted by an agreement entered beforehand. These restrictions of coverture, however, were in practice far less rigorous than would appear from the letter of the law. Mary Cioni, in the first study of what women did do at law, rather than what they could not, concluded, 'it was left to Chancery to begin according female litigants recognition as responsible individuals' (1982, 182).

In 1708 an anonymous lawyer offered to Parliament some proposals to reduce the great charges and delays of suits in equity. At the conclusion of his book, he turns to the particular problems encountered by women, and suggests some alterations in specific laws, 'out of compassion to their natural unfitness to manage suits' (*Proposals* [1708] 1727, 41). His phrase 'natural unfitness' is perhaps nothing more than a platitude of the age, for he concludes with the observation 'the many more hard points of Law, in respect to Women, plainly shew, they never sat in parliament' (*Proposals* [1708] 1727, 43). His conclusion acknowledges the difficulties arose not from some inherent female incapacity but instead from the structuring of society. The evidence of litigation involving women residing in Whitehaven indicates their capacity as litigants to engage responsibly with the law not only in Chancery but in a variety of jurisdictions in order to protect their property rights. The study of litigants residing in one locality provides a means to reveal what the bare legal records of courts leave unstated: it helps re-create the family relationships, patterns of property holding, business activities, and occupations of women litigants.

Notes

1 23 January [1725]. Cumbria Record Office, Carlisle (hereafter CRO) D/ Lons/W2/3/32.

2 E.g., Public Record Office (hereafter PRO) CP40/3441 rot. 708, 3442 rot. 1272, 3442 rot. 1274, and also 3453, rot. 1125, 'Joseph Holdfast to answer to John Goodtitle, that with force and arms Joseph entered a messuage in Whitehaven which Robert Dawe and wife Margaret, Mary Drinkald, spinster, and Anne Morrison widow, demised to John for a term of years, and ejected John,' where the three women are the daughters and co-heiresses of the recently deceased Miles Drinkald.

3 Cf. Harris's account of the frequency with which aristocratic men, in an earlier period, appointed their widows as executors: 'Seventy-seven percent (403) of 523 knights and noblemen with surviving wives selected them as executors and supervisors of their estates. Thirty-five percent of the 403 named them their sole executors' (Harris 2002, 129).

4 Court records for the manor of St Bees at CRO D/Lons/W8.

5 I do not count cross bills put in by defendants in the same cause, nor bills of revivor to bring a lapsed suit back into court.

6 PRO C12/2213/14. C2 Chas I, O14/35 is another specimen, but from outside the period.

7 Spedding to James Lowther, 30 November 1743, 'Parkin her attorney would do nothing without money so she has been forced to make up the affair and to give £40 to the plaintiff, of which he has spent about £35 and she has spent £20. Parkin ... believes the court would have given the cause for her but he would not go on without money.' All correspondence between the Lowthers and their stewards (Thomas Tickell, William Gilpin, and John Spedding) at CRO D/Lons/W2.

8 PRO C7/302/7, C7/33/28, C7/36/71.

9 PRO C5/346/37.

10 James Lowther to Spedding, 8 June 1725.

11 As Lloyd Davis explains in a later chapter in this book, seventeenth-century dramas represent women living in seaports as thriving entrepreneurs.

12 Spedding to James Lowther, 25 March 1739, 'Have talked a good deal with Mrs Lutwidge' and 9 May 1739, 'I called on Mrs Lutwidge this evening but she and her husband were gone to Mr Benn's room.' Benn was their attorney.

13 Scottish Record Office (Edinburgh), Scottish Admiralty Court, AC9/1070, *Lowes v. McFarlane* 1728.

14 Spedding to James Lowther, 11 January 1713, 29 January 1723, and 7 October 1715.

15 PRO CP40/3193, rot. 1130, Mary Addison to answer to Anthony Whiteside. She pleaded not guilty and claimed that they were piling stones to her harm, obstruction, and lessening of her access and that she had merely warned them off her premises.

16 PRO CP40/3200, rot. 740v, Anthony Whiteside to answer to Robert Blackburn, and CP40/3201 rot. 1350, Mary Addison to answer to Thomas Singleton.

17 CRO D/Lons/W8, 10 October 1701, 'Anthony Whiteside complains against Mrs Addison for intruding upon his ground. And we find by the evidence of Mr Thomas Curwen, Mr John Gale sr and William Sanderson that Mrs Addison's new house upon the south side stands partly upon the passage which was formerly between the above said parties. And that the stairs built at the aforesaid New House are properly on Anthony Whiteside's ground.'

18 Sir John Lowther to Thomas Addison, 26 March 1704; Thomas Addison to Sir John Lowther 1 April 1704, CRO D/Lons/W1/27.

19 For her agreement to demolish on request, see CRO D/Lons/W8, 9 April 1703. As I have found no trace of the case in Chancery records, I presume the matter was settled before Lowther actually filed the bill.

20 PRO E112/787/58; CRO D/Lec. Bundle of unsorted correspondence, 1629–19th c., letter dated by year only, 1714.

21 Tickell to Sir John Lowther, 17 April 1669, 7 and 21 June, 6 September
    1669, 18 February 1670, and 6 February 1671.
22 CRO D/Lons/W8, 20 October 1670; Sir John Lowther to Tickell, undated
    November 1670; and Tickell to Sir John Lowther, 12 December 1670.
23 PRO C5/578/47.
24 Tickell to Sir John Lowther, 18 September 1672.
25 Sir John Lowther to Tickell, 19 July 1683. A copy of the bill at CRO
    D/Lons/W4/5, the depositions at PRO C22/214/10.
26 Tickell to Sir John Lowther, 4 June 1691, 'Mr Fletcher sits in custody at
    Carlisle and careless of coming out and his wife as I hear content with his
    restraint which puts the government of the estate into her own manage-
    ment who spares not to report her utter dislike to let you have any part
    thereof.'
27 Will at Lancashire Record Office, Preston, Probate Records, Copeland
    deanery.
28 CRO D/Lons/W5/232 (Street Survey Book), entries for 20 Lowther St.,
    4 Duke St. and 7 Plumblands Lane.
29 James Lowther to Spedding, 29 June and 3 July 1725; Spedding to James
    Lowther, 5 May 1723.
30 Spedding to James Lowther, 5 May 1723.
31 He had probably been Musgrave's lawyer all along, 'lent' to Dorothy for her
    suit against Lowther while her father was still employed as Musgrave's
    election agent. Musgrave was Lowther's political rival and used any oppor-
    tunity to discomfort him.
32 James Lowther to Spedding, 11 April 1728.
33 PRO E112/1095 nos. 3 and 5, C12/1796/56, E127/35, E126/5 no. 25,
    E134 4 Geo 2 Hil 12 and 14, E112/1096 nos. 21 and 27, Spedding to James
    Lowther, 20 February 1737.
34 PRO PROB 11/521 for will of Thomas Addison, PRO C9/220/14 and C11/
    956/2, IND 1/6449, Calendar of Treasury Papers, vol. clxxviii, no. 31,
    13 July 1714.
35 Sir John Lowther to Tickell, 20 April 1688; Tickell to Sir John Lowther,
    1 June 1688, 21 June 1669; Sir John Lowther to Tickell, 24 February 1674;
    and Tickell to Sir John Lowther, 9 March 1674.

Works Cited

Brooks, Christopher. 1998. *Lawyers, Litigation and English Society since 1450.*
    London: The Hambledon Press.

Churches, Christine. 1998. Women and Property in Early Modern England: A Case-Study. *Social History* 23: 165–80.

Cioni, Maria. 1982. The Elizabethan Chancery and Women's Rights. In *Tudor Rule and Revolution: Essays for G.R. Elton from His American Friends,* ed. D. Guth and J. McKenna, 159–82. Cambridge: Cambridge University Press.

Erickson, Amy Louise. 1993. *Women and Property in Early Modern England.* London and New York: Routledge.

Gowing, Laura. 1996. *Domestic Dangers. Women, Words, and Sex in Early Modern London.* Oxford: Clarendon.

Harris, Barbara J. 2002. *English Aristocratic Women, 1450–1550: Marriage and Family, Property and Careers.* Oxford: Oxford University Press.

Proposals humbly offered to the Parliament of Great Britain and Ireland, for remedying the great charge and delay of suits at law: And in equity ... by an eminent lawyer. [1708] 1727. 8th ed. Dublin.

Stretton, Tim. 1998. *Women Waging Law in Elizabethan England.* Cambridge: Cambridge University Press.

Vickery, Amanda. 1998. *The Gentleman's Daughter: Women's Lives in Georgian England.* New Haven: Yale University Press.

3

Women's Property, Popular Cultures, and the Consistory Court of London in the Eighteenth Century

DAVID LEMMINGS

The London Consistory Court was the bishop of London's court and as such one of the network of diocesan ecclesiastical courts that had existed in England since the twelfth century. It applied a modified form of canon law under the administration of civil lawyers. These courts are probably best known because of their reputation in the early modern period as 'bawdy courts' where sexual offences were tried, and for their marginal status in a Whig trajectory of English legal history as deserving losers to the post-Reformation hegemony of secular common and statute law. More recently they have attracted considerable attention from social historians, principally because of their surprising vitality during the century after the Reformation as agencies for the regulation of popular morals and the enforcement of religious discipline by the Church of England. It is in these contexts – the courts' role at the interface of popular and elite cultures, and their endurance in a diminished role despite the travails of the established church – that I wish to examine the London court during the eighteenth century.

Despite the sensitivity of recent studies, with significant exceptions most historians continue to take a perspective on the English church courts that predetermines their inevitable decline with the breakdown of religious consensus and increasing secularism. But as a result of revisionist work on the Elizabethan and early Stuart period, the decline has now been postdated to the eighteenth century. The new story is one of rapid death after post-1689 legislation established a limited form of toleration for Protestant dissenters and supposedly undermined the popular legitimacy of the established church. In fact, until very recently little research had been done on the ecclesiastical courts after the restoration of their jurisdiction in 1660, no doubt because of this unpromising prognosis. But while it is certainly true that they became moribund in the nineteenth century, and their jurisdiction was decimated by Victorian statutes, recent work by Laura Gowing and others has shown that in the early seventeenth century they played a unique role as sites for negotiating plebeian women's issues and representing their values – principally via the rebuttal of oral accusations of sexual incontinence and in the resolution of matrimonial contracts and disputes (Gowing 1996, Ingram 1987, Sharpe 1980). In other words, in the church courts women were protecting and negotiating their 'property' and 'propriety' as women: their special places and individual reputations under contemporary constructions of female roles. By doing so, it could be argued, they constituted a point where female 'social space' intersected and interacted exceptionally with the elite, 'official,' and normally patriarchal cultures of law and governance (Hindle 1994, 393).

At least two questions then arise in relation to the history of the church courts during the eighteenth century. First, if, despite the shock of the Reformation, these courts had become important by providing 'ordinary' women with legal agency, as places where they represented their own cultural values and community norms rather than simply reflecting the pieties and moral standards of the church, why should they be doomed to wither and die with further departures from the ideal of religious consensus after 1689? Indeed, to what extent did this kind of litigation survive into the eighteenth century, and why did it ultimately decline? And second, if the peculiar relevance of the church courts to women diminished, how far was the jurisdiction affected by the significant shifts in social constructions of gender differences and 'respectability' which seem to have occurred over the 'long' eighteenth century? In particular, to what extent were 'ordinary' women able to negotiate their reputations and represent their values publicly during a period when 'politeness,' 'sensibility,' and Enlightenment values appeared to be eroding many characteristic expressions of popular cultures? I suggest below that in London at least the Consistory Court was partly 'de-feminized' with the ultimate dominance of suits for separation over those for defamation and its colonization by more wealthy and genteel litigants whose stories reflected the normal power relations of patriarchy and material property. It appears that the priorities of the church and legal establishment tended to render the courts less open to the representation of plebeian discourse, especially the words of 'silly women,' and therefore

contributed to a general process by which law was becoming remote
from the lived experience of ordinary people. These issues will be ap-
proached by looking first at the dimensions of litigation in the court and
then considering the gender and social characteristics of the litigants.

Patterns of Litigation

Before proceeding to look at the role of women's litigation in the
London Consistory Court it is necessary to take an overall view of
the jurisdiction. There were two sides to the jurisdiction of the court: the
'office' side and the 'instance' side. Office or 'correction' causes were
those brought in the name of the church authorities and approximated
roughly to criminal indictments in the secular courts. Besides regulation
of the clergy and the administration of church fabric and services,
before the eighteenth century they included a whole range of lay offences against the moral discipline of the church, including a variety of
sexual transgressions, along with failures in church attendance and ob-
servances, as well as scolding, wife beating, and drunkenness. Despite
the impact of the Reformation, which might have been expected to
undermine the authority of the church, in many dioceses, prosecutions
of this kind against ordinary men and women seem to have increased
over the period 1560–1640 as the discipline of the church underwent
'reinvigoration' (Ingram 1987, 13–14, 69; Marchant 1969, 230–3, 241).
But there is no doubt that the 'office' jurisdiction of the ecclesiastical
courts became a shadow of its former self after 1700, being confined
largely to strictly ecclesiastical business, such as prosecutions of clergy
and churchwardens for failing to maintain church buildings and furni-
ture, or squabbles among status-conscious parishioners over the rights to
prominent pews. By contrast, the endurance of the 'instance' jurisdiction of the church courts beyond 1700 implies that they continued to
represent practical solutions embedded in cultural expectations which –
like church baptism, marriage, and burial – did not necessarily depend
upon deep spiritual commitment to the established church.[1]

   'Instance' suits in the church courts were complaints of private individuals against other parties, in this corresponding roughly to civil cases
at common law. Theoretically, like the office cases, they could be brought
for a range of spiritual offences and were motivated by concern for the
good of the offender's soul, with reform in mind; but in most church
courts they were confined to disputes over wills, tithes, promises and
breakdowns in matters of marriage, and sexual defamation. Not surpris-

ingly, the last two – matrimonial suits and defamation actions for words alleging sexual misconduct – have attracted most recent scholarly attention; but this is not simply prurient interest. Suits for defamation, in particular, showed the greatest growth among interpersonal actions in almost all the church courts during the Elizabethan and early Stuart period, and they have therefore been the focus of several detailed studies (Ingram 1987, 299–300; Marchant 1969, 61–2, 68, 71; Sharpe 1980, 4, 8–9). The results are remarkable, because it appears that women, most of them wives, increasingly dominated defamation prosecutions. Gowing's study of the London Consistory Court in the later sixteenth and early seventeenth centuries shows that defamation cases constituted two-thirds of the court's business in the 1630s, and around three-quarters were sued by women, among whom a majority were married (1996, 32–4, 61).[2] Everywhere the litigants were mainly from the lower-middling ranks of society: the wives and daughters of tradesmen and craftsmen in the cities and towns, or husbandmen and yeomen in the surrounding countryside (Gowing 1996, 61; Sharpe 1980, 17; Ingram 1987, 304). Such a preponderance of female prosecutors requires some explanation.

For women in early modern England, their property and material interests were closely connected with establishing what anthropologists generally term 'honour,' meaning moral 'character,' or conformity to the cultural norms of behaviour established among peers. In part this was because of their disadvantageous legal position in relation to property. Under common law, married women had no separate legal personality; this meant that full legal ownership and use of property were confined to femes sole – unmarried women or widows. Femes covert had exchanged their legal independence for the status, care, and protection supposedly provided by marriage. So (leaving aside elite women with access to lawyers who could preserve their material property via equitable trusts), for those of plebeian or lower-middling social position, a married woman's most valuable property was her honour or status as a 'good housewife,' who fulfilled her domestic and maternal duties and was faithful and obedient to her husband (Walker 1996, 235–45; Roper 1994, 55–6). The second reason for the crucial importance of feminine honour was that in this period it seems to have been regarded as very fragile and was certainly under stress, especially in marriage, where women's supposedly powerful sexuality and passionate nature, as well as their work and social relations, were necessarily constrained by the demands of the patriarchal household. Even as late as 1743, the author of *The Art of Governing a Wife* complained 'if you keep your Wife at home, she is eternally complaining; if she has liberty to gadd, she is subject to every body's Censure' (1747, 5).[3] Moreover, the burden of material and cultural investment in marriage and the patriarchal ordered household was such that women's transgressions were viewed as threats to the community and the state, as well as to husbands or fathers (Gowing 1996, 185–8; Amussen 1988, chap. 2), as Patricia Parker explains in the introductory chapter to this section.

In these circumstances women's reputations were frequently the subject of public comment by neighbours and associates, and feminine dishonour had serious practical consequences. Wives and daughters were cautioned to avoid giving any excuse for adverse comment: 'A virtous Woman must be very cautious in what she says, and circumspect in all she does; for ... the Opportunity is enough to defame a Woman' (*Art of Governing* 1747, 13–14). It has been argued that critical remarks like 'whore' or 'strumpet' or 'quean' allowed the community to exercise its authority and maintain norms of acceptable behaviour, but they were also easy taunts which could embroider essentially nonsexual disputes. Whether the accusations were genuine or not, single women in domestic service or any women in sociable occupations were particularly exposed to public taunts of unchastity – slurs which might well affect prospects of marriage, or of income, especially if the target was self-employed or in business with her husband (Clark 1989, 239–40). And marriages were vulnerable to these charges too. The potential fragility of marriage, especially among the mobile populations of towns and cities, was a problem in itself which went beyond dishonour: wives were sometimes deserted or treated cruelly; their 'husbands' occasionally turned out to be married previously; and promises or precontracts of marriage might be broken after the woman became pregnant, leaving her honour damaged and her chances of marriage low (Ingram 1987, 147–9). So these were all potentially serious practical issues which might ultimately affect women's material circumstances, as well as their honour as women. No doubt they were most frequently addressed informally, via the intervention of friends and relatives, and inevitably some women must have failed to restore their names or their marriages. But in the later sixteenth and early seventeenth centuries problems like these were the principal issues which women brought to the ecclesiastical courts as suitors in cases of defamation and matrimony.

What, then, was the experience of the ecclesiastical courts in the eighteenth century? They had become exceptional in providing a forum for plebeian women to litigate interpersonal actions at a time when

English law largely denied such women legal agency, in line with the cultural assumptions of a patriarchal society. Historians have labelled the instance side of the ecclesiastical jurisdiction in the early modern period as a species of litigation uniquely appropriated by women, and representing a popular culture of gender relations quite different from the teachings of the church (Gowing 1996, 10–11, 265–8; Ingram 1987, 301–2). So it would be surprising if it simply collapsed with the relative loss of prestige experienced by the established church after 1640 and 1689, especially since the legal status of married women did not undergo fundamental change before the nineteenth century (Staves 1990; Baker 1990, chap. 27). Certainly, it is very likely that there was a decline in the *totals* of litigation business, if office and instance cases are taken into account. But defamation litigation at least was hardly moribund by 1700, according to a series of local studies. The evidence for the church courts at York, Wells, and Norwich suggests that while it was never as buoyant after 1660 as it had been, defamation business only began to fall away seriously in the second quarter of the eighteenth century; and it took another century to disappear altogether, much to the embarrassment of strait-laced early nineteenth-century church officials (Marchant 1969, 62, 68; Sharpe 1980, 8–9; Morris 1985, Table IVa, 245, 247; Amussen 1988, 101–2; Waddams 2000, 195). Indeed, from their hostile and superior comments and the semicontinuous parliamentary opposition to the church courts during the eighteenth century, it appears that plebeian litigants exercised the opportunity to prosecute defamation in the teeth of resistance from their betters (Morris 1985, 236–9, 242; Waddams 2000, 56–7, 65, 66–7). To paraphrase Polly Morris, the instance side of the ecclesiastical courts seems to have died 'a slower, more complicated death' than that predicted by the history of the Church of England (1985, 213).[4]

The eighteenth-century story of the London court is equally complex, although there are clear parallels with the provincial courts. Recent work by Tim Meldrum and Robert Shoemaker suggests that the London Consistory Court never again matched its early seventeenth-century glut of defamation business, when up to 200 cases a year had been heard. But there does seem to have been a limited revival around 1680, when nearly 80 cases were heard in one year, and possibly again in the early eighteenth century, since there were over 60 cases in 1715 and nearly 50 in 1725 (Shoemaker 2000, 101; Meldrum 1994, 2).[5] Thereafter, although the picture is complicated by the cessation of the main series of Act Books and consequent use of evidence from different classes of documents, it is likely that new defamation business declined significantly; there were probably only 15–20 new cases a year from mid-century and hardly any after 1800, by contrast with a continuous trickle in some provincial dioceses (Waddams 2000, 193–5).[6] My own figures (Table 1), which are derived from the surviving Act Books, show that the early decline of defamation suits was part of a general reduction in the volume of instance cases. Whereas there had been over 350 suits in the London Consistory during sample years in the second and third decades of the seventeenth century, by the turn of the eighteenth century there were only about 75 new cases a year, and the volume of cases declined still further to reach less than 35 over the years 1749–53 (Gowing 1996, 33). Defamation suits remained the single most numerous class of actions until at least the middle of the century, however, although 'ecclesiastical' business became much more important as the overall volume of cases declined, especially petitions for the allocation of pews, or the construction and appropriation of burial vaults and monuments. This last increase should be borne in mind, because while it can be interpreted as part of a tendency for the Consistory to become more absorbed with 'church matters,' especially ecclesiastical property, it also suggests the court was attracting a more wealthy clientele, who were prepared to pay handsomely to enhance their families' honour and status (see Meldrum 1994, 3). Moreover, although matrimonial suits (predominantly actions for judicial separation, but also for 'jactitation' or false claim of marriage, and nullification on the grounds of previous marriage or precontract) seem to have declined over the first half of the eighteenth century, both in absolute and relative terms, we know from other sources that the London Consistory Court survived into the nineteenth century by becoming the most important divorce court in the country, and the suits were dominated by clients of wealth and relatively high status (Stone 1990, 43–4, 186; Waddams 1992, 165–6).

But if it appears that the London Consistory Court ultimately went upmarket to survive, despite its overall decline the early eighteenth-century litigation tends to confirm the persistence of its attraction for a particular constituency. In the decades beginning in 1700 and 1735, among suits which reached the stage of generating a 'libel' – a statement of the case by the 'producent' or prosecutor – 60 per cent of the interpersonal suits were for defamation and around 20 per cent were matrimonial cases. And while it has been shown that around 60 per cent of the matrimonial cases at mid-century were prosecuted by women, no less than 95 per cent of the defamation suits had been brought by women,

Table 1
New Instance Business in the London Consistory Court, 1699–1702 and 1749–1753

| | 1699–1702 | | | 1749–53 | | |
Type of case	N	Av/year	%	N	Av/year	%
Defamation	161	40.3	55.0	67	13.4	40.9
Ecclesiastical[a]	36	9.0	12.2	51	10.2	31.1
Matrimonial	68	17.0	23.1	25	5.0	15.2
Testamentary	13	3.3	4.4	19	3.8	11.6
Other/unknown[b]	16	4.0	5.4	2	0.8	1.2
Total	294	74.5	100.0	164	32.8	100.0

[a]Includes many uncontested petitions for faculties or licences, especially to establish burial vaults and monuments.
[b]Includes promoted office cases.
Sources: LMA, DL/C 39, ff. 1–381 (Instance Act Book, Jan. 1699–Dec. 1702); LMA, DL/C 52, ff. 1–428 (Instance Act Book, Jan. 1749–Dec. 1753).

and they also formed 80 per cent of the defamation litigants as a whole (Meldrum 1994, 2, 6; Stone 1990, 428). There are similar findings for the provincial courts, although the London Consistory seems to have been feminized more completely, and earlier (Sharpe 1980, 10, 27; Morris 1985, 7–8; Gowing 1996, 267–8). Although significant numbers of men were still present as defendants, a constituency of women, and wives particularly, appears to have valued the services which the church courts could provide, especially in regard to resolving arguments which involved charges of sexual incontinence, and at a time when they were no longer likely to be prosecuted for sexual offences by the church itself (Meldrum 1994, 6; Shoemaker 1999, 138–9, 140; Clark 1989, 240). And yet the virtual collapse of defamation suits in London around mid-century implies a change either in their values or in the administration of the court – or perhaps both. It will be necessary to look at some examples of the suits to approach an explanation of this apparent paradox.

The Characteristics of Litigation

By the early eighteenth century the London Consistory Court had become even more dominated by women than it had been before 1640: in fact the decline in the number of defamation suits may have been partly a matter of the absolute disappearance of *men* as prosecutors. And the female plaintiffs who prosecuted defamation were overwhelmingly lower 'middling sort' women suing sexual slanders. The following case was typical: in Trinity term 1700 Mrs Mary Grant of the parish of St John's in Wapping sued Mrs Lucy Russell. She alleged that in 1698 Russell had called her a whore in public, and the libel recited the standard form of words 'That by reason of speaking the Defamatory words aforesaid the good Name fame and Reputation of the said Maria Grant is very much hurt and injured amongst her Neighbours Acquaintance and others.' The court had jurisdiction because the words alleged adultery – a spiritual offence which placed the soul in danger – and also because an unfounded allegation of this kind constituted a breach of Christian charity. But the papers in the case suggest a simple and very worldly argument over money. The prosecutor and defendant had lived in the same house, Mary Grant being Mrs Russell's serving maid, and her husband being apprenticed to Mr Russell; and the accusation 'whore' had been flung at the prosecutor out of anger in the context of an ongoing and materialistic quarrel between the two couples. It seems Mr Grant had been arrested at common law for a debt of £30 to Mr Russell, and the defendant alleged that Mary Grant had brought the defamation case in retaliation. Despite these counter-allegations the suit was proved to the satisfaction of the judge, and the defendant Lucy Russell was subsequently excommunicated pending the performance of penance and ordered to pay costs of suit (LMA, DL/C 149, ff. 58–63, *Grant v. Russell*).[7]

Whatever the precise truth of the accusations and counter-accusations in the case, it probably had little to do with the libel's formal declarations about need for 'canonical correction' of any person who uttered 're- proachful scandalous or defamatory words' against another, especially the charge of committing 'the foul crime of adultery Fornication and Incontinency.' In this case at least there is a strong suspicion that the plaintiff did not take her claim to the Consistory Court because she wanted to assert the health of her soul or restore the bond of charity with her neighbour; and the sexual nature of the slander may well have been incidental to the argument. But the issue was a serious one all the same, and on both sides: the two couples seem to have been friends (it was alleged that the Grants were married from the Russells' house and that Mrs Russell had provided a wedding dinner for them); no doubt Mary Grant had attempted to persuade Mrs Russell that the claim against her husband should be dropped so that he could be released from prison, but she would have been relatively powerless in the face of her employer's refusal (LMA, DL/C 149, f. 60). In the bitterness of friendship turned sour, she probably believed the threat of doing a penance in a white sheet (the standard penalty if the suit proceeded to judgment) on pain of imprisonment might change her adversary's mind, because it would undoubtedly be humiliating for the wife of a master craftsman. As a married woman and in the absence of her husband, she looked to the Consistory as the only legal tribunal available to her as a private prosecutor; and in 1700, when defamation suits were still relatively common, other women's experiences might have led her to expect a favourable outcome. Indeed, it was the accusation of sexual impropriety which enabled her to bring her opponent before the court. Certainly, in this case the Consistory Court was probably 'being used as an arena (like the street, shop or stall) for the promotion and resolution of disputes,' but it was a uniquely accessible source of authority for vulnerable women like Mary Grant (Meldrum 1994, 13).

I am suggesting that the church courts continued to remain relatively popular with litigants in the early eighteenth century, despite any relative decline in their moral authority, because they continued to fulfil a practical need, in this case for women to maintain interpersonal actions in their own right under the cover of responding to sexual slander. By no means can all the defamation cases brought by women be reduced to vexatious material disputes of the kind implied by *Grant v. Russell*; many were brought because women genuinely sought to defend their reputations for sexual continence, most likely indeed to sustain their marriages and maintain tenuous employment opportunities, which depended on their credit in the local community (Meldrum 1994, 8–13). But they did not self-evidently manifest any deep personal commitment to the Church of England; rather they represented the culture of plebeian women, negotiating their customary rights and reputations in household, family, and community. Indeed, it was the representation of popular cultures in the church courts which may have rendered defamation cases undesirable to the church authorities, as we shall see.

This secular independence seems to have been equally true of litigants in matrimonial disputes, the second most important species of interpersonal litigation in the early eighteenth-century church courts. For example, in Hilary term 1700 Mrs Frances Abercromby sued her husband John in the London Consistory, seeking a separation from bed and board on the grounds of adultery (LMA, DL/C 39, f. 115, *Abercromby v. Abercromby*). The libel alleged that having married Frances Butler in 1695, John, who was a cabinetmaker of St Giles in the Fields, repeatedly visited 'Whore houses or Bawdy howses,' and thereby 'got the foul disease Gonorrhea or French pox.' After several promises of reformation and cure followed by relapse and reinfection, and the birth of a very sickly child, his wife refused him sexual relations, upon which he allegedly 'fell into a great passion and said he was sorry he had not given it to her, meaning the Distemper he then laboured under.' It was only then that Mrs Abercromby, described according to form as 'a modest virtuous woman,' and the daughter of one Dr James Butler, resorted to the court for a more permanent solution to her problem: judicial separation and alimony. The story is one which must have been familiar to the presiding judge and officers of the court, being repeated in countless other cases. But it was remarkable in at least one instance: both the husband and wife were Catholics. As such, the complainant would hardly have recognized the spiritual authority of the court, but the Church of Rome had no authority in England, and as a married woman who was being abused by her lawful husband, she had no other means of legal redress which might remove him permanently (LMA, DL/C 149, ff. 1–2).[8] In the event, her husband contested the case, and although the court ordered interim alimony on pain of excommunication, and witnesses were summoned to answer interrogatories, the case seems never to have proceeded to a final judgment (DL/C 39, ff. 121, 127, 138, 146). We do not know if she took him back again or returned to live with her father, but in the absence of a decree for permanent separation with maintenance for herself and the child her future options would have been bleak.

The business of the ecclesiastical courts seems to have remained essentially secular and material in substance throughout the eighteenth century. The increase of business concerning ecclesiastical property is one facet of what appears to be a general change in the principal business and social orientation of the court. A gravitation towards a different constituency is certainly apparent in the court's surviving litigation business. Among sixty-eight cases in advanced stages initiated during the years 1789–91, thirty-five were issues of marriage and thirty-three were for defamation (LMA, DL/C 181, ff. 2–486). This slight preponderance of matrimonial cases only partially reflects an important transformation, whereby suits for divorce, rather than defamation, became the main business of the court (Stone 1990, 43–4, 428.).[9] As the statistics in Table 1 show, suits for defamation had gone into recession after the first quarter of the eighteenth century, and although the numbers of new suits were not trifling before 1800, their fairly rapid decline is even more significant in the context of London's rising population, which increased slowly between 1700 and 1750, and more rapidly in the second half of the century (Shoemaker, 2000, 101; Holmes 1993, 403). Moreover, the late eighteenth-century defamation cases which generated a libel (meaning that the 'ministrant,' or defendant, had responded to the suit by appointing a proctor to defend it) were much more rarely taken as far as judgment and sentence than matrimonial cases: twenty-seven of the defamation cases went no further than the libel, while all but eight of the matrimonial suits resulted in the calling of witnesses and/or an eventual judgment and sentence (LMA, DL/C 181, ff. 2–486). Indeed, by contrast with the brief entries for defamation suits, proceedings in some of these cases run to scores of pages in the records, as counter-allegations followed libels, and extensive series of 'interrogatories' were issued to the witnesses on behalf of each party (e.g., LMA, DL/C 181, ff. 133–221, *Augusta Evans v. Thomas Evans* esq [separation]). So the clerks who wrote down the words, the proctors and advocates who acted as lawyers, and the vicar-general who was the judge must have made their livings principally from the fees they received in litigating marital disputes. And litigants able to maintain these suits were relatively wealthy: typically by the later eighteenth century they were members of merchant or professional families, but also not infrequently members of the gentry and nobility.[10] The London Consistory was becoming the principal forum in the country for propertied couples to obtain a practical separation from bed and board on the grounds of adultery or cruelty, often in tandem with an action for 'criminal conversation,' by which the husband sued the wife's lover for damages in the Court of King's Bench (Stone 1990, chap. 9). Appropriately for the eighteenth century, an age whose most obvious feature is arguably hard-headed materialism, like the money for honour transactions over private pews and funerary monuments, this was business which was essentially commercial, rather than pious.

Moreover, there can be little doubt that the increasing predominance of matrimonial suits represented a departure from the position whereby the Consistory Court of London could be characterized as a 'women's court,' insofar as it was dominated by female litigants and allowed women legal space to represent positively distinct feminine cultural values and social contexts. Table 2, which tabulates the gender of litigants in defamation and matrimonial suits for three sample periods in the eighteenth century, shows that the gender balance of the court was shifting. Certainly it is true that despite declining overall caseloads, defamation litigation remained mainly a feminine preserve, for nearly 60 per cent of the suits in each period were all-women affairs. However the complete absence of male prosecutors of defamation after the middle of the century may suggest that eighteenth-century men no longer took sexual slander very seriously, for they were still frequently named in the court's records of defamation suits as defendants, and it has been suggested that they were less restrained than their predecessors when it came to making sexual insults themselves (Shoemaker 1999, 138–45; Shoemaker 2000, 114–15). It appears that men's reputations became less sensitive to accusations of sexual immorality as expectations of male and female conduct diverged after 1700 (Dabhoiwala 1996, esp. 212–13; Meldrum 1994, 5–6, 10–11). Indeed, the very low rate of sentencing in these cases relative to matrimonial suits surely implies that they were rarely fully defended and were taken no more seriously by the men who were proctors, advocates, and judges in the court. The statistics in Table 2 also show that as matrimonial cases came to dominate litigation business, women no longer formed a majority of prosecutors, as they had done since at least the early seventeenth century (Gowing 1996, 35). More detailed figures published by Lawrence Stone show that separation suits brought by men on the grounds of adultery were outnumbering those brought by women citing cruelty or abandonment, as well as actions for breach of contract, which had been common early in the century before being prohibited by the Marriage Act of 1753 (Stone 1990, 187, 428; Lemmings 1996, 346).[11] The stories presented in these cases suggest the shift was hardly favourable for women.

It is true that women who were litigants in matrimonial cases attempted to take advantage of their contemporaries' peculiar interpretation of marriage as a species of polite commerce: a contractual arrangement which implied that wives had rights of maintenance, protection, and respect. Certainly propertied women who were involved in matrimonial disputes sometimes used the opportunity to assert the value of their dowries and inheritances as pressure on the court to approve adequate alimony, thereby stressing their material contribution to the husband's estate. For example, Harriet Ball, who was the defendant in a suit for separation brought by her husband in 1791, alleged that she brought him the interest and dividends of £5,000 bank stock inherited from her father, James Harris Esquire. But although evidence of her dowry may well have raised her standing in the eyes of the court, she nevertheless had to undergo the dishonour of evidence that she was living in adultery with a Wapping brewer, and her own suit for annulling the marriage on the basis of her husband's long-standing impotence was dismissed, thereby preventing her from marrying her lover and becoming respectable again (LMA, DL/C 181, ff. 28–40, *Thomas*

Table 2
Gender of Defamation and Matrimonial Prosecutors in the Consistory Court of London, 1699–1702, 1749–1753, and 1789–1791

Gender	1699–1702		1749–53		1789–91	
	N	%	N	%	N	%
Defamation litigants						
Woman v. woman	92	57.1	39	58.2	19	57.6
Woman v. man	60	37.3	28	41.8	14	42.4
Man v. woman	7	4.3	–		–	
Man v. man	2	1.2	–		–	
Total	161	100.0	67	100.0	33	100.0
Matrimonial litigants						
Woman v. man	47	69.1	15	60.0	17	48.6
Man v. woman	21	30.9	10	40.0	18	51.4
Total	68	100.0	25	100.0	35	100.0

Sources:
1699–1702 and 1749–53: Instance Act Books (see sources for Table 1).
1789–91: Allegation, Libel, and Sentence Books (LMA, DL/C 181, ff. 2–486).

Bannister Ball v. Harriet Ball).[12] Mrs Ball also alleged her husband was 'of a most cruel and vicious disposition' insofar as he had beaten her frequently, and one might have expected the frequent stress on the violence of husbands in marriage to have had great impact in a period when excessive violence of husbands towards wives was regarded as shameful (Hunt 1992, 25–7; Foyster 1996, 219–23). But like the respect due to property, the frequent appeals to Enlightenment standards of civility and reason by wives who sued for separation could hardly compensate for the hard fact that they were always disadvantaged against husbands in cases like these because of the 'double standard' which applied in marriage. Indeed, they were virtually obliged to base their suits on evidence of extreme cruelty rather than adultery; for despite the church's condemnation of adultery by either sex, in the eighteenth century extramarital intercourse among men was frequently winked at, and wives were merely expected to work harder to redeem their errant husbands. As Samuel Johnson said, 'a wife ought not greatly to resent this ... [She] should study to reclaim her husband by more attention to please him' (Boswell 1980, 394; Hunt 1992, 26).

This relative tolerance of male adultery was the consequence of an important transition in understandings about male and female sexuality.

Whereas women's sexuality was previously regarded as potentially insatiable, during the eighteenth century there was an increasing tendency
to see them as sexually passive, while men's sexuality was believed to be
more uncontrollable and its repression even thought to be harmful
(Fletcher 1995, 58, 114, 340–5, 392–4; Shoemaker 1998, 61–7). Thus
women were held responsible for controlling masculine lust, and unlike
men they had no excuses for promiscuity themselves. As Lovelace said in
Richardson's *Clarissa*, 'Men are to ask – Women are to deny' (1811, vii.
313). By contrast with the treatment of unfaithful husbands, among all
but the lowest social groups, female adultery was absolutely unaccept-
able and normally fatal to a woman's character, not so much on the
seventeenth-century grounds that it represented fundamental disorder
and disobedience in the household, as well as sin and masculine
dishonour, but rather because it threatened male property rights (Fletcher
1995, 110–11; Gowing 1996, 185–206). Johnson insisted 'the chastity of
women ... [is] of the utmost importance, as all property depends upon
it,' and Boswell's apologia for an abused wife who succumbed to another
man only elicited the comment 'The woman's a whore, and there's an
end on't' (Boswell 1980, 537, 702). Indeed, as the Court of King's Bench
recognized, the adultery of wives was feared mainly because of its potential for disrupting the transmission of property in the legitimate family
line. Thus, from the mid-eighteenth century the court encouraged the
action of criminal conversation, whereby lawyers made a doctrine of the
common concern held by a man of property and rank 'that no spurious
issue be imposed on his family' (*Two Actions* 1790, 6 [*Cecil v. Sneyd*, King's
Bench, 1790]). Judging by the results of the separation cases which
reached advanced stages in 1789–91, litigation in the London Consistory
was susceptible to the same views, because fourteen of the eighteen
matrimonial cases sued by men led to a sentence in the prosecutor's
favour, whereas only five of the seventeen women won their suits (LMA,
DL/C 181, ff. 2–486).[13]

They certainly had an uphill task. Abused wives who sued in the
Consistory Court were forced to conform to the traditional ideology of
gender relations in marriage, whereby they were expected to be patiently
obedient, submissive, and affectionate, even in the face of maltreatment.
Like Frances Dey, who sued for separation from her allegedly violent
spouse in 1699, their libels always included the standard form that

> the said Frances Dey is a person of a meek quiett and peaceable temper and
> of a vertuous life and conversation and hath during all the time of her

intermarriage with ... John Dey her husband carryed and demeaned her selfe very loving and obediently towards her ... husband and endeavoured by all wayes and meanes to deserve the same vertues of kindnesse and affection.

Although Mrs Dey claimed that her husband had attempted to stab her with a penknife, had beaten her on several occasions, and turned her out of the house so that she was 'destitute of all necessaryes,' the higher expectations of wifely conduct meant that she was very vulnerable to counter-attacks of her own misbehaviour. Her husband alleged that since their marriage she 'has been a person of a very unchast and immodest behaviour and of a very turbulent quarrelsome and provoking temper, nor hath she in all the time aforesaid shewed carried or behaved herself with that duty love or affection towards the said John Dey.' These were offences which contemporaries generally accepted amounted to sufficient justification for 'moderate correction,' if not cruelty. But perhaps more crucially, John Dey also accused her of adultery and of living in a bawdy house since they had separated, and summoned witnesses to prove the allegations. Indeed, while both parties attempted to discredit the testimony of the other's witnesses via accusations of sexual incontinence, theft, and perjury, one suspects that enough damage had been done to render Frances Dey's character suspect in the eyes of her supporters, because her case did not proceed to judgment (LMA, DL/C 149, ff. 27–46, *Frances Dey v. John Dey*). The much higher success rates for men who sued in cases like these suggests the court was more amenable to claims of wifely infidelity and immodesty than it was to evidence of cruelty on the part of husbands, even if they had been unfaithful too.

It appears, then, that by the later eighteenth century the London Consistory Court was much less of a 'woman's court' than it had been one hundred years earlier. Defamation suits brought by plebeian women had declined in numbers and significance, while the increasing dominance of matrimonial suits between propertied litigants represented a culture of marital relations which was clearly disadvantageous for wives. Indeed, the double standard is also clearly visible in the surviving defamation business, as women still brought men to the court for defaming them, but men apparently no longer felt the need to defend their own reputations against sexual insults. Given that the increase in matrimonial business was exactly proportional to the rise in King's Bench criminal conversation suits by husbands seeking damages on the grounds of adultery, it is arguable that the primary interest of the court changed dramatically between 1700 and 1800: from enabling women actively to defend their honour and propriety as women, and even 'to claim a [limited] verbal and legal authority' in the gendered regulation of sexual and social relations, it became preoccupied with a species of litigation which supported male commerce in women's persons as *property*, and at best rendered them as passive victims of abusive husbands (cf. Gowing 1994, 28, 43; Stone 1990, 43–4, 241–3; and Hunt 1992, esp. 19, 24). Moreover, the court had gone up-market decisively in its litigation and administrative business, despite its continuing appeal for a minority of plebeian women. It is necessary to consider now why these shifts had occurred and what they meant for the place of the church courts in negotiating popular cultures.

Explanations and Conclusion

Although the distinction is ultimately unsatisfactory, it is convenient to approach explanations for the shifts in litigation and litigants which have been described by considering separately factors which can be catego-rized as 'internal,' meaning the actions and declarations of the court and its personnel, and those which might be classed as 'external,' signify-ing 'grass-roots' social and cultural changes. Certainly Robert Shoemaker's recent study of the London Consistory Court's records, which concen-trates on defamation proceedings, has emphasized external explana-tions in seeking to account for the decline of these suits in the eighteenth century. The author identifies a tendency for public insult to diminish with increasing refinement and sensibility in English society, a process driven by the emerging middle class: status-conscious people who valued the privacy of their sexual and social relations, and for whom personal honour supposedly became a matter of private contemplation rather than public comment. Such an argument is indeed plausible, and it undoubtedly has added force for women, insofar as the eighteenth-century prescriptions for polite femininity meant that they 'were increas-ingly seen as too pure and delicate to think about sex, let alone talk about it in public, either in the streets or the courtroom' (Shoemaker 2000, 115). But without wishing to deny the ultimate 'progress of polite-ness' in Georgian society, too much reliance on prescriptive literature tends to anticipate the development of Jane Austen's world among the mass of middle-class families by at least fifty years. The evidence of witnesses at the Old Bailey and of Francis Place's autobiography suggests an independent, lower-middling culture of relatively loose sexual relations and ribald discourse survived among men and women in London, at least until Evangelical reform destroyed it in the early nineteenth century (Clark 1989, 235–8; Place 1972, 57–9, 81–2, 90–1). And despite arguments about the declining incidence and power of public insult, in the second half of the eighteenth century newspapers frequently carried apologies from individuals who admitted defaming neighbours or acquaintances. For example, in March 1767 the *Ipswich Journal* included a notice from Agnes Ary, a servant of Jonathan Maston, of Hoxne in Suffolk, for publicly defaming Sarah Garrard, another servant, by accusing her of having 'been towards four natural Children, and [she] had destroyed them all.' As usual in these cases, Agnes thanked Sarah for not proceeding 'as Law directs' (*Ipswich Journal*, 22 March 1767). Indeed, the suddenness of the collapse in defamation litigation at the London Consistory around the middle of the eighteenth century, after the maintenance of substantial numbers between 1670 and 1730, suggests cultural changes were being assisted by something less subtle. And this impression is reinforced by Tim Meldrum's observation of a 'steep decline' before 1740 in the number of defamation cases which went beyond the presentation of a libel by the prosecutor (1994, 3–4; see also Shoemaker 2000, 103). There is little doubt that 'Women seem to have become less willing to contest allegations of sexual immorality in the public forum of the courts' after 1750, but the chronology of decline makes one wonder if their forbearance was entirely voluntary (Shoemaker 2000, 115).

The observed context of this shift deserves to be emphasized: whatever the reality of behaviour in English streets and alehouses, we only know for certain that during the eighteenth century public insult was less frequently represented in the courts of the established church. Moreover, it seems to have occurred earliest in London, at the court which was closest to the institutions of central government. And perhaps most crucially, it happened at a time when the ecclesiastical jurisdiction was the subject of a major assault in Parliament, wherein the bishop of London himself was its principal defender, both via the press and in the House of Lords (Taylor 2000; Gibson 1733). These coincidences surely suggest that 'internal' factors should not be dismissed too readily in seeking to explain the changes in the London Consistory Court's business and may also imply that the state had an important role in the 'civilization' of popular culture, at least in the courts (see Hindle 1996, 237–8; Shoemaker 2000, 130–1; Elias 1994).

I have space here for only a relatively superficial review of these issues, but there is enough evidence to suggest that further research might be rewarding. First, there is the high probability that more dilatory proceedings and rising costs contributed to the disappearance of defamation suits, cases normally maintained by suitors who were certainly not poverty-stricken but hardly affluent either. Costs have been discussed in some of the recent work on the London Consistory, but only very briefly, and not with sufficient rigour to support suggestions that they did not increase significantly.[14] There are clear indications to the contrary. Gowing's study of litigation at the London court in Eizabethan and Stuart times suggests the expense of a defamation suit was much lower then: while examples of costs in the early eighteenth century vary from £7 to £21, she cites a 1592 case which went all the way to sentence and where the defendant was ordered to pay only £2 6s in expenses of suit, and she estimates the expense for an average case was 'around £4' (Gowing 1996, 40; Meldrum 1994, 3, n. 17). And Ingram's study of the Wiltshire church courts provides early seventeenth-century examples of defamation costs which varied between £2 and £5 (Ingram 1987, 57). By comparison, in two of the three defamation cases which reached sentence between 1789 and 1791 the costs of suit were £16 and £19 2s, sums which would have been prohibitive for many (LMA, DL/C 181, f. 58, *Crompton v. Butler*, f. 335, *Myatt v. Allen*).[15] Of course, estimating legal costs is complicated, because the totals depended on the length of the suit, and there was considerable variation. But it would be surprising if the expenses of ecclesiastical justice did not increase. The early eighteenth century was a period of declining litigation in virtually every jurisdiction which has been studied, a dearth which was normally accompanied by rising fees and lengthier proceedings, as lawyers and clerks made the most of high-value cases (Brooks 1986, 357–99; Lemmings 2000). And we know there was a transfer of profitable matrimonial business to the London Consistory from provincial church courts during the eighteenth century, as litigants who were prepared to pay handsomely for the services of the country's top advocates and barristers took advantage of the capital's legal facilities to maintain parallel actions in the Consistory and King's Bench (Stone, 1990, 41; e.g., LMA, DL/C 181, f. 32, *Ball v. Ball*, f. 124, *Duberly v. Duberly*). Indeed, complaints about rising costs and slow processes formed part of the contemporaneous press and parliamentary campaign against the ecclesiastical courts (Sykes 1926, 150). Certainly in the London Consistory the clear evidence of increasing unwillingness to pursue defamation cases beyond the early stages of the suit is more plausibly explained by rising and unsustainable expenses rather than by modesty and restraint.

It should be emphasized once more that the decline of business in the church courts was socially disproportionate: the increasing dominance of lengthy and expensive matrimonial suits among propertied couples makes the lower 'middling sorts' who were the mainstay of the defamation jurisdiction conspicuous by their absence. But their absence may not have been just a matter of high costs. The second 'internal' factor which merits further investigation is the attitude of the court to the social milieu which gave rise to defamation litigation. It is necessary to ask again why defamation suits declined more rapidly in London than elsewhere. Leaving aside for a moment the question of the capital's general precocity as a leader of 'civility,' one must consider whether the eighteenth-century church establishment, especially the chancellors, vicar-generals, advocates, and proctors who ran the courts, were themselves reluctant to entertain defamation cases, or even positively discouraged them in favour of more genteel business. Unfortunately, it is relatively hard to identify the views of the civil lawyers because there are very few published reports of the proceedings in the consistory courts, as opposed to the higher church courts, and hardly any relate to defamation. But there is plenty of evidence that other lawyers and social equals were increasingly intolerant of what they saw as petty disputes among people of little consequence. Indeed, Shoemaker cites 'considerable evidence of judicial disapproval of defamation cases,' although he abruptly dismisses its importance for explaining changes in the London Consistory Court, despite the parallel decline of cases for opprobrious words at the Middlesex sessions and apparent disinterest of the courts at Westminster (Shoemaker 2000, 104–8, 116–17, 118–19). Yet it is surely important that common law judges, magistrates, and grand juries all commonly complained about the insignificance of cases that arose from 'scolding, backbiting, and reproaching' among 'poor people.' Whitlocke Bulstrode, the chairman of the 1718 Middlesex sessions, in his charge to the Middlesex grand jury, delivered in Westminster Hall, the very centre of the English legal world, ridiculed the discourse of the 'crowd,' especially plebeian women, and wondered that the law should pay it any attention:

Our Common Law has condescended so low, as to punish by Indictment or Information, a common Scold, communis Rixatrix: Now this silly Woman only makes a Noise among her Neighbours, and claps her Hands to in-

crease the Sound of impertinent Words; which to the Crowd, is even
Musick, but to nicer Ears, somewhat of Jargon or Caw-Jack. Now if this is an
Offence against the Publick Peace and Quiet of the Nation, which only
grates upon the Organ of Hearing on the tender and distinguishing Ears of
a wise Person, and sinks no deeper; what must be the hearing perpetually
of that Name (which, above all Things in the World, we ought to love,
reverence, and adore) being daily and hourly prophan'd, and vilify'd,
scorn'd, and contemn'd?

These comments were made in the context of an extended diatribe
against common blasphemy. For Bulstrode, a determined moral reformer, the universal practice by which 'ordinary Fellows' were always
punctuating their conversation with curses 'by the Name of Almighty
God' deserved presentation and indictment (Bulstrode 1718, 117–18).
Thus in this case, the magistrate not only derided feminine scolding as
insignificant; at the same time he sought actively to impose civility from
above, in the cause of religion and in the name of the state. If it was
replicated among the civil lawyers who staffed the church courts, such an
attitude can only have acted as a deterrent to the plebeian women and
men who might have considered taking their cases and exposing their
discourse to the Consistory.

Certainly, there is evidence that disapprobation of public insult represented 'official' culture as well as middle-class morality. In 1792 Sir
William Scott, judge of the Consistory Court of London, referred pa-
tronizingly to defamation proceedings as 'that class of causes, founded
on reproachful words, and mostly between the lower orders of the
people' (*The English Reports* 1900–32, clxv. 515n [*Hutchins v. Denziloe*]).
And around the same time JPs were urged not to remit their fees out of
generosity to humble complainants because the result would be an
increase in their workload, especially in dealing with 'squabbles and
contentions among the poor, who would carry every frivolous dispute,
every angry word, to the nearest tribunal' (Gisborne 1795, i. 417).
Ultimately magistrates and officials seem to have resented their courts
being taken up with the verbal abuse which was typical of the streets and
alehouses. In the ecclesiastical courts at Wells, they challenged the use of
the defamation jurisdiction by ordinary people whose proceedings were
'indecorous' and whose ends obviously had no connection with the
respectable pieties of the church. And in the early nineteenth century
several ecclesiastical judges who gave evidence to a parliamentary commission of inquiry 'reacted with embarrassment and revulsion to the

sexual content of defamation, [and] to the sorts of people who brought these suits,' while admitting that they sought to discourage such litigation (Morris 1985, 13, 236–8; Waddams 2000, 57, 66–7). One suspects such prejudices had been prefigured in the early eighteenth century, at a time when the campaign for the 'reformation of manners' among the common people was in full swing. Edmund Gibson, bishop of London from 1723 to 1748, was in the forefront of the campaign, and personally took a hand in the composition of material which was designed to reform language and behaviour, even publishing *An Admonition against Profane and Common Swearing*, a tract wherein like Bulstrode he connected blasphemy with the 'wild, unthinking profligate part of mankind' and encouraged 'honest and sober conversation' (Sykes 1926, 208–9). Moreover, Gibson was a vigorous administrator and an advocate for widespread reforms in the constitution and administration of the church, including the ecclesiastical courts, and was prevented from implementing thoroughgoing changes only by his failure to secure the support of other churchmen and the virulent anti-clericalism of the House of Commons, which came to a head in several bills designed to reduce the powers of the clergy, including attacks on the ecclesiastical jurisdiction (Sykes 1959, 192–204; Taylor 2000, 347–50, 351–2, 354–5). In these circumstances, while defending the ecclesiastical jurisdiction and the latent disciplinary powers of the church over the laity, it would not be surprising if Gibson had instructed his judicial officers to discourage suits which hardly conformed to his own public emphasis on the need for the reformation of manners (Sykes 1926, 69).

Nevertheless, despite the circumstantial evidence that increasing costs and official disapprobation may have materially accelerated the shifts which have been identified in the London Consistory Court's business, it is surely a mistake to consider the courts and their officials as separated from the 'popular cultures,' represented in litigation proceedings, as if they were isolated from the communities which gave them life. There is considerable evidence that the kind of grass-roots popular ordering and freedom of expression which defamation proceedings represented were legitimized by the widespread participation in the legal process which was typical of early modern England. For example, the widespread propensity for urban crowds to enforce popular norms by riot may partly be explained by the empowerment of the citizenry via common law processes and institutions, such as the hue and cry, public forms of punishment, and of course, the jury. Sometimes the rioters explicitly appropriated legal forms and symbols to legitimate their actions (Shoemaker 1987, esp. 287–9). Indeed, there is considerable evidence that ordinary people were keenly aware of their access to official power: Gowing has shown that the popular discourse typical of defamation litigants in the London Consistory occasionally included threats to use its characteristic punishments against their opponents. Clearly such people understood the 'law' as something which was animated by its local and communal context and was available on their own initiative (Gowing 1994, 33). On the other hand, it should be noted that early modern courts were not just spaces for administering official justice: before the eighteenth century, when most people experienced governance via the law and the church rather than through Parliament, they also had important representative functions. As Anna Clark has shown, even at the end of the eighteenth century, when the London Consistory Court was becoming dominated by wealthy litigants, the surviving defamation proceedings clearly reveal the robust mores of plebeian women, albeit to the horror of middle-class judges (1989, 235–8). So it appears that the broadly participatory proceedings of early modern courts and the 'law' which they applied and articulated formed a partial continuum with popular expressions of ordering: legal institutions both represented and helped to legitimize popular cultures. But if this reasoning is correct, and courts were a crucial interface for cultural exchange in English society, official discouragement of popular expression from below would have had a disproportionate effect, as plebeians lost confidence in their right to appropriate the law.

So even if there was a decline in spontaneous public argument during the eighteenth century, as people gradually became more restrained and polite, did this amount to one product of a subtle delegitimization of the communal ordering from below which previously underwrote and was validated by the participatory traditions of English law? Increasing contempt for popular cultures is reflected in early eighteenth-century elite legal discourse, as plebeians in the street became 'the mob' or the 'rabble,' and accounts of witchcraft were ridiculed from the judicial bench (Shoemaker 1987, 273, 282, 284; *A Complete Collection of State Trials* 1809–26, xiv. 639–90, *R v. Hathaway*, 1702; Davies 1999, chap. 1). According to one historian this was 'a period of conscious elite detachment from the beliefs of the "people"' (Davies 1999, 77). Indeed, if plebeian women were henceforth conspicuously silent and disempowered as agents in the courts, was their relative impotence symptomatic of a more general process in English society over the long eighteenth century – a fundamental shift by which rapid social differentiation and the impact of

Enlightenment rationalism increasingly consigned ordinary people to experience 'the rule of law' as remote commands to be internalized and obeyed rather than as participatory justice (Lemmings 2000, 319–20, 328–9; Postema 1986, 309–10)? There is no doubt that around this time plebeians were being priced out of the market for common law litigation, an activity their seventeenth-century predecessors had experienced widely. And later in the century professional lawyers intervened decisively in criminal trials to mediate confrontation between prosecutors and defendants, contrary to common law traditions which privileged their unvarnished expressions (Beattie 1991, 221–7; Langbein 1978, 263–316; Hawkins 1716–21, ii. 400). Certainly after 1800 the ecclesiastical jurisdiction could no longer be stigmatized as a 'bawdy court': accusations arising out of unseemly disputes among the vulgar, where the parties called each other whores or their husbands cuckolds, had been banished to the margins. And plebeian women desiring judicial separation seem to have disappeared altogether: we know from other sources that they were reduced to the customary rituals of divorce by 'wife-sale,' and jumping backwards over the thresholds of their cottages, just as popular cultures of marriage diverged from elite conventions after the Marriage Act of 1753 gave a legal monopoly to the church wedding (Gillis 1985, chap. 7). The eighteenth-century story of the London Consistory Court may well suggest the institutions and culture of law were becoming official and polite 'property,' rather than the currency of Everyman and Everywoman.

Notes

1 Although the mass of people were believers and conformed outwardly to the established church, there is plenty of evidence for a widespread lack of piety among the common people in the sixteenth and early seventeenth centuries, when the church courts were busiest (Ingram 1987, 92–8). Moreover, the continued relevance of the courts to issues of everyday life may help to explain why litigation remained plentiful in Somerset down to c. 1740, despite the proximity of large dissenting communities (Morris 1985, 142).

2 Ingram's figures for defamation cases 1580–1640 in Wiltshire, York, and Ely show only slightly less (60–70 per cent) dominance by female plaintiffs (1987, 301–2).

3 For women's supposedly passionate nature, see, for example, Fletcher (1995, 4–12) and Shoemaker (1998, 61–2).

4 The defamation jurisdiction was abolished in 1855 (18 &19 Victoria, c. 41).

5 Shoemaker's figures to mid-century are derived from the Act Books. Meldrum's are based on the Allegation, Libel, and Sentence Books.

6 The Act Books (Instance) provide the most comprehensive records for suits initiated, but they do not continue beyond 1765. Thereafter historians have tended to utilize the Allegation, Libel, and Sentence Books, which only include cases that reached the stage where a libel was presented, thereby excluding those where the 'ministrant' (defendant) had never answered the citation and nominated a proctor to answer.

7 The usual penalty in defamation cases was penance, but in this case the defamatory words had been uttered more than a year before commencement of the suit, and in these circumstances the penalty of excommunication was declared to apply from the time they were spoken until such time as the defendant satisfied the church by making appropriate penance (Consett 1685, 337–8).

8 The only alternative would have been complaint to a magistrate on the grounds of violence and having him bound over on recognizance to keep the peace (*A Treatise* 1732, 81).

9 I am referring principally to divorce 'a mensa et thoro,' or 'of bed and board,' which practically amounted to legal separation without possibility of remarriage. Only the very wealthy, who could obtain a private act of Parliament, could have fully legal marriages annulled.

10 Although the matrimonial litigants had always been of higher social status than defamation suitors, there seems to have been a marked rise in the social origins of marriage cases by the later eighteenth century, whereby most of the latter were from the higher middle class and above. Compare Gowing (1996, 183–4); Hunt (1992, 11–12); LMA, DL/C 181, ff. 2–486.

11 There was a slight overall majority of female prosecutors again in 1828–57, but wives were more likely to abandon their cases than male prosecutors (Waddams 1992, 163–4).

12 The lover was prosecuted for criminal conversation in King's Bench.

13 Where male prosecutors failed and females succeeded, the issue was usually nullification of marriage (on strict proof of illegality or previous marriage etc.), rather than separation because of adultery or cruelty. See also Stone (1990, 187), Waddams (1992, 164.)

14 Meldrum compares what he implies was the average cost of an early eighteenth-century London defamation suit, as taxed in the sentence (approx. £10) with a single statement by Sharpe, which estimates the average cost of a suit fought 'to its conclusion' at York in the later sixteenth century as £8. Ingram's examples of much lower fees in seventeenth-

century Wiltshire are simply noted (Meldrum 1994, 3, n. 17; Sharpe 1980, 24; Ingram 1987, 57).

15 The third case which went to sentence reserved determination of costs. Early nineteenth-century defamation costs in defended suits 'could easily amount to £20 or £30' (Waddams 2000, 13, 104). In the eighteenth century average earnings of shopkeepers, innkeepers, or domestic tradesmen were estimated at around £50 a year, according to the calculations of King (1688) and Massie (1760). See Holmes and Szechi (1993, 353).

Works Cited

Amussen, S.D. 1988. *An Ordered Society: Gender and Class in Early Modern England.* Oxford: Basil Blackwell.

The Art of Governing a Wife, with Rules for Batchelors. 1747. London.

Baker, J.H. 1990. *An Introduction to English Legal History.* 3rd ed. London: Butterworths.

Beattie, J.M. 1991. Scales of Justice: Defence Counsel and the English Criminal Trial in the Eighteenth and Nineteenth Centuries. *Law and History Review* 9: 221–67.

Boswell, J. 1980. *Life of Johnson,* ed. R.W. Chapman and J.D. Fleeman. Oxford: Oxford University Press.

Brooks, C.W. 1986. Interpersonal Conflict and Social Tension: Civil Litigation in England, 1640–1830. In *The First Modern Society: Essays in Honour of Lawrence Stone,* ed. A.L. Beier, D. Cannadine, and J.M. Rosemheim, 357–99. Cambridge: Cambridge University Press.

Bulstrode, Whitlocke. 1718. The Second Charge of Whitlocke Bulstrode, Esq. To the Grand Jury and other Jurers of the County of Middlesex, at the General Quarter-Session of the Peace, held the Ninth Day of October, 1718, at Westminster Hall. In *Charges to the Grand Jury 1689–1803,* ed. G. Lamoine, 109–26. Camden Society. 4th ser., vol. 43. London: Royal Historical Society.

Clark, A. 1989. Whores and Gossips: Sexual Reputation in London 1770–1825. In *Current Issues in Women's History,* ed. A. Angerman, G. Binnema, A. Keunen, V. Poels, and J. Zirkee, 231–48. London and New York: Routledge.

Complete Collection of State Trials. 1809–28. Ed. W. Cobbett and T.B. Howell. London: R. Bagshaw.

Consett, H. 1685. *The Practice of the Spiritual or Ecclesiastical Courts.* London: T. Basset.

Dabhoiwala, F. 1996. The Construction of Honour, Reputation and Status in

Late Seventeenth- and Early Eighteenth-Century England. *Transactions of the Royal Historical Society*, 6th ser. 6: 201–13.

Davies, O. 1999. *Witchcraft, Magic and Culture 1736–1951*. Manchester: Manchester University Press.

Elias, N. 1994. *The Civilizing Process*. Trans. E. Jephcott. Oxford: Blackwell.

The English Reports. 1900–32. Edinburgh and London: William Green.

Fletcher, A. 1995. *Gender, Sex and Subordination in England 1500–1800*. New Haven, CT: Yale University Press.

Foyster, E. 1996. Male Honour, Social Control and Wife Beating in Late Stuart England. *Transactions of the Royal Historical Society*. 6th ser. 6: 215–24.

Gibson, E. 1733. *Remarks on a Bill Now Depending in Parliament, for the Better Regulating the Proceedings of the Ecclesiastical Courts*. London: G. Sumtor.

Gillis, J.R. 1985. *For Better or Worse: British Marriages, 1600 to the Present*. Oxford and New York: Oxford University Press.

Gisborne, T. 1795. *An Enquiry into the Duties of Men in the Higher and Middle Classes of Society in Great Britain: Resulting from their Respective Status, Professions, and Employments*. London: B. and J. White.

Gowing, L. 1994. Language, Power and the Law: Women's Slander Litigation in Early Modern London. In *Women, Crime and the Courts in Early Modern England*, ed. J. Kermode and G. Walker, 26–47. London: UCL Press.

– 1996. *Domestic Dangers: Women, Words, and Sex in Early Modern London*. Oxford: Oxford University Press.

Hawkins, W. 1716–21. *A Treatise of the Pleas of the Crown*. London: J. Walthoe.

Hindle, S. 1994. The Shaming of Margaret Knowsley: Gossip, Gender and the Experience of Authority in Early Modern England. *Continuity and Change* 9: 391–419.

– 1996. The Keeping of the Public Peace. In *The Experience of Authority in Early Modern England*, ed. P. Griffiths, A. Fox, and S. Hindle, 213-48. New York: St Martin's Press.

Holmes, G. 1993. *The Making of a Great Power: Late Stuart and Early Georgian Britain 1660–1772*. London and New York: Longman.

Holmes, G., and D. Szechi. 1993. *The Age of Oligarchy: Pre-industrial Britain 1722–1783*. London and New York: Longman.

Hunt, M. 1992. Wife Beating, Domesticity and Women's Independence in Eighteenth-Century London. *Gender & History* 4: 10–33.

Ingram, M. 1987. *Church Courts, Sex and Marriage in England, 1570–1640*. Cambridge: Cambridge University Press.

Langbein, J.H. 1978. The Criminal Trial before the Lawyers. *University of Chicago Law Review* 45: 263–316.

Lemmings, D. 1996. Marriage and the Law in the Eighteenth Century: Hard-wicke's Marriage Act of 1753. *Historical Journal* 39: 339–60.

– 2000. *Professors of the Law: Barristers and Legal Culture in the Eighteenth Century.* Oxford: Oxford University Press.

London Metropolitan Archives (LMA)

Marchant, R.A. 1969. *The Church under the Law: Justice, Administration and Discipline in the Diocese of York 1560–1640.* London: Cambridge University Press.

Meldrum, T. 1994. A Women's Court in London: Defamation at the Bishop of London's Consistory Court, 1700–1745. *London Journal* 19: 1–20.

Morris, P. 1985. Defamation and Sexual Reputation in Somerset, 1733–1850. Ph.D. diss., University of Warwick.

Muldrew, C. 1998. *The Economy of Obligation: The Culture of Credit and Social Relations in Early Modern England.* Basingstoke: Macmillan.

Place, F. 1972. *The Autobiography of Francis Place (1771–1854),* ed. M. Thrale. Cambridge: Cambridge University Press.

Postema, G.J. 1986. *Bentham and the Common Law Tradition.* Oxford: Clarendon Press.

Richardson, S. 1811. *The Works of Samuel Richardson,* ed. E. Mangin. London: William Miller and James Carpenter.

Roper, L. 1994. *Oedipus and the Devil: Witchcraft, Sexuality, and Religion in Early Modern Europe.* London and New York: Routledge.

Sharpe, J. 1980. *Defamation and Sexual Slander in Early Modern England: The Church Courts at York.* York: University of York, Borthwick Institute of Historical Research.

Shoemaker, R.B. 1987. The London 'Mob' in the Early Eighteenth Century. *Journal of British Studies* 26: 273–304.

– 1998. *Gender in English Society 1650–1850: The Emergence of Separate Spheres.* London and New York: Longman.

– 1999. Reforming Male Manners: Public Insult and the Decline of Violence in London, 1660–1740. In *English Masculinities 1660–1800,* ed. T. Hitchcock and M. Cohen, 133–50. London and New York: Longman.

– 2000. The Decline of the Public Insult in London 1660–1800. *Past & Present* 169: 97–131.

Staves, S. 1990. *Married Women's Separate Property in England, 1660–1833.* Cambridge, MA: Harvard University Press.

Stone, L. 1990. *Road to Divorce: England 1530–1987.* Oxford: Oxford University Press.

Sykes, N. 1926. *Edmund Gibson Bishop of London 1669–1748: A Study of Politics and Religion in the Eighteenth Century.* Oxford: Oxford University Press.

– 1959. *From Sheldon to Secker: Aspects of English Church History 1660–1768.* Cambridge: Cambridge University Press.

Taylor, S. 2000. Whigs, Tories and Anticlericalism: Ecclesiastical Courts Legislation in 1733. *Parliamentary History* 19: 329–55.

A Treatise of Feme Coverts: or, the Lady's Law. 1732. London: B. Lintot.

Two Actions for Criminal Conversation. 1790. London: M. Smith.

Waddams, S.M. 1992. *Law, Politics and the Church of England: The Career of Stephen Lushington 1782–1873.* Cambridge: Cambridge University Press.

– 2000. *Sexual Slander in Nineteenth-Century England: Defamation in the Ecclesiastical Courts, 1815–1855.* Toronto: University of Toronto Press.

Walker, G. 1996. Expanding the Boundaries of Female Honour in Early Modern England. *Transactions of the Royal Historical Society.* 6th ser. 6: 235–45.

4

The Whore's Estate: Sally Salisbury, Prostitution, and Property in Eighteenth-Century London

LAURA J. ROSENTHAL

In the concluding anecdote of Charles Walker's *Authentick Memoirs of Sally Salisbury*, Salisbury and 'a certain Nobleman' decide to play a trick on a 'Dignify'd' fortune-hunting clergyman. The nobleman introduces Salisbury, who greatly impresses the clergyman with her beauty, wit, and opulent manner of living. Salisbury, however, insists on being honest with him and tells him that 'Notwithstanding she liv'd so genteely as she did, yet she could not boast, nor would she have him think she had a large Estate; for that, in Truth, she has nothing but a very *Small Spot* to which she had any *Hereditary Right*' (Walker 1723, 143). The clergyman dismisses this modesty, for she 'must have a very considerable Number of Acres to defray the Expences of so handsome a Manner of Living, and to be rever'd by so many fine People as he observ'd she was' (Walker 1723, 144). But Salisbury, tired of this banter and ready dramatically to reveal the truth, pulls up her skirts 'and clapping her Hand upon *Madge*, said, *Ecce Signum*, Doctor. This is my only Support, and I hope will continue so to my Life's End' (Walker 1723, 144).

While some writers in early eighteenth-century London moralized about the fate of this famous prostitute who went by the name of 'Sally Salisbury' (she died in jail), most nevertheless also could not resist admiring her wealth, success, fame, and Hobbesian ambition. Three biographies of Salisbury appeared in the same year: *The Genuine History of Mrs Sarah Prydden, Usually Called Sally Salisbury* (1723), *The Effigies, Parentage, Education, Life, Merry-Pranks and Conversation of the Celebrated Mrs Sally Salisbury* (1722–3), and Captain Charles Walker's *Authentick Memoirs of the Life and Intrigue and Adventures of the Celebrated Sally Salisbury*

(1723), a life story told through a series of supposedly true anecdotes sent to Walker by various correspondents. 'Sally Salisbury' herself does not seem to have contributed directly to any one of these: they are not personal confessions like *The Apology for the Conduct of Mrs Teresia Constantia Phillips* (1748) or the *Authentic and Interesting Memoirs of Miss Ann Sheldon* (1790) or *The Life of Mrs Margaret Leeson* (1798). First-person narratives of prostitute lives with convincing claims to some kind of authenticity would only come later in the century with the enhanced possibility of sentimental pity for the whore – as in the narratives about the figure of the penitent 'magdalen' that Eleanor F. Shevlin discusses in a later chapter in this book. Instead, the accounts of Sally Salisbury exploit the fame and legendary status of a clearly well-known public figure, similar to prostitute narratives such as *Memoirs of the Celebrated Miss Fanny M[urray]* (1759) or *The Uncommon Adventures of Miss Kitty Fisher* (1759) or *The Life and Intrigues of the Late Celebrated Mrs Mary Parrimore* (1729). All of these narratives offer sensationalized accounts of real women who became (in)famous in the eighteenth century; most contain a minimum of erotic description, which suggests that the titillation of a voyeuristic peek into a whore's life cannot entirely explain their popularity. Salisbury became so famous that stories about her continued to appear after her death. In another prostitute narrative, *The Velvet Coffee-Woman: Or, the Life, Gallantries and Amours of the Late Famous Mrs Anne Rochford* (1728), the author laments that death has 'now possessed himself of our Female Triumverate, (*Sally Salisbury*, the *Royal Sovereign*, and Mrs *Rochford*)' (1728, 25). In the anonymous *View of London and Westminster*, the narrator notes that the parish of St Andrew in Holbourn 'has rendered its Name famous to all succeeding Ages, for retaining the Ashes of that great and wonder Woman Mrs *Sarah Salisb—y* ... She was a remarkable Instance of to what a height of Reputation the *free Use of natural Parts* will carry People' (*View of London* 1725, 27). Salisbury's dead body again drew public attention in 1747 when the vault of Dr Sacheverell was opened. The location of Salisbury's coffin in the same vault right next to her former rector inspired some witty verses:

> Lo! to one grave consigned, of rival fame,
> A reverent Doctor and a wanton dame.
> Well for the world both did to rest retire,
> For each, while living, set mankind on fire.

And:

A fit companion for a high-church priest;
He non-resistance taught, and she profest. (Holmes 1973, 267)

In his *Foreign View of England in 1725–1729,* César de Saussure reports how 'some time ago a courtesan, of the name of Sally Salisbury, famed for her rare and wonderful beauty, her wit and fun, became the fashion in London, and was favoured by distinguished personages' (1995, 119). Sources vary in their levels of admiration and disdain; they disagree on certain facts. They dispute, for example, whether she was, like Nell Gwyn, a 'protestant whore' or a Jacobite and how she ended up with the name 'Sally Salisbury.' Nevertheless, they share several anecdotes and offer similar accounts of their subject's personality, which suggest that, even if they do not offer an unmediated portrait, they at least report a somewhat consolidated cultural myth about this woman.

According to John Richetti, early eighteenth-century popular narratives like these 'set out to flatter and exploit rather than to challenge or redefine the assumptions of its implied audience ... Criminal and whore biographies, travel narratives of merchants, pirates, or hermits, scandal chronicles, and amatory or pious novellas all delivered certain predictable satisfaction to their audiences' (1969, 263). All three accounts of Salisbury in certain ways indeed flatter their audience and exploit their subject material. Perhaps unlike the standard criminal biography, however, prostitute narratives, while sometimes similarly enforcing cultural norms, do not *necessarily* offer predictable satisfaction; they *do* sometimes challenge or refine the assumptions of their audiences, as certain famous whores appear intriguingly to have done as well. While the anonymous *Genuine History* and the also anonymous *Effigies, Parentage, Education ...* offer fairly conventional moral interpretations of Salisbury's life story, Walker's *Authentick Memoirs* leaves more of a clue as to why prostitutes' lives so fascinated readers in this period. While not the complex literary achievement of Defoe's *Roxana,* Walker's *Memoirs* nevertheless (and perhaps inadvertently) goes beyond voyeurism and bawdy humour (although it includes these as well) and suggests the ways in which a career like Salisbury's represents a new kind of social and economic mobility. Courtesans who rose through their charms were of course nothing new; Salisbury, however, prospered as an independent agent with neither a permanent bawd nor keeper. In describing her career, the narrative offers in some ways a more direct and demystified (or not *yet* mystified) vision of shifting class relations, social mobility, and the meaning of capital than do many novels. Other kinds of criminal biographies may offer more conventional punishments for property violation; prostitution, by contrast, actually involves a contractual agreement (unless the whore is also a thief) and thus more closely resembles the mainstream experience of the marketplace. Further, prostitute careers exemplified the uncertainty and chimerical qualities that contemporary critics associated with early modern capitalism. At a time when, as J.G.A. Pocock has argued, civic humanists insisted upon the connection between estate and virtue (1985, 103–23), Salisbury and the nobleman make a fool out of the clergyman because he cannot tell the difference between a respectable lady and a whore; her wealth, after all, looks exactly the same as if it had indeed sprung from the income from a landed estate. The cultural work of this story, as well as the cultural work of the prostitute narrative in general and the significance of the life of the real 'Sally Salisbury,' thus does not end with simply a ribald joke or punishment for crime, for Salisbury's shocking but defiant gesture, as well as the story of her rise from a bricklayer's daughter to a wealthy woman who moved freely through the aristocratic social scene, demystified both aristocratic ideology *and* certain middle-class claims to a relationship between commerce and manners. Like so many other writers in the eighteenth century, Walker represents prostitution as a comic epitome or microcosm of market relations in general, as the popular slang term for female genitalia – 'the commodity' – might suggest; he also represents this marketplace as a scene of both rapacious greed and heroic, liberating possibilities. The whore embodies these extreme possibilities. Intentionally or not, the anecdotes that Walker gathers construct the whore as a demystifying force in early modern capitalism.

The eighteenth century has been widely characterized as the cradle of modern domesticity, most prominently by Nancy Armstrong's seminal *Desire and Domestic Fiction.* As Armstrong argues, since modesty ideally characterizes the domestic woman, then any kind of female self-display becomes anathema: Salisbury's gesture of throwing up her skirts and clapping her hand on 'Madge' marks an extreme version of this. Arguing against an earlier feminist overvaluation of social outcasts, madwomen, and disreputable girls as inherently radical figures in women's novels, Armstrong maintains that such characters feed the same domestic ideology as does the virtuous woman, only as complex negative rather than positive examples (1987, 77, 182–3, 252–3). In this essay, however, I want to argue that even though prostitute figures in literary and cultural texts do not necessarily represent female rebellion against patriarchal norms in any simple way, their stories, rather than simply enforcing domestic ideology by their negative example or adding to the century's broad collection of misogynistic, exploitative, scandalous, and porno-graphic literature, nevertheless often explore the fundamental problems of property in the world of emergent capitalism.[1] A wide range of writers, from respectable novelists like Samuel Richardson and Charlotte Lennox to scandalmongers, pornographers, and prostitutes (apparently) moved to tell their own life stories, could not resist telling stories about whores. The interest in these narratives, as the case of Sally Salisbury will demon-strate, exceeded voyeuristic pleasure and moralistic warning, for as con-fusion over Salisbury's estate in the preceding anecdote shows, prostitution suggests the instability not just of sexual values but of value itself. In fact, prostitution in general – at least in the form that developed in the eighteenth century – necessarily demands reflection on property rela-tions and gender, for prostitutes exchange the very epitome of bourgeois privacy – heterosexual sex – in the public marketplace.[2] So while I thus want to complicate and expand the narrow meaning Armstrong reads in prostitute figures, I am indebted to her overall insight that female sexual-ity bears a highly significant political and culturally symbolic meaning in the eighteenth century.

Walker's *Authentick Memoirs* represents the whore as a challenge to gendered divisions of property, aristocratic privilege, and middle-class hypocrisy. The *Memoirs* bawdily but quite explicitly proposes the poten-tial confusion over modes of property that Sally Salisbury creates with her wicked sense of humour and thus raises disturbing political ques-tions inherent in prostitute narratives. In the sexual contract that Nancy Armstrong describes as gaining prominence in the middle of the cen-tury, middle-class female virtue functions as the emblem for the middle class itself. Thus bourgeois women gain authority as members of the increasingly dominant class, but at the same time must subordinate themselves to their husbands. For Armstrong, women's limited ability to own property and participate in the public sphere positioned them culturally as apolitical subjects; as such, they could in the domestic novels of the era rise in class status and challenge aristocratic dominance without posing the kind of explicit threat a male challenger would. Lack of access to property, then, empowered middle-class women in certain ways. But if the upward mobility of domestic women (in Richardson's *Pamela*, for example) could provisionally pass in fiction as apolitical, the upward mobility of the whore in similar kinds of narratives could not get away with this kind of mystification.[3] In fact, prostitute narratives often plunge headlong into the political implications of such mobility, fleshing out anxieties rather than smoothing over conflicts.

The *Authentick Memoirs of Sally Salisbury* tells the story of the child of a bricklayer who rose to great heights of wealth, luxury, and prestige through prostitution. *The Genuine History of Mrs Sarah Prydden, Usually Called Sally Salisbury* represents a similar trajectory of upward mobility but seems to place its heroine somewhat higher on the social scale. *The Genuine History*, for example, reports that Sally/Sarah excelled at dancing lessons in her youth. Nevertheless, in both narratives she grows up with the expectation that she would work for a living, even as a child. In *The Genuine History*, she sells oranges in the theatre and sells books on the street; in *Authentick Memoirs*, she works as an apprentice to a seamstress. Both narratives observe that her beauty, wit, and talent attracted so much attention that she could have been a success on stage; Walker, however, argues that pride prevented her from pursuing this option (1723, 7). Both biographies, though in different ways, record her progress from her work as an ordinary prostitute in a brothel to her establishment of her independence to her extraordinary wealth and luxurious lifestyle that allowed her to mingle freely with the aristocracy. At the height of her career, however, Salisbury dramatically captured public attention when she stood trial for stabbing her lover, one Mr Finch. At the trial, the proceeding of which drew enough attention to merit publication in *Select Trials at the Sessions-House in the Old-Bailey* (Trumbach [1742] 1985), the defence argued that Salisbury stabbed Mr Finch because he had offered her sister a ticket to the opera. As the defendant had provided her sister with a virtuous education and feared that Mr Finch had designs on her, Salisbury merely acted to protect her sister. Salisbury immediately regretted this impetuous act and helped care for Mr Finch. But according to the prosecution, 'Persons of the Prisoner's Character can scarce be supposed to be capable of a sincere Friendship' (Trumbach [1742] 1985, 1: 342). The King's Council argued that the sister had no virtue to protect and that Salisbury's regret came from her fear of prosecution rather than concern for Mr Finch. The jury found her guilty of assaulting Mr Finch, but innocent of the greater charge of attempted murder. The court sentenced her to pay £100 and spend a year in prison, but she died in Newgate and 'left behind her the Character of the most eminent Punk that ever the Hundreds of *Drury* could boast of.' Both biographies, as well as the broadside *The Effigies, Parentage, Education ... of Mrs Sally Salisbury* end with her trial.

This trial brought to the attention of the general public a woman who seems to have had a widespread underground notoriety already. Both the prosecution and the defence used Salisbury's character as a key issue: while the prosecution, not surprisingly, represented Salisbury as dangerously passionate, the defence attempted to assert her essential domesticity. In the court of public opinion, however, her combination of mobility, success, and outlaw status had already earned her a certain level of celebrity and even of a folk hero status.[4] Walker's *Authentick Memoirs* itself does not tell her story through a single narrative but rather weaves together various anecdotes in the form of letters from men who had met, heard stories of, or been clients of the celebrated Sally Salisbury and could be persuaded to tell them. Walker probably did not simply fabricate these letters: in the 8–10 January 1722/3 issue of *The Post Boy*, he placed an advertisement asking that

> Those Gentlemen who can communicate any useful Particulars towards perpetuation the memoir of the eminent Person [Sally Salisbury], are desired to transmit them to the Author, directed to Jones's Coffee-House in Drury Lane.

In the 15–17 January issue, he thanks 'the Gentlemen who have honour'd me with their Letters, and hopes those who can illustrate the History of this LADY with any agreeable Adventures, will be pleas'd to communicate them.' The same newspaper reports the publication of a poem called 'The Ghastly Wound. A Tale, inscribed to the Celebrated Mrs S— S—,' which presumably tells the story of her stabbing Mr Finch (12–14 February 1722/3); the paper also reports the availability of 'A Curious Print in Metzotinto of Mrs SALLY SALISBURY' (28 February–2 March 1722/3). *The Post Boy* updated its readers on Salisbury's health while she was in prison.[5] According to Saussure, her lovers 'crowded into the prison, presenting her with every comfort and luxury possible.' Finch himself forgave her and requested her discharge (1995, 120).

In the broadside, which features a beautiful, full-length sketch of Salisbury, the author finds this popular heroism of hers perplexing, given her association with aristocrats:

> Quickly after [going on the town] she was so much in Vogue, that even the Populace compos'd a Song about her, call'd Salley in our Alley.[6] What Reason the Vulgar had to do this I do not know, for nothing is more certain than that they had very little knowledge of her; Her whole Time being

spent in the Society of nothing Inferior to Gentlemen, and I blush heartily
to think what I dare not Write, viz. that so many of our Noblemen could
delight in the Carcass of a Prostitute, and yet nothing is more sure than
several of them did, for otherwise she could never have liv'd in that Pomp
and made the appearance which all the World is too Sensible of. (*Effigies*,
1722/3)

The author finds the class 'miscegenation' suggested by Salisbury's story
disturbing but irrefutable, given the evidence of her wealth. But if even
half of the anecdotes in Captain Walker's biography have any truth to
them, then her apparent popularity with the populace might not be such
a mystery. In *The London Hanged*, Peter Linebaugh shows how several
high-profile male criminals became folk heroes in the early eighteenth
century out of a flamboyant refusal to accept emergent redefinitions of
property, a phenomenon that John Gay captured in *The Beggar's Opera*.
Female criminals have attracted less critical attention than their male
counterparts, but the historical Sarah Prydden/Sally Salisbury may have
elicited some of those popular sentiments that Linebaugh describes.
Salisbury, according to the author of the broadside, managed to move
freely amidst the aristocracy in spite of her common birth; she coupled
with them and took their money; she had no respect for aristocratic
superiority or middle-class virtue. The whore biography, then, offers a
more intimate, and thus perhaps more threatening, version of the class
warfare inherent in the criminal biography in general.

   In both biographies, but in Walker's in particular, Salisbury does not
attempt quietly to blend in with the worlds of her elite and middle-class
clients; rather, she takes particular pleasure in both unmasking hypocrisy and challenging any equations between birth and human worth,
although she does both in characteristically lewd and crude ways. In one
anecdote from Walker's biography, Salisbury dresses herself as a lady
and attends an elite ball. Her dancing, however, reveals her class origin;
as Walker puts it, 'though she Dances well enough in a Country-Dance,
her Talent does not lie in French Dances' (1723, 125). One lady, jealous
from suspecting Salisbury had slept with her husband, mocks her dancing, implicitly exposing the inferiority of her origins. Sally, however,
lashes back: 'I perceive your Ladyship does not approve of my Manner of
Dancing: But I can assure you, Madam, my Lord – (naming her own
husband) admires my Dancing above all Things, and has often told me,
that he had much rather Dance or – (speaking mighty plain English)
with me than with your Ladyship at any time' (Walker 1723, 125).

Another lady teasingly exclaims that Salisbury will take all of their husbands, to which Sally replies, 'Not much to yours, indeed, Madam ... I try'd him once, and but once, and am resolv'd I'll never try him again; for I was forc'd to kick him out of Bed, because his – e'en good for nothing at all' (Walker 1723, 126). Rather than accepting the lady's class putdown, Salisbury asserts the superiority of her sexual skill to humiliate the lady in return. Further, she reduces all men, regardless of the class, to their bodies as the basis for human differentiation. If the historical Sarah Prydden/Sally Salisbury consistently behaved this way, then her folk heroism becomes less mysterious. For Salisbury, sexual desire serves as irrefutable evidence of the radical equality of all human beings.

Salisbury uses this strategy not only to shock proper ladies but to defend herself against male insult as well. At the same party, a certain naval commander recognizes her and tries to humiliate her by asking if the smock she was wearing was the same one that she won in a dancing contest at Bath. (Both biographies describe Salisbury's famous triumph in this dancing competition.) By referring to the smock, the naval commander also believes he can triumph over Salisbury by exposing her class origins. No, she replies, 'this is not the Shirt you mean; I sent that, with the rest of my Linen to your Mother to be wash'd last Week, and she has not brought it home' (Walker 1723, 127). His mother, it turns out, secretly *did* work as a laundress as her fortune had become depleted; none of his elite friends, however, knew this.[7] With this remark, Salisbury turns all the mockery away from herself and to the commander, who sneaks off like 'a Dog ... with his Tail between his Legs' (Walker 1723, 128). As a whore, Salisbury could have gathered this knowledge through her privileged access to gossip or through continuing to move through the world of laundresses as well as the world of ladies. Either way, her response reveals both her extraordinary mobility and refusal to mystify the origins of wealth. If Richardson's *Pamela*, then, challenged aristocratic privilege from the perspective of middle-class ideology by using the (apparently) apolitical figure of the virtuous servant girl, then Sally Salisbury, in history and in the narratives she inspired, challenged the same claims to inherent superiority of birth from a perspective that had nothing to do with middle-class virtue as traditionally understood and could not possibly disguise itself as apolitical. In the mobile world of the whore, money functions as the universal equivalent and holds transformative powers.

While Walker's narrative explores Salisbury's destabilizing potential and demystifying wit, the broadside and the anonymous biography both

attempt to contain the disturbing possibilities of her extraordinary financial success by representing prostitution as both the egregious violation of domestic virtue and the relatively passive commodification of the
female body itself (as opposed to the whore's active commodification of
sexual service in Walker's narrative). The author of the anonymous
biography, for example, pleads on Salisbury's behalf in the face of her
murder trial by representing her lack of agency and wisdom:

> If Mrs Pryddon [Salisbury] was seduced to wander in the softer Paths of
> Pleasure at a tender Age, unable to distinguish between Good and Evil: If
> she has believed too long, that Gaiety was Happiness, and that to be Great,
> was to be Honourable: Let us pity her, and blame, if any, those who, when
> she was young and innocent, first betray'd her Innocence and Youth:
> Blame those Men, who by a sweet and gentle Villany, the soonest undo the
> softest of Hearts. If she has acted any thing Criminal since those Days, the
> Law is open; she'll be adjudged by those who are faithful and impartial.
> (*Genuine History* 1723, iv)

Prostitution, no doubt, had serious negative consequences for many
women in the eighteenth century: for many it did not substantially
relieve poverty and exposed them to disease and violence. Some prostitutes endured social marginalization, isolation from familial support,
harassment by reformers, attacks on their houses by marauding appren-
tices, sailors, or rakes, and punishment by the authorities. But then, as
now, victimization is not the only available lens through which to view
commercial sex, for this perspective tends to overlook the agency of the
women themselves.[8] *The Genuine History,* however, represents prostitution as the total commodification of the woman, comparable to the
objectification of the slave trade. In recalling her entrance into Mrs
Wisebourn's brothel,

> Mrs Salisbury has often, with Laughter, said herself, That the Old Maid-
> Merchant [Mrs Wisebourn] caused her to pluck off all her Cloths, felt
> every Limb one by one, touch'd her to see if she was sound; as a Jockey
> handles a Horse or Mare in Smithfield; or as the Planters in America, the
> Features of the Negroes before they purchase 'em. (1723, 22)

While *The Authentick Memoirs* tells various stories of the impish tricks
that Salisbury played on those who offended her, *The Genuine History* tells
stories of tricks played on Salisbury as well as the hideous abuse of some

prostitutes. This abuse ranges from the relatively harmless to the chillingly violent. In one rather playful example, some associates put Salisbury to bed with the castrato Niccolini rather than the appealing young lord she was expecting to find there (*Genuine History* 1723, 34–5), giggling at her disappointment. Another anecdote, however, ominously tells the story of egregious violence against a different prostitute, who apparently gave the pox to a person of quality. His friends sought her out, stripped her, tied her to the ground, strewed corn all over her body, and released a turkey to peck at the corn. She died of her injuries within three weeks. While the author of *The Genuine History* cannot entirely erase the agency, ambition, and defiance that seem to have characterized the historical Sally Salisbury, he represents prostitutes as commodities sold by bawds into precarious situations. Thus, while claiming to defend the 'celebrated' Sally Salisbury and acknowledging her extraordinary class mobility and accumulation of wealth, this biography nevertheless attempts to reinscribe a more traditional conception of women, virtuous and otherwise, as not owners of property but property themselves.

The Genuine History thus reconciles the challenges that Salisbury's career posed to both class stability and gendered divisions between the owners and the owned; *The Authentick Memoirs*, by contrast, takes full advantage of destabilizing possibilities that her life and livelihood potentially suggest.[9] Let us return, then, to the meaning of Salisbury's shocking gesture of lifting her skirts. First and perhaps most obviously, this anecdote has Salisbury claim a kind of self-possession generally absent in the anonymous biography. In *The Genuine History*, Salisbury enters the brothel as herself a commodity, little different from a prized animal or a slave. In the *Memoirs*, by contrast, Salisbury expresses a Lockean sense of self-possession and a relentless, Hobbesian, possessive individualism. As in Locke – although Locke does not necessarily extend these rights to women – the body differs from the self, providing the fundamental alienation necessary for the alienation of labour in general (Macpherson 1962, 194–262). Thus the *Memoirs* proposes the prostitute less as a victim of seduction and poor education than as a woman who disturbingly can claim property in her own body in a way that the virtuous woman cannot.[10] Since Salisbury transgresses against virtuous womanhood, it might be tempting to dismiss her claims of self-possession as simply either a vilification of possessive individualism or as misogynistic representation in which women making this claim cannot merit sympathy.[11] But given the historical Prydden/Salisbury's folk heroic status and the numerous comical and bawdy situations in which the narrative encourages the reader to laugh *with* the whore rather than *at* her (including the closing anecdote), I think that either of these readings would miss the force of the *Memoirs*.

Through her shocking gesture, Salisbury not only claims a kind of self-possession generally unavailable to women, but she also mocks the ideology of civic humanism that the clergyman clearly presumes. As J.G.A. Pocock explains, civic humanists placed owners of mobile property under suspicion and held that the possession of a landed estate alone reliably created the conditions for virtue (1985, 103–23). Both Salisbury and her friend the nobleman know that the clergyman will assume her virtue on the basis of her property. He becomes 'smitten' not only with her person but with her 'pretty Manner of Living.' The clergyman assumes that he has fallen into the company of a landowning heiress, for only a vast estate could support her opulence. But he also, as Pocock might suggest, assumes her inherent virtue on the basis of her supposed land. To become her husband would position him as well to attain this civic humanist virtue, for such an estate would liberate him from the tiresome and potentially corrupting demands of earning a living. In the narrative, however, the clergyman can see no difference between wealth generated by, arguably, the trade that in the eighteenth century symbolized all other forms of corruption – think, for example, of Swift's ominous floating island *La Puta* – and the elegance and virtue made possible by acreage. Wealth does not betray its origins in the *Authentick Memoirs*; it has become both mobile and anonymous. And the clergyman's error is not just the blindness caused by love, for the *Authentick Memoirs* offers several examples of the delicious scandal of the anonymity of value. Earlier in the narrative, Salisbury similarly catches the eye of a 'very grave, genteely-dress'd, sober-looking Matron' (Walker 1723, 94), who stops her in the street to admire her beauty. The matron offers a low, highly respectful curtsy and showers her with compliments over her dress, charm, and manners, for Salisbury was then apparelled 'like a little Princess, in Crimson Velvet, with abundance of Jewels about her' (Walker 1723, 94). Rather than accepting this courtesy, however, Salisbury decides to 'banter' her, deceptively leading the matron into an obscene joke about her own private parts. Salisbury trips away laughing, leaving the gentlewoman shocked. Then her mistake dawns on her: 'Sweet *Jesus* have Mercy upon me! As I live she is a vile Whore in all this Finery! Who could have thought it? She looks as much like a Woman of Reputation, as any I ever saw in my Life' (Walker 1723, 97). Like the incident with the clergyman, this incident with the proper gentlewoman is entirely gratuitous. In both cases, Salisbury takes extraordinary pleasure in disabusing 'respectable' people of their assumptions about the connection between wealth and virtue. She shocks both of them because they assume that an estate lies behind her wealth and supports her virtue.

As Pocock points out, early eighteenth-century literature abounds with anxious images that embody the instability of emergent capitalism in the allegorical figure of a woman – a figure Pocock (1975) traces back to the female embodiment of Fortune. But I think the satire here goes beyond reproducing anxieties about the anonymity and mobility of property, for such a reading would assume that the narrative encourages us to identify with the matron and the clergyman and share their shock that a beautiful, elegant lady could turn out to be a whore. The *Authentick Memoirs*, however, consistently places the reader on the other side. Not that Salisbury emerges as an ideal: the narrative represents her as a crude, ambitious, and ungrateful woman with a wicked sense of humour. Both biographies, after all, seem to have been inspired by her trial for attempted murder. Still, the *Authentick Memoirs* falls generally into the libertine tradition, taking pleasure in rather than simply offence at the whore's outrageousness. Men and women tangle with Salisbury at their own risk, for the obsequious petitioner, rather than the whore, becomes the butt of the joke. But the *Authentick Memoirs* overall has less of a stake in satirizing particular versions of propriety than it does in comically, ruthlessly, and quite crudely refusing the civic humanist link between virtue and an apparent level of material comfort. Salisbury's identification of her estate as her genitals – the very small spot to which she has any hereditary right – satirizes the estate's ability to generate a particular kind of virtue. Thus her closing gesture not only mocks the clergyman's greed but also defiantly refuses landed pretensions to inherent superiority.

The gesture ending the *Authentick Memoirs*, then, bawdily mocks the popular image of the estate that generates virtue. At the same time, however, it inevitably raises questions about the estate that generates Salisbury's income and the nature of the economic exchanges in which she participates. The *Memoirs* offers no stable, virtuous alternative to Salisbury's Hobbesian aggression and Rabelaisian sense of humour, from either an emergent middle class or a respectable aristocracy. A nobleman friend, in fact, sets up the prank with the clergyman. Salisbury moves through a world of breathtakingly mobile property, which she draws to herself through no visible commodity exchange, so to speak. In fact, the very question of the commodity – of what exactly the vendor exchanges for money – has long vexed discussions of prostitution. The author of the anonymous biography represents prostitution as the sale of a woman's body, generally by a third party. Salisbury's humorous comparison of her inspection by Mother Wisebourn in the brothel represents sexual commerce as a form of slavery, objectification, and sale of the very self. In this representation, then, the commodity sold is the woman herself. Indeed, some contemporary feminists would make this argument as well about prostitution in general. In perhaps the most forceful of these arguments, Carole Pateman (1988, 189–218) insists that since society defines one's core being so closely with sexuality, commercial sex inevitably traffics in the self. Other feminists, however, as part of a larger project to defend the rights of sex workers, have argued that prostitutes instead sell a service that happens to be sexual but that does not differ inherently from any other. Wendy Chapkis, for example, makes a compelling case for the structural similarity between sex work and the work of flight attendants, for both involve a combination of emotional and physical labour which the worker usually learns to balance against a sense of privacy (1997, 69–82; see also Nagle 1997, McClintock 1993, Chancer 1993, and Rubin 1984).

The *Authentick Memoirs* offers a more complicated view of sexual commerce than simply the sale of the woman's self, in sharp contrast to the anonymous *Genuine History;* even here, though, the nature of the commodity remains elusive. As if searching to identify the mysterious commodity, *Authentick Memoirs* offers several analogies, none of which suggests that a prostitute sells her body or herself. In fact, they tend to suggest, albeit comically, that prostitution is instead comparable to other ways of making a living in the marketplace, but also implicitly reject the emergent mystification of financial success as in part a result of highly developed manners or a middle-class version of virtue. Salisbury at one point in fact compares her trade to manual labour in a way that we might dismiss as a bawdy pun if not for another reference to her labour in the same letter. One 'W. Rider' wrote to Captain Walker with an anecdote about the time a bookseller, curious about the famous prostitute, disguised himself as a shoemaker in order to get the chance to measure her foot and look up her dress. In good humour that day, Salisbury put up with his antics and laughed when her lover let the cat out of the bag after the counterfeit shoemaker left enraptured. But then one day she passes his bookshop, stops in, and humiliates him in front of his customers by demanding her shoes. When a 'grave Clergyman' insists that she must have mistaken him for someone else, she persists, '*What you lousy Pimp? are you asham'd to own your Trade?*' (Walker 1723, 132). Embarrassed in front of respectable company, he tries to beat her at her own game (always a mistake): '*Now you talk so much of Trades, Madam, pray what Trade are you of?*' to which she responds, '"Why don't you know," says she, "don't you know my Trade? *I am a* Stone-Cutter *you pimping Son of a Bitch*"' (Walker 1723, 132).

While this analogy mainly works as an aggressive pun, it nevertheless suggests the possibility of the commodity in prostitution as labour. Earlier in the anecdote we find the same possibility. After peeking at her perfection, the bookseller swears that '*The Mould in which that dear Creature was cast, is broke!*' (Walker 1723, 130). The letter writer, however, digresses that old Mrs Priddon (Sally's mother) still lives, 'and Cants, Prays, and Plunders her Daughters of what they have *Earn'd* with the *Sweat of their Brows*, as much as ever, notwithstanding her exclaiming against the *Partakers of the Wages of Sin*' (Walker 1723, 130). Before the punch line, then, the writer sets up the possibility of prostitution as a form of labour from which the woman herself retains the right to benefit. The letter also resembles the closing one, for the bookseller wants to retain his prestige and respectability while peeking up Salisbury's skirt. Salisbury does indeed come across as a 'stone-cutter' throughout the *Memoirs*. She also, however, comes across as refreshingly honest in contrast with the hypocritical bookseller and her hypocritical mother. Thus, while both references to prostitution as labour participate in the bawdy humour of the narrative, at the same time they leave Salisbury herself on the higher ground. Rather than living off the work of another and refusing to acknowledge the origin of those profits, Salisbury consistently declines to mystify the origins of either her luxuries or her necessities. She has nothing financial to gain by exposing the bookseller, and although she calls herself a 'stone-cutter,' she does not actually harbour particular hostility to men *as men*. She lives up her to name as a 'stone-cutter,' however, whenever a man tries to look down on her for her uncloseted sexuality and demystified exchange of labour for money.

In other stories, the *Authentic Memoirs* compares prostitution to more professional activities. Salisbury not only refuses to mystify her work in any way; she also displays professional pride and even develops arrogance in her visibility. One letter reports that she frequently declared that '*It was always my Ambition to be a First-Rate Whore, and I think I may say, without Vanity, That I am the greatest, and make the most considerable Figure of any in the Three Kingdoms*' (Walker 1723, 98). In a confirmation of sorts, the narrator adds his 'private Sentiments': 'she is the most conspicuous *Punk*, that has shin'd in a *Side Box*, or empty'd the *Privy Purse of a PEER*, for this last Century.' In one anecdote, the famous Colley Cibber apparently compared his own professional stature to Salisbury's. Out for revenge after he contracted the clap from sleeping with Salisbury,

> he took an Opportunity, upon the Stage, of saying somewhat, that almost, as bitterly stung her Ladyship, and the eyes of the whole Audience were immediately fix'd on her; not long after, they met at the Masquerade, where, with great Scorn, she flung from him, and, in the Saucy Tone of a fine Lady, call'd him *Player!* he reply'd, *our Professions, Madam, are very like one another, any one may see the best we can do for Half a Crown.* (Walker 1723, 39)

In this anecdote, Cibber quips at least in part at his own expense, for actors in general and Cibber in particular came under the suspicion of irregular sex practices (Straub 1992). To compare his own profession to that of a prostitute also participates in an emerging vocabulary in which a range of economic transactions could be signified as potentially degrading or alienating. Critics, for example, accused commercial writers of prostituting themselves when they would professionally articulate political positions that they did not necessarily hold, or even just for writing for money (Gallagher 1994, 1–48). Yet Cibber's analogy works the other way as well: here the prostitute does not sell *herself* but sells a *performance*, a fantasy created for the pleasure of the client. Prostitution becomes just another form of entertainment available on the marketplace. Cibber describes the actor/whore commodity as essentially visual and not exactly either physical labour or a service; nevertheless, he certainly imagines Salisbury's performance, like his own, as active creative work rather than the passive objectification of the body. The commodity sold, however, emerges here as not just mobile but imaginary (see Pocock 1985, 103–23).

The *Authentick Memoirs* not only imagines the commodity of prostitution as imaginary in the sense that it fulfils, like the commodity of an actor, the fantasies of the paying customer, but it also proposes Mrs Wisebourn's 'academy,' where Salisbury gets her start, as a model of capitalist circulation:

> Within thy *Walls* the RICH were ever pleas'd,
> And from the *Gates* no *LAZAR* went unfed!
> *South-Sea Directors* might have learnt from *Thee*
> How to pay Debts, and wear an honest Heart!
> From *Thee* the *Lawyer* might have learnt strict Justice,

Thy Hand ne'er grasp'd a CLIENT's *Fee* in vain;
And when the Cash *ran low* and Blood *ran high,*
The Man in such a Plight thy Bounty felt!
Thy Darling Girls were offer'd to his view,
And with the Chosen Nymph to Bed he flew. (Walker 1723, 15)

Other critics have noticed the ways in which eighteenth-century writers so commonly compared prostitution to legitimate forms of business. But in looking at Richardson's *Clarissa* and Bernard Mandeville's *Defence of the Publick Stews,* Beth Kowaleski-Wallace (1997, 129–43) and Laura Mandell (1999, 64–83) respectively conclude that these authors use prostitution as essentially a negative example that excuses the exploitative practices in sanctioned forms of commerce. The whores in *Clarissa,* in Kowaleski-Wallace's argument, represent female participation in the marketplace as inherently illegitimate; in Mandell's argument, Mandeville appears to defend women but in fact misogynistically blames all the ills of capitalism on the figure of the female prostitute. But clearly something different is going on in this poem, for Walker proposes Mother Wisebourn's house (comically) as a model of business itself. And if, as Pocock argues, other writers expressed profound anxieties over the mobility of property, Walker proposes this brothel as admirable for the way it maximizes circulation. Thus Wisebourn succeeds in extracting money out of clients; unlike the directors of the South Sea Company, she pays off her creditors. She also, however, keeps the business moving through credit when her clients run out of cash. Rather than treating Salisbury as a slave, here she actually rescues her from the 'bondage' of a 'merciless Creditor' and takes her on as an investment (Walker 1723, 16). Mother Wisebourn buys her attractive clothes, presumably frees her from her debt, and keeps vigil over her venereal health. While Walker clearly expresses all this in satiric and bawdy terms, at the same time I think prostitution in the *Memoirs* functions as a trope not for the negative potentials of capitalism that can be misogynistically abjected, but for a demystified version of commerce itself. Thus prostitute narratives can sometimes offer explorations of labour, exchange, circulation, and mobility more directly and more ambivalently than other genres.

By contrast, throughout most of the early modern era, writers in general defined female prostitutes by their sexuality rather than by their economic activity. As Ruth Mazo Karras has pointed out, in the Middle Ages a woman could be identified as a 'prostitute' or 'whore' even without any suggestion that she accepted money for illicit sex

(1996, 13–31).[12] This remained true at least through the seventeenth century: even for reformers, the insatiable desire for sex drove women into prostitution. Reformer, poet, and constable Humphrey Mill put it starkly:

> Widow, maid, or wife,
> If once she does affect a whorish life
> Then like a Bitch she in her lust will burne,
> Takes up a rogue, and he must serve the turne. (Mill 1640, 27)

For Mill, in fact, some prostitutes have no interest in money at all and only walk the streets seeking their own sexual pleasure:

> I must turne
> Unto the Whore; now she with lust doth burne,
> And takes her time to walk about the street;
> If any letcher do's this Harlot meet,
> Few words will serve; she'l quickly give consent.
> Those ways of darknesse, give this whore content.
> Nor do's she stand upon't, though she be fine,
> And but bare; nor do's she trade for coyne;
> She wants not gold, or any thing beside. (Mill 1640, 173)

Similarly, in John Dunton's *Nightwalker*, a prostitute confesses to the reformer that she took to the streets because she was 'unable to master her desire' ([1696] 1985, 2.2.15). In Walker's narrative, however, Salisbury not only lands in Mrs Wisebourn's brothel as a result of debt, but initially runs away from her family for similar reasons: first she loses a valuable piece of lace when working as an apprentice to a seamstress, and later her father wrongfully accuses her of stealing twenty pounds from him.

Salisbury occasionally takes a lover for pleasure in the *Authentick Memoirs*, but generally speaking money rather than sexual pleasure drives her. In fact, for a narrative that appears at first glance to promise bawdy, voyeuristic entertainment for men, the *Authentick Memoirs* offers relatively little explicit erotic titillation. While the *Authentick Memoirs* in general, as I have argued, represents mobile property as liberating rather than just anxious, at the same time it shows Salisbury's excesses as financial rather than just sexual. Salisbury consistently represents the extremes of both getting and spending:

> There is no expressing the violent Avarice that appear'd in her on the one
> Hand, to get whatever she could out of the Persons, that her Charms had
> any Power over, and she had, on the other Hand, such a Spirit of Profusion,
> and took such a Wantonness in Prodigality, that she seem'd form'd by
> Nature to make the most exquisite Example of Consummate Ingratitude.
> Hence, in Proportion, as she more or less touch'd the Heart of any Ad-
> mirer, she got the Command of his Purse, and then made his Generosity
> the Measure of her Extravagance. (Walker 1723, 70)

Thus her 'wantonness' here describes consumer rather than sexual
indulgence. The same letter tells an anecdote about her refusal to lend
five pieces at the gaming table to a gentleman who had been keeping her
in lavish style. Anecdotes like this appear throughout the *Authentick
Memoirs*, for clients seem to have a sense that their exchanges with her
entitled them to some kind of enduring relationship of credit and debt –
a view that Salisbury clearly does not share. She uses men instrumentally,
and rather than becoming a piece of property or selling herself, she
instead makes, as one of her former clients complains, a 'property of
[him]' (Walker 1723, 99). Money drives her and even provides erotic
pleasure: another letter writer notes that Salisbury took 'a greater kind
of Wantonness in Ingratitude, than even in the Acts of Wantonness
themselves' (Walker 1723, 90). Yet this greater wantonness of lust for
money and passion for consumption does not so much condemn prostitution in order to preserve the dignity of mobile property in general, but
rather describes the flow of capital itself as essentially libidinal. In the
Authentick Memoirs, the whore does not lurk at the margins of legitimate
business, justifying its virtue by her negative example; rather, the whore's
combination of avarice and prodigality – or getting and spending –
epitomizes the mobile and imaginary qualities of property itself in the
emergent capitalist economy.

Perhaps nothing in the *Authentick Memoirs* illustrates this point so
dramatically and summarizes the economic theme of the narrative as the
volume's most pornographic scene. One of Salisbury's lovers – Senior
Gambolini, identified in the key as Bolingbroke – takes another mistress,
a move that infuriates Salisbury. In revenge, Salisbury tells Gambolini's
wife about the new mistress. Not having seen Salisbury for a while,
Gambolini agrees to join his friends in an 'Old Game' played in a 'New
Manner' (Walker 1723, 67). Upon entering the room, he sees Salisbury
naked, upside down upon a bed, with a peer holding on to each of her

legs; 'thus every Admirer pleas'd with the Sight, pull'd out his Gold, and with the greatest Alacrity pursued the agreeable Diversion':

> Between two Marble-Pillars, round and Plump,
> With Eye intent, each Sportsman took his Aim;
> The merry Chuck-Hole border'd on the Rump,
> And from his Play Sally deriv'd a Name.
> Within her tufted Chink, the Guineas shone,
> And each that she receiv'd was all her own.
> With ecchoing Shouts the vaulted Chamber rung,
> Belle Chuck was now the TOAST of ev'ry Tongue.
> Sally no more her Christian Name could boast,
> And Priddon too, to that of Chuck was lost. (Walker 1723, 68)

Salisbury plays an 'old game' in at least two ways here. First, the posture comically echoes Zeus's appearance to Danae in a shower of gold, offering a pornographic version of a classical story.[13] Second, as James Turner points out, the inverted woman posture appears in several seventeenth-century bawdy texts, which this one now self-consciously repeats. Turner reads these seventeenth-century images as expressions of male power over women and money (2002, 144); the context in which Salisbury's 'game' appears in *Authentick Memoirs*, however, opens up other readings as well. Salisbury, after all, plays the game to take revenge on her former lover; through it, she suggests her own indifference to his money over anyone else's. The men clearly find the naked, upside-down Salisbury sexy, but instead of pulling out their 'yards,' as they might in a more explicitly pornographic narrative, they pull out their gold and toss it into her genitalia. Thus the flow of gold entirely replaces the flow of semen here. We witness a form of prostitution, but one in which sexual contact does not actually take place. It is almost as if sex itself has become superfluous, and the more interesting erotic action consists of the direct flow of money. Salisbury pornographically literalizes here the famous image that Defoe's Moll Flanders offers when she describes a woman as a bag of gold. But while Moll uses this image to describe the danger women face without protection in the world, Salisbury instead insatiably draws the gold to herself with no sense of danger or even any sense of obligation to offer something in return. The 'estate' that she elsewhere exposes to the clergyman is not just mobile but imaginary, as none of the men have any actual contact with it. Men receive nothing for their money, except the purely libidinal pleasure of 'spending' itself.

Notes

1 On early modern capitalism, see Pocock (1985), Dickson (1967), and Braudel (1992).

2 Radin (1996) discusses capitalism's potentially contradictory tendency toward the extreme of universal commodification.

3 While the *Authentick Memoirs* was published before the cultural dominance of the domestic novel, stories of the upward mobility of women through prostitution persist throughout the century. See, for example, Lyons (1995), *Uncommon Adventures of Miss Kitty Fisher* (1759), *The Secret History of Betty Ireland* (c. 1750), *Memoirs of the Celebrated Miss Fanny M[urray]* (1759), *Memoirs of a Demi-Rep of Fashion* (1776).

4 Prostitutes endured an outlaw or marginal status in the eighteenth century, although technically prostitution was not itself illegal. Authorities and reformers, however, found various strategies for arresting, harassing, and convicting prostitutes. See Henderson (1999) and Trumbach (1998).

5 For example, the issue of 9–12 March 1772/3 reports that 'Sally Salisbury continues out of Order and is much troubled with Vapours, and sudden Palpitations of the Heart, proceeding, as 'tis thought, from abstaining too much from Repletion, to which she was formerly used. Her chief Complaint is Want of Motion, and that, like the Cameleon, she was always gaping for fresh Air, tho' to no purpose.'

6 Wood (1930) attributes 'The Ballad of Sally in Our Alley' to Henry Carey, although the comments here suggest that it could have had a folk origin or at least become popular as a song about Sally Salisbury. Carey himself acknowledges this popular association, although he denies that the ballad refers to the famous prostitute: 'A vulgar error having long prevail'd among many persons, who imagine Sally Salisbury the subject of this ballad, the author begs leave to undeceive them and assure them it has not the least allusion to her ... as innocence and virtue were ever the boundaries of his muse.' He claims that the ballad describes an apprentice's love for a young woman, and while the speaker announces his intention to marry Sally in the last stanza, other parts of the ballad suggest a commercial transaction: 'When Christmas comes about again, / O, then I shall have money; / I'll hoard it up, and box and all, / I'll give it to my honey; / And would it were ten thousand pounds, / I'd give it all to Sally; / She is the darling of my heart, / And she lives in our alley.'

7 According to Karras, in the Middle Ages laundresses had an unsavoury reputation and were associated with prostitutes (1996, 54). Thus it is possible that Salisbury is also revealing this man's mother as a whore.

8 On prostitution in the eighteenth century, see Trumbach (1998) and
Henderson (1999). On alternatives to reading sex workers as victims, see
Davidson (1998), Delacoste and Alexander (1987), Chapkis (1997), Nagle
(1997), McClintock (1993), Chancer (1993), and Rubin (1984).

9 As Salisbury's passing comparison of herself to a 'Negroe' in *The Genuine
History* (1723) suggests, prostitute narratives can also disturb 'racial' categories as well. This becomes explicit in later centuries with the euphemism
'white slavery.'

10 Aphra Behn makes a similar claim about her own position. See Gallagher
(1994, 1–48).

11 For a study of this sort of mobilization of misogyny, see Mandell (1999).

12 Karras (1996) makes the point that sexuality rather than money defined
prostitution in the Middle Ages.

13 I thank Margaret Ferguson for this point.

Works Cited

Armstrong, Nancy.1987. *Desire and Domestic Fiction: A Political History of the Novel*.
New York and Oxford: Oxford University Press.

Braudel, Fernand. 1992. *Civilization and Capitalism, 15th–18th Century*. Trans.
Siân Reynolds. 3 vols. Berkeley: University of California Press.

Chancer, Lynn Sharon. 1993. Prostitution, Feminist Theory, and Ambivalence:
Notes from the Sociological Underground. *Social Text* 37: 143–71.

Chapkis, Wendy. 1997. *Live Sex Acts: Women Performing Erotic Labor*. New York:
Routledge.

Davidson, Julia O'Connell. 1998. *Prostitution, Power, and Freedom*. Ann Arbor:
University of Michigan.

Delacoste, Frederique, and Priscilla Alexander. 1987. *Sex Work: Writings by
Women in the Sex Industry*. Pittsburgh, PA: Cleis Press.

Dickson, P.G.M. 1967. *The Financial Revolution in England: A Study in the Development of Public Credit, 1688–1756*. New York: St Martin's Press.

Dunton, John. [1696] 1985. *The Night-Walkers: or, Evening Rambles in Search of
Lewd Women*. Facsimile ed. New York and London: Garland Publishing.

*The Effigies, Parentage, Education, Life, Merry-Pranks and Conversation of the Cele-
brated Mrs Sally Salisbury*. 1722–3. Cornhill: J. Wilson.

Gallagher, Catherine. 1994. *Nobody's Story: The Vanishing Acts of Women Writers in
the Marketplace, 1670–1820*. Berkeley: University of California Press.

The Genuine History of Mrs Sarah Prydden, Usually Called Sally Salisbury. 1723.
London: Andrew Moor.

Henderson, Tony. 1999. *Disorderly Women in Eighteenth-Century London: Prostitution and Control in the Metropolis, 1730–1830.* London and New York: Longman.

Holmes, Geoffrey. 1973. *The Trial of Doctor Sacheverell.* London: Eyre Methuen.

Karras, Ruth Mazo. 1996. *Common Women: Prostitution and Sexuality in Medieval England.* Oxford: Oxford University Press.

Kowaleski-Wallace, Elizabeth. 1997. *Consuming Subjects: Women, Shopping, and Business in the Eighteenth Century.* New York: Columbia University Press.

The Life and Intrigues of the Late Celebrated Mrs Mary Parrimore. 1729. London.

Linebaugh, Peter. 1992. *The London Hanged: Crime and Civil Society in the Eighteenth Century.* Cambridge: Cambridge University Press.

Lyons, Mary, ed. 1995. *The Memoirs of Mrs Leeson.* Dublin: Lilliput Press.

Macpherson, C.B. 1962. *The Political Theory of Possessive Individualism: Hobbes to Locke.* Oxford: Clarendon Press.

Mandell, Laura. 1999. *Misogynous Economies: The Business of Literature in Eighteenth-Century Britain.* Lexington: University Press of Kentucky.

McClintock, Anne. 1993. Sex Workers and Sex Work. *Social Text* 37: 1–10.

Memoirs of the Celebrated Miss Fanny M[urray]. 1759. London: J. Scott.

Memoirs of a Demi-Rep of Fashion; or, the Private History of Miss Amelia Gunnersbury. 1776. 2 vols. Dublin: United Company of Booksellers.

Mill, Humphrey. 1640. *A Night's Search, Discovering the Nature and Condition of Night-Walkers with Their Associates, Digested into a Poem by Humphrey Mill.* London: Richard Bishop for Laurence Blaicklock.

Nagle, Jill, ed. 1997. *Whores and Other Feminists.* New York: Routledge.

Nocturnal Revels: Or, the History of King's-Place and Other Modern Nunneries. 1779. 2 vols. London.

Pateman, Carole. 1988. *The Sexual Contract.* Stanford: Stanford University Press.

Phillips, Teresia Constantia. 1748–9. *An Apology for the Conduct of Mrs Teresia Constantia Phillips.* London: Printed for the Author.

Pocock, J.G.A. 1975. *The Machiavellian Moment: Florentine Political Thought and the Atlantic Republican Tradition.* Princeton: Princeton University Press.

– 1985. *Virtue, Commerce, and History: Essays On Political Thought and History, Chiefly in the Eighteenth Century.* Cambridge: Cambridge University Press.

The Post Boy. With Foreign and Domestic News. 1665–1726. London.

Radin, Margaret Jane. 1996. *Contested Commodities. The Trouble with Trade in Sex, Children, Body Parts, and Other Things.* Cambridge, MA: Harvard University Press.

Richetti, John J. 1969. *Popular Fiction before Richardson: Narrative Patterns 1700–1739.* Oxford: Clarendon Press, 1969.

Rubin, Gayle. 1984. Thinking Sex: Notes for a Radical Theory of the Politics of

Sexuality. In *Pleasure and Danger: Exploring Female Sexuality*, ed. Carole S. Vance, 267–319. Boston: Routledge and Kegan Paul.

Saussure, César de. 1995. *A Foreign View of England in 1725–1729*. Trans. Madam Van Muyden. London: Caliban Books.

The Secret History of Betty Ireland. n.d. (1750?). London: Printed for S. Lee.

Sheldon, Ann. 1790. *Authentic and Interesting Memoirs of Miss Ann Sheldon*. London: Printed for the Authoress.

Straub, Kristina. 1992. *Sexual Suspects: Eighteenth-Century Players and Sexual Ideology*. Princeton, NJ: Princeton University Press.

Trumbach, Randolph, ed. [1742] 1985. *Select Trials at the Sessions-House in the Old-Bailey*. Facsimile ed. 4 vols. New York and London: Garland Publishing.

– 1998. *Sex and Gender Revolution*. Vol 1: *Heterosexuality and the Third Gender in Enlightenment London*. Chicago: University of Chicago Press.

Turner, James Grantham. 2002. *Libertines and Radicals in Early Modern London: Sexuality, Politics, and Literary Culture, 1630–1685*. Cambridge: Cambridge University Press.

The Uncommon Adventures of Miss Kitty Fisher. 1759. London: Thomas Bailey.

The Velvet Coffee-Woman: Or, the Life, Gallantries and Amours of the Late Famous Mrs Anne Rochford. 1728. Westminster: Simon Green.

A View of London and Westminster; or, the Town Spy. 1725. London.

Walker, Capt. Charles. 1723. *Authentick Memoirs of the Life and Intrigue and Adventures of the Celebrated Sally Salisbury*. London.

Wood, Frederick T. ed. 1930. *The Poems of Henry Carey*. London: The Scholartis Press.

Part Two

Women, Social Reproduction, and Patrilineal Inheritance

5

Primogeniture, Patrilineage, and the Displacement of Women

MARY MURRAY

Recent legal histories of inheritance practices in England from 1300 to 1800 focus on the ascendancy of primogeniture among large landholders, that is, the aristocracy and gentry. In *Law, Land, and Family*, for example, Eileen Spring argues that various legal devices, including the use and strict settlement, can be described as 'primogenitive devices' that provided practical means to ensure property was transmitted in the patriline. Primogeniture and these legal devices, she argues, can be theorized as the practical means to implement 'the family logic' that guided landholders' behaviour (Spring 1993, 2). She uses statistics to document her analysis of landholders' inheritance practices that, she argues, aimed to subordinate the common law right of a daughter, as heir-general, to inherit before a collateral male relative. Instead of conforming with the common law, landholders practised primogeniture in order to transfer property between the eldest male of each generation and, thereby, maintained a family's relationship to the land. In Spring's analysis patrilineal inheritance practices displaced women's common law rights to land, not only daughters' rights to inherit but widows' rights to dower, in order to implement that family logic.

This chapter offers an alternative approach to the subject of inheritance practices that ensured property was transmitted patrilineally and 'displaced' women; I analyse primogeniture and 'primogenitive devices' as 'resurrective practices' that illustrate cultural understandings of the fact of death. Death is an indivisible component of inheritance practices; it marks the moment of the transmission of property from one generation to another. In his research on death, property, and ancestry Jack

Goody (1962; 1998) analyses inheritance as the means by which the social system is reproduced. I want to explore the resonance of the word 'reproduce' in this study of primogeniture as an inheritance practice derived from feudal tenures of landholding in England. I will suggest that a link between death and historically specific forms of property relationships can be analysed in two interrelated ways: first, by utilizing the concept of 'resurrective practice,' and second, by 'conceiving' a more general link between death, fertility, and birth.

Despite the fact that primogeniture became the predominant method of inheritance for real property among the aristocracy during what is commonly described as the feudal period in England, it is not a subject discussed in *The Place of the Dead* (Gordon and Marshall 2000), a recent book in which social historians evaluate mortuary customs and wills, for example, as evidence of medieval and early modern societies' ideas of the relationships of the living and the dead. Their research, like my own, however, acknowledges the seminal, if flawed, theorization of death by Philippe Ariès in *The Hour of Our Death* (1981). I will use Ariès's typology of different concepts of death in premodern and modern Western European societies in order to evaluate the significance of primogeniture as a system of inheritance fostered in medieval and early modern England by the feudal system of land tenure. Ariès's basic thesis was that a shift occurred from the medieval and early modern concept of death as 'tamed' to the modern understanding of death, which, if not 'taboo,' is, he argues, certainly 'invisible.' Ariès contends that in medieval and early modern European societies fear of death was greatly reduced because it was understood as part of human existence. Death was a communal, public act accompanied by ritualized expression of mourning by family and community at the deathbed. Religion theorized death as collective salvation and bodily resurrection. In modernity, Ariès posits, death became increasingly 'invisible' and denied as individuals died not at home but in hospitals in conditions of unparalleled isolation.

Ariès's thesis is, of course, contestable. However, Houlbrooke (1998, 7–10) among others, provides evidence that supports Ariès's observation that death was a familiar part of life in medieval times because people were more frequently exposed to the deaths of others. It is difficult, however, to verify Ariès's thesis that death was tamed and fear of it much reduced. At the very least high rates of mortality due to warfare, famine, or plague, for example, could have seriously disruptive effects upon individuals and society (Seale 1998, 51). Similarly, Ariès's observation that death is hidden or invisible in modern society may be supported insofar as the site of death has moved, we have less contact with the dead and dying, and expression of emotions associated with death have been discouraged. Elias (1985) also argues that in modernity the expression of grief has become regarded as morbid behaviour to be discouraged if not shunned. Gorer (1955) argues that taboos surrounding death are analogous to those about sex in Victorian England. However, Ariès's thesis that there is a 'denial of death' in modern societies is more problematic. Death may be hidden from public space but we cannot therefore assume that individuals engage in the psychological denial of death. Indeed, with meaning increasingly relocated in the privatized realm of individual subjective experience, death, Mellor (1993) argues, may in fact be *more* present for individuals.

The significance of inheritance practices is not addressed by Ariès or scholars who have more recently studied social attitudes and practices surrounding death. Inheritance, however, stands in uncanny contiguity to the fact of death and does aim to maintain not just the memory but also the existence of a family lineage linking the living and the dead. Inheritance practices are only one of many social practices related to death, such as mortuary rituals and the making of wills, for example; inheritance is also a means to 'place' the dead in relationship to the living. Inheritance practices, I suggest, can be meaningfully classified among the various activities that Benedict Anderson (1983) describes as 'resurrective practices,' which include religion and mortuary ritual as well as nationalist ideologies. These, as Anderson has pointed out, connect the dead with the living and those yet to be born through the construction of imagined communities. Resurrective practices can restore a sense of basic security fractured by death, which threatens to undermine the security of individuals and 'society' alike. Death not only challenges the existential and ontological security of individuals; it also poses a threat to the social order. Just as death can raise fundamental issues of meaning for individuals, it also poses a threat to the continuity and stability of the social order. Resurrective practices enable individuals to ward off the terror of meaninglessness while affirming wider social bonds. As social and cultural activity, a resurrective practice may be seen as a defence against death, turning away from its inevitability towards an affirmation of life. Resurrective practices transform the threat to basic security posed by mortality into an orientation towards continuing meaningful existence (Seale 1998, 1).

While it is widely acknowledged that inheritance practices function as a means of social reproduction, I would suggest that the symbolic significance of inheritance practices in early modern England may be more fully appreciated if we also think of them as resurrective practices that confer immortality upon the community and its members. Viewed as a resurrective practice, inheritance effects reincorporation and revitalization of the dead into the world of the living. Inheritance is the 'medium' through which the apparent opposition between life and death becomes part of a process of regeneration. Through the 'alchemy' of inheritance the dead are transformed into the living and connected to those yet to be born. To detail the way in which this was achieved in medieval England we need to move to a historical consideration of inheritance practices and property law.

By the end of the thirteenth century, primogeniture had become the law of England for free tenures. Lawyers applied the rule of primogeniture unless special proof of a custom of partibility could be shown. According to Bracton, writing in the thirteenth century, 'in the matter of succession the male sex must always be preferred to the female' and 'Proprietary right lies with the older' (Thorne 1968, 190, 188). In the previous century Glanvill had stated, 'if he was a knight the eldest succeeds to his father in everything' (Hall 1965, 75). By the sixteenth century primogeniture spread, as Thirsk notes (1976, 186–91), downwards to the gentry and by the eighteenth century to members of the yeomanry.

Primogeniture does not appear to have been popular among the peasantry and seems to have been related to the degree of manorialization, probably developing under strong seigniorial pressure and associated with large demesnes and heavy labour services (Thirsk 1964, 12). Nevertheless on partible holdings elder sons might become the sole heirs by buying out younger brothers' shares, while younger children and other relatives could be provided for, either by settling land on them before death or, very often, by use of the will (Faith 1966–7, 85–6). What was effected by such inheritance practices was the maintenance of social bonds and a degree of stability in the social order. Inheritance practices in medieval England maintained the feudal class hierarchy, ties of kinship, and a patriarchal gender order. Death did not threaten the matrix of class, kinship, and patriarchy that defined the feudal social order. On the contrary, that matrix was reproduced and resurrected despite, and because of, the fact of death.

The establishment of primogeniture needs initially to be understood in terms of the political exigencies of the patron–client relationship that became the basic organizing principle of feudal England. Following the

Norman Conquest, primogeniture was the rule where military tenants-in-chief owed personal service in the king's army for land and rights of jurisdiction. The permanent commutation of personal service into money had by the thirteenth century replaced the former military relevance of primogeniture. However, the interests of the wealthy landowners ensured the preservation of the principle of primogeniture (Creighton 1980, 146). Both before and after the Norman Conquest, primogeniture facilitated the preservation and accumulation of property, sustaining and reproducing relations of class power. The strict settlement, as A.R. Buck explains in a subsequent chapter, was designed to protect and preserve the principle of primogeniture, particularly after the abolition of feudal tenures. This legal device, as Christopher Hill has argued, was crucial for the development of agrarian capitalism. It 'led on to the great consolidation of landed property which made the Whig oligarchy of the eighteenth century ... it also contributed to the relative depression of the lesser gentry' (Hill 1969, 146–7).

Insofar as primogeniture sustained and reproduced relations of class power, and in so doing maintained the essence of the feudal mode of production as an exploitative relationship between landowners and subordinated peasants in the face of the potentially destabilizing effect of death, we may view primogeniture as a resurrective practice. Without strict rules of succession and, in this instance, rules of succession that facilitated the consolidation and accumulation of property, death could potentially undermine the fundamental social relation of property at the heart of the feudal mode of production. Moreover, insofar as inheritance practices contributed to the buildup of landed estates that were crucial to the development of agrarian capitalism in early modern England, we may even view such practices as *reincarnating* historically specific forms of class relations. In medieval and early modern England, the 'alchemy' of inheritance practices entailed the reincarnation of earlier forms of class power as new forms.

Inheritance practices also maintained and asserted the social bond of kinship in the face of death. Joan Thirsk suggests that among the nobility primogeniture 'seems to have been deemed by common consent the most acceptable practice for *family reasons* ... it reduced strife among brothers when the eldest automatically took the leading positions; it maintained the status of the family' (1976, 186; emphasis added). She cites Starkey's *Dialogue between Pole and Lupset* (c. 1532–4) in which it is asserted: 'if the lands in every great family were distributed equally betwixt the brethren in a small process of years the great families would decay and little by little vanish away' (Thirsk 1976, 184). Similarly, she notes that in the sixteenth century Powell argued: 'Partition in a populous country already furnished with inhabitants is the very decay of the great families, and ... the cause of strife and debate' (Thirsk 1976, 188). As far as the peasantry was concerned, Thirsk points out that in 'the weakly manorialized districts of England and Wales family cohesion was aided by the practice of partible inheritance, which involved much cooperation within the family, in the working of jointly owned land' (1964, 118). Faith suggests a similar reading: 'However much peasant inheritance customs varied by the thirteenth century, they shared one basic principle. They placed great importance on the concept of keeping the name on the land ... the emphasis on family landholding is as strong in areas of partibility as elsewhere' (1966–7, 86). Medieval inheritance practices, then, made good sense in terms of class and family because primogeniture, in particular, functioned as a resurrective practice that reasserted and furthered the interests and bonds of class and kinship.

At the same time medieval inheritance practices and the class and family relations that they maintained and resurrected were infused with patriarchal privilege. Even though women might inherit property as residual heirs, and were provided for by means of dowry, dower, and later by jointure, the bulk of real strategic property in medieval and early modern England was held by men, affording men rather than women the hugely significant advantages of material and economic resources as well as social status. In fact, although the common law practice of daughters inheriting before a collateral male relative did prevail in early feudal times (Milsom 1981; Holt 1985), during the sixteenth, seventeenth, and eighteenth centuries practices changed. Drawing on research by Stone and Stone (1984), Spring alerts us to the fact that landowners cut the rate of female succession quite dramatically – to less than a third of what might be expected if common law rules had prevailed (1993, 14). As Spring puts it, 'since the common law itself when compared to equal division cut female inheritance in half, landowners had actually cut it to less than one-sixth. As for the number of women who were disherisoned, whereas 33 percent of women would have inherited from their fathers if the common law had prevailed, less than 10 percent actually did so; and whereas 42 percent would have inherited all told if the common law had prevailed, less than 13 percent actually did so' (1993, 14). Drawing on Barbara English's 1990 study of great landowners of East Yorkshire, Spring points out that between 1530 and 1919, out of a total of 127 successions, only 7, that is, about 5 per cent, went to women (1993, 16).

Spring also draws on Lloyd Bonfield's (1983) study of strict settlements, alerting us to the fact that from all the strict settlements made before 1740, 78 per cent favoured collateral male relatives over daughters (1993, 17).

By the sixteenth century disputes between collateral male and direct female heirs from large landholding families had become frequent. Sometimes the female heir was successful, as in the case of the Dacre family, where sisters who were heirs-general succeeded over the claims of their uncle, Leonard Dacre (Spring 1993, 105). It seems, however, that compromise was the more usual outcome in such disputes, as in the case of the Stanley family. When the fifth Earl of Derby died in 1594, he left his estates to his eldest daughter rather than his brother. His brother, however, began legal proceedings against his niece, claiming that the land had been entailed. Ensuing developments suggest that if the land had in fact been entailed then the land involved was not particularly substantial, or a disentailing could be alleged because the Earl offered his niece a financial inducement to forgo a legal contest. Only after elaborate negotiations was a final agreement achieved (Spring 1993, 106–7). It seems that compromise generally followed the Statute of Wills, according to which an heir-at-law could expect to receive one-third of land held by knight service. By the late fifteenth century, property that was originally transferred in the female line came to be transferred patrilineally (Spring 1993, 107). This, as Mary Chan and Nancy E. Wright explain in a subsequent chapter in this book, seems to have been the situation in the case of Anne Clifford.

The struggle between male and female heirs extended beyond the peerage. Although records for untitled families are not as complete or reliable as those for titled families, it is clear that the same struggle was played out among untitled landowning families. In the case of *Sharington v. Strotton* (1565), Andrew Baynton, who had no sons, excluded his daughter from inheriting by means of a covenant with his brother Edward. While the case has been seen as establishing the principle that natural affection (in this case between brothers) is sufficient ground for making a settlement, as Spring puts it: 'From the family historian's point of view the case demonstrates the growth of an order of succession not natural' (1993, 109). In the complicated and notorious *Shelley's Case* (1579) the intention was to defeat a female heir. The case ended up being a conflict between a posthumously born son and his uncle. The end result was that Edward Shelley's manifest intentions were carried out with the succession of his posthumous grandson (Simpson 1986, 96–102; Spring 1993, 110). In the case of *Dormer v. Parkhurst* (1740), John Dor-

mer, in a collateral branch of the Dormer family, challenged the possession of land by three sisters as heirs-general. The courts dispossessed the
three sisters after they had been in possession for some twelve years
(Spring 1993, 111). As Spring sees it: 'We may be sure that had Fleetwood's
heirs not been female the case would never have arisen. John Dormer
would not likely have challenged a male in the senior branch of the
family who was in possession' (1993, 112).

Commenting on these trends, Spring observes:

> Clearly the history of the heiress in gentry and aristocratic families is of a
> great downward slide. From once succeeding according to common law
> rules, she came to succeed about as seldom as possible. With the strict
> settlement of the eighteenth century she reached her nadir. She was not to
> succeed except as a last resort; inheritance would not be traced through
> her except as a last resort; and her portion, calculated before her birth, was
> calculated at a time when the interests of the patriline were uppermost. In
> short, English landowners had moved from lineal to patrilineal principles.
> (1993, 18–19)

Primogenitive devices can be viewed as resurrective practices that ensured the preservation and perpetuation of male privilege and advantage in, and through, the potentially destabilizing effect of death.

Moreover in symbolic terms we may view medieval and early modern
inheritance practices – primogeniture and the shift to patrilineal rather
than lineal principles – as patriarchal acts of *birth*. In the preceding
discussion of inheritance as a resurrective practice a linkage was made
between inheritance and the symbolism of rebirth and reincarnation
with death being seen as a source of the renewal of life. Primogeniture
and inheritance according to the patriline, I suggest, can be viewed as an
act of birth albeit of social rather than biological life. Connections
between death and symbols of fertility and birth have, of course, been a
focus for anthropological analysis (Bloch and Parry 1982). But anthropologists have tended to limit this connection to mortuary rituals in non-
Western, preliterate, and preindustrial societies. Such an approach,
however, can be applied to a wide range of social practices and institutions, including inheritance practices. Seen in this light, what is particularly remarkable – miraculous, perhaps – about primogeniture and
adherence to patrilineal principles is that it is men rather than women
who give birth.

There is in fact a tradition of masculine birth in Western society, a birth in which miraculously the laws of nature and biology are defied and inverted. Lying at the heart of Western belief systems in the Judaeo-Christian creation story in Genesis, for instance, we see Adam as the first male giving birth – Eve being created out of Adam's body. Later, because of her association with the serpent, Eve, as the first woman, becomes associated with death. A psychological interpretation of the relationship between Eve and the serpent is that the serpent is actually a phallic symbol and that the sin of Adam and Eve is not just one of disobedience but of sexual transgression (Condren 1989, 4). Adam and Eve are cast out of Eden as a place of divine, asexual fertility (Bloch and Parry 1982, 19). Because of her association with the serpent (which in pre-Christian religions was a symbol of immortality), Eve, the 'Mother of all the Living,' becomes a carrier of death (Condren 1989, 15). Female sexuality here is associated with death, and sexuality is set in opposition to fertility as something to be overcome – a theme which, of course, is echoed in the story of the virgin birth of the Christian Messiah.

It is my argument that these same disjunctions were, in symbolic terms, embedded in the principle and practice of primogeniture and the shift to patrilineal rather than lineal principles and practices. By interpreting fertility as 'fecundity' or 'productiveness' (rather than in a restricted or technical sense), and interpreting birth symbolically (rather than literally), we can view primogeniture and patrilineality as component parts of an ancestral fertility rite controlled by men: one having 'seminal' significance in the production and reproduction of the feudal social order. What is notable about this particular type of fertility is the absence of sexuality. Clearly, in the first instance, it is women who give biological birth to the men that inherit. But it is men who appear to be the principal agents in social and economic generation. As equivalents to parthenogenesis, primogeniture and patrilineality enabled men to give birth to the body social and its economic and jural relationships.

Patriarchal inheritance practices in feudal England were not simply involved in the birth and resurrection of the body social, they were also central to the birth and resurrection of the body politic. Death presents a problem of an essentially political nature to do with the legitimation of traditional authority. Because positions of authority are conceptualized as belonging to an eternal and unchanging order, within systems of traditional authority death threatens the continuity of the eternal social order (Bloch and Parry 1982, 11). An uncontrolled event of such centrality as death puts into question the extent to which the social order can really govern the lives of its members. 'In such systems positions of authority are conceptualized as belonging to an eternal and unchanging order ... it is thus that things have always been and must always remain' (Bloch and Parry 1982, 11). How then did primogeniture and patrilineality as an act of birth and resurrection offer a solution to this problem?

Patron–client relations were integral to state formation in feudal England. Pollock and Maitland argue that the near absolute and uncompromising form of primogeniture which emerged in England was not characteristic of feudalism in general but of a highly centralized version of feudalism in which, theoretically, the king had little to fear from even his mightiest vassals. Although subinfeudation may have encouraged lesser tenants to conceive of themselves as fighting for their mesne lords, all military service was performed for the king (Pollock and Maitland 1898, 2: 264–5). Primogeniture was also crucial to determining the taxable capacity of subjects of the English state – the distribution of land being of central importance for the imposition of taxes (Holdsworth 1923, 3: 55). The permanent commutation of personal service into money had by the thirteenth century replaced the former military relevance of primogeniture. The interests of wealthy landowners, however, ensured the preservation of the principle. Primogeniture was profoundly political. John Aubrey pointed out that entails were a good prop for monarchy (Hill 1969, 147). In the sixteenth century Starkey's *Dialogue between Pole and Lupset* highlights the way in which the stability of the state depended on the existence of well-rooted and well-endowed families in positions of authority (Thirsk 1976, 183).

Even in the nineteenth century it was stated that primogeniture 'had a peculiar value in preserving the aristocratic branch of the constitution.' The absence of primogeniture and settlement 'would leave many peerages without an estate to support their honours' (Thompson 1963, 69). When in the nineteenth century it was proposed that the law on intestacy in connection with real estate be made the same as for personal property, where equal division occurred, such proposals were violently and successfully resisted by the landed interest. Any interference with primogeniture would, it was felt, by leading to the division of estates, 'destroy that fair and reasonable influence which the property and aristocracy of the country was allowed to possess.' According to Palmerston, such changes would be incompatible with the existence of the landed gentry and 'tended to republicanism' (Thompson 1963, 69). Theorists in seventeenth-century England related different property relationships to aristocracies and republics: 'If Montesquieu approved entails and primogeniture as means to preserve noble families themselves essential to true monarchies, he also expressed the republican tradition, partly derived from Harrington, that such devices were inimical to republican regimes which required more or less egalitarian partible inheritance' (Cooper 1976, 195).

Carole Pateman's comments on Sir Robert Filmer's defence of monarchical power in *Partriarcha* (1680) are also apposite to the discussion in hand: 'Filmer's account is only one version of a long Western tradition in which the creation of political life can be seen as a masculine act of birth: as a male replica of the ability which only women possess ... Eve's procreative, creative capacity is denied and appropriated by *men* as the ability to give *political birth*' (1989, 44). In *Patriarcha,* Filmer invokes divine will and age differentials underpinning the law of primogeniture. All title to rule originated in the divine grant of kingly right to Adam. Pateman notes how the biblical creation narrative in Genesis 2: 4 was read by Filmer as a story of sovereignty and descent arising solely from the male parent; Eve 'is not created *ab initio* but from Adam, who is thus in a sense her parent. Filmer is able to treat all political power as the right of a father because the patriarchal father has the creative powers of both a mother and a father. He is not just one of two parents; he is *the* parent' (1989, 38). The historical development of nation-states was seen by Filmer as a process of descent from Adam, the first father and supreme patriarch, who divided up the world between his sons, who themselves became fathers and patriarchs (Ryan 1984, 14). Political right in Filmer's theorization, Laslett explains, is transmitted upon Adam's death to his son, who 'inherited all his property as he inherited all his power' (1949, 12–13). Where the principle and practice of primogeniture prevail, the death of the 'father' does not threaten political security and stability. On the contrary, it preserves and furthers the life of the political community. The life of the father is resurrected, if not reincarnated, in the *polis.* Indeed, metaphorically speaking we might even view Adam's 'son' as a spirit medium, harnessing the magic of the dead to conjure up the theatre of the state.

Benedict Anderson (1983) has alerted us to the significance of nationalism in invoking an 'imagined' community. He suggests that as religious modes of thought waned, nationalism articulated a link between the dead and the living, regenerating and embracing community in and through the nation-state. Ordinary citizens not only believe themselves to be part of a larger community which will continue to exist after their death, they may also be willing to die in the interests of the life of that imagined community. The concept of nationalism obviously cannot be applied to feudal England. The nation-state and the nationalist ideologies that accompany it have been features of modern but not medieval and early modern social formations. It would therefore be inappropriate to argue that nationalism as a resurrective practice pertained in feudal England. The English Crown, however, has been seen as the strongest medieval monarchy in the West. Whereas Continental Europe featured semi-independent territorial potestates, Norman feudalism was administratively centralized. Moreover, Perry Anderson suggests that by the sixteenth century the Tudor dynasty had made a 'promising start towards the construction of an English absolutism' (1974, 119). Although Parliament acted as a counterweight to the Crown, and government in the Tudor period was developed through Parliament and statute, in comparison with Continental Europe, English feudalism was highly centralized. Though not yet a nation-state proper, the political nation that comprised this highly centralized version of feudalism invoked the dead to legitimize their political authority. Instead of posing a threat to the continuity of order and government, by means of the medium of lineage and inheritance, death was turned into an act of birth and resurrection, becoming the elixir of political life. Through inheritance the dead were reincorporated and revitalized into the living world of the political order. Inheritance was the medium through which the apparent opposition between life and death became part of a process of political generation and regeneration.

The principle and practice of primogeniture were integral to feudal property (for which ideas of absolute ownership and absolute title are anachronisms) because they contained the threat to the stability and security of the feudal social order which death posed. The principle and practice of primogeniture resurrected and gave birth to the economic, political, and kinship ties that defined feudal England. The fecundity and resurrective thrust of primogeniture may have been afforded particular potency by the directly political nature of feudal society; 'the elements of civil life for example, property, or the family, or the mode of labor, were raised to the level of political life in the form of seigniority, estates and corporations' (Marx quoted in Sayer 1987, 100). If, as Ariès suggests, death was a familiar part of life in medieval and early modern times because people were more frequently exposed to the death of others, the interconnecting vertical and horizontal ties of landholding together with the directly political nature of feudalism made the fecundity and resurrective potency of inheritance practices more apparent.

That fecundity and potency, like the 'patriarchal' set of gender relations it effected, were all-pervasive and 'publicly' visible.

I will briefly posit a hypothesis about Ariès's typology of 'invisible' death in relation to inherited property in a capitalist society. It is Ariès's thesis that death has become invisible, if not taboo, in modern society. Preceding this shift, with the development of capitalism property became private property affording individuals the right to exclude others. In contrast to medieval and early modern society, a separation of public and private spheres occurred in modern society. Meanwhile, with perhaps the exception of the monarchy and aristocracy, inheritance is in twenty-first-century Western societies no longer tied to the exercise of political right. Given the degree of material inequality that exists in modern society, inheritance undoubtedly continues to play an important role in the perpetuation of privilege. But its full significance as a fecund and resurrective practice in this respect is difficult to assess. To the extent that inheritance has, like the family, become privatized, it has, like death itself, attained a degree of invisibility. At the same time a dominant ideology of capitalism is that of equality of opportunity involving competition in an apparently meritocractic society for achieved rather than ascribed position. It is perhaps unsurprising then that full acknowledgment of the fecundity and resurrective potency of inheritance practices is something of a 'taboo' subject, its discussion considered as distasteful as discussion of death. However, whether death is 'tamed' or 'invisible,' through the practice of inheritance the dead are still present as members of the political, economic, and social community.

In their recent book *The Place of the Dead*, Gordon and Marshall (2000) ask what obligations did the living owe the dead in medieval and early modern England, and 'how in fulfilling those obligations did the living allow the dead to shape patterns of social organization ... In what circumstances did the dead threaten the living, and in what ways could the living exploit the dead for their own social and political purposes? If we speak, as perhaps we must, of a "relationship" between the living and the dead, what, in specific historical contexts, were the parameters of that relationship, its successes and failures, functions and dysfunctions?' (2000, 2–3). My analysis of primogeniture and 'primogenitive devices' in medieval and early modern England suggests one way of exploring such questions. By analysing primogeniture and 'primogenitive devices' as resurrective practices, and by 'conceiving' a more general link among death, fertility, and birth, I have been exploring the boundary between life and death. It has been my argument that through the 'medium' of inheritance the dead were very much part of the living community. Their ability to significantly shape patterns of social organization ensured that the dead transcended any limitations that might be placed upon them by a mere ghostly presence.

Acknowledgments

I would like to thank Nancy Wright for originally inviting me to present a paper at the conference from which this chapter has developed. I would also like to thank Nancy, Margie Ferguson, and two anonymous reviewers for their helpful comments and additional references which have been incorporated into the chapter.

Works Cited

Anderson, B. 1983. *Imagined Communities: Reflections on the Origin and Spread of Nationalism.* London: Verso.

Anderson, P. 1974. *Lineages of the Absolutist State.* London: NLB.

Ariès, P. 1981. *The Hour of Our Death.* London: Allen Lane.

Bauman, Z. 1992. *Mortality, Immortality and Other Life Strategies.* Cambridge: Polity Press.

Berger, P.L. 1973. *The Social Reality of Religion.* Harmondsworth: Penguin.

Bloch, M., and J. Parry, eds. 1982. *Death and the Regeneration of Life.* Cambridge: Cambridge University Press.

Bonfield, L. 1983. Marriage, Property and the Affective Family. *Law and History Review* 1: 297–312.

Clark, D., ed. 1993. *The Sociology of Death: Theory, Culture, Practice.* Oxford: Blackwell.

Condren, M. 1989. *The Serpent and the Goddess: Women, Religion and Power in Celtic Ireland.* San Francisco: Harper and Row.

Cooper, J.P. 1976. Inheritance and Settlement by Great Landowners. In *Family and Inheritance: Rural Society in Western Europe,* ed. J. Goody, J. Thirsk, and E.P. Thompson, 192–327. Cambridge: Cambridge University Press.

Creighton, C. 1980. Family Property and Relations of Production in Western Europe. *Economy and Society* 9.2: 129–67.

Cressy, David. 1997. *Birth, Marriage and Death: Ritual, Religion and the Life-Cycle in Tudor and Stuart England.* Oxford: Oxford University Press.

Durkheim, E. 1965. *The Elementary Forms of the Religious Life.* Trans. Joseph Ward Swain. New York: Free Press.

Elias, N. 1985. *The Loneliness of the Dying.* Trans. Edmund Jophcott. Oxford: Blackwell.

English, B. 1990. *The Great Landowners of East Yorkshire, 1530–1910.* London: Harvester Wheatsheaf.

Faith, R. 1966–7. Peasant Families and Inheritance Customs in Medieval England. *Agricultural History Review* 14: 14–15.

Gittings, C. 1984. *Death, Burial and the Individual in Early Modern England.* London: Croom Helm.

Goody, J. 1962. *Death, Property and the Ancestors.* Stanford: Stanford University Press.

– 1998. Dowry and the Rights of Women to Property. In *Property Relations: Renewing the Anthropological Tradition,* ed. C.M. Hann, 201–13. Cambridge: Cambridge University Press.

Gordon, Bruce, and Peter Marshall, eds. 2000. *The Place of the Dead: Death and Remembrance in Late Medieval and Early Modern Europe.* Cambridge: Cambridge University Press.

Gorer, G. 1955. The Pornography of Death. *Encounter* 5: 49–53.

Hall, G.D.G., trans. 1965. *The Treatise on the Laws and Customs of the Realm of England Commonly called Glanvill.* Oxford: Oxford University Press.

Hill, C. 1969. *Reformation to Industrial Revolution, 1530–1780.* Harmondsworth: Penguin.

Holdsworth, W. 1923. *A History of English Law.* 3rd ed. 17 vols. London: Methuen.

Holt, J. 1985. Feudal Society and the Family in Early Medieval England: The Heiress and the Alien. *Transactions of the Royal Historical Society.* 5th ser. 35: 1–28.

Houlbrooke, R. 1998. *Death, Religion and the Family, 1480–1750.* Oxford: Oxford University Press.

Laslett, P., ed. 1949. *Patriarcha and Other Political Works.* Oxford: Blackwell.

Mellor, P. 1993. Death in High Modernity: The Contemporary Presence and Absence of Death. In *The Sociology of Death: Theory, Culture, Practice,* ed. David Clark, 1–30. Oxford: Blackwell.

Milsom, S.F.C. 1981. Inheritance by Women in the Twelfth and Early Thirteenth Centuries. In *On the Laws and Customs of England: Essays in Honor of Samuel Thorne,* ed. Morris S. Arnold, Thomas A. Green, Sally A. Scully, and Stephen D. White, 60–89. Chapel Hill: University of North Carolina Press.

Pateman, C. 1989. *The Disorder of Women: Democracy, Feminism and Political Theory.* Cambridge: Polity Press.

Pollock, F., and W. Maitland. 1898. *History of English Law before the Time of Edward I.* 2 vols. Cambridge: Cambridge University Press.

Ryan, Alan. 1984. *Property and Political Theory.* Oxford: Blackwell.

Sayer, D. 1987. *The Violence of Abstraction: The Analytic Foundations of Historical Materialism.* Oxford: Blackwell.

Seale, C. 1998. *Constructing Death: The Sociology of Dying and Bereavement.* Cambridge: Cambridge University Press.

Simpson, A.W.B. 1986. *A History of the Land Law.* 2nd ed. Oxford: Clarendon Press.

Spring, Eileen. 1993. *Law, Land, and Family: Aristocratic Inheritance in England, 1300 to 1800.* Chapel Hill: University of North Carolina Press.

Stone, L., and J.C. Fawtier Stone. 1984. *An Open Elite? England 1540–1880.* Oxford: Oxford University Press.

Thirsk, J. 1964. The Common Fields. *Past & Present* 29: 3–25.

– 1976. The European Debate on Customs of Inheritance 1500–1700. In *Family and Inheritance,* ed. J. Goody, J. Thirsk, and E.P. Thompson, 177–91. Cambridge: Cambridge University Press.

Thompson, F.M.L. 1963. *English Landed Society in the Nineteenth Century.* London: Routledge and Kegan Paul.

Thorne, S.E., trans. 1968. *Bracton on the Laws and Customs of England.* Vol. 2. Cambridge, MA: Harvard University Press.

6

Isabella's Rule: Singlewomen and the Properties of Poverty in *Measure for Measure*

NATASHA KORDA

In act 1, scene 4, of *Measure for Measure*, Isabella stands poised on the threshold of a nunnery, learning of the 'strict restraint' to which she must succumb if she is to join the 'votarists of St Clare' (1.4.4–5).[1] Yet the Rule that defines and structures the Clarissan order is left unarticulated in the play. The scene begins *in medias res,* just after a nun named Francisca has explained it to her. We are told only of Isabella's desire to submit to the Rule – or more precisely, to submit to 'more,' which within the Clarissan economy, as we shall see, means less:

> *Isab.*   And have you nuns no farther privileges?
> *Nun.*   Are not these large enough?
> *Isab.*   Yes, truly; I speak not as desiring more,
>   But rather wishing a more strict restraint
>   Upon the sisters stood, the votarists of Saint Clare. (1.4.1–5)

In spite of the fact that, in J.W. Lever's words, Shakespeare's 'presentation of Isabella as a novice of the strict order of St Clare' represents his 'most important innovation' or departure from the play's source texts, this innovation has received surprisingly little commentary (1989, xliv). Yet *Measure for Measure*'s specification of the Poor Clares as the particular order Isabella seeks to enter suggests that the singularity of the Clarissan Rule may not be insignificant to an understanding of the play. What was the Rule that bound English nuns of the order of St Clare, and why is it invoked, only to be effaced, in *Measure for Measure*? This question is of more than merely antiquarian interest; indeed, I shall argue that it *was* of more than merely antiquarian interest to a playwright who, after all, was writing some sixty years after the demise of the female religious houses in England. For the regulation of singlewomen – many of whom had formerly lived in, around, and, in the case of those who were impoverished, by the good graces of, the nunneries – was a pressing concern in post-Reformation England. *Measure for Measure* manifests a profound preoccupation with the place of singlewomen in post-Reformation society. What was at stake in this preoccupation, I shall argue, was the threat that placeless singlewomen posed to an emergent, newly paternalistic state (one that had taken over, secularized, and centralized the task of provisioning the poor, a task that had formerly been presided over by the religious houses) and to a patrilineal property regime under the pressure of demographic change.

Where did singlewomen reside in early modern England and how did they subsist following the dissolution of the nunneries? Who provided for impoverished singlewomen (a category including maids, unwed mothers, 'masterless' women, and widows), many of whom had found institutional support in and around the religious houses? How were these women regulated by the state? What particular cultural anxieties were associated with the figure of the propertyless and the propertied singlewoman? Such questions pose important challenges to materialist feminist criticism. Perhaps most crucially, at a methodological level, they lead us to contemplate what is at stake in articulating what remains unarticulated in a literary text. In *Measure for Measure*, I shall argue, what remains unarticulated regarding singlewomen's regulation, modes of habitation, and property relations nevertheless surfaces through pointed silences, absent presences, and temporal displacements in the text. In tracing the history that produces these textual fissures, I follow Jonathan Dollimore's suggestion that materialist criticism is concerned not only with the 'history in the text including the historical conditions of its production' but with that which 'even if not addressed directly by the text can nevertheless still be said to be within it, informing it' (1985, 85). In articulating what remains unarticulated in *Measure for Measure*, my hope is to gain a new understanding of what is at stake in the play's action and to rebalance the scales of critical and historical inquiry by giving due weight to the place of singlewomen in post-Reformation society.

Following early modern usage, I deliberately employ the peculiar compound form of the term 'singlewoman' as a single word, in order to emphasize the singularity of this category in the period. For to be a singlewoman in post-Reformation England was to be something of an anomaly.[2] This is not to suggest that singlewomen were rare. Indeed, recent historical demography has demonstrated that never-married singlewomen were far more numerous in northern Europe (and in England in particular) than in southern Europe, and that their numbers continued to grow during the sixteenth century, reaching a peak of between 20 and 30 per cent of all adult women in England during the seventeenth century (the numbers being higher in urban than in rural areas) (Kowaleski 1999, 52–3; Froide 1999, 236–7).[3] If we add widows or 'ever-married' women to this calculation (who made up some 15 per cent of the adult female population), we arrive at the rather astonishing aggregate figure of between 35 and 45 per cent of adult women living without husbands (Froide 1999, 237). What made singlewomen anomalous was thus not their rarity, but rather what Ruth Karras has termed their 'lack of social space or social identity' (1999, 127). Amy Froide has likewise suggested that in a society in which marital status was a primary 'category of difference,' singlewomen who no longer had the option of becoming nuns quite literally had no social place (1999, 237). Historians have only begun to ask 'How did these lone women live in a society which theoretically had no place in its social hierarchy, its "great chain of being," for the unattached female?' (Erickson 1992, xxxv).

Unmarried 'maids' in early modern England were expected to live as household dependents (i.e., with family, kin, or as servants in other men's households) and, of course, to remain chaste until marriage. Those who lived independently risked being classified as 'masterless women,' witches, or prostitutes (the term 'singlewoman' was in fact often used synonymously for prostitute in the period) (Karras 1999, 131). Such women were singled out for various forms of punitive attention, such as corporal punishment and compulsory labour in 'bridewells' or houses of correction (women 'vastly outnumbered men in most of the urban bridewells') (Froide 1999, 241–3, 254–5). The preponderance of women in such institutions in part resulted from singlewomen's susceptibility to poverty. Those singlewomen not living as household dependents who could not find work as servants had few legitimate employment options; they often had to get by on unlicensed, ad hoc forms of economic activity (such as victualling, huckstering, and pawnbroking), or were forced into prostitution or onto the poor rates (see Froide 1999, 243–52). Yet poor relief was available only to singlewomen who were accounted 'deserving poor' (a category that included the elderly, impotent, pregnant, or widowed). Never-married singlewomen who were deemed able-bodied were classified as 'undeserving' and were therefore not eligible.

Only recently have historians begun to look at the feminization of poverty – or what Amy Erickson has termed 'the systemic economic vulnerability imposed to varying degrees on all women' – in early modern England. The available evidence suggests, in Erickson's view, that singlewomen 'were the social group most vulnerable to poverty' (Erickson 1992, xxxvii). While this statement includes both never-married and ever-married (i.e., widowed or separated) women, the former, as suggested above, were even more economically vulnerable than the latter. Because widows were considered deserving poor, however, we have more accurate information about them as reflected in records of parish poor relief. According to the census of the poor taken in Norfolk in the seventeenth century, more than 60 per cent of those in receipt of poor relief were women, most of them widows with young children (Wales 1984, 380). In Holkham in 1600–1, women represented 75 per cent of those on poor relief (66.6 per cent of these were widows); and in Wighton in 1614–15, a staggering 90 per cent of all recipients were women (of which 70 per cent were widows) (Wales 1984, 360–1). The economic plight of never-married or lifelong singlewomen, and in particular those without children, is more difficult to assess, since they were deemed undeserving of poor relief. There is evidence that many of them migrated to cities in search of a living (Brodsky Elliott 1981, 90–1). Those who did so, however, risked being apprehended en route, punished as 'masterless women' (by branding, whipping, or, if repeat offenders, even death), and then sent 'home' (although many had no homes to which to return).[4] Impoverished singlewomen who made their way to towns and cities, but who were unable to find work as servants or in various ad hoc trades (and who, without dowries were unlikely to find husbands), were liable to be arrested as vagrants or prostitutes and incarcerated in the local bridewell. In an age that had little comprehension of the systemic causes of poverty and unemployment (and perhaps even less of their gendered determinants), unemployed or 'masterless' singlewomen were viewed as wilfully idle and in need of discipline or correction.

The notion that these placeless singlewomen should be the responsibility of the state, however, was a relatively recent one at the time *Measure for Measure* was written (c. 1604). The gradual secularization of poor relief and emergence of the poor laws following the dissolution of the monasteries had been cobbled together by local authorities up until the passage by Parliament of the famed Elizabethan Poor Laws of 1598 and

1601.[5] In its final form, the 1601 Act (which would remain largely unchanged until 1834) had three essential features (Slack 1985). First were the poor rates, compulsory tax assessments in each parish to finance the 'deserving' poor. The second feature, which Paul Slack describes as 'the quid pro quo in return for public taxation,' was the criminalization of 'masterless' women and men or the 'undeserving' poor (1985, 222). Finally, there were the provisions for putting the latter to work, a strategy which included the erection of houses of correction.

At first glance, the state's role in provisioning the poor, on the one hand, and in punishing them, on the other, would seem to be represented in *Measure for Measure* by the politics of the Duke and Lord Angelo, respectively. At the start of the play, the Duke likens his paternalistic benevolence towards his subjects to that of a 'fond father' (1.3.23), whose excessive affection for his children/subjects prevents him from exacting due justice. As a result, he complains, the punishing 'rod' of the state has become 'more mock'd than fear'd ... / The baby beats the nurse, and quite athwart / Goes all decorum' (1.3.27; 1.3.30–1). The Duke blames his 'nursing' of his subjects for the lack of domestic decorum that plagues his state, which is populated not by families but by single men and women, unwed mothers, and illegitimate children. Fearing that a sudden shift in his own style of governance will appear 'too dreadful' to his people, he deputizes Angelo, hoping that he 'may in th'ambush of [the Duke's] name strike home' (1.3.41). The phrase 'strike home' aptly describes the early modern state's increasingly interventionist role in policing domestic conduct (Kent 1973). The 'precise' Angelo's assumption of this role within the play would seem to align him with the Puritan magistrates whose 'determination to shape a godly commonwealth,' in Slack's words, put them at the vanguard of the effort to enforce social discipline (1985, 237; see also Bond 1985). Yet the binary opposition set up at the start of the play between the Duke's reluctant and Angelo's overzealous policing of domestic conduct is soon complicated by the Duke's own surreptitious policing of the 'dark corners' of his realm. For it is the Duke's shadowy surveillance and manipulation of his subjects, a policy that is repeatedly defended within the play as a form of 'charity,' that perhaps best exemplifies the lengthening arm of the state in domestic governance and, in particular, its 'growing use of poor-relief as a means of social control' (Slack 1985, 238). Ironically, the secularization of poor relief following the dissolution of the monasteries and culminating in the Elizabethan Poor Laws (which became the model for the state's increasingly interventionist role in domestic governance) finds expression in *Measure for Measure* in a pre-Dissolution setting. In his disguise as a mendicant friar, the Duke extends the reach of the state into the dark corners and recesses of his realm, exerting control over subjects who had hitherto evaded its grasp, all under the rubric of monastic charity. Moreover, the subjects over whom the disguised Duke exerts the most complete and effective, but also the most coercive, control within the play are all placeless singlewomen.

In foregrounding *Measure for Measure*'s singlewomen, I am intentionally moving against the grain of previous criticism, which has instead largely focused on the play's 'broken nuptials' or failed marriages, thereby reproducing the period's positioning of marriage as a 'primary category of difference.'[6] To clarify the obstacles impeding marriage in the play, commentators have mainly concentrated on the laws governing the intricacies of marital contracts or what were termed 'spousals.' While such criticism has made an important contribution to our understanding of the play, I would suggest that while this body of law is necessary to understand *how* these marriages fail, it is nonetheless insufficient to explain *why* they do.

In the case of all three of the broken nuptials in the play (those of Claudio and Juliet, Angelo and Mariana, and Lucio and Kate Keep-Down), the obstacle upon which marriage founders is not juridical but rather economic: the lack of a sufficient dowry. In Juliet's case, the dowry is wilfully withheld (not by her parents, for she has none, but by certain 'friends,' presumably her deceased father's executors); in Mariana's, it is fortuitously lost at sea; and in Kate Keep-Down's it is systemically absent due to abject poverty.[7] To comprehend the play's preoccupation with placeless singlewomen, we must therefore explore the economic, as well as the legal, barriers impeding marriage in the period. The former, moreover, may provide us with a more dynamic view of spousals law than that elaborated by previous criticism. For while it is true that the law of spousals remained largely unchanged from the twelfth through the eighteenth centuries, its enforcement shifted dramatically in the late sixteenth and early seventeenth centuries, when ecclesiastical courts began prosecuting cases of premarital fornication with greater zeal. This shift can be understood, however, only if it is situated in relation to social and economic factors, such as the sharply increasing levels of poverty and illegitimacy (Ingram 1981, 54–5; Wrightson and Levine 1995, 127). Church authorities were willing to turn a blind eye to premarital pregnancy as long as 'expectations of housing, a settlement, land or employment were met and marriage ensued' (Wrightson and Levine 1985,

128). During the economic crisis of the 1590s, however, when such settlements were often not forthcoming, the number of marriages declined and officials began to prosecute such cases with greater frequency (Wrightson and Levine 1985, 133). Ingram, Wrightson, and Levine all attribute this shift to widespread poverty and to a 'growing hostility towards bastard bearing' occasioned by the 'explosion of illegitimacy' (Wrightson and Levine 1985, 127, 131; see also Ingram 1981, 54).

Measure for Measure's preoccupation with the policing, prosecuting, and provisioning of singlewomen likewise seems to centre on the threat illegitimacy posed to a newly paternalistic state and patrilineal property regime pressured by demographic change. This is perhaps most clear in the case of Juliet, who at the start of the play is incarcerated for conceiving a child out of wedlock. Significantly, it is Juliet's pregnancy that makes her visible, and therefore subject, to the state; her crime is quite literally written 'with character too gross' (1.2.143) on her belly. As an unwed and dowryless mother, Juliet has become an economic burden to the state: 'What shall be done, sir, with the groaning Juliet?' the Provost of the prison asks Angelo, who responds, 'Dispose of her / To some more fitter place; and that with speed ... Let her have needful, but not lavish means; / There shall be order for it' (2.2.15–17, 2.2.23–5). Almost as soon as she appears, this spectre of the placeless singlewoman is whisked away, removed from view until the end of the play. The dilemma posed by her lack of social space and identity is marked within the play by the peculiar imprecision of the site to which she is to be removed, which is designated only as 'some more fitter place.'

The Jacobean statute books were far less imprecise about designating the social space befitting unwed mothers: 'Every lewd woman which shall have any bastard which may be chargeable to the parish, the justices of the peace shall committ such woman to the house of correction, to be punished and set to work, during the term of one whole year' (cited in Laslett, Oosterveen, and Smith 1980, 73). By contrast, the punitive regulation of singlewomen in *Measure for Measure* is effectively invisible except when the object of such regulation is defined as a prostitute. At the start of the play, all eyes are on Claudio, not Juliet, as the culprit to be punished by Angelo. While Claudio is paraded in public as a criminal, Juliet is notably silent onstage. We are immediately informed that 'within these three days his head [is] to be chopped off' (1.2.62), but no mention is made of Juliet's punishment. When the Provost informs the disguised Duke of their situation, he makes this discrepancy clear: '*She* is with child,' he says, 'And *he* that got it, sentenc'd' (2.3.13). The punishment of the father, rather than the mother, of the illegitimate child in *Measure for Measure* runs counter to contemporary legislation, which viewed 'bastardy ... as the exclusive responsibility of women and a sign of their promiscuity' (Breitenberg 1996, 19). Yet the inhabitants of the prison in *Measure for Measure*, who are described as former customers of Mistress Overdone's (4.3.1–20), are all men. While it is true that Juliet temporarily resides in the prison at the start of the play, she is kept there just long enough to confess to the Duke that her offence, in spite of her more lenient treatment, is 'of heavier kind' (2.3.28) than Claudio's, even though the sin was 'mutually committed' (2.3.27). Thus, while the play refrains from staging the forms of punishment meted out to singlewomen who conceived bastards during the period, it nevertheless suggests in more subtle ways their greater culpability for this crime.

Women were more vulnerable to punishment for bastard bearing, of course, because paternity was always open to doubt in a way that maternity was not. The double standard regarding extramarital sex likewise found support in the commonplace misogynist notion that women provoke men to intemperate lust. This notion is woven throughout the Angelo/Isabella narrative, most famously in Angelo's 'Is this her fault or mine? / The tempter, or the tempted, who sins most' (2.2.163–4) speech, but later lent support by Isabella's plea for Angelo's life: 'I partly think / A due sincerity govern'd his deeds / Till he did look on me' (5.1.443–4). Contemporary writers were quite aware of this double standard and were at pains to justify its legitimacy by explaining the cultural stakes of the ideological overvaluation of female chastity: namely, the security of a patrilineal social order and property regime, as Mary Murray and A.R. Buck explain in chapters in this section.

It is the threat of undermining patrilineal property transmission that determines which singlewomen are subject to penal regulation in *Measure for Measure* and which are not. It is only the prostitute and the bawd who feel the full weight of Angelo's newly instituted 'proclamations.' The play's other singlewomen are all protected from this fate by their removal to another scene (Isabella to a nunnery, Mariana to a moated grange, and Juliet to some 'fitter place'); they are thus protected from being branded as singlewomen by the law. For to be interpellated within this category was to be immediately confused with a prostitute or 'lewd woman' and therefore to become disqualified as a guarantor of patrilineality. This risk is particularly clear in the case of Mariana: as soon as she leaves the moated grange and confesses to being 'neither maid, widow nor wife' (5.1.181), she is accused of being a 'punk' (5.1.180).

The Duke must then prove that she does not belong to this category by insisting 'I have confess'd her, and I know her virtue' (5.1.524). When Isabella leaves the sanctuary of the nunnery, she is likewise confused with her vulgar other (prostitutes were known as 'nuns of Venus') by Angelo, who offers her brother's life as payment for her sexual favours.

Yet if what characterizes the play's singlewomen at the start of the play is their impoverishment (they are all apparently dowryless), and hence unvendibility on the marriage market, how can their status as guarantors of patrilineal property transmission be at issue? The ideological ruse of Juliet's, Mariana's, and Isabella's impoverishment, I would maintain, is that, like the Duke's, it is 'usurped' (Lucio accuses the Duke of 'usurp[ing] the beggary he was never born to' [3.2.90]). While it may be true that they, like Kate Keep-Down, lack dowries, unlike the latter they are clearly designated as being of elite status. Isabella and Claudio, we are informed, 'had a most noble father' (2.1.7). Mariana's elite status is likewise emphasized when her brother Frederick is described as 'noble and renowned' (3.1.219). From this perspective, the 'poverty' of the play's female protagonists appears to be nothing more than a romantic fiction, a temporary obstacle impeding marriages that appear all the more miraculous when they are achieved.

My analysis of the play's treatment of singlewomen has thus far followed previous criticism of *Measure for Measure* in focusing almost exclusively on the state's punitive function, as represented by the 'severe' Angelo's repressive statutes. Yet the play suggests by its outcome that such severity is not the most effective form of governance; in the end, it is the Duke's surreptitious surveillance and manipulations of his subjects, not the archaic, draconian statutes that Angelo resurrects and enforces, that achieve order in the state. In his disguise as a mendicant friar, the Duke extends the reach of the state into the 'dark corners' of his realm, exerting control over subjects who had hitherto evaded its grasp. To what end does the state, in the person of the Duke, exert this control? I would suggest that the Duke's surreptitious strategy of surveillance and suasion works to reposition the play's impoverished gentlewomen so that they are removed from the category of placeless singlewomen. First, he works to instil in his female subjects the notion that they bear primary responsibility for the crime of bastardy. Juliet proves an eager recipient of the Duke's counsel, promising 'I'll gladly learn' (2.3.23) when he offers 'I'll teach you how you shall arraign your conscience' (2.3.21). She not only immediately confesses the truth of his estimation of her greater culpability and 'repent[s] it,' she reassures the Duke that her repentance results not from a 'fear' of the repercussions of her act, but simply because the act itself was 'evil' (2.3.29; 2.3.34–5). The malleability of the play's 'poor gentlewom[e]n' (3.1.218–19) to the Duke's manipulations ensures their positioning by the state as guarantors of patrilineal property transmission. Within the play, the quid pro quo for the singlewoman's provisioning by the state would thus appear to be her interpellation as one who bears greater culpability for the crime of producing illegitimate subjects. Paradoxically, by accepting her culpability Juliet is rendered legitimate, for she buys into the system of value sanctioned by the state. Juliet's interpellation as a criminalized singlewoman is thus only temporary; her reputation and property are restored and her child rendered legitimate at the end of the play by the state in the person of the Duke. In the end, Juliet's status as a singlewoman is thus effectively erased.

The trajectory traced by Mariana likewise demonstrates the Duke's power to transform a propertyless, placeless singlewoman into a propertied bride. At the start of the play, Mariana epitomizes the singlewoman's lack of social space or identity. Residing – in what has become perhaps the most memorable of all liminal literary spaces – 'at the moated grange' (3.1.265), Mariana, like Juliet, is removed to the margins of a society in which sexually ambiguous singlewomen had no place. Mariana herself calls attention to her lack of identity at the end of the play, when she appears, veiled, for her interrogation by the state's governors. Until her putative husband hails her, she remains unclassifiable within what were the only socially recognized and legitimated categories of female subjectivity in the period – maid, wife, or widow:

Duke. Is this the witness, friar?
         First, let her show her face, and after, speak.
Mar. Pardon, my lord; I will not show my face
         Until my husband bid me.
Duke. What, are you married?
Mar. No, my lord.
Duke. Are you a maid?
Mar. No, my lord.
Duke. A widow, then?
Mar. Neither, my lord.
Duke. Why, you are nothing then: neither maid, widow, nor wife!
Lucio. My lord, she may be a punk; for many of them are neither maid,
         widow nor wife.
Duke. Silence that fellow! (5.1.169–82)

The Duke's bald statement that a woman is 'nothing' if she does not fit into the categories of maid, widow, or wife recalls Isabella's earlier remark that a woman in this situation is better off dead: 'What a merit were it in death to take this poor maid from the world!' (3.1.231–2). While Isabella knows Mariana to be a 'poor maid,' the rest of the world does not; as an impoverished singlewoman living alone, her chastity is immediately cast into doubt, as Lucio's insinuation that she is a 'punk' or prostitute makes clear. Mariana's putative promiscuity is cemented when Angelo 'pretend[s] in her discoveries of dishonour' (3.1.227), thereby removing her from the category of maid and effectively rendering her unmarriageable.

In certain respects, Mariana bears closest resemblance to a widow, mourning the loss of her husband. The figure of the widow was less threatening to the social order than that of the never-married singlewoman, according to Amy Froide, in spite of the fact that many of them lived alone, choosing not to remarry: 'Widows had a public and independent place within the patriarchal society, singlewomen did not' (1999, 237). Froide's observation applies only to propertied widows, however, for impoverished, propertyless widows, like unwed mothers, as we have seen, placed a significant burden on parish poor rates.[8] In the play's final scene, the Duke seeks to transform Mariana into a propertied widow. Having married her to Angelo, he immediately orders the latter put to death and designates Mariana as the recipient of his property: 'For his possessions, / Although by confiscation they are ours, / We do instate and widow you with all' (5.1.420–2).

In his next breath, however, the Duke makes clear that Mariana is not to remain a propertied widow but is to use her newly acquired estate to remarry, or in his fiscal terms, 'To buy you a better husband' (5.1.423). As satirical representations of propertied, 'merry' widows in the period make clear, while such women may have had a 'public and independent place' within early modern culture, their sexual and economic independence was itself perceived as threatening and was subject to pervasive criticism. In *Measure for Measure*, this criticism is deflected onto the figure of Mistress Overdone, who having been widowed nine times chooses to remain single and earn her living as a brothel- and alehouse-keeper. Her economic and legal vulnerability as a widow is emphasized from the start, however, when she complains of her 'poverty' (1.2.76), only to learn of Angelo's 'proclamation' dictating that her house 'must be plucked down' (1.2.89). Because Mistress Overdone may be classified within the socially proscribed categories of 'punk' and bawd, the play does not hesitate to send her off to prison. As a 'poor gentlewoman,' however, Mariana faces a different destiny; she is preserved at the moated grange until such time as she may be repositioned as a wife and thereby serve as a vehicle of property transmission between men.

It is the Duke's restoration of the play's singlewomen as propertied brides that appears to balance the scales of justice within the play. At a rhetorical level, this balancing is reflected in the reciprocal, chiastic exchange of value that marriage represents in the Duke's final cautioning of Angelo: 'Look that you love your wife: her worth, worth yours' (5.1.495). What is elided, of course, by the ideal equality of 'worth' that marriage represents in the Duke's utterance, is the wife's loss of propriety (both her property and her legal identity) under coverture. As a contemporary commonplace regarding this legal fiction held, 'the husband and wife are one, and that one is the husband.' Isabella is likewise transformed from singlewoman into wife by the balancing rhetoric of the Duke's 'measure for measure': 'Dear Isabel,' he says, 'I have a motion much imports your good; / Whereto if you'll a willing ear incline, / What's mine is yours, and what is yours is mine' (5.1.531–4). The ruse of *Measure for Measure*'s solution to the problem posed by the figure of the placeless singlewoman is that marriage represents a reciprocal exchange of value or 'worth' between husband and wife and that this exchange 'imports' the wife's own 'good.' From this perspective, the play's narrative works effectively to ensure that property never remains in the hands of its placeless singlewomen.

Thus far, I have outlined some of the ways in which the predicament of singlewomen in post-Reformation England constitutes a kind of absent presence in *Measure for Measure*. Their placelessness is at once evoked and elided through Juliet, Isabella, and Mariana's indeterminate status and temporary removal to indeterminate or liminal zones. The pauperization of singlewomen is likewise both presented and absented through the play's impoverished gentlewomen. The regulation of singlewomen by the state is both evidenced and eclipsed through Juliet's brief imprisonment. More elusive in the play, however, is the figure of the propertied singlewoman, fleetingly represented by Mariana when she is instated with Angelo's estate before she begs to marry him. It is here that I would like to return to the temporal displacement referred to at the beginning of this paper. If the play, as I have argued, is so profoundly preoccupied with the place, or more properly, the placelessness of singlewomen in post-Reformation society, what are we to make of its pre-Reformation setting? This question leads us to consider the ambiguous figure of the novice, Isabella, who is and is not a nun, whom we find poised at the start of the play on the threshold of a Clarissan nunnery, superannuated in Shakespeare's time, having learned the particulars of a Rule which remains unarticulated to the audience, and who famously responds to the Duke's final proposal of marriage with silence. When compared with the play's other singlewomen, Isabella might appear a kind of wishful, nostalgic relic of a former age and therefore removed from the present, pressing dilemma such women posed during the period in which the play was written. Yet (as Freud teaches) the most far-fetched displacements and most disfigured figures often point to that which is most present and pressing.

Like Juliet, Mariana, and Kate Keep-Down, Isabella too suffers a broken nuptial in the play: when we first encounter her she is in the midst of taking her vows as a bride of Christ. Her interview is immediately interrupted by Lucio, however, who removes her from the cloister before her vows are complete. What might appear to distinguish this broken nuptial from that of Juliet and Mariana is that it does not seem to hinge on the bride's status as a vehicle of property transmission. For the play makes no mention of Isabella's dowry, or lack thereof. Like Juliet and Mariana, Isabella might appear to fall within the category of the 'poor gentlewoman' – a woman of elite social status, but in financial hardship. If we think of Isabella as poor, however, it is because of her association with the order of the Poor Clares; for the play curiously offers no indication of her economic status as either propertied or propertyless. It might be objected that the play makes no mention of Isabella's dowry simply because she is entering a nunnery and therefore would have had no need of one. Yet *Measure for Measure*'s silence on the subject of Isabella's dowry should not be read as simple evidence that she has none, because nuns *were* in fact generally required to have dowries, and often trousseaus as well, to recompense nunneries for their expenses and to signify their symbolic marriages to Christ. To understand what is at stake in this silence, in the context of a play that goes into great detail on the status of its other female protagonists' dowries, we will need to have a clearer sense of what Isabella's choice of a Clarissan nunnery represents.

Women who became nuns in medieval and early modern England, according to Marilyn Oliva and Barbara J. Harris, were generally speaking neither terribly impoverished nor terribly wealthy; most were drawn from the middling ranks of society, including the parish gentry, yeomanry, and in the case of urban monasteries, from the families of merchants, burghesses, and tradespeople.[9] In general, poor women en-

tered nunneries as lay sisters, servants, labourers, and, at the lowest end
of the social scale, as recipients of monastic hospitality and alms. Maureen
Connolly McFeely has suggested that the nunnery of the Poor Clares in
Measure for Measure is an exception to the commercial and socially strati-
fied structure of other female religious houses, because the order was
distinguished by its strict vow of poverty; it is on this basis as well that she
asserts Isabella would have had 'no need of a dowry to become a Poor
Clare' (1995, 214, n. 26). The assumption that the Poor Clares were in
fact poor, however, confounds what Penelope D. Johnson has called
'documents of theory' (such as the order's written Rule) with 'documents of practice' (records of what property they actually possessed)
(1987, 29). For the Poor Clares, who were commonly referred to as the
Poor Ladies, in fact had far stronger ties to the aristocracy than other
orders and amassed considerable wealth through their commercial interests throughout England. This was particularly true of the London
house called the Minories, located without Aldgate (Bourdillon 1926,
16). It is perhaps more than a coincidence that several of the order's
noble patrons, founders, and abbesses were, like Shakespeare's young
Clarissan novice, named Isabella. Isabella of Gloucester, granddaughter
of Edward III, for example, became abbess of the London Minories in
1421. The contents of her monastic 'trousseau' demonstrate the dispar-
ity between the theory and practice of pious poverty and the misconcep-
tion that a Poor Clare would have had no need of a dowry; as a novice,
she brought with her 'a bed of cloth of gold of cyprus, black and red,
with a testa, coverlet, curtains, and tapestries; a French Bible in two
volumes, with two gold clasps enamelled with the arms of France ... £40
in money, a belt of black leather with a buckle and pendant, and twelve
plain round bars of gold' (Bourdillon 1926, 41, 44, 52). In 1539 (the year
of its dissolution), the house received £185 7s. 10d. in profits from its
various commercial interests – including land, tenements, shops, and
even a tavern and brewery – which it owned in London (an amount
which does not include the income it earned from properties possessed
in nine other counties), making it one of the wealthiest nunneries in
England (Bourdillon 1926, 29).[10]

The history of the divergence between the 'theory' or doctrine of
pious poverty as set forth in the life and Rule of St Clare, on the one
hand, and the commercial practices of the London Minoresses, on the
other, is a complex one. A disciple of St Francis of Assisi, St Clare
modelled her life and the sisterhood she founded on the strict interpretation of pious poverty followed by the Franciscans, for whom religious

poverty assumed a new and far stricter form, including not only individual or private property (and in particular, movables), but landed property and property held in common as well (Fiege 1909, 27).[11] Like Francis, Clare neither was born poor nor had poverty thrust upon her; she willingly chose to lead a life of poverty as a sign of her piety. In the words of Sister Magdalen Augustine, a nun of the Order of the Poor Clares in Aire, in her early seventeenth-century translation of Luke Wadding's *The History of the Angelicall Virgin Glorious S. Clare,* Clare founded her order on the 'singular Prerogative of Evangelicall Povertie, both in proper and in common, (which never any other Religious Foundresse professed before her)' (Wadding 1635, sig. A3r). Yet this strict rule was apparently adhered to during Clare's lifetime only by her own monastery and that of her sister, Blessed Agnes, in Prague (Wadding 1635, 146). It is clear in Clare's last testament that she feared her death might mean the death of the strict observance of pious poverty: 'I admonish you all my Sisters, who are, and shall be, that you labour to follow the way of simplicity, humility, & Poverty' (*Rule* [1621] 1975, 58–9, 61–2). Her premonition in fact came true, for as the later history of the order attests, after her death, strict pious poverty was a custom more honoured in the breach than in the observance. The great majority of Clarisses followed more moderate versions of the Rule which did away with absolute poverty and allowed the order to own real property from which they might earn an income (Moorman 1968, 208).

In France and England the moderated Rule followed by the order was known as the Isabella Rule. This Rule was named after another Poor Clare of elite parentage who bore the name of Shakespeare's heroine: Blessed Isabella, sister of Lewis, King of France, who composed this version of the moderated Rule for her monastery at Longchamp in France in the mid-thirteenth century. The Isabella Rule was transported to England around 1293–4 by Blanche, Queen of Navarre, who was Blessed Isabella's niece and who founded the house of Minoresses in London (Bourdillon 1926, 3, 16). This Rule quite explicitly sanctioned the holding of communal property from which the Minoresses might receive an income (Seton 1914). When Isabella professes to desire 'a more strict restraint' (1.4.4) than the moderated Rule followed by the Poor Clares in *Measure for Measure,* she thus voices what might have been Clare's own response to her commercially minded, property-holding English disciples. Isabella's evocation of St Clare, which hinges on her implied critique of the moderated Rule that bears her name, creates an ideological tension that may help to account for the textual indeterminacy of her silence at the end of the play. On the one hand, her professed desire for a 'more strict' Rule casts her as·a figure of religious reform, distancing her from the commercial ventures of the English Minoresses, who had fallen away from the 'strict path of poverty' envisioned by Clare. According to this reading, Isabella's disillusionment with the Poor Clares leads her eventually into the arms of the Duke, thereby tracing a well-worn ideological path from chastity to Christian matrimony. From this perspective, Isabella is appropriated to the Duke's project of reform. The absent (and by implication, insufficiently strict) conventual Rule at the start of the play is replaced by the state's successful regulation and subjection of its placeless singlewomen. The aim of this regulation, to reposition the play's singlewomen as propertied brides, is dissimulated, however, by the fiction of reciprocity underlying the institution of Christian matrimony in the Duke's balancing rhetoric ('her worth, worth yours,' 'what's mine is yours, and what is yours is mine,' 'measure for measure,' etc.). According to this reading, the play elides the threat posed by the figure of the propertied singlewoman by remaining silent on the subject of Isabella's dowry until the Duke secures her hand.

From another perspective, however, *Measure for Measure*'s evocation of the figure of Saint Clare troubles the Duke's project of containment. For Clare's strict adherence to the doctrine of pious poverty, which casts her as an ideal figure of reform, also positioned her as a threat to patrilineality. Although the play's interruption of Isabella's initiation into the order at the precise moment when a Clarissan novice would have invested her property in her spiritual Bridegroom (Christ) appears to preserve it for her worldly suitor (the Duke), the circuit of property transmission remains incomplete; Isabella never assents to the Duke's proposal. From this perspective, Isabella's association with the figure of St Clare recalls the most significant and defining feature of her hagiography, namely, her refusal as an elite, propertied singlewoman to serve as a vehicle of patrilineal property transmission. According to Wadding, Clare 'despiced and trampled under foot all honours, dignities, mariages, sumptuous apparell, Jewells, and all wordly pelfe ... to dedicate her selfe a living temple to Christ Jesus taking him for the only spouse of her body' (1635, 101). Wadding's account emphasizes the lineage and patrimony which Clare and her disciples forsake to embrace the doctrine of pious poverty. Her order attracts elite disciples, who sacrifice their wealth and status to marry Christ: 'gentle woemen and Ladies,' he says, have 'contemn[ed] their faire houses and sumptuous tables' and 'refused the most honorable and advantageous allyances in the world, for to bind themselves, according to the example of her povertie, to an austere life' (Wadding 1635, 119, 132). Wadding grounds his justification of Clare's subversion of patrilineality rhetorically in an oxymoronic transvaluation of material into spiritual values: 'Is it not a wonder, that this Angelicall Virgin, having cast away all care of temporall things, should be in continuall care, how she might leave this *Patrimonie* to her children, that they might enjoy *Nothing* ... And yet they will cease to wonder, that consider, what extraordinary *priviledges* this sacred *Poverty* hath annexed to it ... 'Tis easily proved *Povertie* is the *Riches* which purchases Heaven' (1635, 95). By describing Clare's strict adherence to the doctrine of pious poverty as her 'Patrimonie' to her 'children,' Wadding rhetorically disarms the threat that she poses to patrilineality.

In *Measure for Measure*, the Duke's program of reform consolidates secular and religious power in the person of the prince and seeks to prove the scope and efficacy of that power through its stealthy repositioning of the play's propertyless singlewomen as propertied brides. Yet the indeterminacy of Isabella's destiny at the end of the play resists this forced solution and in so doing echoes the divergent destinies of the inhabitants of dissolved nunneries in post-Reformation England. Lyndal Roper has argued that 'as the Reformation was domesticated – as it closed convents and encouraged nuns to marry, as it lauded the married state ... and as it execrated the prostitute – so it was accomplished through a politics of reinscribing women within the family' (1989, 3). While we can certainly see the politics of domestication at work in the enforced marriages at the end of *Measure for Measure*, in assessing the play's resistance to closure we should again be careful not to conflate ideology with material practice. For while ex-nuns were certainly encouraged to marry, there is very little evidence that many of them in fact did. Marilyn Oliva estimates the average age of nuns at the time of the Dissolution to have been about forty, which would have made most ex-nuns about fifty in 1549, when legislation released them from their oath of chaste living (1998, 193, 201).[12]

Although most nuns were not impoverished when they entered nunneries, many experienced extreme financial hardship when they were forced to leave. The pensions and stipends of female ex-religious were far more meagre than those of their male counterparts.[13] Faced with few financial options, many ex-nuns chose to set up house together in their new locations (Oliva 1998, 201–3). While it was financial necessity in part that kept these nuns together, there is evidence that wealthier nuns who were supported by their families likewise chose to live with other ex-religious. Thus, Elizabeth Throckmorton, who had been the abbess of Denny, a Clarissan house in Norwich, 'retired to her family ... in Warwickshire with 2 or 3 of her nuns where in a private chamber of the family seat, she ever after to her death in 1547 lived a conventual life and in their proper habits, hardly ever appearing in the family ... but pre-scribed to themselves the Rules of the Order as far as it was possible in their present situation' (Bourdillon 1926, 83). The case of Elizabeth Throckmorton and other ex-nuns of elite and middling status who chose to set up house together makes clear that some singlewomen did resist the Reformation's 'politics of reinscribing women within the family.' Perhaps, then, we may read Isabella's silence at the end of *Measure for Measure* as registering this rift between political theory and material practice.

The rift widens with each step down the social ladder; while ex-nuns of elite or middling status had the option of either marrying or setting up alternative domestic arrangements, the many lay sisters who worked as servants and labourers in female religious houses, having lost their means of support, probably fell into abject poverty. According to the pension rolls for the London house of Minoresses, the six lay sisters who served the professed nuns received no pension at all. Of these, Elizabeth Martin, who was 68, Joan Crosby, who was 95, and Julia Heron, who was only 13 and described as an 'idiot,' may have been deemed elderly or impotent enough to receive parish poor-relief; but Rose Lightfoote and Joan Cresswyth, who were both 50, and Katherine Donnyngton, who was 31, would probably have been considered able-bodied and thus unde-serving (Bourdillon 1926, 90–1). 'If any of the ex-religious were reduced to beggary,' according to John Pound, 'they were drawn from those in this category [women who received meagre pensions or none at all], but how often and in what proportion we shall probably never know' (1971, 19). Those female ex-religious who were reduced to beggary would have joined the ranks of women who had depended on monastic hospitality and alms, but who would increasingly become the burden of the state. Those deemed undeserving of poor relief and who were unable to find employment, as we have seen, were criminalized as 'lewd' or 'masterless' women. By the time *Measure for Measure* was written, such women would have been incarcerated and set to work in bridewells. The material history of this institutional shift is traced in the post-Dissolution history of the London house of Minoresses, which during the Commonwealth became a 'great workhouse' set up by the Corporation for the Poor of the City of London (Bourdillon 1926, 84).[14] The female beggars, prostitutes, and masterless women who inhabited these bridewells are only obliquely represented in *Measure for Measure*, which displaces the problem posed by placeless, impoverished singlewomen onto its elite, female protagonists, whose miraculously restored dowries permit them to avoid the fate of the bridewell by becoming brides themselves in the end. Yet the silences that surround Isabella nevertheless register the failure of the early modern state, through its domestic policies, to solve the intractable problem posed by its growing population of placeless singlewomen.

Notes

1 A longer version of this essay appears in Korda (2002).

2 The compound term 'singlewomen' is likewise deployed in Bennett and Froide (1999). This groundbreaking volume has made a significant contribution to our understanding of various aspects of the predicament of singlewomen living in early modern Europe, and my discussion in what follows is deeply indebted to several of the essays contained in it.

3 On the high percentage of men and women never marrying (between 10 and 20 per cent of the population) see Wrigley and Schofield (1981); on women remarrying less frequently than men, and the higher number of widows than widowers see Dupaquier and others (1981).

4 On the various forms of punishment legislated by the vagabond acts, and for an instance of a 'masterless woman' sentenced to be hung as a repeat offender, see Leonard (1965, 70). While only just over half as many singlewomen on average were arrested under the vagabond acts as single men (in Salisbury in 1598–1638, 171 singlewomen were apprehended as compared with 343 single men; Beier's study of eighteen counties lists 246 singlewomen and 483 single men), this number, according to Beier, may in part reflect the fact that vagrant males 'were feared more than females and greater efforts were made to capture them' (Beier 1974, 6). For Salisbury figures, see Slack (1974, 366). A significant number of 'masterless women' received punitive attention by authorities. The 1572 statute is at pains to include women under its purview: 'all and every person ... being whole and mighty in body and able to labor, having not land or master, nor using any lawful merchandize, craft or mystery whereby *he or she* might get *his or her* living, and can give no reckoning how *he or she* does lawfully get *his or her* living' (my emphasis). Nevertheless, scholars have assumed a male subject in discussions of vagabondage. Paul Slack thus complains that previous 'histo-

rians have seldom been able to penetrate the haze of rhetorical abuse to see the vagabond as *he* was, to define *his* status, or assess the significance of *his* mobility. The first problem for the historian ... is to know who the vagrant actually was, to define *his* status' (my emphasis). While Slack does a great deal to demystify the category of the vagabond, that category is still presumptively male in his own rhetoric (Slack 1974, 360–2). Beier's (1985) important study of the subject is likewise titled, *Masterless Men: The Vagrancy Problem in England 1560–1640.*

5 In response to the increasingly pressing problems of poverty and vagrancy during the last decade of the sixteenth century, some seventeen bills were exhibited in the 1597–8 parliamentary session, including proposed legislation for 'erecting of Houses of Correction and punishment of rogues and sturdy beggars and for levying of certain sums due to the poor,' for the 'necessary habitation and relief of the poor, aged, lame, and blind in every parish,' for 'relief of Hospitals, poor prisoners and others impoverished by casual losses,' for 'the better governing of Hospitals and land given to the relief of the poor,' for 'extirpation of Beggary,' 'against Bastardy,' for 'setting the poor on work,' and 'for erecting of hospitals or abiding and working houses for the poor' (Leonard 1965, 75).

6 According to Martin Ingram, 'cases concerning the *formation* of marriage, not marital breakdown, normally constituted the bulk of matrimonial litigation in the English ecclesiastical courts' (Ingram 1981, 36). On marriage and 'broken nuptials' in the play, see Caciedo (1995), Friedman (1995), Harding (1950), Hayne (1993), Nagarajan (1963), Neely (1985, 92–102), Ranald (1979), Schanzer (1960), Scott (1982), Scouten (1975), and Wentersdorf (1979). A recent exception to this trend is Theodora A. Jankowski's discussion of the 'queerness' of Isabella as a virgin who 'repudiates' marriage (2000, 170–7).

7 Refusing to marry a prostitute, Lucio leaves his illegitimate child to be brought up in a brothel (3.2.192–7). As what Jonathan Dollimore has termed the play's 'most exploited' singlewoman, Kate Keep-Down is likewise its most invisible; although she is referred to several times, she never actually appears onstage. Beyond the pale of dramatic representation, Kate nevertheless functions as a crucial, negative place-holder, for she represents, if only in absentia, that which renders the extramarital sexual activity of the play's other singlewomen (Juliet, Mariana) virtuous by comparison (Dollimore 1985, 85–6).

8 In spite of the fact that, in Erickson's words, 'for a substantial number of women, widowhood meant poverty,' the plight of the impoverished widow has been largely ignored by early modern scholarship (1992, xxxvi–xxxvii).

B.A. Holderness, who observes that 'Destitute or insolvent widows and old maids [*sic*] almost certainly outnumbered those who had property to live upon or savings to invest,' thus nevertheless excuses his 'neglect of their plight' in his study of widows in preindustrial society with the assertion that 'the poor widow ... is less important as a historical phenomenon than her wealthier contemporaries' (1984, 428). On the existence of a 'poor widow subculture in the less wealthy London parishes,' see Brodsky (1986, 123).

9 Marilyn Oliva calculates that 89 per cent of nuns in the diocese of Norwich between 1350 and 1540 were of the middling sort (of which 64 per cent were from parish gentry families, 20 per cent from urban families, and 5 per cent from freeholder and yeomen families), while only 10 per cent came from upper gentry families and a mere 1 per cent from the aristocracy (1998, 54–9). See also Harris (1993, 92–4).

10 Bourdillon includes a table of gifts of real property to the three endowed Clarissan houses in England (the London house, Denny, and Bruisyard) (1926, 94–9). On the relative wealth of the nunneries at the time of the Dissolution, see Oliva (1998, 20).

11 'Francis enjoined on his followers ... to be poor, not only individually, but also in common. Their houses were to be modeled, not after the palaces of the rich, but after the humble dwellings of the poor. They were to own neither houses nor lands; they were to have no fixed income or revenue of any kind. And even the little they had for their use was to be held by others ... They were to live by the labor of their hands, humbly accepting as an alms, whatever was given them in recompense. And should, at any time, the recompense not suffice for their daily needs, they should then not be ashamed to beg their bread from door to door, as veritable paupers' (Fiege 1909, 27).

12 Although some ex-nuns may have opted to marry in spite of their vows of celibacy, Oliva describes such cases as 'rare' (1998, 193, 201).

13 Oliva argues that 'the Dissolution entailed a greater change in lifestyle for nuns than it did for their male counterparts,' as 'the male religious who were pensioned were awarded substantially larger pensions than their female counterparts received.' Male religious could also 'prosper even more by combining their pensions with the money derived from the many new benefices they were now able to hold,' an option not available to women (Oliva 1998, 200).

14 Robert Copland, in a popular poem written in the year the Dissolution commenced (1536), likewise traces the singlewoman's path from the convent to the brothel to the 'spital-house,' describing the hordes of masterless women who 'Every day / ... come so thick that they stop the way. / The

sisterhood of drabs, sluts and callets / To here [the hospital or almshouse]
resort ... / And be partners of the confrerie / Of the maintainers of ill
husbandry' (Judges 1930, 24).

Works Cited

Beier, A.L. 1974. Vagrants and the Social Order in Elizabethan England. *Past &*
    Present 64: 3–29.
– 1985. *Masterless Men: The Vagrancy Problem in England 1560–1640*. London:
    Methuen.
Bennett, Judith M., and Amy M. Froide, eds. 1999. *Singlewomen in the European*
    Past, 1250–1800. Philadelphia: University of Pennsylvania Press.
Bond, Ronald B. 1985. 'Dark Deeds Darkly Answered': Thomas Becon's Hom-
    ily against Whoredom and Adultery, Its Contexts, and Its Affiliations with
    Three Shakespearean Plays. *Sixteenth Century Journal* 16: 190–205.
Bourdillon, Anne Francis Claudine. 1926. *The Order of the Minoresses in England.*
    Manchester: Manchester University Press.
Breitenberg, Mark. 1996. *Anxious Masculinity in Early Modern England.* Cam-
    bridge: Cambridge University Press.
Brodsky, Vivien. 1986. Widows in Late Elizabethan London: Remarriage,
    Economic Opportunity and Family Orientations. In *The World We Have*
    Gained: Histories of Population and Social Structure, ed. Lloyd Bonfield, Richard
    M. Smith, and Keith Wrightson, 122–54. Oxford: Basil Blackwell.
Brodsky Elliot, Vivien. 1981. Single Women in the London Marriage Market:
    Age, Status and Mobility, 1598–1619. In *Marriage and Society: Studies in the*
    Social History of Marriage, ed. R.B. Outhwaite, 81–100. New York: St Martin's
    Press.
Cacicedo, Albert. 1995. 'She Is Fast My Wife': Sex, Marriage, and Ducal Au-
    thority in *Measure for Measure. Shakespeare Studies* 23: 187–209.
Dollimore, Jonathan. 1985. Transgression and Surveillance in *Measure for Mea-*
    sure. In *Political Shakespeare: New Essays in Cultural Materialism*, ed. Jonathan
    Dollimore and Alan Sinfield, 72–87. Ithaca and London: Cornell University
    Press.
Dupaquier, Jacques, and others. 1981. *Marriage and Remarriage in Populations of*
    the Past. London: Academic Press.
Erickson, Amy. 1992. Introduction to *Working Life of Women in the Seventeenth*
    Century by Alice Clark. 1919. New ed. New York: Routledge.
Fiege, Father Marianus. 1909. *The Princess of Poverty: Saint Clare of Assisi and the*
    Order of Poor Ladies. Evansville, IN: The Poor Clares of the Monastery of S.
    Clare.

Friedman, Michael D. 1995. 'O, Let Him Marry Her!': Matrimony and Recompense in *Measure for Measure*. *Shakespeare Quarterly* 46: 454–64.

Froide, Amy M. 1999. Marital Status as a Category of Difference: Singlewomen and Widows in Early Modern England. In *Singlewomen in the European Past, 1250–1800*, ed. Judith M. Bennett and Amy M. Froide, 236–69. Philadelphia: University of Pennsylvania Press.

Harding, Davis P. 1950. Elizabethan Betrothals and *Measure for Measure*. *Journal of English and Germanic Philology* 49: 139–58.

Harris, Barbara J. 1993. A New Look at the Reformation: Aristocratic Women and Nunneries, 1450–1540. *Journal of British Studies* 32: 89–113.

Hayne, Victoria. 1993. Performing Social Practice: The Example of *Measure for Measure*. *Shakespeare Quarterly* 44: 1–29.

Holderness, B.A. 1984. Widows in Pre-Industrial Society: An Essay upon Their Economic Functions. In *Land, Kinship and Life-Cycle*, ed. R.M. Smith, 423–42. Cambridge: Cambridge University Press.

Ingram, Martin. 1981. Spousals Litigation in the English Ecclesiastical Courts, c. 1350–c. 1640. In *Marriage and Society: Studies in the Social History of Marriage*, ed. R.B. Outhwaite, 35–57. New York: St Martin's Press.

Jankowski, Theodora A. 2000. *Pure Resistance: Queer Virginity in Early Modern English Drama*. Philadelphia: University of Pennsylvania Press.

Johnson, Penelope D. 1987. The Cloistering of Medieval Nuns: Release or Repression, Reality or Fantasy? In *Gendered Domains: Rethinking Public and Private in Women's History*, ed. Dorothy O. Helly and Susan M. Reverby, 27–39. Ithaca and New York: Cornell University Press.

Judges, Arthur V. 1930. *The Elizabethan Underworld*. London: George Routledge and Sons.

Karras, Ruth Mazo. 1999. Sex and the Singlewoman. In *Singlewomen in the European Past, 1250–1800*, ed. Judith M. Bennett and Amy M. Froide, 127–45. Philadelphia: University of Pennsylvania Press.

Kent, Joan. 1973. Attitudes of Members of the House of Commons to the Regulations of 'Personal Conduct' in Late Elizabethan and Early Stuart England'. *Bulletin of the Institute of Historical Research* 46: 41–71.

Korda, Natasha. 2002. *Shakespeare's Domestic Economies: Gender and Property in Early Modern England*. Philadelphia: University of Pennsylvania Press.

Kowaleski, Maryanne. 1999. Singlewomen in Medieval and Early Modern Europe: The Demographic Perspective. In *Singlewomen in the European Past, 1250–1800*, ed. Judith M. Bennett and Amy M. Froide, 38–81. Philadelphia: University of Pennsylvania Press.

Laslett, Peter, Karla Oosterveen, and Richard M. Smith. 1980. *Bastardy and Its Comparative History*. Cambridge, MA: Harvard University Press.

Leonard, E.M. 1965. *The Early History of English Poor Relief.* New York: Barnes and Noble.

Lever, J.W. 1989. Introduction to *Measure for Measure* by William Shakespeare, ed. J.W. Lever. Arden Shakespeare. New York: Routledge.

McFeely, Maureen Connolly. 1995. 'This Day My Sister Should the Cloister Enter': The Convent as Refuge in *Measure for Measure.* In *Subjects on the World's Stage: Essays on British Literature of the Middle Ages and the Renaissance,* ed. David G. Allen and Robert A. White, 200–16. Newark, NJ: University of Delaware Press.

Moorman, John. 1968. *A History of the Franciscan Order from Its Origins to the Year 1517.* Oxford: Clarendon Press.

Nagarajan, S. 1963. *Measure for Measure* and Elizabethan Betrothals. *Shakespeare Quarterly* 14: 115–19.

Neely, Carol Thomas. 1985. *Broken Nuptials in Shakespeare's Plays.* New Haven: Yale University Press.

Oliva, Marilyn. 1998. *The Convent and the Community in Late Medieval England: Female Monasteries in the Diocese of Norwich, 1350–1540.* Woodbridge: Boydell.

Pound, John. 1971. *Poverty and Vagrancy in Tudor England.* London: Longman.

Ranald, Margaret Loftus. 1979. 'As Marriage Binds, and Blood Breaks': English Marriage and Shakespeare. *Shakespeare Quarterly* 30: 68–81.

Roper, Lyndal. 1989. *The Holy Household: Women and Morals in Reformation Augsburg.* Oxford: Oxford University Press.

The Rule of the Holy Virgin S. Clare. [1621] 1975. London: Scolar.

Schanzer, Ernest. 1960. The Marriage-Contracts in *Measure for Measure.* *Shakespeare Survey* 13: 81–9.

Scott, Margaret. 1982. 'Our City's Institutions': Some Further Reflections on the Marriage Contracts in *Measure for Measure.* *ELH* 49: 790–804.

Scouten, Arthur H. 1975. An Historical Approach to *Measure for Measure.* *Philological Quarterly* 54: 68–84.

Seton, Walter W., ed. 1914. The Rewle of Sustris Menouresses Enclosid. [MS. Bodl. 585] In *A Fifteenth Century Courtesy Book and Two Franciscan Rules,* ed. R.W. Chambers and Walter W. Seton, 63–119. Early English Text Society. London: Oxford University Press.

Shakespeare, William. 1989. *Measure for Measure,* ed. J.W. Lever. Arden Shakespeare. New York: Routledge.

Slack, Paul. 1974. Vagrants and Vagrancy in England, 1598–1664. *Economic History Review* 2nd ser. 27: 360–79.

– 1985. Poverty and Social Regulation in Elizabethan England. In *The Reign of Elizabeth I,* ed. Christopher Haigh, 221–41. Athens: University of Georgia Press.

Wadding, Luke. 1635. *The History of the Angelicall Virgin Glorious S. Clare.* Trans. Sister Magdalen Augustine. Douay.

Wales, Tim. 1984. Poverty, Poor Relief and the Life Cycle: Some Evidence from Seventeenth-Century Norfolk. In *Land, Kinship and Life-Cycle*, ed. R.M. Smith, 351–404. Cambridge: Cambridge University Press.

Wentersdorf, Karl P. 1979. The Marriage Contracts in *Measure for Measure*: A Reconsideration. *Shakespeare Survey* 32: 29–44.

Wrigley, E.A., and Roger Schofield. 1981. *The Population History of England, 1541–1871: A Reconstruction.* London: Edward Arnold.

Wrightson, Keith, and David Levine. 1995. *Poverty and Piety in an English Village: Terling 1525–1700.* Oxford: Clarendon Press.

7

Marriage, Identity, and the Pursuit of Property in Seventeenth-Century England: The Cases of Anne Clifford and Elizabeth Wiseman

MARY CHAN and NANCY E. WRIGHT

The first marriage of Lady Anne Clifford (1590–1676) and the remarriage of Elizabeth Wiseman (1647–1730) confirm that courtship and marriage, among the elite in seventeenth-century England, can be characterized as the pursuit of property.[1] Ideals of romantic love and conjugal affection, as their own diaries and letters confirm, played little part in the conduct of these two heiresses, their families and suitors. To say the property that they inherited, Lady Anne Clifford's £15,000 and Elizabeth Wiseman's £20,000, made them eminently marriageable does not sufficiently emphasize the consequences of owning property for these women. In their contemporaries' eyes, the role of property owner was an 'office' that endowed an individual with particular legal rights necessary in order to fulfil obligations and duties not simply to oneself but more importantly to one's family and class. In their own eyes, as their writings indicate, Lady Anne and Elizabeth Wiseman assumed that as marriageable women of property they had, and should exercise, 'the liberty' of that office, meaning, as Conal Condren has explained, the legal rights and other conditions necessary for the fulfilment of its responsibilities.[2] The liberty of this office consequently implied that, to its owner, property had a greater importance than its economic value.

It is a mistake to assume, however, that the economic or commodified value of their substantial inheritances, or property, was irrelevant to the pursuit of these women. In the memorable words of Elizabeth Wiseman's brother, Roger North, an heiress's possession of property, to her contemporaries, clearly made her 'one of the good things ... to be gott' (Chan 1998, 80).[3] His language nicely clarifies one of the consequences of property ownership for a marriageable woman; while she occupied the privileged subject position of a property owner before marriage or during widowhood, she could also become, to potential suitors, an 'object' to be 'gott' and, to her own family, an 'object' to be transferred between owners. Nevertheless, the fact that a woman and her property were not simply opposed as dichotomous subject and object is eloquently articulated in the writings of Lady Anne Clifford and Elizabeth Wiseman. Indeed their letters and diaries, despite their seemingly 'private' genres, were in fact, produced and collected as documents relevant to public audiences engaged in legal disputes about their property and marriage.

Recent studies by Staves, Spring, and Erickson, among others, have established the rules of law regarding inheritance and marriage settlements most relevant to married and marriageable women of property in seventeenth-century England. Our chapter directs attention to a different, but equally relevant, facet of the cases of Lady Anne Clifford and Elizabeth Wiseman, namely, how commodification threatened their legal rights as property owners and their own ideas of personhood. Despite legal provisions that, in the seventeenth century, could enable a woman to control her own property after marriage, the cases of Lady Anne Clifford and Elizabeth Wiseman demonstrate, in practice, the offices of married woman and property owner conflicted. We draw upon Margaret Jane Radin's analysis of commodification in order to clarify the consequences of competing ideas of property informing their marriage and marriage negotiations addressed in the letters and diaries written by Lady Anne Clifford, and letters and other documents written by Elizabeth Wiseman and her relatives.

Radin directs attention to the ways in which commodification can collapse distinctions between a subject and an object – a dichotomy customarily drawn in Western law in order to differentiate alienable and inalienable property. Alienable property is understood as a commodity. In general, Radin explains, 'commodities are socially constructed as objects separate from the self and social relations' (Radin 1996, 6). Commodities, or in Radin's terminology, 'object-property,' customarily can be exchanged for any other kind of fungible, or saleable, property without loss or damage to the owner (1993, 192). Inalienable property, however, is implicitly understood as 'a constitutive property of a subject,' meaning it is an attribute of a person which cannot be sold or exchanged, such as a legal right. Radin calls these 'attribute-properties' (1993, 192). In the practice of societies, however, commodification can transgress this subject/object dichotomy and, consequently, threaten the well-being and personhood of individuals. An attribute-property, Radin posits, cannot be commodified or alienated without affecting an individual's sense of self. Consequently, she argues, two senses of the word 'alienation' might be drawn together: alienation of property – in the strictly market-legal sense of sale or transfer – and alienation in the social and moral sense of estrangement (1993, 200–2). It is the blurring of the distinction between alienable and inalienable property and the drawing together of the two meanings of 'alienation' which throws into relief some important implications in, and inferences to be drawn from, the personal writings of Lady Anne Clifford and Elizabeth Wiseman.

The Commodification of Legal Rights in the Case of Lady Anne Clifford

Many histories document the protracted legal disputes of Lady Anne Clifford, who was the only lineal heir of George Clifford, third Earl of Cumberland.[4] In 1605, her father in his will left the family estates, amounting to 90,000 acres, to his brother and his male heirs. Lady Anne contested that will, which provided her with a portion of £15,000 and, if her uncle and his son should die without a male heir, the remainder of the family estates. Her father's will exemplifies the ends sought by the practice of aristocratic inheritance in England from 1300 to 1800. During this period, inheritance practice, in Eileen Spring's words, did not follow the 'rules of common law' but instead the 'rules of landowners.' According to common law rules of inheritance 'land descended to the eldest son to the exclusion of his siblings ... If there was no son, land descended to daughters. The common law ... chose son over daughter, but daughter over collateral male' (Spring 1993, 9). During the twelfth and thirteenth centuries, despite common law rules of inheritance, a collateral male often came to be the successor rather than the daughter. This became the customary practice of inheritance, Spring notes, long before 1540, when the Statute of Wills allowed the devising of real property, or land, by will and thereby enabled fathers to ignore common law rules of inheritance. Spring's study of rules of law in relation to inheritance practices usefully sets gender and property within the context of legal rights. This was the context in which Lady Margaret Russell, Lady Anne's mother, encouraged her daughter to view the claim to the barony of Westmorland. As a result, they first petitioned the king to assert Lady Anne's right of succession in 1606. A firm conviction in her legal right as heiress subsequently led Lady Anne to reject a settlement arbitrated in 1617 by King James I, who awarded the family property to her uncle and £21,000 to her. Despite the king's decision, she refused to sign over her claim to the remainder of the estate as her husband and uncle demanded. She publicly pursued what she called 'the right of mine Inheritance' until 1643, when she came into her inheritance after her cousin, the fifth Earl of Cumberland, died without a male heir.

What needs to be examined, we suggest, is Lady Anne's understanding of her legal right of inheritance, or succession. Her understanding of that common law right is all the more striking because, as Spring explains, it had not been customary among the aristocracy for four centuries. In fact, since the Statute of Wills in 1540, common law rules of succession that Lady Anne believed secured her right as heir-general were, at best, 'default rules' that applied only in cases of intestacy.[5] Consequently, our concern is the question: what meanings did that right have to Lady Anne?

In her diaries Lady Anne described her right of succession as a legal right that should not be commodified. Radin's analysis of commodification provides particular insight into Lady Anne's negotiation of her legal right of succession. Commodification functions in Lady Anne's inheritance dispute, as Radin contends it does in other contexts, as an index of multiple and unstable concepts of property interacting (1996, xiii). In her diaries and will, Lady Anne described the effects she attempted to forestall by refusing to alienate and commodify her right of succession to the hereditary office and estate of the barony of Westmorland. When she described her right of succession as an attribute of her office or duty, she expressed an idea common to her seventeenth-century contemporaries for whom, Condren explains, 'the world was less a market place of competing rights ... than a forum of duties requiring rights' (1997, 467). Because, in seventeenth-century England, the self, in Condren's words, 'extended to a perception of standing, *dignitas*, what was due to the role of aristocrat ... [in] an office driven world' (1997, 467), Westmorland was, for Lady Anne, an attribute of her 'self.'[6] Indeed it is not simply the ownership of real property, or Westmorland, that is at issue for Lady Anne but instead the attribute-property of her legal right to succeed to the barony.

During Lady Anne's extensive negotiation of her legal rights of dower and inheritance with her first husband, Richard Sackville, third Earl of Dorset, she differentiated her inheritance as an attribute essential to her self-constitution. In contrast, her willingness to have her dower lands conveyed to another owner and to have her jointure cancelled indicates her understanding of these legal rights (and the use of real property that they bestowed upon her) as objects separate from herself. The different meanings that she associated with dower and inheritance initially seem surprising because they were both legal rights. That she differentiated them is clearly indicated by her willingness to treat her right of dower as a commodity transferred by contract and, in contrast, by her refusal to agree to accept an award that, like a contract, allocated her an increased portion in exchange for her right of inheritance.

After Sackville married Lady Anne, he predictably did not support her legal efforts to claim her inheritance. Because coverture vested in her husband only the use of her real property during his lifetime, Sackville did not attempt to help his wife secure the barony of Westmorland. Instead he attempted to coerce her to relinquish her claim to the inheritance so that he would immediately receive her award of £21,000, which was, to him, far more lucrative. When she refused to agree to his demand, Sackville threatened to cancel her jointure. This was of consequence to Lady Anne because she had previously allowed fines to be passed upon her dower (see Clifford 1992, 38). Dower was the ancient right enshrined in English law which afforded a married woman the use of one-third of the freehold lands of her husband, to be enjoyed during her widowhood. In the fifteenth century dower was fixed in law and seen as a moral right (Buck 1987, 90–1). Lady Anne had agreed to fines upon her dower (that, in essence, conveyed the property to another owner) upon the condition that Sackville settle upon her a jointure that was of equal value.[7] Subsequently, she chose to forfeit her jointure rather than relinquish her claim to the legal right of heir-general to Westmorland as her husband demanded (see Clifford 1992, 56). This negotiation indicates, on the part of both Sackville and Lady Anne, the coexistence of commodified and noneconomic understandings not only of real property but also of particular legal rights.

Sackville's use of contract law to limit his wife's dower exemplifies an early modern idea of property that viewed dower as a restriction upon the testamentary capacity of the landowner to perpetuate the land–family bond in patrilineal succession. In the early modern period, as A.R. Buck has explained, land was not valued solely because of its economic value by the aristocracy because the landowner's

position depended, in large measure, on the perpetuation of a secure nexus between landownership on a vast scale and an aristocratic title premised on patrilineal succession ... To be able to claim one-third of that estate as her own [dower] – even though an ancient right legitimised by law – would weaken the mechanics of corporate inheritance, whereby the estate and the title were maintained intact, both for the individual family and for the class which those families comprised. (1987, 91)

The benefit to accrue to Sackville by having his wife relinquish her dower was clear: it enabled him upon his death to transmit his entire estate intact to his heir and thereby maintain the land–family bond. What, however, were the consequences for Lady Anne of allowing the commodification of her right of dower?

Dower, which originated in feudal law and became a legal right in the fifteenth century, had long been evaded in practice. By the early seventeenth century, jointure stipulated in a marriage contract had all but replaced dower (Harris 2002, 23). In the later seventeenth century, the strict settlement had, among the landed aristocracy, circumvented dower. Lady Anne's use of her dower and jointure as commodities to be negotiated, that is, transferred to other owners, in fact, was not a radical alteration of her contemporaries' understanding of those legal rights of women. In essence women's common law right of dower had been defined previously not only as a right but also as a commodity, or an object to be transferred among owners, from the fifteenth to the seventeenth centuries. Lady Anne's resistance to a similar economic dimension that her husband (and others) introduced when negotiating her right of inheritance directs attention to her understanding of the consequences of that particular instance of commodification. Sackville's attempt to coerce his wife to renounce her claim to Westmorland so that he would receive a large cash settlement indicates that he accepted the idea of real property as a commodity for commercial exploitation by way of a market transaction or free transfer. His negotiations indicate, however, that he held a commodified understanding not only of his wife's property but also of her common law right as heiress to an ancient barony.

Lady Anne's diaries articulate the different conflicting meanings – that is, commodified and noneconomic meanings – of both real property and legal rights, evident in her negotiation of her inheritance. Her rhetoric, which described her legal rights as attributes of her office of baron, clarifies her understanding of the consequences of commodification. Radin has argued that 'To conceive of something personal as fungible assumes that the person and the attribute, right, or thing, are separate' (1996, 93). Rather than accepting such a dichotomy, Lady

Anne uses language to assert that her right of inheritance is inalienable, that is, essential to her office and its duties. Entries in her diaries refer, in her words, to the 'Inheritance of my forefathers,' 'my Right,' and 'my Right of the Lands' (1992, 36–7). She uses economic and commercial terms, in contrast, to refer to the transactions undertaken by the king, the Archbishop of Canterbury, the Lord Chancellor, and her husband when arbitrating a settlement with her uncle against her wishes. She uses the terms 'business' and 'businesses' when dismissing their negotiations (1992, 49–57). In several of the passages in which she uses the noun 'business' to describe their negotiations she uses the place name 'Westmorland' (1992, 45, 47, 53) in order to articulate her own understanding of the contested barony as an office that conferred upon her legal rights and duties – attributes that defined her – rather than an object to be commodified. For example, in April 1617, she records: 'Sometimes I had fair words from him [my Lord] & sometimes foul, but I took all patiently, & did strive to give him as much content & assurance of my love as I could possibly, yet I told him that I would never part with Westmoreland upon any condition whatever ... I sat by my Lord & my Brother Sackville in the Drawing Chamber & heard much talk about my Businesses' (1992, 53). Westmorland, which was not only the place name of the estate but also the title of the person who fulfilled the hereditary office of sheriff of the barony, enabled her to communicate, in her diaries, that money was incommensurable with her right of inheritance.

Lady Anne also uses a rhetoric of personal affinity and genealogy that suggests why she is unable to accept the assumption implied by the language of commodification – the assumption that her relation to her legal right of inheritance is that of a subject to an external object. Lady Anne articulates her right as heir to the ancient barony of Westmorland as a status embedded in the context of a fixed hierarchy, that is, not only of her class, the aristocracy, but also of her genealogy. The most characteristic feature of Lady Anne's rhetoric in her later diaries is her explanation of how, as Sheriff of Westmorland, she restored and reconstructed the social order of her ancestors. For example, the first night that she resides at Pendragon Castle, after she had it repaired, she records:

> it had layen desolate ever since the 15th yeare of Edward the third in 1341, which is 320 yeares ago, for then (as [in] old Records and Chronicles it appears) the Scotts made an Inroad into the West of England totally destroying it and pulling down all the timbere and a greate parte of the Stone building of it. But before that it was the chiefe and beloved habitation of

Idonea the younger Daughter and Coheire of Robert de Viteriponte, my
Auncestor, she dying without issue (as appears by Inquisition) later after her
death in the 8th year of Edward the third ... all her Inheritance in Westmerland
came to her eldest Sister Isabella's Grandchild, Robert, Lord Clifford, and
his posteritie to whom I am heire by a lineal descent. (1992, 154)

The place names of the landscape and the residences located within it, to
Lady Anne, are the means to articulate her own location within a genealogy that determines her office, familial identity, and status.[8] In this
passage (and others) she records the precedents for her inheritance as
the lineal female heir and successor to the ancient barony.

The arbiters of her inheritance in 1617 commodified her common law
right as heiress as a 'business' transaction facilitated by recent statute law
and confirmed by landholders' practice. The Statute of Wills allowed
landed property to be transferred between generations not by common
law rules of succession but instead by will. Statute law, which introduced
greater flexibility of testamentary capacity maintained the aristocracy's
power based on the land–family bond. The flexibility introduced to the
laws of succession, as Lady Anne's case illustrates, exaggerated the potential for the commodification, subordination, and unequal distribution of
rights as well as property among men and women of her class. Lady
Anne, like other female heirs, within a flexible system of land transfer
found her potential for self-constitution more limited than in a fixed
system ensured by common law rules of inheritance. Her response to
that limitation was to use a rhetoric that articulated attributes, including
duties and legal rights, which constituted her office and sense of self.
Her own rhetoric attempted to counteract the market rhetoric that
commodified and reduced her legal right to succeed to the office of
Baron of Westmorland to mere 'business.'[9] Lady Anne's rhetoric alluded
to the ideas of the immemorial origins of common law and its unchanging continuity, represented by her own genealogy. The significance of
that rhetoric – its resistance to commodification – is most poignantly
expressed when, after having come into her inheritance, she records her
hope that her daughters who '(if it bee the Will of Almightie God) ... are
to succeed mee in these places, for a Wife and Lady ... make their owne
houses the place of Selfe fruition and bee comfortably parte of this Life'
(1992, 112). Her diaries confirm the need to dissociate commodification
from her legal rights that she understood to be inalienable attributes
invested in the person who fulfilled the office and duties of the barony of
Westmorland.

The Alienation of a Woman's Personhood in the
Case of Elizabeth Wiseman

Different, competing ideas of property occur in the personal letters among papers of the North family preserved at Rougham Hall, Norfolk, as documents relating to a suit of jactitation of marriage prosecuted in 1687 on behalf of Elizabeth Wiseman by members of her family. Elizabeth Wiseman was the seventh surviving child of Dudley (fourth Baron North) and Anne (neé Montague). Her eldest brother was Charles, Lord North and Grey; and she was sister to Francis, first Baron Guilford and from 1682–5 keeper of the Great Seal, to the lawyer Roger North, best known for his *Lives* of three of his brothers, and to Sir Dudley and to Mountague North, merchants. In 1684, at the age of 37, she was left a widow in London with an inheritance of £20,000 from her first husband, Sir Robert Wiseman, Dean of the Arches. In 1686, she was courted by a number of men – in particular, by one who became very troublesome to her, Robert Spencer, cousin to the Earl of Sunderland. Robert Spencer was a younger son with limited financial means. His courtship of Elizabeth Wiseman was promoted and encouraged by Elizabeth's eldest brother, Charles Lord North and Grey, because Spencer had promised him favours at court and influence with the Earl of Sunderland if the match was successful. But Elizabeth claimed that from the first meeting she disliked Spencer and wished not to see him again; so Charles, his wife Lady Katharine, and Spencer were put to considerable trouble to organize surprise meetings between them. At one such meeting, Charles allegedly locked his sister and Spencer in a room together and then claimed that, when they came out, he and his wife Lady Katharine had witnessed a verbal contract of marriage between them. Elizabeth was so appalled at this claim that she involved her brothers, Roger and Dudley, in her plight asking for their legal and brotherly advice. These brothers advised her to move to her sister's house (that of Christina and Sir George Wenyeve) in Brettenham, Suffolk, for a time to escape from Spencer's claims and harassment; and they also suggested the possibility of taking a case of jactitation of marriage against Spencer, which meant that Elizabeth would sue for Spencer to cease claiming that he was contracted to marry her. Spencer, for his part, said that he would sue Elizabeth not only for breach of contract but also for damage to his reputation, which he believed Roger and Dudley North had maligned in advising their sister not to marry him.

Spencer's was not the only suit to Elizabeth at the time. When he was first introduced to her, Roger North was arranging a marriage for her and investigating the property of Sir John Thorold in order to draw up a settlement. Spencer visited Sir John and told him that 'Elizabeth was his wife before God' and that no one else could marry her. This scared Sir John off; but it did not deter the persistence of a man called Mr Neale or of another called Danvers, both of whom pursued Elizabeth Wiseman to her retreat in Suffolk. Eventually, six months after she had been introduced to Spencer, Elizabeth Wiseman married William Paston, second Earl of Yarmouth (in March 1687). After her marriage to Yarmouth, and since Spencer still pressed his claims, legal measures were taken to silence him and to make Charles, Lord North, retract his claim that he had witnessed a contract between his sister and Spencer.

Because of the competing claims, and the possibility of their own case for jactitation of marriage, Roger North kept all letters and documents relating to the affair and asked anyone who was involved in discussion of it to write an account of what was said and heard. These documents, which form an unfolding narrative of the affair, provided plausible, and thus legally defensible, evidence at a time when legal theorists were beginning to write about circumstantial evidence. North deliberately preserved these documents, which together narrate a story, in order to defend his sister's reputation and, indeed, her life.

The case, as the documents reveal, is largely a contention about property: Elizabeth's inheritance of £20,000. From Elizabeth Wiseman's point of view, however, it is not merely her £20,000 that is at issue, but, more importantly, herself. The documents draw attention to the crude and market-driven nature of marriage and marriage portions in the late seventeenth century: the common law doctrine of coverture in marriage and the fact that a married woman's property belonged to her husband. But in drawing attention to the fact that her inheritance was valued as a commodity to be transferred or alienated to another owner – the man she wed – the documents also make clear the subject's point of view: Elizabeth's sense of herself, her legal rights, duties, and obligations.

Elizabeth had a commodified 'market value' as a widow in a way she did not before her first marriage. When she married Sir Robert Wiseman, she had a marriage portion of £1,500 that he promised to double at his death (see Chan 1995, 192). The marriage had been arranged through her elder brother, Francis North (the Lord Keeper), and her family considered her most fortunate to make such a 'good' match. Her 'value' was not in her portion, which was small (nor, really, in herself as an individual), but in the good name of her family. As a very rich widow,

Elizabeth suddenly has a new status; she is no longer reliant solely on her family. Many of the documents reveal her understanding of the burden (and responsibilities) such wealth places on a widow alone in London, with all the 'sharks' (Chan 1998, 90), as Roger North calls them, after her. Before her first marriage, her marriage portion ensured her marriageability – that is to say, her father would pay it only when she married someone of whom he approved. As a widow, however, her inheritance of £20,000 is hers, to do with as she pleased. Herein lies her dilemma, for the very means by which she has market value (i.e., her inherited fortune) is also the means that allows her self-determination and self-expression. Her property gives her a voice, both literally and literarily, and her voice reveals her awareness of the ambiguity of her position.

Her office as a woman of property endows her with legal rights, or liberty, but such notions, as Condren explains, 'left precious little room for valuing liberty in its own right and no room for the autonomous individual' (1997, 461). Her letters indicate that she assumed that the liberties of her office as a woman of property were for the fulfilment of its functions, such as accruing both honour and status to her family to whose best interests she remained subordinate.[10] This is implied by the fact that she intends to marry. When the 'story' opens, her lawyer brother, Roger North, is arranging a marriage settlement for her with Sir John Thorold.

Before she remarries, as a widow with an inheritance, she has new economic and social status. Regarded from the point of view of Radin's discussion of alienable and inalienable property, Elizabeth Wiseman becomes the focus for competing concepts of identity. Who, or what, is she? Elizabeth's identity, before her widowhood, had been largely defined by her family's social standing – that is, both the family of her father and of her former husband. Because as a widow she is financially independent, the correspondence between Elizabeth and her brothers reveals her own struggle with her concept of personhood. From her point of view, on the one hand, she still owes responsibility to her family, a strongly felt need not to be the centre of public gossip and thus to preserve the 'honour' of the family; on the other hand, she has a new responsibility to herself. The family 'good' is presented in two guises. First is Charles, Lord North's, view of her as a marketable commodity which he can 'sell' (the word is actually used, ironically, by one of the Norths' cousins, Peregrine Bertie [Chan 1998, 38]) to Spencer in exchange for favours for himself (and, he claims, to his other brothers) at the court of James II; second is the vaguer ideal of the family's honour and reputation. In either case she is being asked to act for good beyond herself. Against these is her own sense of her property as an attribute that is part of her identity, inalienable except insofar as she herself gives it freely, with herself, in marriage. In other words, while in Charles North's view she is now very much 'for sale,' from her point of view, the very fact of her wealth gives her status, independence, and identity. Charles's is the legal and social view of women; hers is more complex for she understands that her inheritance blurs the distinction between subject and object. It is not only object-property, that is, an external object that can by convention be transferred to another owner, but also attribute-property, that is, a constitutive element of her social role as a widow who belongs to multiple families, her natal and marital family.

Furthermore, while she agrees with the necessity for family solidarity in all matters of significance and therefore in this consults her supportive brothers, she is acutely aware that this necessity conflicts with her individual choice. But her dilemma is more subtle than simply a choice between family and self. She makes clear that 'self' is very slippery in such a context. In other words, she is conscious of what Radin has called the 'contextual aspect of personhood,' the need to find 'self-determination within the group' (1996, 56). The way in which all the Norths (except Charles) regard self-determination of members within their family includes concern for the family as a whole.

Her dilemma can be illustrated by contrast. The Norths have an aunt, their father's sister Lady Dorothy Dacres, who enters the story late and who counsels complete liberty and independence. She is appalled at the way in which Elizabeth has felt forced to retreat to the Suffolk home of her sister for protection and is all for Elizabeth braving out the gossip, and Spencer's threats, and coming back to her house in London, in defiance of everyone. It is clear that Elizabeth finds this an attractive suggestion: but her brothers dissuade her, saying 'your education, nor temper is not that way, having most of the oblidging and complyant' (Chan 1998, 83). Lady Dacres's solution is an extreme that the supportive North brothers are anxious their sister not follow. They represent their aunt as a bold, noisy, and tyrannical woman. Roger North describes her reaction to the news of Elizabeth's harassment and consequent flight from London as 'mightily upon the rant' (Chan 1998, 77).

Charles, Lord North, who is trying to promote this marriage, reveals most clearly the late seventeenth-century stereotypical view of his sister and her wealth. She can be alienated in both senses of the word for all he cares. For him she is a commodity which he, as eldest brother and (as he points out to her) head of the family, can dispose of. Elizabeth does not really question this attitude to her: what she does balk at is Charles's unashamed intent to sell her for his own personal gain, with no regard either to her interests or, actually, to those of the family. Charles also tries to make out that Elizabeth's supportive brothers really regard her as a commodity too. Their interest, he claims, is to discourage her from marriage in order that her wealth remain in the family. This attitude of Charles's is reflected in his letters by their artificiality of style and by the way in which they characterize his sister as a two-dimensional figure, a character from Restoration comedy, playing hard to get and almost indecently desperate to marry again. He writes to Elizabeth at one point claiming that Spencer is ill because of her 'unkind' treatment of him and that this illness is because 'his honour and conscience [have] stood in his light' (Chan 1998, 14): in other words, he should have raped Elizabeth. It is not in Charles's own interest to take Elizabeth seriously, to regard her as more than a marketable 'object.' Charles and Lady Dacres represent two extreme – and competing – views of Elizabeth.

Although Robert Spencer, the suitor, is the main focus of the letters, there exists only one letter from him in the series.[11] At the very end of the series, after Elizabeth has married the Earl of Yarmouth, he challenges the earl to a duel. He appears in the letters only through the eyes of others. Elizabeth says that she disliked him from the first meeting and had asked her servants not to admit him to her house. Later she says she 'hates' him. Nevertheless, he is brought, uninvited, by Lady Katharine North and is present on several occasions when Elizabeth visits Lady Katharine, on one occasion emerging from a closet when the company is seated in the drawing room. It is obvious that Spencer is a fortune hunter; but Charles North claims to his sister that Spencer 'desires only you, not yours. Leaves your own estate to your private disposition and menage' (Chan 1998, 8), implying that an arrangement by which Elizabeth can control her own property is his wish. In reality, such an arrangement was a possibility: whether Elizabeth could (or would) also have had control over the testamentary disposition of that property is uncertain. Since she had no children by her first marriage and at the age of thirty-nine might be unlikely to survive childbed, we can infer that Spencer might have counted on winning in the end! Despite his apparently more subtle attitude to her property, Spencer believes, once he claims that a marriage contract has taken place at Charles North's house with Charles and his wife as witness, that he is 'married' to Elizabeth and that she and all she owns is his. He is reported to use market rhetoric to refer to her on several occasions just as Charles does. For example, he sends a message to Sir John Thorold to tell him that 'that lady [is] his wife before God and not fit for any man else to have' (Chan 1998, 17, 53). Spencer also claims that he will 'seize her in the streets, church, or anywhere' (Chan 1998, 53) and that he will 'prosecute at law for her' (Chan 1998, 17).

Elizabeth's three supportive brothers (Dudley, Roger, and Mountague) occupy a middle ground in this matter. They acknowledge her right to make her own choices when they write to her saying, 'If ever, we desturbe you in any thing that you positively determine concerning yourself farther then by telling you our thoughts of it, or refuse to assist you in your owne way all that in us lys, we will give Lord [North] leav to print what he commonly talks' (Chan 1998, 82); and later, 'wee doe neither desire, nor pretend to sway you, in anything against your owne perswasion' (Chan 1998, 89). They and Elizabeth are also in accord in their view of the matter as one of family significance and therefore one requiring expert legal advice. So they write to her at length with advice on how to conduct herself in this affair, and do indeed attempt to dissuade her from returning to London when she wishes to do so. In her replies, Elizabeth acquiesces in this subordinate role. When Charles writes to her, on two occasions she asks Roger and Dudley to write for her an answer to him, which she then writes out in her own hand. In other words, they regard Elizabeth as unworldly, as not sufficiently able to manage her own affairs.

Elizabeth's view of the matter is not quite that of her supportive brothers. Certainly, she appears to be in accord with them when she makes a veiled reference in one of her letters to her brothers' arrangements for her eventual marriage to the Earl of Yarmouth, where she writes of 'your matching me to that excellent man' (Chan 1998, 33) as though she has no say in the matter. She also makes no reference to Sir John Thorold, with whom her brothers are arranging a marriage settlement when the Spencer affair starts. Clearly she does not regard marriage in a romantic light.[12]

Elizabeth certainly makes clear that she would like a say in the matter, and although she agrees that marriage is best for the family honour (a rich single woman living alone in London is open to gossip) she makes clear too that she must marry only someone she can respect and like: that she must give her fortune freely with herself. Further than this, she regards her fortune as part of herself – rather than, as Charles does, herself as a rather troublesome and unfortunate part of her fortune. She never writes of it as such, although several of her letters to Roger contain discussion about the investments of her fortune. But she does regard her independence as important, writing of the irksomeness of having to stay so long with her sister, since she (Elizabeth) is someone 'who does not love to hang' (Chan 1998, 86). She is very concerned when her brothers suggest that she give up her house in Soho Square and not live by herself and she refers to her late husband's advice never to 'putt my selfe out of a house and home' (Chan 1998, 85). She goes on to say, 'I knowe my selfe so much in my owne powr that I will not doe anything to make my life vneasy' (Chan 1998, 85). In one letter, full of exasperation and despair, she writes: 'Lett him [Spencer] do what he can, and when I come to town if he dares come neer me Ile spit in his beastly face. After that lett him take his course. I know so well my selfe and my behauour that I feare not the worst that he or his associates can be guilty of, lett them doe what they can' (Chan 1998, 85). Further on in the same letter she writes: 'The sparks are of the mind I will marry. I never de[c]lared my selfe of that opinion yett nor shall they find it so. But lett them say what pleases them I reguard it not: but they shall never find my discourse or actions tending that way' (Chan 1998, 87). She is torn between her admiration of the forthrightness of her aunt, Lady Dacres, a desire to act like her, and a recognition that her concern for her family honour and standing will mean that she is confined only to words.

To herself, then, Elizabeth's inheritance is not simply an alienable commodity or object-property. In regarding it (and her) as alienable in a market sense Charles North and Spencer would also alienate or estrange her from her family and her sense of self. She is aware that the very ownership of that property makes her, in others' eyes, a commodity; that as a result of her inheritance, she, in Roger North's words, is 'look't upon as one of the good things now to be gott' (Chan 1998, 80). She is also aware, however, that ownership of that property is what gives her specific legal rights that constitute her liberty of office and that inform her own idea of her identity. When her first marriage with Sir Robert Wiseman is discussed by Roger North in his *Life* of the Lord Keeper (Francis) North, even allowing for the fact that he is writing from the point of view of Francis's role, he makes very little mention of Elizabeth herself or her wishes or feelings. Presumably the emotions of Elizabeth, a singlewoman with a very small marriage portion, were, in his eyes, of little relevance. There is some irony in the fact that Elizabeth gains a (literary) voice (i.e., her letters are of significance) only when she also becomes 'one of the good things.' And that voice – subtle, affectionate, good-humoured, and forceful – is what complicates Charles North's simple view of the case. While in the end she remains the late seventeenth-century exemplary woman – deferential to her supportive brothers' wider knowledge of 'the world' and submitting to the greater family good – nevertheless, Radin's theories about property and personhood provide an approach which draws the reader's attention to the significance of Elizabeth's responses to her situation and, consequently, to the underlying struggle in her letters to define her idea of her own life.

Conclusion

As a result of a law case that caused her letters to be produced and preserved, Elizabeth Wiseman became a literary figure for six months of her life (at least from our modern point of view, for her letters about this dilemma in her life are, unlike others which survive by her, all directed towards a single theme – her second marriage).[13] Furthermore, the events represented in her letters, although temporarily catastrophic for her, did provide an occasion for her to define, in her own words, her social role and place. She obviously was not otherwise voiceless. Rather, she inhabited (as many like her did) a nonliterary world, and it is this that her letters allow us to glimpse: a personality and not a commodity, as Charles North would have her. Her common, day-to-day life, revealed in the 'news' she tells her brothers and her way of telling it, is as integral a part of herself as is her property, as inalienable as that is.

By contrast, Lady Anne Clifford existed as a literary figure for most of her life; as Paul Salzman explains in a later chapter in this book, she is the author and subject of many different genres of writings, including her family chronicles *The Great Books of the Clifford Family*, letters to her mother, and voluminous diaries that document her life from youth to old age. Nevertheless the fact that she saw her life in terms of documents, evidence, and records was, perhaps, a consequence of her thirty-eight-year legal struggle to claim her right of succession. Indeed, Barbara Lewalski argues, 'by definition the diary is a private genre, yet it seems likely from the format that Anne ... may have decided to preserve the segment we have as a record for posterity of her most momentous years in the struggle over her lands' (1993, 141). In her detailed study of Lady Anne's diaries, Lewalski notes that they record not only public duties (typical subjects pertaining to men's roles and activities in travel and military diaries) but also household and family activities (the customary subjects of women's domestic diaries). More surprisingly, her diaries describe her motives and emotions – intimate statements of self-revelation atypical of the genre in the seventeenth century. As a result, her diaries blur the conventions and boundaries of public and private genres of writing.

In letters and her diaries, Lady Anne, to modern readers, seems to find a private context in which she can articulate her personhood and contest others who deny her legal rights. In letters written to Lady Anne, her mother Lady Margaret Russell advised her about the conduct and expression of her affairs because her letters, in fact, could function as legal documents rather than private writings. For example, when Sackville cancelled Lady Anne's jointure, her mother wrote, on 22 September 1615, that he respected neither his duty to his wife and child nor their rights: 'it seems he hath not tasted of true spiritual comforts that so much forget that saying of the apostle, he is worse than an infidel that provides not for his wife and family. Then he that hath not a heart to defend their rights, wants the true spirit of God.' Nevertheless, while confidently referring to the Bible as the authority that condemned Sackville and affirmed her daughter's rights, Lady Margaret advised discretion:

Lay all on me and neither cross him in words but keep your resolutions with silence and what gentle persuasion you can, but alter not from your own wise course ... You have written to Masters Crackenthorpe which letter was opened by chance, that whether my Lord would let you or not, if I would have you come [to visit me] you would come against his will. Dear heart be very wary what you say but most wary what you write for they desire to have advantage and to sever my Lord and you, as they let me from my Lord. (cited from Lewalski 1993, 135)

Lady Margaret's counsel indicates her knowledge that the diaries and letters in which her daughter voiced her grievances were not, as might be assumed, private genres but were, potentially, documents that could be used publicly as evidence. As a result of her awareness of the different, possible functions of her letters and diaries, Lady Anne, with the aid of her mother, produced and preserved written documents which, for modern readers, constitute a narrative that clarifies her understanding of herself, particularly her legal rights.

Elizabeth Wiseman and her brothers, similarly, wrote and collected a variety of genres, private and legal, that used a rhetoric of liberty as an attribute and right of the self in order to protect their sister from commodification. Her letters show her as an intelligent woman, aware of her independence but also aware that her social context is an aspect of her self-definition. She wishes to remain within that context (unlike her aunt, Lady Dacres). She is not, in principle, opposed to a second marriage if that is what her supportive brothers think best, but she recognizes her wealth as part of herself: it will buy her property, certainly, and to that degree is alienable, but it will also secure for her social status, respect, and independence, and to that degree it is, to her, inalienable.

Both Elizabeth Wiseman and Lady Anne Clifford refer to marriage and family in a manner that indicates these institutions and their office of wife, in particular, in Radin's terms, define the contextual aspect of their personhood. This explains why Elizabeth Wiseman, once married to the Earl of Yarmouth in a marriage which had mostly to do with family honour, petitioned the Queen in 1690 to be permitted to join her husband, who had been committed to the Tower as an open supporter of James II (Chan 1998, 103). It also explains, what many modern readers cannot comprehend, Lady Anne's loving and deferential references to her coercive first husband. She understood marriage as an office that was the context in which she must define herself. Lady Anne accepts her subordination to her husband in all matters excluding her right of succession. Her obedience and deference to him in all other matters most clearly reveals her belief that her right of succession should not be alienated to a collateral male relative. In defying her husband, she exercised the liberty of her office as an heir and property owner in order to fulfil her obligations and duties to her family – a family that, her diaries indicate, she believed included both deceased as well as living and unborn persons. To Lady Anne, her female ancestors, in particular, not only represented legal precedents for her to claim her right of succession but also imposed upon her an obligation to contest the commodification and possible alienation of her rights to Westmorland.

The courtship of Elizabeth Wiseman and the first marriage of Lady Anne Clifford both reveal the conflict of the offices of property owner and married woman. The liberty of a property owner – that is, the legal right to succeed to a property, in Lady Anne's case, and the right to dispose of her fortune through a marriage to which she consents, in Elizabeth Wiseman's case – conflicted with their obligation as marriageable women of property to subordinate those rights to the potential honour, status, and wealth of their families. In these cases different notions of their inheritances – their understanding of them as inalienable attribute-properties and some of their male relatives' view of them as alienable and marketable objects to be transferred to others – interact and conflict. Most tellingly it is the commodified view of these women's property that, according to their writings, both women identify as the cause of their estrangement from the roles and duties they desire to fulfil.

Notes

1 On property-based marriages among the aristocracy and gentry see Erickson (1993), Harris (2002), Spring (1993), and Staves (1990).
2 Condren explains that in seventeenth-century England, 'The activities of ruling, obeying, leading, following, advising, trading, administering, nurturing, nursing, marrying, curing (souls and bodies), were all offices compounded of rights and duties' (1997, 466).
3 All the letters and documents written by Elizabeth Wiseman and her family about her pursuit by Spencer are collected in Chan (1998).
4 See discussions of Lady Anne Clifford's inheritance in Acheson (1995, 1–14), Clay (1905, 387–92), Coward (1971, 194–215), English (1990, 81), Lamb (1992, 346–68), and Lewalski (1993, 125–52).
5 Spring explains the consequences of the Statute of Wills (1540) to an heiress: with that statute 'the common law rules of succession, long evaded in practice, were officially on the way to becoming default rules, rules that would apply only upon intestacy' (1993, 32).
6 See Lamb (1992, 366), who argues that Lady Anne used iconography in order to attribute to herself the agency customarily wielded by a noble, male landlord.
7 See Staves (1990, 33, 43) on the use of fines to convey dower lands.
8 Condren (1997, 461) explains the interrelation of the concepts of office, liberty, and identity.
9 See Radin's analysis of the consequences of using market rhetoric to describe things not customarily valued solely in economic terms (1996, 1–15).
10 Cf. Harris's conclusions about marriage among aristocratic women: 'although individual aristocratic women might criticize or quarrel with their male relatives, there is no evidence that as a group they imagined an essential difference between their interests and those of their male kin or that they articulated ambitions for themselves that were incompatible with their duties in the family. Instead, they contributed to the social reproduction of their families' (2002, 9).
11 Spencer's deposition before the Consistory Court survives in the London Metropolitan Archives (DL/C/144) and is reproduced in part in Travitsky and Prescott (2000, 403–11).

12 Her marriage to Yarmouth might well have been promoted, at least partly, as a family convenience. In 1684 Dudley North as Commissioner of Customs had refused to support a renewal of Yarmouth's timber farm, a lucrative source which would have assisted the earl's financial affairs, and so a marriage to the wealthy sister might well have been a sort of compensation. The Earl of Yarmouth is known to have accumulated 'vast debts' by 1708. See Ketton-Cremer (1944, 22–57). When Yarmouth died in 1732 he was declared bankrupt.

13 Some letters to her sister, Anne Foley, and to her niece, also Anne Foley, survive in British Library MSS Additional 32500 and 32501.

Works Cited

Acheson, Katherine O. 1995. Introduction to *The Diary of Anne Clifford 1616– 1619: A Critical Edition*, ed. Katherine O. Acheson, 1–14. New York and London: Garland.

Buck, A.R. 1987. 'A Blot on the Certificate': Dower and Women's Property Rights in Colonial New South Wales. *Australian Journal of Law & Society* 4: 87–102.

Chan, Mary, ed. 1995. *The Life of the Lord Keeper North by Roger North*. Lewiston: Edwin Mellen.

– ed. 1998. *Life into Story: The Courtship of Elizabeth Wiseman*. Aldershot: Ashgate.

Clay, J.W. 1905. The Clifford Family. *The Yorkshire Archaeological Journal* 18: 354–411.

Clifford, Lady Anne. 1992. *The Diaries of Lady Anne Clifford*, ed. D.J.H. Clifford. Stroud: Alan Sutton.

Condren, Conal. 1997. Liberty of Office and Its Defence in Seventeenth-Century Political Argument. *History of Political Thought* 18.3: 460–82.

Cooper, J.P. 1955–6. The Counting of Manors. *The Economic History Review* 2nd ser. 8: 377–89.

Coward, B. 1971. Disputed Inheritances: Some Difficulties of the Nobility in the Late Sixteenth and Early Seventeenth Centuries. *Bulletin of the Institute of Historical Research* 44: 194–215.

English, Barbara. 1990. *The Great Landowners of East Yorkshire 1530–1910*. New York: Harvester Wheatsheaf.

Erickson, Amy Louise. 1993. *Women and Property in Early Modern England*. London and New York: Routledge.

Harris, Barbara J. 2002. *English Aristocratic Women, 1450–1550: Marriage and*

Family, Property and Careers. Oxford: Oxford University Press.

Ketton-Cremer, R.W. 1944. *Norfolk Portraits.* London: Faber.

Lamb, Mary Ellen. 1992. The Agency of the Split Subject: Lady Anne Clifford and the Uses of Reading. *English Literary Renaissance* 22: 346–68.

Lewalski, Barbara Keifer. 1993. *Writing Women in Jacobean England.* Cambridge: Harvard University Press.

Radin, Margaret Jane. 1993. *Reinterpreting Property.* Chicago: University of Chicago Press.

– 1996. *Contested Commodities.* Cambridge: Harvard University Press.

Spring, Eileen. 1993. *Law, Land, and Family: Aristocratic Inheritance in England, 1300 to 1800.* Chapel Hill and London: University of North Carolina Press.

Staves, Susan. 1990. *Married Women's Separate Property in England, 1660–1833.* Cambridge, MA: Harvard University Press.

Travitsky, Betty S., and Anne Lake Prescott, eds. 2000. *Female and Male Voices in Early Modern England: An Anthology of Renaissance Writing.* New York: Columbia University Press.

8

Cordelia's Estate: Women and the Law of Property from Shakespeare to Nahum Tate

A.R. BUCK

Much has been written on the dramatic differences between Shakespeare's *King Lear* and Nahum Tate's *King Lear*.[1] The different fate of Cordelia in the two plays, for instance, is striking. In Shakespeare's play, Cordelia is stripped of her inheritance at the beginning, never to recover it, and, like Lear, ultimately dies. In Tate's play, Lear lives to give away the bride (to Edgar) and the inheritance passes smoothly from one generation to the next. In this intergenerational passing of property, it is not Cordelia who inherits in her own right; she is, however, the conduit through which the property stays in the family. Greater emphasis is placed on issues of 'legitimacy' and 'virtue' in Tate. As we shall see, this is crucial to understanding not only important differences between the two versions of *King Lear* but also aspects of the relationship between women and property in late seventeenth-century England. Between the early seventeenth century, when Shakespeare wrote, and the later seventeenth century, when Nahum Tate wrote, there were dramatic changes to the laws of property and to the legal status of aristocratic women and men – changes which had significant implications for the status and agency of women. Those changes would, moreover, have informed the values and attitudes of Tate's audience. Consequently, if we examine the question of Cordelia's inheritance in historical context, what might it reveal? This is the question with which this chapter is concerned.

Cordelia's Estate

In order to grapple with that question we need to have some understanding of the character of society and property at the beginning of the seventeenth century, when Shakespeare wrote *King Lear*. A historical example, known to literary scholars, may serve as a useful template. Brian Annesley, the Queen's Master of Harriers, and substantial Kentish landowner, had three daughters, Grace, Christian, and Cordelia.[2] In a will he made in April 1600, Annesley left the vast bulk of his estates to Cordelia, with significantly lesser shares to the other daughters. Annesley had become senile by 1603 and lived with Cordelia, who managed both his affairs and his estates. The eldest daughter Grace and her husband, Sir John Wildgoose, sought to have the will overturned. Had this happened the property would have devolved on Annesley's death by virtue of the inheritance custom of Kent, known as gavelkind, whereby equal partibility prevailed. From the perspective of Lady Grace and Sir John Wildgoose, this was the only way to undo the unequal division of Annesley's estates. Since the Statute of Wills in 1540, the common law recognized testamentary disposition, something previously denied by the common law. But since the amendment to that statute in 1543, the testator had to be of 'perfect health and memory' for the will to be valid. Lady Grace and Sir John argued before the prerogative Court of Canterbury that Annesley's mental infirmity was sufficient ground to invalidate the will; they failed, however, when the Court decided to uphold the will, arguing that Annesley had never been declared a lunatic.

The case of Brian Annesley's will suggests tantalizing connections between the state of the law of inheritance in early seventeenth-century England and the representation of the law of inheritance in Shakespeare's *King Lear*. The similarity between reality and literature is striking; indeed, it has been suggested that Shakespeare was aware of the Annesley case.[3] The possible connections between the case of Annesley's will and Shakespeare's *King Lear* are of less interest, however, than what the Annesley case reveals about the state of both the law of property and women's legal status at the time. Annesley's daughter Cordelia, like Shakespeare's Cordelia, exercises considerable power and influence. Annesley's daughter succeeds in managing the affairs and estates of her invalid father and successfully resists legal attempts to wrest the estates from her. Shakespeare's Cordelia reenters the kingdom with an army to avenge her wronged father, although she ultimately fails in her efforts. Both narratives reveal the predatory nature of social relationships, but in the Annesley case the legal dispute is fought out within the boundaries of the law as they existed in the early seventeenth century. In order to understand how much had changed by the time of Tate's *King Lear*, it is important to understand the state of the law as it existed in Shakespeare's age.

The Laws Regulating Inheritance and Succession in
Early Seventeenth-Century England

In the early seventeenth century lawyers and landowners had not yet responded effectively to the impact of the Statute of Uses of 1535 on inheritance and succession. In the sixteenth century the common law did not recognize testamentary capacity, only the common law rules of inheritance. The most important rule was that of primogeniture. When an heir came into his or her inheritance, moreover, the Crown could exact heavy feudal incidents. As a result landowners and their lawyers designed ways of securing testamentary capacity while at the same time avoiding feudal taxation. They did this by way of the conveyancing instrument known as the use. The use was a procedure in which the legal interest in the estate was divested from the owner and vested in another party (a group of trustees) and the land was held for 'the use of' the owner and whoever else was indicated in the settlement which effected the use. In this way the estate was entailed, for one purpose of the settlement was to allow for the testamentary capacity that the law prohibited. The estate was held by the trustees on behalf of (usually) the eldest son, who would resettle the estate on taking up his inheritance on his majority. With respect to the struggle between the aristocracy and the Crown over the payment of feudal taxation, the implications of the use were profound. As the legal estate was divested from the owner, then the owner's death and the subsequent transfer of the estate to his heir did not affect the legal estate. As a result all the feudal incidents normally payable when the heir came into his inheritance could be avoided, because under the use the heir was not the legal owner. Moreover, the secrecy of the transactions provided by the use masked the identification of the true owner, further facilitating the evasion of feudal taxation. Consequently, the use facilitated the perpetuation of family estates over many generations, protecting the estate from both without and within.

In 1529 Henry VIII began a concerted campaign to regain his depleted feudal incidents. The result was a victory for Henry when Parliament agreed to pass the Statute of Uses in 1535 (see Buck 1990). The Statute of Uses invalidated the use by simply enacting that the equitable owner was also the legal owner. Notoriety replaced secrecy, making the evasion of taxes more difficult. Also, without the use land could not be transferred from one generation to the next by will, only by the inflexible rules of inheritance. Concessions were wrought from the Crown by Parliament in the Statute of Wills in 1540, most notably the legitimacy of

devisory capacity. Henceforth, it was possible to make a will. But lawyers
and landowners were to struggle to replace the use (and all that it
provided) for many decades. It was only with the rise of the strict settlement in the second half of the seventeenth century that they succeeded
in doing this. Consequently, the ability of the landed aristocracy, who
were the principal landowners, as well as the lesser gentry, to secure their
landed status and power through the law was considerably different at
the turn of the century when Shakespeare wrote than it was in the early
1680s when Nahum Tate wrote his version of *King Lear*. The legal strategies available to the aristocracy were circumscribed by the state of the law
at the time. Women had, perhaps, a less definite role in the relationship
between law and aristocratic inheritance at the beginning of the century
than at the end. In order to understand the changing legal status of
women in relation to property and inheritance during the seventeenth
century it is necessary to first understand the broad contours of social,
economic, and legal change.

Property Law and the Aristocratic Ascendancy of the Late Seventeenth Century

When Charles II was invited back to restore the monarchy it was not
without important concessions. In 1660 the Restoration Parliament enacted 12 Car. II, c.24, An Act Taking Away the Court of Wards and
Liveries, and Tenures in Capite, and by Knight Service, and Purveyance,
and for Settling a Revenue upon His Majesty in Lieu Thereof, commonly
know as the Statute of Tenures. That piece of legislation swept away
feudal tenures, along with the Court of Wards and Liveries. It has long
been realized that the consequences of that Act were profound. For Sir
William Blackstone the Statute 'was a greater acquisition to the civil
property of this kingdom than even *Magna Carta* itself; since that only
pruned the luxuriances that had grown out of the military tenures, and
thereby preserved them in vigour; but the Statute of King Charles extir-
pated the whole, and demolished both root and branches' ([1766] 1979,
2: 77). Harold Perkin has claimed that through a process of political and
economic consolidation culminating in the Statute of Tenures, 'the
landed aristocracy and gentry defeated the claims of the peasants, the
Church and the Crown, and turned lordship into absolute ownership'
(1968, 135). Indeed, he goes on to claim that 'This was the decisive
change in English history which made it different from the continent.
From it every other difference in English society stemmed' (1968, 135).

When the landowners of the Restoration Parliament abolished the oner-
ous incidents of military tenures along with those tenures themselves,
they were careful to preserve those incidents that they could call upon
from their own tenants. In such a context of aristocratic ascendancy it
was crucial that legal titles be sound and secure. With this in mind we
may understand the importance of the Statute of Frauds of 1677, the rise
of the strict settlement, and the establishment of the rule against perpetuities in 1681.

The importance accorded to the marketable potential of landed property after the Restoration had troubling legal consequences. As Sir Matthew Hale, Chief Justice of the King's Bench, observed from the Bench
in *Buckridge v. Shirley* (1671): 'It is come to pass now, that every thing is
made an action on the case, and actions on the case are become one of
the great grievances of the nation; for two men cannot talk together, but
one fellow or other, who stands in a corner, swears a promise or cause of
action. These catching promises must not be encouraged' (Simpson
1987, 603). Such a state of affairs could be seen as particularly troubling
in a litigious age – and the mid-seventeenth century was particularly
litigious. When one considers the rapidly expanding commercial potential of landed property and of commerce generally, it should come as no
surprise that a property-owning Parliament should consider reforming
the law so as to discourage verbal commercial agreements with relation
to land. The type of impetuous division of the land undertaken verbally
by King Lear in Shakespeare's play was precisely the type of activity that
law reformers wished to discourage in the second half of the seventeenth
century. In 1677 a property-owning Parliament passed the Statute of
Frauds. Its object was to prevent fraudulent dealings of a commercial
nature, particularly with respect to landed property. Its most important
provisions were, first, that all conveyances of land be in writing in order
to be enforceable in a court of law. Second, it required that when the
value of an estate exceeded thirty pounds, a will be attested to by three
witnesses, and that no verbal will could revoke a written will. In this way,
'truth' and 'virtue' were to be incorporated into dealings involving land
and wealth. This also facilitated the commercialization and commodification
of landed property. But the commodification of property was tempered in
aristocratic eyes by the desire for dynastic succession.

As the political and economic power of the landed aristocracy grew in
the late seventeenth century, it came to be realized that landed property
(and all the political, social, and economic power that it afforded)
needed to be on a substantial – indeed massive – scale to effectively

secure its privileges. 'Nothing,' commented Edmund Burke at the end of the eighteenth century,

> is a due and adequate representation of a state, that does not represent its ability as well as its property. But as ability is a vigorous and active principle, and as property is sluggish, inert and timid, it can never be safe from the invasions of ability, unless it be, out of all proportion, predominant in the representation. It must be represented too in great masses of accumulation, or it is not rightly protected. ([1793] 1969, 140)

The importance placed on this landed status ensured that the mechanics of preserving estates through generations was of crucial concern. The principal method of intergenerational estate preservation was achieved by the strict settlement, a conveyancing procedure developed in the second half of the seventeenth century.[4]

The purpose of the strict settlement was to remove the power of alienation from the owner of the estate, placing it in trust for his eldest son. This was achieved by drafting an instrument that placed the legal interest in the estate into the hands of trustees for a long period of time (usually 500 to 1,000 years). The fee simple was then held in trust for the eldest son, while the owner retained a life interest over the estate. A new interest had thereby been created: the fee tail, or entail, and the settlor had become the tenant in tail. The trustees were usually empowered under the settlement to use their control of the legal interest in the estate to raise mortgages to provide for the owner's wife and children. As the settlement would normally be made at his majority or at his marriage, the settlor would provide for an ultimate retainer, in default of children, to himself in fee simple. When the son obtained his inheritance he was persuaded to resettle the estate, as his forefathers had done, by placing the fee simple in trust for his (perhaps unborn) eldest son. In this way no one actually possessed the power to sell the estate except when a new settlement was being drawn up. Although the system was voluntary, familial and social expectations could be buttressed by the son's prospects of suffering a lack of funds during his father's lifetime, consequent upon the father's life interest in the estate. The strict settlement was, in essence, a more sophisticated version of what 'the use' had achieved in the sixteenth century. With respect to the position of women, it should be obvious that the settlement manifested a language of the market; marriage was, in a very real sense, a market transaction.[5] This is shown clearly in those legal cases where the family of either the groom or the bride borrowed clandestinely in order to be able to represent themselves as being good for the portion expected.[6] Together, the strict settlement and the custom of primogeniture as it applied to the aristocratic title ensured that the aristocracy remained landed, just as great estates remained aristocratic. The perpetuation of the nexus between land and title, moreover, secured what E.P. Thompson has called 'corporate inheritance – the means by which a social group has extended its historical tenure of status and of privilege' (1976, 360). But the desire for dynastic succession was, in turn, tempered by the commercial advantages to be derived from freedom of alienation. It is with this in mind that we can understand the importance of the rule against perpetuities.

The rule against perpetuities established that an interest would not be tied up for longer than twenty-one years after the life in being at the creation of the interest. The rule is designed to address fetters on alienability yet provide a period of suitable length in which strategies of dynastic succession might be implemented. The rule was established by Lord Nottingham's decision in *The Duke of Norfolk's Case*[7] and subsequent decisions.[8] During the Middle Ages the courts favoured freedom of alienation. Landowners, however, had dynastic pretensions, which conflicted with freedom of alienation. This led to a tension, both among the landowners themselves and in the law, between the desire to secure dynastic succession, which required restricting freedom of alienation, and the desire to exploit one's land commercially, which necessitated freedom of alienation. Lawyers attempted to design 'unbreakable' entails for their landowner clients, which required the courts to introduce rules against such 'perpetuities.' Perpetuities, therefore, are best understood as an entail or trust that could potentially last forever.[9] But these rules against perpetuities, laid down in response to specific cases brought before the courts in the sixteenth and seventeenth centuries, were simply negative: they provided no positive guide as to what limitations on freedom of alienation were valid. Herein lies the importance of Lord Nottingham's judgment in *The Duke of Norfolk's Case*.

The facts of the case are interesting in themselves, as they provide a fascinating analogue to some of the issues of Tate's *King Lear*. In 1647 the Earl of Arundel and Surrey decided to draft a will that accommodated the interests of his three sons: Thomas, the eldest son who would inherit the title; Henry; and Charles (see Haskins 1977). The problem was that Thomas was insane, and the earldom and the landed status of the earldom might have been jeopardized were Thomas to succeed to the property. So the earl instructed his conveyancer, Sir Orlando Bridgman (who is often credited with the invention of the strict settlement), to construct an instrument whereby Henry should have substantial income

from the property during Thomas's lifetime, and if Thomas predeceased
Henry without issue and the title thereby passed to Henry, then Charles
should, in turn, have substantial income from the property. Bridgman
accordingly constructed an instrument whereby, after the death of the
earl, the property was to be held in trust for the benefit of the second
son, Henry, and the heirs male of his body, but if Thomas predeceased
Henry without issue, then the trust was to be for the benefit of the
younger brother Charles and the heirs male of his body. The earl died in
1651 and Thomas succeeded to the earldom. Arrangements were made
for Thomas to live out his life in Padua and he never took possession of
the estate. In the early 1660s, following the Restoration, Henry occupied
Arundel House. In 1675, when Thomas died, Henry instigated proceedings to forestall the trust passing to his brother Charles. Charles brought
a proceeding in Chancery to protect his interest and Henry argued that
Charles's interest was a perpetuity and therefore void. The presiding
judge, Lord Nottingham, had to decide what constituted a perpetuity.
Nottingham ruled in favour of Charles, and subsequent decisions established that the appropriate period was a life or lives of those 'in being'
when the deed or will took effect, plus twenty-one years (Simpson 1986,
225–6). As in Tate's *King Lear*, it had become crucial that the landed
estate be protected from those who lacked the mental capacity to care
for and improve it. The financial stakes alone were too high to do
otherwise. And the best way to protect it was through an inheritance
strategy based on legitimacy of title.

The collective importance of these legal developments on the culture
of property, and on the legal roles and status of both women and men in
late seventeenth-century England, was considerable. The changes to the
law had established strategies for aristocratic and elite succession in a
world where, increasingly, as Burke was to note in the following century,
property was 'predominant in the representation.' By the late seventeenth century a confident, aristocratic age had dawned, a world where
the demands of commerce and power were articulated in a language
that alluded to 'truth' and 'virtue.' This is the legal context in which we
may appreciate the literary representation of women, such as Cordelia,
in seventeenth-century England.

Cordelia in Context

In Shakespeare's *King Lear* inheritance is notable by its failure. Lear's
attempt to divide the kingdom ends in chaos. All is lost. But if one

focuses on the question of inheritance in Tate the differences are striking. In Tate's *King Lear* a land–family nexus has been brought into existence – defined and effected through inheritance. This is not to say that Cordelia has acquired individual property rights, but rather that her legal status as legitimate wife and daughter allows for the perpetuation, not just of the land, but of the family, or more to the point, the landed family.

The problem of securing landed estates from alienation that preoccupied landowners among Shakespeare's audiences was magnified within his play by having not one aristocrat's estate but the entire kingdom threatened with alienation from the king and his heirs. Lear improvises a ceremony intended to implement an inequitable division of property among his three daughters. That ceremony, spoken and incomplete, results in an insecure title to the family lands and an insecure entitlement to the Crown. No complete written document records the title to the estates that Lear bequeaths to his two heirs, the husbands of Goneril and Regan. Lear's hastily spoken words 'With my two daughters' dowers digest the third' (1.1.122) are the only clear statement of the title to the land. He wastes his words on denouncing his youngest daughter, divesting her of his love and honour as well as her potential inheritance. It is important that in Shakespeare's play Cordelia seeks to recover not her landed inheritance but instead her honour:

> I yet beseech your majesty ...
> that you make known
> It is no vicious blot, murder, or foulness,
> That have deprived me of your grace and favour. (1.1.218–24)

When France takes her as his wife it is with the belief that Cordelia, although a 'dowerless daughter,' is a worthy bride; it is her 'virtue' that makes her an appropriate consort and 'queen of us, of ours, and our fair France' (1.1.252). On her marriage she does not transmit to her husband a clear title to landed estates or other wealth, only her virtue. Ultimately, Cordelia's marriage leads to France's invasion of England. It is a vivid representation of the threats to the land–family bond. It was the land–family bond that the aristocracy sought but, before the legal developments of the later seventeenth century, lacked the means to secure.

The radical insecurity of the land–family nexus in Shakespeare's tragedy is displaced from Tate's *King Lear*, in which the kingdom is transmitted to the legitimate, married heir, Cordelia's husband. For Tate's audiences secure and *legitimate* title to landed estates was of paramount importance. With the Restoration the aristocracy secured the abolition of feudal incidents, which preserved landowners' wealth for investment and improvement of their own lands and the enclosed commons. In addition, the Statute of Frauds enabled them to rely on clear and legiti- mate titles to land. This was perhaps of more importance, in their view: new statute law prevented fraudulent transactions that could deplete estates. Impediments to legal devices for maintaining continuity of the land–family bond in this period arose not from the Crown but from judges, whose decisions sought to maintain a balance between landown- ers' desire to prevent alienation of their estates and the nation's need for a market in land. After the Restoration the aristocracy, although pre- vented from creating perpetual entails, could rely upon the strict settle- ment to prevent alienation of their estates and statutory law to protect them from fraudulent titles to land.

Those are the twinned issues that Tate's *Lear* presents as secured within the world of the play. Continuity of the land–family bond is secured by Cordelia's marriage, which represents the transmission of the kingdom/land by legitimate title. The pun upon 'title' is crucial to an appreciation of the play's representation of the discourses of property and family circulating in legal and aristocratic culture at this time. Gloucester's legitimate son retains his own title as earl and gains through marriage to Cordelia a clear and legitimate title to her family's land. It is also worthy of note that while Cordelia's 'virtue' is foregrounded in Tate, it is now inextricably bound to the spoils of inheritance. In the opening scene of Shakespeare's *King Lear* Cordelia is concerned for her honour, not her inheritance. In the final scene of Tate's *King Lear*, with the prospect of legitimate marriage to Edgar and the attendant inheritance, Cordelia's final line is imbued with the language of market rhetoric: 'Nor do I blush to own myself o'paid / For all my sufferings past' (5.6.143–4).[10]

In Shakespeare, Cordelia stands alone, exercises power, and loses all. In Tate, Cordelia is defined by her purity, her love for Edgar, and her legitimacy as Lear's 'true' child. She exercises little power but is enor- mously important in effecting the smooth transition of Lear's estates from one generation to the next. The parallels with the changes to property law and the status of the landed classes during the seventeenth century are striking. As the landed aristocracy in particular consolidated the gains made consequent upon the passage of the Statute of Tenures in 1660, new demands upon, and expectations of, property required legal adaptation. The rise of the strict settlement, the passage of the Statute of Frauds in 1677, and the rule in the *Duke of Norfolk's Case* in 1681 respecting perpetuities were all evidence of the changing constellation of rights and roles of landed women and men in a society where property and power were inextricably intertwined. Were these legal developments gendered? Here I would agree with Mary Murray that:

> Where individual legal subjects – citizens – are empowered by property ... *state regulated individualism,* rather than calculated disempowering of women as a category, provided the soil in which gendered divisions were nurtured. The working out of *class* relations, notably around ownership as a condition of legal individuality, was basic in defining the parameters of women's access to political power within the state. (1995, 96)

If one compares Shakespeare's Cordelia with Tate's Cordelia, she seems, by 1681, to have taken on a defined (and confining) role as virtuous and legitimate daughter and betrothed, in order that the expectations of a social order based on property be fulfilled.

Conclusion: 'Fine word, "legitimate"'

The growing emphasis on legitimacy, of birth and of title, was crucial in an age when so much depended on correcting defects of title. In Tate's *King Lear* the emphasis shifts, from the very beginning, to the question of inheritance and of the bastard, Edmund.

> Well then, legitimate Edgar, to thy right
> Of Law I will oppose a bastard's cunning.
> Our father's love is to the bastard Edmund
> As to legitimate Edgar. With success
> I've practised yet on both their easy natures.
> Here comes the old man chafed with th'information
> Which last I forged against my brother Edgar:
> A tale so plausible, so boldly uttered,
> And heightened by such lucky accidents
> That now the slightest circumstance confirms him,
> And base-born Edmund spite of law inherits. (1.1.11–21)

The word 'legitimate' in Shakespeare's *King Lear* resonates with ambiguities as Edmund questions the grounds of authority upon which the aristocracy's practice of primogeniture rests. Bastardy, baseness, and illegitimacy are unquestionable impediments to his attainment of the title of 'Gloucester.' However, his father, like Lear, ignores legal rules, custom, and precedent in order to act upon his own judgment and thereby loses his own life and endangers that of his 'legitimate' heir, Edgar. It is the chaos that follows upon that abandonment of law and precedent rather than the eventual righting of the true heir that Shakespeare emphasizes.

Tate treats the issue of inheritance in a more direct manner than Shakespeare. In Tate's *Lear*, Edmund's 'crime' of illegitimacy is compounded by his sexual libertinism. His behaviour can be contrasted with Cordelia's fidelity to her one true love, Edgar. Indeed, in stark contrast to the sexually rapacious, 'untrue' son, Edmund, who covets the entire kingdom, Cordelia is willing to forgo her inheritance rather than compromise either her romantic love for Edgar or her 'true' filial love for her father:

> Now comes my Trial, how I am distrest,
> that must with cold speech tempt the chol'rick King
> Rather to leave me Dowerless, than condemn me
> To loath'd Embraces! (1.1.92–5)

It is not without meaning that just as Tate's *King Lear* begins with a speech by the illegitimate son, Edmund, who coveted the inheritance, it concludes with a speech by the legitimate son, Edgar, who, in marriage to the virtuous Cordelia, comes into an even larger inheritance. It is, moreover, a concluding speech full of references to legitimacy, virtue, triumph, and even sexual potency – all applauded in a context of legal legitimacy and moral virtue. It, like the play as a whole, indicates the important, yet confined, role of Cordelia in this confident future:

> Our drooping country now erects her head,
> Peace spreads her balmy wings and Plenty blooms.
> Divine Cordelia, all the gods can witness
> How much thy love to empire I prefer!
> Thy bright example shall convince the world
> (Whatever storms of fortune are decreed)
> That truth and virtue shall at last succeed. (5.6.154–60)[11]

Legitimacy of legal title was merely one side of a doubled-sided coin; in a world where the mechanics of corporate inheritance were of paramount concern to the landed elite, both sexual licentiousness and the possibility of illegitimacy were potentially as worrying as a defect in the title. Tate's juxtaposition of Edmund's illegitimacy and licentiousness to Cordelia's purity – indeed, her purity being an indication of legitimacy – would have captured the concerns of a late seventeenth-century audience. It is only fitting, in such a play, that it be Cordelia who is rewarded for her virtue. Tate's Cordelia, as Jean Marsden (1991, 50) astutely points out, does not, like Shakespeare's Cordelia, appear at the head of an army to avenge the wrongs done to her father, but instead relies on her beauty and her tears. It would be unthinkable to Tate's audience that Goneril and Regan, both competing for the illegitimate sexual favours of Edmund, would benefit from the inheritance. Rather, Cordelia has shown her fitness for her role, which is to be the conduit by which the inheritance passes from one generation to the next in a world of confident, aristocratic, propertied values. At the end of the play Lear lives, Cordelia lives, but perhaps of more importance, the landed status of the family survives. And it survives precisely because Cordelia's role is not to lead an army but to take her place in a complex inheritance grid.

Notes

1 See, for example, Hardman (2000), Massai (2000), Strier (1995), Maguire (1991), Nameri (1976), and Spencer (1972).
2 The name is spelled both Cordelia and Cordell in the documents. The case has received detailed treatment by Wilson (1993, 215–30). I would like to thank Arthur Kinney for bringing this reference to my attention.
3 This is particularly so with regard to the legal challenge by his daughter Lady Grace Wildgoose and her husband, Sir John Wildgoose, when the Fool warns Lear of how children might perceive a father's actions, as: 'Winter's not gone yet, if the wild geese fly that way' (2.4.43) (Halio, 1992, 4).
4 The literature on the strict settlement is extensive. See English and Saville (1983), Bonfield (1983), and Spring (1993). The following passage draws on Buck (1995).
5 Cf. the discussion of commodification or 'market rhetoric' in the section on the marriage of Elizabeth Wiseman in chapter 7 this book.
6 *Redman v. Redman* (1685) 1 Vern 348; *Gale v. Lindo* (1687) 2 Vern 475. See further, Pottage (1998).
7 (1681) 2 Swanst. 454.
8 *Stanley v. Leigh* (1732) 2 P. Wms. at p. 689 (Jekyll, M.R.); *Stephens v. Stephens* (1736) Ca. Temp. Talbot, 228; *Heath v. Heath* (1781) 1 Bro. C.C. 147 (Lord

Thurlow); *Jee v. Audley* (1787) 1 Cox, 324 (Kenyon, M.R.); *Caldell v. Palmer* (1833) 1 Cl. & F. 372.

9 Although fee tails could potentially last forever, they could be 'barred,' that is, transferred into a freely alienable fee simple by means of the legal strategies known as a 'fine' or 'recovery.' Consequently, the rules against perpetuities were not concerned with entails per se, but instead with fetters on alienability.

10 All references are from Tate (1976).

11 I have normalized spelling of the word 'viture' in Black's edition (Tate 1976), which seems to be a typographical error, as the word is spelled 'vertue' in the facsimile of the 1681 edition (Tate [1681] 1969).

Works Cited

Blackstone, William. [1765–9] 1979. *Commentaries on the Laws of England*, ed. A.W.B. Simpson. 4 vols. Facsimile ed. Chicago: University of Chicago Press.

Bonfield, Lloyd. 1983. *Marriage Settlements, 1601–1740: The Adoption of the Strict Settlement.* Cambridge: Cambridge University Press.

Buck, A.R. 1990. The Politics of Land Law in Tudor England, 1529–1540. *Journal of Legal History* 11: 200–15.

– 1995. Property, Aristocracy and the Reform of the Land Law in Early Nineteenth Century England. *Journal of Legal History* 16: 63–93.

Burke, Edmund. 1969. *Reflections on the Revolution in France*, ed. Conor Cruise O'Brien. Harmondsworth: Penguin.

English, Barbara, and John Saville. 1983. *Strict Settlement: A Guide for Historians.* Hull: University of Hull Press.

Halio, Jay L. 1992. Introduction to *The Tragedy of King Lear*, ed. Jay L. Halio, 1–89. Cambridge: Cambridge University Press.

Hardman, C.B. 2000. 'Our drooping country now erects her head': Nahum Tate's *History of King Lear. Modern Language Review* 95: 913–23.

Haskins, George L. 1977. Extending the Grasp of the Dead Hand: Reflections on the Origins of the Rule against Perpetuities. *University of Pennsylvania Law Review* 26: 19–46.

Maguire, Nancy Klein. 1991. Nahum Tate's *King Lear*. 'The king's blest restoration.' In *The Appropriation of Shakespeare: Post-Renaissance Reconstructions of the Works and the Myth*, ed. Jean I. Marsden, 29–43. New York: Harvester Wheatsheaf.

Marsden, Jean I. 1991. Rewritten Women: Shakespearean Heroines in the Restoration. In *The Appropriation of Shakespeare: Post-Renaissance Reconstructions of the Works and the Myth*, ed. Jean I. Marsden, 43–56. New York: Harvester Wheatsheaf.

Massai, Sonia. 2000. Nahum Tate's Revision of Shakespeare's *King Lear*. *Studies in English Literature, 1500–1900* 40: 435–50.

Murray, Mary. 1995. *The Law of the Father? Patriarchy and the Transition from Feudalism to Capitalism.* London: Routledge.

Nameri, Dorothy E. 1976. *Three Versions of the Story of King Lear.* 2 vols. Salzburg: Institut fur Englische Sprache und Literatur.

Perkin, H.J. 1968. The Social Causes of the British Industrial Revolution. *Transactions of the Royal Historical Society* 5th ser. 18: 123–43.

Pottage, Alain. 1998. Proprietary Strategies: The Legal Fabric of Aristocratic Settlements. *The Modern Law Review* 61: 162–87.

Shakespeare, William. 1992. *The Tragedy of King Lear*, ed. Jay L. Halio. Cambridge: Cambridge University Press.

Simpson, A.W.B. 1986. *A History of the Land Law.* 2nd ed. Oxford: Oxford University Press.

– 1987. *A History of the Common Law of Contract.* Oxford: Clarendon Press.

Spencer, Christopher. 1972. *Nahum Tate.* New York: Twayne Publishers.

Spring, Eileen. 1993. *Law, Land and Family: Aristocratic Inheritance in England, 1300–1800.* Chapel Hill: University of North Carolina Press.

Strier, Richard. 1995. *Resistant Structures: Particularity, Radicalism and Renaissance Texts.* Berkeley: University of California Press.

Tate, Nahum [1681] 1969. *The History of King Lear.* Facsimile ed. London: Cornmarket Press.

– 1976. *The History of King Lear*, ed. James Black. London: Edward Arnold.

Thompson, E.P. 1976. The Grid of Inheritance: 'A Comment.' In *Family and Inheritance: Rural Society in Western Europe, 1200–1800*, ed. Jack Goody, Joan Thirsk, and E.P. Thompson, 328–60. Cambridge: Cambridge University Press.

Wilson, Richard. 1993. *Will Power: Essays on Shakespearean Authority.* Detroit: Wayne State University Press.

Part Three

*Women's Authorship and Ownership:
Matrices for Emergent Ideas of
Intellectual Property*

9

Writing Home: Hannah Wolley, the Oxinden Letters, and Household Epistolary Practice

JENNIFER SUMMIT

Many genres in which early modern women wrote strike an uneasy balance between the realms of property and writing. Letters, for example, are not 'intellectual property' in the ways in which that term has been historically defined; existing as manuscript documents whose presumed privacy exempted them from legal protection, they were at the same time written, circulated, and understood within communal circuits that belie the notions of individual authorship on which intellectual property has historically been grounded. But letters, like wills, participated in a world of tangible property, along with the objects and artefacts that made up the everyday life of early modern women. In so doing, like other genres of writing discussed by chapters in this section, letters challenge us to reconsider the particular kind of 'property' that written texts represent. Like the movables and 'paraphernalia' that constituted early modern women's property, letters occupy a grey area of ownership. If literary texts made authors into owners, letters represent an alternative model of property – one whose defining characteristic is not individual ownership but the state of ongoing negotiation and exchange to which letters owe their existence.

What gives early modern letters an especially complicated relation to property is also what makes them difficult to read within conventional models of literary authorship: their historical and material location within the household. Despite the gendered rhetoric of privacy through which it was frequently described by contemporaries, the early modern household was in fact the centre of extended, communal relationships, supporting Penelope Allison's assertion that households need to be recognized less as private zones than as 'social and productive units in the wider community' (1999, 2). As Helen Wilcox finds, the writings that early modern women produced within these household settings reflect a social world that is 'so communal ... that it is hardly accurate to term it "private"' (1992, 57). Read within the communal structures of the early modern household, women's letters do not offer autobiographies of individual selves so much as they map relationships that extend outward into broader social and textual networks. Furthermore, as perhaps the defining genre of the household, letters demand a reexamination of the place of writing – in the most literal sense – in the early modern period.

As a sphere of activity, the early modern household has long been considered marginal to literary culture, an assumption supported by the contemporary opposition between the needle, with which women pursued the quintessentially domestic art of embroidery, and the pen, the instrument of male eloquence and literary self-assertion (Orlin 1999; Jones and Stallybrass 2000). Yet just as the early modern household defies oppositions between public and private, the letter – as an example of what Susan Frye calls 'household writing' (2000) – defies oppositions between literary art and domestic craft. In letters, writing exists not in opposition to women's household activities but in tandem with them, taking its place as a female 'accomplishment' alongside the domestic practices of needlework and cookery.

Considering the meanings and uses of one early modern epistolary collection, the Lisle letters, Karen Newman finds in the letters' preoccupation with the stuff of everyday life a corrective to scholarship in Renaissance material culture. Critiquing what she sees as a tendency to privilege objects as sources of 'fully readable' meanings over the rhetorical readings of texts, she concludes from the Lisle letters that objects achieve meaning 'through language' and therefore need to be read rhetorically (Newman 1996, 148). While sharing Newman's desire to recover textuality as a relevant term for the study of material culture, this essay approaches early modern letters from the opposite direction, by considering not how they make things into texts but how, in letters, texts become things. This is not to make their meanings any more transparent, but rather to foreground texts' place among the material objects and practices that made up household life in the early modern period. Letters do not merely represent material culture, I argue, but participate in it as objects themselves whose material modes of fashioning, use, and exchange hold meanings that exceed the limits of what they actually say. In pursuing this analysis, I turn to two sources of seventeenth-century letters. The first is Hannah Wolley's instructional work for women, *A Supplement to the Queen-Like Closet* (1674), which followed from Wolley's immensely popular cookbook, *The Queen-Like Closet* (1670) and expanded the earlier book's scope of instruction from cookery to other household arts, including lace making, cleaning, interior decoration, and – in a section on which I will focus – letter writing. The second is a contemporary collection of seventeenth-century letters from the minor gentry Oxinden family, who lived outside Canterbury and maintained and preserved an extensive correspondence from 1607 to 1670. The Oxinden letters reflect a household milieu similar to those that formed the primary context for Wolley's work; not only were many of them written by and to women, they illustrate how letters helped to structure the seventeenth-century household and the relationships within it, thus producing what we could call a rhetoric of property.

Hannah Wolley's Serviceable Letters

Hannah Wolley's works of instruction, together with their phenomenal popularity, reflect a historically specific condition of the seventeenth-century household: the network of nonfamilial relationships loosely classified under the category of service, which became central to household organization and thus to many women's lives. As she reveals in her *Supplement to the Queen-Like Closet*, Wolley herself had worked as a servant for seven years before her marriage, during which time she 'had the fortune to belong to a Noble Lady in this kingdom' and there learned skills of household management, medicine, cookery, and other domestic arts that she details in her published works (Wolley 1674, 10). In the seventeenth century women entered service as a reflection less of their class than of their stage in life. Marking a period between puberty and marriage, service provided a formal structure by which young women were taken from their parents' homes and placed in the homes of their social superiors. The practice grew out of an ongoing Tudor 'child exchange,' which, as detailed by Lawrence Stone, Grant McCracken, and Patricia Fumerton, served the complex function of establishing bonds between the ranks of the Tudor hierarchy while also differentiating lines of unequal obligation between them – since children always moved from subordinate to superordinate households – at the same time that it civilized the children themselves. From serving at table and assisting in other household tasks, children were able to observe adult models of polite conversation and behaviour; 'thus,' as McCracken remarks, 'the honest yeoman's son, raised in the plain style of his own home, was perhaps expected to undergo a "civilizing" process in the home of a gentleman' (1983, 10). In the seventeenth century, while boys increasingly entered university and the Inns of Court as an intermediary stage between puberty and marriage, service became a disproportionately female occupation that served a pedagogical function parallel to young men's, while marking the unequal expectations of male and female education (Mendleson and Crawford 1998, 94–7). As servants, young women learned the domestic skills that would prepare them to lead their own households and even employ servants of their own (O'Day 1994, 177–9). At the same time, they entered into relationships of surveillance and subordination intended to regulate young women's sexuality before they could be safely married.

Hannah Wolley's *Supplement to the Queen-Like Closet* promotes and participates in the 'civilizing process' of service. Addressing 'Gentlewomen, or other Maids, who desire to go forth to service, and do want Accomplishment for the same' (Wolley 1674, n.p.), it describes the roles and functions of female servants from the lowest scullery maid to the 'Waiting-Gentlewoman' and offers primary instruction in a range of skills necessary to their various ranks, such as cooking, serving, cleaning, and decorative crafts. Among the domestic skills in which Wolley instructs her readers is letter writing, by which she emphasizes the importance not only of penmanship – the focus of other similar domestic guides – but of rhetoric: 'I do da[i]ly find that in Writing most Women ... spend their time in Learning a good Hand; but their English and language is, The one not easie to understand, the other weak and impertinent' (1674, 148). In turn, Wolley produces a collection of 'forms or patterns of Letters' purportedly drawn from correspondence between women of various ages and stations and their friends, benefactors, or families.

The book of letters was a popular genre in its own right by the mid-seventeenth century. Books such as Nicholas Breton's *Conceyted Letters, Newly Layde Open* (1618) and John Massinger's *The Secretary in Fashion, or, A Compendious and Refined Way of Expression in all Manner of Letters* (1640) produced sample letters to be read as both instruction and literary entertainment. The rise of epistolarity in seventeenth-century popular print runs parallel to developments in the material conditions of letter writing, as the English postal service became more efficient and cheap, allowing personal letters to be more commonly adopted as forms of written conversation (Wright 1989, 553). As Anna Bryson points out, letter-writing manuals were increasingly dominated by concerns about polite interaction, taking on the cultural function of the sixteenth-century conduct book as general handbooks of civility (1998, 156–9). Above all, the letter-writing manual was valued for its instruction in the finer points of how to translate relative social positioning and hierarchical status into appropriate forms of address. As Jonathan Goldberg argues, early modern letter writing 'begins with an awareness of the person, not as an individual but rather as a social category'; by offering a taxonomy of these categories and a rhetoric for their negotiation, the letter-writing manual teaches its users how to enter 'the fictions defined by the generic classifications that embrace the social domain' (1990, 252, 254). Thus such manuals could be read as both instruction and literary entertainment: their point was to turn social intercourse into a living literature.

If women bore an often vexed relation to literary culture in the seventeenth century, they became privileged subjects and objects of writing within these emergent epistolary genres. In the most popular examples, women's letters were given meaning almost exclusively within quasi-literary narratives of romance; Breton's *Conceyted Letters* includes a number of love letters both to and by women that recount miniature courtship dramas, as do many other letter books that followed suit. The collection of love letters ostensibly by women updated the *Heroides* for seventeenth-century readers; when a work such as *The Academy of Complements* (1640) addresses itself to ladies and their 'chambermaids and waiting-gentlewomen' by offering them sample letters whereby they can respond to suitors, it clearly courts a secondary readership for whom such letters represent an erotically charged glimpse into the secret affairs of women. Henry Care's *The Female Secretary: or, Choice New Letters* (1671) likewise offers sample letters to 'Ladies of Noble Birth and Education' and their 'Waiting Gentle-women' 'for the expressing themselves aptly and handsomly on any occasion proper to their sex,' while it includes a section entitled separately 'Courtship a-la-mode; or Love in Fashion,' revealing the extent to which letters by women had come to be classified as romantic popular literature (1671, 34–7).

The books' emphasis on courtship could be dismissed as an effort to sensationalize their topic and pander to the romantic or more prurient interests of a popular readership; but in their address to 'waiting gentle-women' lies a clue about women's actual practices of letter writing within the household structures of service. *The Gentlewoman's Companion* (1672), a work that was falsely attributed to Wolley herself, demonstrates on its title page the connection between letter writing and female service. Addressing itself to 'Gentlewomen' as well as to 'the Female Sex in

General,' the work announces 'directions in behaviour' suited to every form of hierarchical relationship in which women might find themselves, including 'Huswives to the House' and 'Mistresses to Servants.' Moreover, it offers 'A Guide for Cook-maids, Dairy-maids, Chambermaids, and all others that go to Service, The whole being an exact Rule for the Female Sex in General.' In bold capital letters running between these two stated aims, it further promises 'LETTERS & DISCOURSES upon all Occasions.' Whereas the visual layout of the page makes letters coextensive with the roles of service that structure women's places within the household, in the book itself letters become a medium of service and the civilizing function that it exercises on young women.

Within the household, writing is a domestic skill especially associated with 'waiting-Gentlewomen,' the highest-ranking office of female domestic service. *The Gentlewoman's Companion* instructs its female reader, 'If you desire to be a waiting-Gentlewoman, it will be expected that you can Dress well; Preserve well; and write well a legible hand, good language, and good English' (1672, 205–6). As Wolley would also stress, here 'good writing' includes both the manual skill of penmanship and the rhetorical skill of 'good language, and good English.' The instruction echoes that of another work that has been likewise misattributed to Wolley (although more likely by recent cataloguers than by contemporaries), *The Compleat Servant-Maid; or the Young Maiden's Tutor*, which offers 'directions for Preserving, Conserving, and Candying' as well as 'for writing the most usual hands for Women, as Mixt Hand, Roman and Italic Hands' (1677, A4r–v). Classified with these other household skills, writing is neither a particularly masculine act nor one outside of women's domestic purview. To the contrary, it becomes, as *The Gentlewoman's Companion* observes of 'Candying, Conserving and Preserving,' a 'Curiosity' that is 'requisite and necessary in young Ladies and Gentlewomen' (1672, 183).

The sample letters in *The Gentlewoman's Companion* offer letter writing as an ornamental skill, exemplifying the book's lesson, 'in letters of Complement supply the barrenness of your matter with the smoothness of your rhetoric and exornations' (1672, 228). Here rhetoric is a feminine decorative practice akin to needlework, as illustrated in an exchange of letters that is presented as occurring between two absent female friends. As one writes to the other, 'I have laid aside the exercise of my Needle, that I may employ my hand some little time in the management of my Pen' (1672, 232). In response, her friend praises her rhetorical skills as evidenced by her letter, assuring her 'Were I to be judg, I know not which to give the greater praise or encomium, the

Flourishes of the Pen, or the Flowers of the Needle' (1672, 233). Letters like these become noteworthy not for what they say – indeed, they exemplify the instruction to 'supply the barrenness of your matter with the smoothness of your rhetoric' – but for their production of 'Complements' as objects of exchange. Thus they produce, in Lynne Magnusson's words, 'a stylistics of interaction' whose key function is to mediate social relationships (1999, 36).

Wolley's decision to include sample letters in her *Supplement to the Queen-Like Closet* may well have been prompted by a desire to recapture the readership that was attracted by the fraudulently authored *Gentlewoman's Companion*; while she vigorously denies writing the book in the preface to her *Supplement*, she nonetheless follows the earlier work's example by promising 'A Little of Everything, presented to all Ingenious Ladies, and Gentlewomen,' including letters, which are prominently announced in a separate section listed on the book's table of contents. But Wolley's letters differ from those in the *Gentlewoman's Companion* as well as from those in popular 'literary' works like Care's *Female Secretary*. These are not, with one exception, letters of ornamental or amorous 'complement'; rather, in Wolley's letters household service becomes both the context for and the explicit subject of women's writing. In one letter a mother writes to a daughter who is 'in a ladies service' (Wolley 1674, 151), and the daughter replies by describing the conditions of her daily work: 'My Lady likes my Dressing very well, and also what I starch; but she would fain have me more curious in my Point work. She will not let me wash her chamber because I should not spoyle my Hands for work. If she like me well I shall be glad, for I like her service very well' (Wolley 1674, 152–3). Here needlework is an exercise not simply of ornament but of service; like the Elizabethan gifts of needlework that Lisa M. Klein examines, it negotiates relationships of unequal power between women (1997).

Networks of service play a similarly structuring role in Wolley's other letters: a sister writes to her brother, telling him, 'I thank God I am in a very good Place, where I have the Love and good word of the People I served' (1674, 154). An aunt writes to her orphaned niece at her place of service, counselling her 'Be carefull in the first place to serve God, and to please those whom you serve,' to which the niece responds by assuring her, 'My Lady finds little or no fault with me, therefore I presume I do please her' (1674, 162). And, illustrating the exchange of children on which networks of service were grounded, in a letter written 'From a lady to a Gentlewoman, whom she hath a kindness for,' the former assures the latter, 'if you can condescend that your Daughter shall be a servant to me, you shall find that I will be more a Mother than a Mistress to her. I doubt not of her Abilities, since I know your care hath been very much for her Education,' and promises 'I shall not spare my Purse to give a full Accomplishment to her' (1674, 157–8). In response, the mother consents to send her daughter, thanking her correspondent for 'your goodness and Charity towards me and my poor Child, that we are even transported with joy' (1674, 159). Supporting Rosemary O'Day's assertion that in the seventeenth century, '"servant" described a relationship rather than a job of work,' Wolley's letters reveal how that relationship was complexly structured through the exchange of texts as well as of children (1994, 175). Indeed, her letters retrace and reinforce the lines of exchange that children travelled to become servants. An exchange of letters precedes and secures an exchange of daughters, who learn to become servants by writing letters themselves. In letters, Wolley's servants find a textual form that reflects their own condition: both are constituted through their circulation.

Although they appear at the end of *The Supplement to the Queen-Like Closet*, Wolley's letters establish the thematic centre of her book. Promising 'A Little of Everything,' the *Supplement* appears to be a haphazardly organized miscellany of household skills: its table offers instruction on topics such as 'to wash the face,' 'to keep the hair clean,' 'to make clear points or laces,' 'to adorn a room with prints,' as well as expanding the recipes that she produces in *The Queen-Like Closet*, by including instructions for making 'dressed mutton,' marmalades, and a 'sirop of violets.' But the contents of the *Supplement* are not as random as they appear; rather, they extend the arts of refinement that Wolley's earlier work located in the kitchen to the rest of the household and finally to the very body of the female servant herself.

As a writer of cookbooks, Wolley shows how food preparation is central to the production of civility; offering elaborate menus for households and guests of varying ranks in *The Queen-Like Closet*, she reproduces social hierarchy at the table by differentiating between classes of eaters. For example, 'A Bill of Fare in Winter in Great Houses' includes as its first course, 'A Collar of Brawn,' 'A Capon and White Broth, or two boiled Rabbits,' 'Two rosted Neats Tonges and an Udder between them,' 'A Chine of Beef rosted,' 'A Shoulder of Mutton stuffed with Oysters,' 'An Eel Pie or some other Pie,' 'Three young Turkies in a dish,' and 'A dish of Fish' (1670, 323–4). Contrasting with this aristocratic menu, Wolley also offers 'A Bill of Fare for Gentlemens Houses of Lesser

Quality, by which you may also know how to order any Family beneath another, which is very requisite' (1670, 327). According to Wolley's directions, such 'Houses of Lesser Quality' should serve a first course of 'A Collar of Brawn,' 'A Rosted Tongue and Udder,' 'Leg of Pork Boiled,' 'A piece of rosted Beef,' 'A Venison Pasty or other Pie,' 'A Marrow Pudding,' 'A Goose, or Turkie, or Pig,' and 'A Sallad of what's in Season' (1670, 328–9).

The table generates refinement not only in its seating plans and class-differentiated menus, but also in the very food that formed its centrepiece. As Grant McCracken observes, 'it was here, after all, that the raw food-stuff of the land, air, and sea completed the process of transformation' (McCracken 1983, 311). The recipes that Wolley provides detail above all such transformative arts: the eel pie that graces the table of great houses (but not the 'houses of lesser quality') in winter demonstrates the transformation of living animals into a work of culinary art:

> To make an Eel-Pie.
> Take your largest Eels, and slay them, and cut them in pieces, then having your Pie ready with Butter in the bottom, season your Eels with Pepper, Salt and Nutmeg, then lay them in and cover them with butter, so close it and bake it, if you please, you may put in some Raisins of the Sun, and some large Mace, it is good hot or cold. (1670, 219)

In *The Supplement to the Queen-Like Closet* the most refined culinary arts are not even necessarily meant for eating: some processes of candying, which are appropriate to the skill level of a 'waiting-Gentlewoman,' involve soaking fruits in gum arabic and thus turning them into inedible ornaments for visual display; comments Wolley, 'This is an extraordinary pretty way, and looks very delicately; and as they lie in the Sun they will sparkle like Diamonds' (1674, 125). Recipes like this 'defamiliarize' eating, as Wendy Wall puts it, and turn cooking into a 'performance art' (2002, 2).

Such recipes artfully teach processes of refinement and transforma-tion that refashion animals and plants into material forms that will serve the social rituals of class and civility – thus transforming objects of nature into objects of culture. As expanded and elaborated in Wolley's *Supple-ment to the Queen-Like Closet*, these processes of refinement are also central to the household structures of service itself, through which young women are brought into the houses of their social superiors as part of a larger civilizing process. Significantly, this process takes place when young women are at an age between adolescence and marriage, as a means of controlling their sexuality. Through training in accomplishments appropriate to their status, like candying, lace making, cleaning, and – as I have stressed here – letter writing, service transforms young women into wives.

By facilitating the transformation of women into wives, Wolley's *Supplement to the Queen-Like Closet* shares an interest in female sexuality with the contemporary letter-writing manuals that produce female epistolarity as a romantic, literary form. Where popular letter books like Breton's or Care's associate women's letters almost exclusively with courtship, Wolley's *Supplement* translates this concern with the sexuality of young women into the material realm of the household, where young women are held and trained in preparation for marriage. It thereby makes explicit the social context of seventeenth-century epistolary practice that the popular letter collections obscure. Locating letter writing among the material practices of female service, Wolley reveals the shaping role that letters play in young women's domestic education. She thus opens a way to read letters in and as material culture by refusing to differentiate them from the realm of household goods and practices from which they spring. And, as Wolley shows, like other household objects that women learned to fashion as domestic servants, letters in turn fashioned women as prospective housewives.

The Oxinden Letters and the Romance of Service

As Wolley's letters make clear, the business of turning young women into wives involves the transformation of property: not just the household stuff that they learn to manipulate during their service, but the property that they represent in themselves. Until marriage, young women were held to be the property of their parents, transferred to the husband at marriage. Thus *The Gentlewoman's Companion* reiterates a contemporary commonplace when it asserts: 'Children are so much the Goods and Chattels of a Parent, that they cannot without a kind of theft give themselves away without the allowance of those that have the right in them' (1672, 24). The Oxinden letters, to which I now turn, show how the charged questions of property and ownership that revolved around courtship, marriage, and service found an especially appropriate rhetoric and form in letters.

In what becomes perhaps the defining domestic drama of the Oxinden household and its letters in the early 1640s and thereafter, the transformation of young women into wives is a central concern. As the Oxinden family correspondence reveals, letters became not only the medium through which this problem was expressed but the instruments with which it was enacted and resolved. In late November of 1641, Henry Oxinden, then a thirty-three-year-old widower with three children, wrote to his relation, Lady Oxinden of Deane, to express his frustration over a vexing situation: without his consent or knowledge, his sixteen-year-old ward, Katherine Culling, had been abducted or enticed away by an impoverished local gentry couple, Sir Thomas Baker and Frances, Lady Baker, who took the girl to London to contract her in a marriage of their making. This drama constituted a complicated legal offence: Katherine was the daughter of a local yeoman family, and at her father's death, Henry Oxinden became her legal guardian through the Court of Wards. In the sixteenth and seventeenth centuries, wardships extended vestigial feudal bonds of service into formal legal relationships; by agreeing to tend to wards' education while they were minors, guardians secured the right to control their inheritance and dispose of them in marriage, a remunerative privilege that made wards into 'chattels which could be bought and sold,' as Joel Hurstfield observes (1958, 128). Like servants, with whom they shared functional and definitional similarities – recall Wolley's assertion that as a young servant she 'had the fortune to belong to a Noble Lady in this kingdom' – wards were the objects of a system that bound early modern families by making children into exchangeable property.

By taking Katherine away and appropriating the right to marry her, Sir Thomas and Lady Baker committed a serious offence known (and punishable) as 'the ravishment of a ward' (Hurstfield 1958, 143) – that is, the unlawful assumption of the right to marry a ward – which Oxinden correctly recognized as both a legal and a financial violation perpetrated against him: 'if anie thing fall out without my knowledge it will bee a 100[l] out of my way' (Oxinden 1933, 1: 225), he complains, adding, 'it will be a great dishonor to me to have [Katherine] disposed of, though never soe well, if it bee agt. my knowledge; and not small will bee my losse if it should soe fall out' (1933, 1: 228).

Yet despite Oxinden's assertion of his proprietary rights over Katherine, her legal status as a sixteen-year-old ward was more ambiguous than he allows. According to *The Lawes Resolutions of Womens Rights*, wards who reach the age of sixteen without being married hold a claim to their inheritance: 'So soone as they come to the age of fourteene yeares if the Lord for covetousness will not marry them, yet he shall not keepe their

land above two yeares after they have accomplished 14 within which two
yeares if they be not married by their Lord, they make take action against
him for their inheritance' (1632, 16). Whether or not Oxinden was
motivated by 'covetousness' in failing to marry her – after all, as long as
she remained unmarried, he controlled her inheritance – the fact that
she was still unmarried at sixteen meant that Katherine could potentially
be considered 'out of ward,' allowing her to take the matter of her
marriage into her own hands.

Indeed, this appears to be what happened. During her time in London Katherine seems to have been contracted – and quite possibly
secretly married – to a man named Shelton. Yet after ten days Oxinden
was able to dispatch her brother to retrieve her. Upon her return on the
seventh of December, Katherine met with Oxinden in a private conference. Oxinden recounts the scene to his literate and witty cousin, Elizabeth Dallison, whom he wrote frequently with the knowledge that she
would share his letters with her mother and father, his aunt and uncle,
who maintained considerable interest in his estate:

> I had but little conference with her but that I had was as followeth. After I
> had stood a while strange to her and accused her of taking her journy, she
> sd she hoped it was not a fault unpardonable, and herein she served the
> Ladie in that every maide (I sayd, when I was most angry with her, if they
> take not away her natural sences) she would in the winding up. (1933, 1:
> 243)

The substance of this 'little conference' is difficult to parse. In anger,
Oxinden accuses Katherine of disobedience and perhaps worse: when
Katherine begs his pardon and apparently protests that she 'served the
lady' (Lady Baker) as a 'maide,' Oxinden parenthetically recalls his own
angry (if opaque) response, 'if they take not away her natural sences,'
which seems to call her purity as a 'maide' into question. Such a suggestion would have legal ramifications; a female ward whose virginity was
violated was held to have 'forf[e]it[ed] with her body' her inheritance,
which would then accrue to her 'parceners' – in this case, her brother
(*Lawes Resolutions*, 1632, 22). Katherine delicately defends her virtue by
translating the question into a point about clothing; when, according to
Oxinden, 'I told her I heard she was growne a great gallant in London,'
she protests: 'she sd shee only bought a blacke silke gownd there'
(Oxinden 1933, 1: 244). And when Oxinden asks 'why you did not by a
coloured silke gownd,' he reports, 'shee sd it was not so fitting to her'

(1933, 1: 244). Thus assured, through the symbolic language of clothing, of Katherine's virginity, Oxinden's mood and manner of address shift dramatically; as he reports in his letter, 'I began to wonder how one of less then 17 should have so much discretion as to say iust so much as was fitting to be sd and no more' (1933, 1: 244–5). In short, after the conference, he confesses to his cousin – and thus to his other relations who shared his letter – 'you may adjudge me to be in love' (1933, 1: 245).

Oxinden's abrupt shift from anger to love signals a shift in his legal relationship to Katherine. Whatever affective bond between them – and from the evidence of Oxinden's later letters, they appear to have enjoyed a warm and loving relationship – marrying Katherine himself would enable Oxinden to retain control over her inheritance (the hundred pounds to which he refers) after she falls 'out of ward.' But renegotiating their relationship requires rhetorical, as well as legal, finesse. When Oxinden's relations resist his match with a yeoman's daughter, Oxinden attempts to win their approval by writing an epistolary romance. Again using his cousin Elizabeth Dallison as intermediary, in a second letter written some weeks later, Oxinden retells the scene of falling in love with Katherine Culling, this time embellishing it in verse:

When I censored her for her jurney to London (which fault I never could impute properly to her)
 To make amends poore Cate with yielding eies
 Shee offer'd up herself a sacrifice,
 To slake my anger if I were displeased,
 O what God would not therwith be appeased. (1933, 1: 264)

By recounting the scene thus, Oxinden hopes that verse will accomplish what prose could not and persuade his relations to accept Katherine's new role as his bride-to-be, while at the same time recoding his control over her property in the quasi-religious, erotic language of 'sacrifice.' But the family continued to resist the match, forcing Oxinden to write them, through Elizabeth Dallison, a third time. After reassuring them of his financial well-being, he once again slips into a self-consciously literary register to recount the critical scene of his reconciliation with Katherine, this time as a novelistic narration replete with dialogue:

But noght of these [financial considerations] moved any heart of mine to resolve to entre into that (by me feared and abhorred) condition of life, which I now can by no means avoyd; itt was only her selfe, and unexpected answeare to me when I advised her to beware how and to whom she married, and told her that her fortune and selfe deserved a good match, five to one better then myself; to which (casting her eies upon mee and as soone casting them down againe), she replyed, I know noe man I can thinke a better match or can [MS torn] so well as your selfe; this amazed mee, insomuch that where [MS torn] before I loved her as my child and friend, I now was forced [to] consider of loveing her as a wife. (1933, 1: 277–8)

Acknowledging the change in his relationship with Katherine – '[where] before I loved her as my child and friend, I now was forced [to] consider of loveing her as a wife' – Oxinden claims to have been scripted into a romantic narrative that he is powerless to rewrite. Recalling the popular letter collections and their epistolary conventions of love and courtship, Oxinden attempts to persuade his relations to accept the shift in his legal relationship with Katherine by shifting the rhetorical register of his letters. Where Oxinden's earlier letters refer to Katherine in coldly legal language as 'this party' and 'Culling's heir,' his later letters enlist the literary topoi of romance in order to facilitate her transformation from ward to wife. They thus show how through letters Oxinden learns to negotiate, as Goldberg puts it, 'the fictions defined by the generic classifications that embrace the social domain' (1990, 254).

The self-conscious literariness of Oxinden's letters about Katherine reflects his own cultural aspirations and background. Educated at Cambridge, Oxinden was the author of minor Latin verse and, in 1628, a key to *The Countess of Pembroke's Arcadia*. His letters likewise adapt contemporary poetry to describe his affairs, as when he cites Donne's lament for lost love, 'The Expostulation,' while changing Donne's first line, 'Curst may he bee that so our love hath slain' to 'Curst may she bee that tryd my Charge to staine' to excoriate Lady Baker for her part in Katherine's abduction (1933, 1: 245). If Henry Oxinden in many ways typifies a seventeenth-century consumer and producer of high literary culture, Elizabeth Dallison's own letters represent a striking contrast in tone and vocabulary and bring us closer to the household contexts of letter writing that Wolley's examples illustrate. As Dallison writes to Oxinden in response to his first complaint of Katherine's disappearance,

Noble Cosin,
    My last letter was written in such hast as indeed I know not well what it wase; I beseech you to excuse my presumption that dare to writ to one that

doth exselle in that. Now I must tell you I am my mother's scribe, who craves your favor in excusing her that cannot answer your most compleat lines, full of discreation and judgment. (1933, 1: 233)

Elizabeth Dallison writes for her mother because her (presumably illiterate) mother cannot write herself; yet Dallison's mother is no less a participant in this scene of household literacy than she would be if she wrote herself. To the contrary, her inability to write makes Henry Oxinden all the more aware that his letters are in no way private exchanges but rather are read communally – as they are written to be – just as Dallison's letters are communally authored. While apologizing for her own seeming lack of skill in contrast to Oxinden's 'most compleat lines, full of discreation and judgment,' Dallison appears to set up a contrast between Oxinden's masculine writing – as skilled, literary, and independent – and the feminine, communal contexts of her own household epistolarity.

In what is to my knowledge the only critical study of the Oxinden letters, Carol L. Winkelmann observes that the men's writing evidences a more self-consciously literary style than does the women's, concluding 'as reading and writing skills were being more widely distributed across the female population, the criteria for acceptable literacy were being elaborated in a direction which made invisible or devalued women's participation in the household economy' (1996, 18). Such a conclusion is indeed supported by the letters of Henry Oxinden, with their literary references and motifs, and Elizabeth Dallison, which apologize for their own poor quality relative to Oxinden's by calling attention to 'my presumption that dare to writ to one that doth exselle in that' and contrasting the limited literacy of Dallison's mother with Oxinden's own 'most compleat lines, full of discreation and judgment.' Thus both Henry Oxinden and Elizabeth Dallison seem to collude in the distinction, and gendering, of the categories 'literary' and 'nonliterary' writing. But considered collectively, the Oxinden letters also show that the two categories are not exclusive; rather, they are mutually productive. Oxinden's 'literary' letters are produced in a dialectical relationship with Dallison's household letters, becoming ever more artful and self-conscious in response to his family's resistance to his marriage, as communicated by Dallison. Indeed, 'women's participation in the household economy' forms both the backdrop and the subject of his letters, as Oxinden attempts to persuade his family to accept his former ward as his new wife.

After Oxinden and Katherine marry, the family letters resume a more explicit focus on the material concerns of the household, of which, naturally enough, service forms a major theme. While none of Katherine's own letters survives in either the published collection or the original manuscripts housed in the British Library, Katherine remains a vivid presence in the family correspondence as an addressee and overseer of Oxinden's daughters' education. Thus Oxinden writes her to express the hope that his daughters will learn 'singing (if they have voices) and writing (and to cast account which will be usefull to them hereafter)' (1937, 2: 128). He likewise asks Katherine to instruct his younger daughter Elizabeth to 'beethinke her selfe of a service' (1937, 2: 174), presumably one in which she can put her education – including her writing – to use. In later years, Katherine also becomes the guardian and surrogate 'mother' (for so she is addressed) of the young wife of Oxinden's recreant son, whom he abandons into her care. As mistress of the household, Katherine is thus charged with reproducing the lines of female education and surrogacy that she experienced herself during her own time in the family as Oxinden's ward.

In their continual references to the material and relational structures of the seventeenth-century household, the Oxinden letters recall Hannah Wolley's *Supplement to the Queen-Like Closet* and the epistolary collection it presents. Like Wolley's letters, those of the Oxinden family illuminate the extent to which the household, with its extended relations of service and surrogacy, became a centre of writing. They also show how even self-consciously 'literary' letter writing like Oxinden's derives from and responds to the household circuits of exchange and negotiation that formed the primary context of seventeenth-century epistolarity. In the process, these letters challenge us to reconsider the relationship between writing and property that historical definitions of 'intellectual property' have implied. If those definitions have stressed the autonomy of literary work, household letters show us how texts, like their writers, find meaning within a world of things.

Works Cited

Academy of Complements. 1640. London.
Allison, Penelope M. 1999. Introduction to *The Archaeology of Household Activities: Dwelling in the Past*, ed. Penelope M. Allison, 57–77. London: Routledge.
Breton, Nicholas. 1618. *Conceyted Letters, Newly Layde Open*. London.
Bryson, Anna. 1998. *From Courtesy to Civility: Changing Modes of Conduct in Early Modern England*. Oxford: Clarendon Press.

Care, Henry. 1671. *The Female Secretary: or, Choice New Letters.* London.

The Compleat Servant-Maid; or the Young Maiden's Tutor. 1677. London.

Frye, Susan. 2000. Maternal Textualities. In *Maternal Measures: Figuring Caregivers in the Early Modern Period,* ed. Naomi J. Miller and Naomi Yavneh, 224–36. Aldershot: Ashgate.

Fumerton, Patricia. 1991. *Cultural Aesthetics: Renaissance Literature and the Practices of Social Ornament.* Chicago: University of Chicago Press.

The Gentlewoman's Companion. 1672. London.

Goldberg, Jonathan. 1990. *Writing Matter: From the Hands of the English Renaissance.* Stanford: Stanford University Press.

Hobby, Elaine. 1989. *Virtue of Necessity: English Women's Writing, 1649–88.* Ann Arbor: University of Michigan Press.

– 1996. A Woman's Best Setting Out Is Silence: The Writings of Hannah Wolley. In *Culture and Society in the Stuart Restoration: Literature, Drama, History,* ed. Gerald Maclean, 179–200. Cambridge: Cambridge University Press.

Hurstfield, Joel. 1958. *The Queen's Wards: Wardship and Marriage under Elizabeth I.* Cambridge: Harvard University Press.

Jones, Ann Rosalind, and Peter Stallybrass. 2000. *Renaissance Clothing and the Materials of Memory.* Cambridge: Cambridge University Press.

Klein, Lisa M. 1997. Your Humble Handmaid: Elizabethan Gifts of Needlework. *Renaissance Quarterly* 50: 459–93.

The Lawes Resolutions of Womens Rights. 1632. London.

MacLean, Gerald. 2000. Re-Siting the Subject. In *Epistolary Histories: Letters, Fiction, Culture,* ed. Amanda Gilroy and W.M. Verhoeven, 176–97. Charlottesville: University Press of Virginia.

Magnusson, Lynne. 1999. *Shakespeare and Social Dialogue: Dramatic Language and Elizabethan Letters.* Cambridge: Cambridge University Press.

Massinger, John. 1640. *The Secretary in Fashion, or, A Compendious and Refined Way of Expression in All Manner Letters.*

McCracken, Grant. 1983. The Exchange of Children in Tudor England: An Anthropological Phenomenon in Historical Perspective. *Journal of Family History* 8: 303–13.

Mendelson, Sara, and Patricia Crawford. 1998. *Women in Early Modern England: 1550–1720.* Oxford: Clarendon.

Newman, Karen. 1996. Sundry Letters, Worldly Goods: The Lisle Letters and Renaissance Studies. *Journal of Medieval and Renaissance Studies* 26: 139–52.

O'Day, Rosemary. 1994. *The Family and Family Relationships, 1500–1900: England, France, and the United States of America.* London: Macmillan.

Orlin, Lena Cowen. 1999. Three Ways to Be Invisible in the Renaissance: Sex, Reputation, and Stitchery. In *Renaissance Culture and the Everyday,* ed. Patricia

Fumerton and Simon Hunt, 183–203. Philadelphia: University of Pennsylvania Press.

Oxinden, Henry. 1933. *The Oxinden Letters, 1607–1642: Being the Correspondence of Henry Oxinden of Barham and His Circle*, ed. Dorothy Gardiner. London: Constable and Co.

– 1937. *The Oxinden and Peyton Letters, 1642-1670: Being the Correspondence of Henry Oxinden of Barham, Sir Thomas Peyton of Knowlton, and Their Circle*, ed. Dorothy Gardiner. London: The Sheldon Press.

Stone, Lawrence. 1977. *The Family, Sex, and Marriage in England, 1500–1800*. New York: Harper and Row.

Wall, Wendy. 2002. *Staging Domesticity: Household Work and English Identity in Early Modern Drama*. Cambridge: Cambridge University Press.

Wilcox, Helen. 1992. Private Writing and Public Function: Autobiographical Texts by Renaissance Englishwomen. In *Gloriana's Face: Women, Public and Private, in the English Renaissance*, ed. S.P. Cerasano and Marion Wynne-Davies, 47–62. Detroit: Wayne State University Press.

Winkelmann, Carol L. 1996. A Case Study of Women's Literacy in the Early Seventeenth Century: The Oxinden Family Letters. *Women and Language* 19: 14–20.

Wolley, Hannah. 1670. *The Queen-Like Closet, or Rich Cabinet: Stored with All Manner of Rare Receipts for Preserving, Candying and Cookery*. London.

– 1674. *A Supplement to the Queen-Like Closet; or A Little of Everything, Presented to All Ingenious Ladies, and Gentlewomen*. London.

Wright, Susan. 1989. Private Language Made Public: The Language of Letters as Literature. *Poetics* 18.6: 549–78.

10
Women's Wills in Early Modern England

LLOYD DAVIS

Women made approximately 20 per cent of the two million wills that survive from the 1550s to the 1750s (Erickson 1993, 204). Wills can accordingly be regarded as one of the main genres in which women wrote, or dictated, during the early modern period. Wills exemplify a notion of genre conceived less as a category of text than as a range of factors that encompass stylistic conventions; interpersonal contexts of authorship and response; key institutions such as religion, the law, and the family; gender relations; along with practices of textual production, dissemination, and reception. A further element underscoring the generic quality of wills is that they must be proven; like all genres and texts, they are subject to interpretation and dispute over meaning and intention. Conceived generically, wills thus exemplify the interaction of discursive, historical, and social factors now regarded as central to notions of textuality and meaning. Thinking about wills in such terms in no way diminishes their importance in legal and social history; nor does it aim to substitute one disciplinary approach for another. It does, however, allow wills to be considered as texts that position authors and readers in socially and personally important ways that reveal the workings of powerful institutions and discourses, while also contributing to and intervening in them, and that interact with other genres in the period, such as plays and advice books. By examining these issues, the following discussion seeks to complement an important scholarly tradition and evolving debate over the significance of wills in understanding early modern property and gender relations.

While the majority of people in the early modern period did not make them, wills were widely known about and their purpose was respected. They are a paradoxical kind of text – a part of everyday life and death that is infrequently encountered by the majority of people. Because of the situations in which they are made and made known, their rarity in no way lessens their symbolic and real import: 'An outward and visible sign of wealth and a check upon the "wrongful" disposition of property, [a will] enshrines the wishes of the individual holder as against the demands of the potential heir. It is in effect the written version of the "dying words," the permanent expression of the deathbed wish' (Goody 1976a, 15). Jack Goody's description captures the life-and-death drama inherent in making and executing wills as well as the micro and macro effects that they can have, from structuring interpersonal relationships to reproducing the social system (1976b, 1). Indeed, as Shakespeare sensed when he opened such plays as *Hamlet* and *King Lear* amid crises of family succession and settlement, any system of inheritance – with the laws and codes that implement it – struggles, in J.H. Baker's words, 'to hold a balance between the living, the dead, and the unborn' (1990, 308). Baker's summation of the functions of a will as a legal device mindfully understates what is at stake. As Mary Murray suggests in an earlier chapter in this book, inheritance can best be theorized as a set of customs produced by different attitudes to death and dying in feudal and early capitalist societies. Since land could only be devised by will after the 1540 Statute of Wills, the genre of the will provides an important illustration of shifting inheritance practices that reflect not only economic and political change but also cultural change in early modern England.

The 'cosmic' significance of wills and succession that drives Shakespeare's great tragedies is also tied to the legal and material aspects of interpersonal, family, and gender relations. In this light, wills exemplify the complicated connections between religious and temporal discourses that pervade everyday life in the period. *The Book of Common Prayer* and tracts such as Thomas Becon's *The Sicke Mans Salve* (1558–9; 28 reprints by 1632), William Perkins's *A Salve for a Sicke Man* (1595), William Perneby's *A Direction to Death* (1599), and Christopher Sutton's *Disce Mori, Learne to Die* (1600) all exhorted readers to die well. An important part of doing so was to piously make a will. Christopher Marsh sums up the tenor of Becon's influential work as follows: 'it is the Christian's essential duty to settle his estate, on loan from God, in a manner which demonstrates gratitude and faith, and serves to signal – but not cause – his salvation ... The real duty a testator performed in making his will was to dispose of his wealth in a godly fashion' (1990, 219). The godly disposal of wealth implies that religious and moral aspects of will making are fundamentally linked to social and material concerns. The difficult critical-historical task is, I suggest, to avoid elevating one set of concerns at the expense of the other and instead to grasp their interdependence. Often it is only when a dispute arises over a will that the complex of personal, moral, material, and other motives can be revealed and placed under scrutiny. In recounting a court case between family members in Douai in 1434, Martha Howell observes: 'This was ... a suit between intimates, people closely bound to one another by shared experiences, shared property, shared affections' (1998, 2). Her words are an important reminder not only of the cultural conditions in which self, kinship, and property are situated, but also of the experiential and affective facets of people's lives that both permeate property relations and are constituted by them.

In the early modern period, the various situations in which married women could make wills paralleled their restricted legal and social rights to hold and exchange property. Sara Mendelson and Patricia Crawford summarize the situation thus: 'unmarried daughters and married women were rare as testators, since each needed male permission – a father or husband, respectively – to dispose of personal property. Married women required a husband's consent to dispose of personal property, apart from bequests of pin money ... A widow's power to bequeath her possessions depended upon how much of the family wealth her husband had left to her' (1998, 197). On this reading, it is impossible not to conceive married women's wills as framed and ordered by authoritative, masculine speech acts of consent, permission, and bequest.

Such authority derived from the common law, which restricted married women's rights to hold property and to pursue other modes of social activity. The opening pages of *The Law's Resolutions of Women's Rights* succinctly sums up the situation for married women: '*baron* and *feme* ... are but one person. And by this a married Woman perhaps may either doubt whether she be either none or no more than half a person' (T.E. [1632] 1998, 373). The author goes on to describe vividly the overarching property rights of the husband: 'the prerogative of the Husband is best discerned in his dominion over all external things, in which the wife by combination divesteth herself of propriety in some sort and casteth it upon her governor ... For thus it is, if before Marriage the Woman were possessed of Horses, Neat, Sheep, Corn, Wool, Money, Plate, and Jewels, all manner of movable substance is presently by conjunction the husband's to sell, keep, or bequeath if he die' (T.E. [1632] 1998, 388–9). Legal writers also considered situations in which married women were and were not empowered to make wills. Henrie Swinburn suggests that it was just as well that a wife was unable to bequeath real property; if she could, she would more than likely be pressured to 'deuise the same to her husband ... if this gappe were lefte open, fewe children should succeede in the mothers inheritaunce' (1590, 46). Swinburn later observes that a wife could bequeath goods and chattels as long as she had the husband's consent (1590, 48) and that there were some situations in which she could bequeath movables without consent – for example, if a betrothed woman died before marriage, or if a married woman was an executrix and needed to pay off debts for the deceased (1590, 49). Ultimately, Swinburn compares the position of the *feme covert* with other figures not always able to make testament, including prisoners and 'deafe and dumbe' people. Swinburn does note that single women could make wills involving movables from the age of twelve (1590, 35–6). Writing later in the seventeenth century, John Godolphin reiterates the general rules and the exceptions: 'That *Women Covert* are Intestable for want of Freedom, is not such a general Rule in Law as to exclude all Exceptions' ([1674] 1685, 29). The details he provides agree with Swinburn's position that most of the exceptions depend on the husband's consent. Godolphin also points out that 'If a *Feme Sole* make Will, and after take a Husband, the same is Revocation thereof' ([1674] 1685, 32).[1] Early modern women's wills comprised a highly contingent genre, affected by the interests and responses of the living.

But in some respects contingency was a feature of much will making in the period. Though the idea behind a will was generally understood, in legal terms the purposes and consequences of wills were rather unclear. They had not been allowed under feudal land law and had only recently been formally instituted as part of the inheritance system; the legal power to devise land was not introduced until 1540 (Baker 1990, 232). Trusts had been used to avoid this restriction on bequeathing estates. Theoretically, trusts could provide all single and married women with access to separate property, though in practice they applied only to those who belonged to the landed classes. Even this legal strategy did not assure women's positions. Any trust might of course be challenged in the Court of Chancery, where the results could not be predicted, and trusts could also be established to benefit males. Susan Staves attributes the employment of trusts to protect a wife's property from the husband less to concerns about securing her position than to 'the desire of the wife's

father to continue to exercise some control over the property he gave
the wife to bring into the marriage ... to ensure that at least some of it
remained for the wife's father's grandchildren' (1990, 169).[2] The gradual
development of the succession strategy of strict settlement through the
sixteenth and seventeenth centuries (discussed in more detail below) is a
further sign of the instability of the inheritance system. Existing strategies with conservative patriarchal and dynastic goals did not work and
underwent continuing change and review until a regularly effective
device was developed. (Strict settlement continued to be used until the
mid-nineteenth century, when its effectiveness was curtailed by legal
reforms.) Yet despite the potential for financial and familial advantage
and sustained moral-religious pressure from the church, it is estimated
that less than 20 per cent of the adult population made wills throughout
the period (Honigmann and Brock 1993, 11–12). Though wills had well-
known temporal and spiritual benefits, making one was an unusual act,
especially for a woman. According to Amy Erickson, men were up to six
times more likely than women to make wills (1993, 204).

Changing legal and social conditions throughout the 1500s and 1600s
do not diminish the significance of making a will. The fact that few men
and almost no women made wills may increase the value of the ones that
were made as documents of attitudes and practices. The total number of
wills, with their long-recognized role in interpersonal, familial, and social relations, makes them key texts for examining, in Erickson's words,
'the ingenuity of many ordinary women in working within a massively
restrictive system' of inheritance and marital property laws (1993, 20).
Simultaneously exceptional and unexceptional, private and public, individual and collective, wills illustrate elite and ordinary women's involvement in producing texts, entering discourse, and representing themselves
as capable of acting constructively in interpersonal and institutional
contexts. Marcia Pointon writes that reconsidering wills made by women
during the eighteenth century 'permit[s] a new understanding ... of how
women felt about the things they owned, and how they employed the fact
of their possession in the expectation of exercising influence' (1997, 49).
In short, as authors of wills, early modern women of diverse social levels
inscribed and exercised agency in personal, family, and social relations.

A brief account of the role of wills and succession in two popular plays
from the early 1600s can demonstrate the multiple values and relationships over which characters, as well as audiences, might struggle. Neither
of the comedies – *The Widow's Tears* by George Chapman (c. 1605) and
part one of Thomas Heywood's *The Fair Maid of the West* (c. 1603) –

ventures into the evocative, existential realms of windblown heaths or profound soliloquies or aspires to tragic perceptions of mortality. They do, however, present a range of concerns over the social and personal stakes of inheritance, particularly in relation to women. While at times Chapman's drama resonates somewhat more grandly – near the end a character pronounces, 'in this topsy-turvy world, friendship and bosom-kindness are but made covers for mischief' (5.4.33–4) – Heywood's cross-dressing adventure enacts a wider range of moves and intrigues over wills and bequests. Taken together, the two plays demonstrate many of the prevalent attitudes and practices relating to early modern women's wills and their roles in the inheritance system.

The opening scenes of Chapman's play are dominated by the malcontent Thrasalio, who in his scheming echoes outsiders like Iago and Edmund. He feels unjustly disadvantaged by the primogeniture system that has privileged his elder brother Lysander: 'you were too forward when you stepped into the world before me, and gulled me of the land that my spirits and parts were indeed born to' (1.1.45–7). This conflict, imposed by common law, generates the ensuing sequence of misogynist attitudes and acts by both brothers. First, Thrasalio plots to marry a widow to escape his predicament. His cynicism towards widows, supported by the play's title, flows from this family position and legitimates his plan: 'how short-lived widows' tears are ... they mourn in their gowns, and laugh in their sleeves' (1.1.141–4). His second ploy is to undermine Lysander's faith in his wife Cynthia's fidelity. As in *Othello*, the effect is almost immediate and suggests the credit men are prepared to grant each other over the words and actions of women: 'that ill-relished speech ... hath taken so deep hold of my thoughts,' Lysander readily admits after hearing Thrasalio's remarks (2.1.1–3).

This strand of Thrasalio's misogyny again stems from what he perceives as family disenfranchisement. Though he admires Cynthia, he holds that her virtue has so impressed his brother that 'he hath invested her in all his state, the ancient inheritance of our family, and left my nephew and the rest to hang upon her pure devotion, so as he dead, and she matching (as I am resolved she will) with some young prodigal, what must ensue, but her post-issue beggared, and our house, already sinking, buried quick in ruin' (2.3.80–5). By invoking the 'ancient inheritance,' Thrasalio couples his own aspirations with the 'dynastic ambition' of the 'house,' a motive that largely drove aristocratic succession through strict settlement for over two hundred years (Habakkuk 1994, 51). Not naming himself, Thrasalio effaces his interest behind that of the family, positioning himself and his nephew, rather than his older brother, as its authentic heirs. His views about widows, along with the conception of the family that underlies those views, are triply supported by the rest of the action. The widowed countess Eudora initially rejects Thrasalio for what may sound like overly strong antiromantic reasons: 'am I now so scant of worthy suitors that may advance mine honour, advance my estate, strengthen my alliance (if I list to wed)?' (2.4.164–6). Yet she soon falls for him after being told by the bawd Arsace of Thrasalio's remarkable potency. Notwithstanding the apparent decline in remarriage rates for widows from the sixteenth to the late seventeenth centuries (Staves 1990, 100–1; Erickson 1993, 196), Eudora's response reinforces the popular misogynist image of the lusty widow, as does Cynthia's desire for a burly soldier following her brief period of mourning after her husband's death. That soldier ends up being Lysander after all, trying to test his wife's chastity. At the last Cynthia manages to turn the tables and dismiss any charge of infidelity by claiming she knew who it was all the time (5.5.84).

The play's sardonic view of husband–wife relations rests on various assumptions about property, succession, and marriage. The primogeniture system leads more or less inevitably to rivalry between males, which is waged in large part through manipulating and exploiting women. Thrasalio does not consider working for a living, for he has been imbued with the aristocratic ethos that exaggerates his family's reputation despite its sinking fortunes (Staves 1995, 204). His scheme to wed Eudora (which the Revels editor, writing in the early 1970s, can label 'a good practical purpose' [Yamada 1975, liv]) indicates acceptance that marriage, even if not to a widow, was always the best way for a man 'to improve his financial condition' (Erickson 1993, 90). More significantly, the justification of antifeminist sentiments about wives and widows through dynastic invocation of house and family suggests the kind of patriarchal class-consciousness that could foster and support the practices of strict settlement. Through avoidance of dower and preference for sons, this mode of succession, so Eileen Spring argues, was primarily responsible for the 'decline of women's rights over land' throughout the period (1993, 93; see also Staves 1990, 69). Yet notwithstanding its significance, this set of concerns does not tell the whole story of women, wills, and property in the early modern period. The antifeminist impacts of strict settlement among the aristocracy and gentry, as Erickson and Cicely Howell note, are often not reproduced in the wills of ordinary people.[3] *The Fair Maid of the West* offers a theatrical version of some of these contrasting attitudes to gender and succession.

As in *The Widow's Tears*, the action in Heywood's play is importantly tied to questions of inheritance and family background. In the opening scenes, Captain Goodlacke admonishes his companion Spencer for being infatuated with the beautiful barmaid Besse Bridges: 'you forget your selfe, / One of your birth and breeding, thus to dote / Upon a Tanners daughter: why, her father / Sold hydes in Somersetshire, and being trade-falne, / Sent her to service' (1.2.15–19). His words assume that personal, moral, and material worth can all be equated. Spencer is a gentleman but owns no estate; he is a younger son, like Chapman's Thrasalio, but he has been left financially independent. Forced to flee England, and with no pressing family obligations, Spencer initially leaves all his movables to his beloved Besse – 'Money, apparell, and what else thou findest, / Perhaps worth my bequest and thy receiving, / I make thee mistresse of' (1.4.39–41) – including a tavern, The Winde-mill, in the Cornish town of Foy. Besse runs the tavern very profitably – her beauty draws in many customers and she treats her staff well. Her success suggests popular recognition that the *feme sole* or widow faced no legal restraints on trade and could be a thriving entrepreneur (see also Prior 1985, 102). Meanwhile, overseas, a seriously wounded Spencer tells Goodlacke that he has left a will giving Besse £500 per year while she remains chaste (2.2.74–5). The terms recall the occasional practice of permitting dower or jointure only while the widow remained unmarried. Besse's continued financial success brings social praise and risks: Goodlacke hopes to lead her into wantonness so he can inherit Spencer's money; the mayor of Foy admires and envies her wealth and good name – 'I could wish a match / Betwixt her and mine one and only sonne' (3.3.12–13). In particular, Goodlacke's presumption that he might be able to claim the inheritance hints at the vulnerability of heiresses, widows, and other female beneficiaries to legal challenge from interested male relatives and parties (a predicament illustrated by the well-known inheritance dispute of Anne Clifford). Goodlacke perhaps hopes to elevate his own relationship with Spencer to a perfect bond, one that surpasses the love between his friend and Besse. To Spencer's request that he disclose news of the legacy to her, Goodlacke replies, 'I shall performe your trust as carefully, / As to my father, breath'd he' (2.2.80–1). He intimates that the ambiguity of masculine friendship and rivalry is akin to the paradox of succession – that in wanting to fulfil the father's will, the son must await his demise.

Distraught at news of Spencer's death (which later proves to be false), Besse resolves to search for her beloved's resting place. Yet, before departing she uses her own will to announce a series of munificent social acts, similar to idealized portrayals of benevolent Elizabethan merchants, such as Simon Eyre in Dekker's *The Shoemaker's Holiday*. Her will is 'committed to the trust of the Mayor and Aldermen of Foy' (4.2.30) and includes bequests 'To set up yong beginners in their trade ... To relieve such as have had losse by Sea ... To every Maid that's married out of Foy, whose name's *Elzabeth* ... [and] To relieve maimed Soldiers' (4.2.32–6), along with legacies to all her servants and to Spencer's own dependants. The terms of Besse's will appear to illustrate recent claims that women tended to bestow charitable legacies more regularly than did men (Erickson 1993, 155, 211; Mendelson and Crawford 1998, 173, 198, 221). Like Spencer's initial gift, the will clearly conveys the liberty open to bachelors and single women in making bequests if they had no immediate family responsibilities (Howell 1976, 141).

Heywood's *Fair Maid* depicts a number of will- and succession-related situations in which early modern women could find themselves, as either beneficiaries or testators. In each case, a degree of vulnerability or exposure to male challenge surfaces. It is the power of Besse Bridges's 'fairness' – her beauty as much as her honesty – that enables her to overcome these threats. Most of her male antagonists end up comparing her to Queen Elizabeth. In this sense, Heywood's play is a useful corollary to Chapman's darker comedy. If the latter shows women largely subject and reactive to men's social and legal manoeuvring, suspect motives, and flawed execution, then Heywood's lighter world allows for female initiative and agency in interpersonal, economic, and legal relations. What is perhaps most striking is Besse's ability to act in public. In Chapman's drama Cynthia is constrained by the codes of the 'house' into which she has married. The widowed countess Eudora, though controlling the estate and admitting visitors, remains ensconced in a largely domestic setting and is reliant on her attendants. (In this sense, her position can be compared to that of Olivia in Shakespeare's *Twelfth Night*. Though she is not a widow, with the death of her father and brother, Olivia has inherited the estate. Yet apart from enabling her to refuse offers of marriage from Duke Orsino and Aguecheek, Olivia's social power does not seem to extend beyond the household and by the end of the play she is married.) Eudora's submission to Thrasalio takes place within the household, mysteriously offstage. The secrecy might suggest the potentially binding force of domesticity and privacy over women's lives. In contrast, Besse almost constantly participates in public activities and discourse. The play opens with her in service, and Spencer's and her own wills dramatically increase her civic role and influence to quasi-royal status.

Heywood stages the significant possibility that wills can have striking, determining social outcomes for women. Again, it is partly a generic effect; as noted earlier, wills are at once highly private and public texts – personal sentiments moulded by considerations of family and community expectations, embodied by the presence of witnesses and a notary or scrivener. The content is commonly secret until their announcement, followed by probate in the ecclesiastical courts. Through this process, wills transform their makers, inheritors, and the relationships they share from familial and interpersonal to communal and public contexts. The legacies comprise not only real and personal property but also new kinds of identities and roles for the parties involved. In particular, a will characterizes the testator as someone not only with a history of relationships with others but also with social and cultural capital, and, regardless of the amounts, with the power and right to dispense it. People have these attributes before making a will but doing so places them on the record. A will signifies the past, present, and future agency of its author. It exemplifies the remarkable power of texts to mean and do things for oneself and for others and thereby underscores the capacity for social action that rests with a speaker or author. As authors of wills, even if within a predominantly patriarchal and homosocial system, different kinds of women – single, married, and widowed; from disparate class groups and localities with specific customs – were able in varying degrees and ways to act upon their intentions and to participate formally in processes of interpersonal and social exchange. In doing so, they illustrate the role that female authorship, conceived more generally, could play in early modern discourse and institutions.[4]

Wills can be usefully compared with other written genres in the period in terms of the conditions in which they were produced. Some years ago, Margaret Ezell noted that an unwillingness to publish one's writings, and then using the modesty topos when doing so, was not restricted to female authors (1987, 65, 88). Men too might have had reservations about public authorship. Ezell's observations can also be applied to wills – the reluctance to write one was shared by men and women, and both used formulaic phrases and conventions to convey a final humility. In concert with these customary features, variations in preambles, prefaces, and the main parts of wills and other texts meant that a distinct 'personality can break through the set phrases, as when a will transmits what sounds like an authentic voice from the death-bed' (Honigmann and Brock 1993,

10). Traces of a distinct persona may emerge in the conspicuous spiritual formulas used, though, in reality, the person or persons behind these words could be the testator, the scribe, or a combination of all those present as the will was made (Marsh 1990, 247). Personalities also seem to emerge, reflected in the care with which certain goods or duties are bequeathed to particular people, while others are named as definitely not to receive bequests. When hearing 'an authentic voice' in such details, it is important for modern scholars to appreciate that the voice and identity do not exist separately from a complicated network of relationships between people, objects, and entitlements; wills 'enmesh the personal and individual with the legal and the statutory (of the State) around the crucial issue of accumulated wealth and property' (Pointon 1997, 142). In this light, women's will making offers a powerful instance of early modern individuality as social identity in action. The testator's voice seems 'authentic' the more completely it distinguishes, and is mediated by, relationships with others.

The examples of theatrical wills collected by Honigmann and Brock illustrate many of these features of personality, voice, identity, and concern for others. Margaret Spufford has suggested that a key motive in making a will was 'to provide for children who were not yet independent' (1976, 171). This purpose influences the frequent naming of daughters, married or unmarried, as beneficiaries. For example, Margaret Brayne left all belongings to her creditor Robert Myles, but charged him to 'keepe, educate & bringe vpp Katherine Brayne my husbandes daughter' (Honigmann and Brock 1993, 61). Jane Poley left a small annual amount to her eldest son, who may well, like many eldest sons, have received 'preferential treatment by the common law of inheritance' (Erickson 1993, 71).[5] The large sum of £40 was given to her daughter Frauncis Wibard 'for the maintenance of her and her poor children and the bringing up of them' (Honigmann and Brock 1993, 65). To her apparently childless second daughter, Anne Gibbes, Poley left a number of valued personal possessions, including 'a hope ring of gold ... her best petticoat guarded with velvet ... one bolster which belongs to her bed' (Honigmann and Brock 1993, 66). Agnes Henslowe, the recent widow of theatre manager Philip, bequeathed money to a group of 'eighty poor widows and women,' with different amounts going to various other people and the 'Rest to only and well beloved daughter Joane Allen' (1993, 104). Elizabeth Cundall made the sharpest provisos in her will, leaving her 'goodes' to her daughter Elizabeth ffinch and £50 to her granddaughter Elizabeth Cundall. She then declared, 'I doe intend the same as that my said sonne in lawe Mr herbert ffynch shall neuer have possession of the same' (1993, 183), and 'I would have no parte of my estate neither prodigally spent, nor lewdly wasted by' her son, William Cundall (1993, 183).

The detail of these bequests is all the more notable because neither the amount of money nor the value of the items is especially huge. The 1686 will of Sarah, Duchess of Somerset, is no less specific in itemizing which female relatives and servants will get what. Yet the mass of goods and clothes that is dispensed seems to cloud the bequest's moral rationale and personal motives (see Briscoe 1973, 213–18). Due to the much smaller quantities of money and property and the specificity with which they are distributed, the wills of ordinary women, Mendelson and Crawford conclude, seem to evince a deep concern for 'both people and things at their deaths' (1998, 198). With limited means, they strive to balance attitudes about each beneficiary's character with the worth and amount of goods and the emotive value they hold for all parties.

In this light, wills disclose the potential impact of women's moral judgments in the familial and social spheres. They signify the interaction of emotive, ethical, and material considerations that guided women's conduct and that, through their texts as much as their behaviour, affected others in and beyond the family network, 'both as permanent legal record and as declaration of sentimental attachment' (Pointon 1997, 40). Wills are an excellent example of the variable influence that women's texts could have for their authors and for others. In her will, which was written in 1735 and proved in 1742, Dame Rebecca D'Oyly could reassert the power of independent decision making 'reserved to me in certain articles made on my marriage with the said Sir John D'Oyly' (Pointon 1997, 314). Dorothy Howard might respect and reward the long years of attention offered by a loyal servant while also conveying a moral message to her relatives:

> as the rest of my estate is very inconsiderable and all my ffriends and near relations greatly provided for and I have a poor servant named Margaret White who in a course of years in sickness and in health has given me undeniable proofs of her honesty uncommon ffidelity and concern for me I am persuaded my friends and relations will not blame me for bestowing upon my said servant all the residue of my estate I do therefore give devise and bequeath unto the said Margaret White all the rest residue and remainder of my goods cloaths moneys or securities. (1997, 360–1)

Howard signed her will in 1748 and it was proved in 1760; through this twelve-year period she combined affection for her kin and friends with an ethical concern that both displayed and modelled a right way to act.

Mary Prior finds parallels between the increase in the number of women's wills during the seventeenth century and the increase in women's published writings: 'Economic freedom gave to some wives the freedom to make wills, to others the confidence and the cash to write and publish their own work in a way never before possible' (1990, 223). Yet Prior stops short of declaring the writing of wills as a mode of female authorship, and so perhaps also occludes the possibility of recognizing the wider material, economic, and social effects of women's publishing. She notes, 'No wives who made wills were writers' (1990, 223), although one, Dame Mary Compton, was the granddaughter of Elizabeth Jocelin, the author of the 1624 advice book, *The Mothers Legacie*. In revealing this lineage, Prior all but names the final point I wish to raise: as the most consequential form in which women wrote, wills inform many of the issues, relationships, and conventions with which female authors were dealing in another notable early modern genre, the mother's advice book or 'legacy' to her children. I suggest that advice books are a kind of discursive adaptation of the will, developing the latter's complex of familial, moral, and material concerns and its hybrid private–public address into a personally voiced, socially oriented genre.

It is in fact Jocelin's *Mothers Legacie* which makes the connection between wills and advice books most explicit: 'Our lawes disable those, that are under *Couert-baron*, from dispensing by will and Testament any temporall estate. But no law prohibiteth any possessor of morall and spirituall riches, to impart them vnto others' (1624, sig. A3). A woman who takes up this opportunity becomes a 'truly rich bequeather' (1624, sig. A3v), and the text she produces is a 'will' that is registered 'among the most publique Monuments' (1624, sig. A4v). These lines draw on the material, moral, and religious values intrinsic to wills. The ensuing tract is example and incentive to wives to work around the social-legal restrictions that confront them by using the hybrid legacy genre to enter public discourse. Jocelin goes on to advise her husband and her child on a wide range of social, moral, and religious topics. She assumes her mortal right to some 'dying words' to justify authorship: 'I could not chuse but manifest this desire in writing, lest it should please God to depriue me of time to speake ... not knowing whether I shall liue to instruct thee when thou art home, let me not be blamed though I write to thee before' (1624, 8–10).

Jocelin's text is analogous to a wife's will that co-opts the husband's consent. In an initial contrast, Dorothy Leigh's *The Mother's Blessing*, first published in 1616, is the work of a widow, intent on continuing her dead husband's paternal nurturing of their sons. Leigh constantly underscores her pious motives as an author, 'to write them the right way that I had truly obserued out of the written Word of God' (1618, sig. A2v). In a prefatory letter to her sons, Leigh stresses 'I could not chuse but seeke (according as I was by duty bound) to fulfill his will in all things' and the 'care I had to fulfill his will in this' (1618, sig. A5–A5v). She plays on the dual meaning of will as desire and testament to support her taking over the father's role. But in fulfilling his will, she gradually starts to assert a critical perspective on many details of masculine conduct in the world, including hypocrisy, idleness, covetousness, and the mistreatment of wives. Finally, her focus turns to the inheritance system itself, and paternal preoccupation with bequeathing estates to sons: 'A thousand waies may separate thy sonnes and their goods farre asunder' (1618, 202); 'Seeke ye the heauenly treasure, and a little of this earthly trash will serue the turn' (1618, 213). With these words, Leigh attacks patriarchal values entrenched in early modern society and naturalized by common law. The widow's exclusion from the rules of inheritance affords a critical viewpoint on masculine property and identity, which for all their worldly sway remain subject: 'thou art but a tenant at the will of the Lord' (1618, 245).

A later example of the advice book appears involved less in pressuring paternal inheritance than in consolidating succession among women. The title of Elizabeth Richardson's *A Ladies Legacie to Her Daughters* reflects the emphasis on female bequests in the wills of women from all classes. Yet in some significant ways, the text shows that any case of female succession might serve to problematize inheritance norms. Richardson explains the circumstances that led her to publish the book – initially it was conceived as a private work but she was 'over persuaded by some that much desired to have them' (1645, 3). The hybrid genre of the legacy is again at issue and grants the author a special licence to write publicly. Richardson positions herself explicitly as a widow, and her text is a counter to those who, since the death of her husband (Sir Thomas Richardson, former Lord Chief Justice to the King's Bench), have worked against her: 'But though I am so unhappy as to be left destitute, not able to raise you portions of wealth, yet shall I joy as much to adde unto the portion of Grace' (1645, 4). She hints at a history of legal dispute that has deprived her and her daughters of the estate. Richardson deliberately refrains from addressing her sons, intimating the conflict that could arise between the male heirs and the widow, that so-called 'clog on the estate' in much legal history (Staves 1990, 203): 'And howsoever this my endeavour may be contemptible to many, (because a womans) which makes me not to joyne my sons with you; lest being men, they misconstrue my well-meaning; yet I presume that you my daughters will not refuse your Mothers teaching' (1645, 6).[6] Like Dorothy Leigh, she shifts the terms of inheritance away from material to spiritual value and in doing so challenges an inheritance system that works against women's right to property. The critique is reinforced within the text in 'A sorrowfull widowes prayer': 'having in thy mercifull goodnesse made me see with comfort all my children, who were left destitute, now by thy provident provision and blessing, well settled for this life ... so may I turne this freedome from the bond of marriage only the more to thy service' (1645, 134). Religious, moral, legal, and gendered viewpoints come together in subtle but critical response to worldly events.

Freedom from the bonds of marriage and property was perhaps more difficult to achieve through legal and social avenues than through spiritual means. Nonetheless, the way in which Leigh, Jocelin, and Richardson use religious and ethical discourse first to legitimate publishing their texts then to offer various kinds of critique of patriarchal inheritance and property laws builds upon the hybrid private–public address of early modern women's wills and the moral authority in interpersonal, familial, and social relations signified in the wills' careful bequests. Women's wills are an important example of female social and discursive agency. Through the seventeenth century and beyond, they provide a fundamental context for apprehending the ethical and material rights that were being addressed in the proliferating genres in which growing numbers of early modern women were starting to write.

Notes

1 Mary Prior notes the case of Margaret Lane, whose will was made 'without the consent of her husband, disposing ... freely of money and other goods, and even of the upbringing of her daughter' (1990, 221).

2 On limited class access to trusts, see Baker (1990, 554); Eileen Spring argues against regarding trusts as unilaterally aiding women: 'Equity protected

trusts whatever their purpose, and not all trusts were in favor of women'
(1993, 121). A contrasting and positive view of support for women through
equity is presented by Cioni (1985).

3 For example, Katharine Warner Swett notes that 'most ordinary north
Welshman left their wives with most of their property and their family
responsibilities' (1996, 199). Cicely Howell observes that provision for the
widow was the 'overriding' consideration of husbands in sixteenth- and
seventeenth-century Kibworth, in the English Midlands (1976, 143);
Erickson concludes that widows were principal beneficiaries in the majority
of cases and usually received more than the common law right of dower to
one-third of the estate (1993, 162).

4 See Wendy Wall's discussion of the way various female authors used the
'rhetoric of will-making' to realize different modes of 'self-authorization' in
the period (1991, 40–1).

5 Barbara J. Harris likewise suggests that some women 'ignored their eldest
sons in their wills or left them only token bequests and used their estates to
provide for their other children' (1990, 623).

6 See Harris on the 'delicate' position widows could find themselves in if they
disagreed with their eldest sons about the estate (1990, 629). Compare her
discussion of quarrels between heirs and aristocratic widows (2002, 114–16).

Works Cited

Baker, J.H. 1990. *An Introduction to English Legal History*. 3rd ed. London:
Butterworths.

Briscoe, A. Daly. 1973. *A Stuart Benefactress: Sarah, Duchess of Somerset*. Laven-
ham: Terence Dalton.

Chapman, George. 1975. *The Widow's Tears*, ed. Akihiro Yamada. Revels Plays.
London: Methuen.

Cioni, Maria L. 1985. *Women and Law in Elizabethan England with Particular
Reference to the Court of Chancery*. New York: Garland.

Erickson, Amy Louise. 1993. *Women and Property in Early Modern England*.
London: Routledge.

Ezell, Margaret J.M. 1987. *The Patriarch's Wife: Literary Evidence and the History of
the Family*. Chapel Hill: University of North Carolina Press.

Godolphin, John. [1674] 1685. *The Orphans Legacy: Or, A Testamentary Abridg-
ment*. London.

Goody, Jack. 1976a. Inheritance, Property and Women: Some Comparative
Considerations. In *Family and Inheritance: Rural Society in Western Europe*,

1200–1800, ed. Jack Goody, Joan Thirsk, and E.P. Thompson, 10–36. Cambridge: Cambridge University Press.

– 1976b. Introduction to *Family and Inheritance: Rural Society in Western Europe, 1200–1800*, ed. Jack Goody, Joan Thirsk, and E.P. Thompson, 1–9. Cambridge: Cambridge University Press.

Habakkuk, John. 1994. *Marriage, Debt, and the Estates System: English Landownership 1650–1950*. Oxford: Clarendon Press.

Harris, Barbara J. 1990. Property, Power, and Personal Relations: Elite Mothers and Sons in Yorkist and Early Tudor England. *Signs* 15: 606–32.

– 2002. *English Aristocratic Women, 1450–1550: Marriage and Family, Property and Careers*. Oxford: Oxford University Press.

Heywood, Thomas. 1975. *The Fair Maid of the West, Part 1*, ed. Brownell Salomon. Salzburg: Institut für Englische Sprache und Literatur.

Honigmann, E.A.J., and Susan Brock. 1993. *Playhouse Wills 1558–1642: An Edition of Wills by Shakespeare and His Contemporaries in the London Theatre*. Manchester: Manchester University Press.

Howell, Cicely. 1976. Peasant Inheritance Customs in the Midlands, 1280–1700. In *Family and Inheritance: Rural Society in Western Europe, 1200–1800*, ed. Jack Goody, Joan Thirsk, and E.P. Thompson, 112–55. Cambridge: Cambridge University Press.

Howell, Martha C. 1998. *The Marriage Exchange: Property, Social Place, and Gender in Cities of the Low Countries, 1300–1500*. Chicago: University of Chicago Press.

Jocelin, Elizabeth. 1624. *The Mothers Legacie, To Her Unborne Childe*. London.

Leigh, Dorothy. 1618. *The Mother's Blessing: Or, the Godly Counsel of a Gentlewoman, not long since deceased, left behind her for her Children: Contayning many good exhortations, and godly admonitions, profitable for all parents, to leave as a Legacy to their Children*. 4th ed. London.

Marsh, Christopher. 1990. In the Name of God? Will-Making in Early Modern England. In *The Records of the Nation: The Public Record Office 1838–1988, The British Record Society 1888–1988*, ed. G.H. Martin and Peter Spufford, 215–49. London: Boydell.

Mendelson, Sara, and Patricia Crawford. 1998. *Women in Early Modern England 1550–1720*. Oxford: Clarendon Press.

Pointon, Marcia. 1997. *Strategies for Showing: Women, Possession, and Representation in English Visual Culture 1665–1800*. Oxford: Oxford University Press.

Prior, Mary. 1985. Women and the Urban Economy: Oxford 1500–1800. In *Women in English Society 1500–1800*, ed. Mary Prior, 93–117. London: Methuen.

– 1990. Wives and Wills 1558–1700. In *English Rural Society, 1500–1800: Essays in Honour of Joan Thirsk*, ed. John Chartres and David Hey, 201–26. Cambridge: Cambridge University Press.

Richardson, Elizabeth. 1645. *A Ladies Legacie to Her Daughters*. London.

Spring, Eileen. 1993. *Law, Land, and Family: Aristocratic Inheritance in England, 1300–1800*. Chapel Hill: University of North Carolina Press.

Spufford, Margaret. 1976. Peasant Inheritance Customs and Land Distribution in Cambridgeshire from the Sixteenth to the Eighteenth Centuries. In *Family and Inheritance: Rural Society in Western Europe, 1200–1800*, ed. Jack Goody, Joan Thirsk, and E.P. Thompson, 156–76. Cambridge: Cambridge University Press.

Staves, Susan. 1990. *Married Women's Separate Property in England, 1660–1833*. Cambridge, MA: Harvard University Press.

– 1995. Resentment or Resignation? Dividing the Spoils among Daughters and Younger Sons. In *Early Modern Conceptions of Property*, ed. John Brewer and Susan Staves, 194–218. London: Routledge.

Swett, Katherine Warner. 1996. Widowhood, Custom and Property in Early Modern Northern Wales. *Welsh History Review* 18: 189–227.

Swinburn, Henrie. 1590. *A Briefe Treatise of Testaments and Last Willes*. London.

T.E. [1632] 1998. *The Law's Resolutions of Women's Rights: Or, the Law's Provision for Women*. In *Sexuality and Gender in the English Renaissance: An Annotated Edition of Contemporary Documents*, ed. Lloyd Davis, 371–406. New York: Garland.

Wall, Wendy. 1991. Isabella Whitney and the Female Legacy. *ELH* 58: 35–62.

Yamada, Akihiro. 1975. Introduction to *The Widow's Tear* by George Chapman, xix–lxxxv. Revels Plays. London: Methuen.

11

Spiritual Property: The English Benedictine Nuns of Cambrai and the Dispute over the Baker Manuscripts

CLAIRE WALKER

For th' observance of povertie it will be sufficient to practise what our hollie father hath ordained in divers passages of his Rule ... where his Religious are strictlie forbidden, to give, take, lend, send, beg, aske, receave, or c[laim?] ... neither cloathes, monney, letters, tokens, [or] gifts ... And the reason given by our hollie father St Bennett is, because by there [*sic*] profession they have lost all right, power, and disposition of there [*sic*] owne bodies and soules, much more to other externall thinges. And therfore we ordaine that this be kept carefullie, and that whatsoever is gotten or given to the Monastarie, must be appropriated to the wholl communitie, and be immediatlie brought to the Superiour and be whollie left to her disposition. (ADN 20 H 10, f. 30)

When a seventeenth-century woman pronounced her solemn vows of religious profession, she renounced any right to inherit the property of her secular kin and committed herself to a life of communal ownership within a religious cloister. All monastic goods had to be held in common. Individual possessions were forbidden. This denial of personal property rights was a vital element of monastic poverty. However, in the Benedictine order, poverty was not interpreted literally. Benedict's nuns required adequate housing, clothing, and sustenance in order to focus on their principal apostolate of prayer and contemplation. Therefore property was permitted, so long as all goods were held in common. It was the abbess's responsibility to administer the convent's assets, but she could not alienate lands or substantial goods without the consent of her council of senior nuns and the approval of the house's clerical overseer.

However, as the above extract from the 1631 constitution of the English Benedictine nuns of Cambrai suggests, monastic property was defined in very broad terms. Alongside the communal ownership of clothes, gifts, and money was a prohibition on individual possession of letters. Nuns were not permitted to either send or receive mail without the permission of their superior. This ban was principally intended to preserve the integrity of monastic enclosure. Letters linked individual nuns to their worldly friends and might well distract them from their contemplative vocation. Moreover, indiscreet gossip imparted to secular friends via correspondence might well tarnish the reputation of a religious community. Any hint of scandal often translated into economic hardship for a convent because potential novices would take their dowries elsewhere, and patrons would choose to bestow their alms upon more worthy recipients. Therefore in early modern convents there was a complex relationship between tangible property in the form of goods and income, and 'incorporeal property' represented by the nuns' reputation and, as we shall see, their spirituality (Lowie 1929, 224–32).

For the Benedictine nuns at Cambrai, prayer and anything which might facilitate it were extremely important. The nuns did not perform the active apostolate of nursing, teaching, or offering welfare in the local community. The cloister was contemplative, meaning its primary function was to pray for its patrons and society at large. Therefore the nuns conducted the formal canonical hours of prayer eight times a day. I have discussed the commercial nature of the communally recited divine office and its importance as a source of income for the English cloisters elsewhere (Walker 1999, 404–8). Here I am more interested in the other element of the contemplative vocation, which was personal meditation. Obviously in contemplative monasticism individuals were expected to achieve a fulfilling spiritual relationship with the divine. At Cambrai several nuns attained this goal by following a prayer regimen attributed to Augustine Baker, an English Benedictine monk who was a spiritual guide at the convent during its first nine years. Baker's religious treatises were retained by the convent after he left in 1633, and the nuns copied and circulated them among other cloisters. However, doubts were raised concerning the orthodoxy of Baker's teaching. Although the manuscripts were examined and deemed to be free of any heretical tendency in 1633, questions resurfaced in 1655, when Fr Claude White, the president of the English Benedictine congregation, unsuccessfully attempted to censor the manuscript material. After Baker's death in 1641, as co-founders of his spiritual method and its chief exponents and promoters, the Cambrai nuns were inevitably caught up in altercations over its validity.

The disputes over Augustine Baker's writings raise interesting questions about some of the new forms of property which developed in the early modern period, and women's relationship to them. The manuscripts clearly constituted 'intellectual property' as we would understand it. But the 1655 controversy highlighted the difficult issue regarding ownership of them and their content. What rights did the religious women have to the documents held in their possession, which arguably they had jointly created with Baker? Such considerations were further complicated by the monastic principle of all goods being held in common. In addition, there was the wider issue of the spirituality delineated in the manuscripts and the benefits or dangers it posed to the nuns and the Benedictine order at large. To address these points, I will first explain the wider political and religious context of the 1655 dispute. Then I will explore issues surrounding the ownership of the documents and their contents. Finally, I want to evaluate the relationship between this spirituality, the Benedictines' reputation, and the cloister's assets.

The Benedictine Nuns of Cambrai, Augustine Baker, and Claude White

The Cambrai Benedictines were just one of several English contemplative communities for women established abroad in the seventeenth century. In the aftermath of Henry VIII's dissolution of the monasteries, English women who wanted to take the veil had to enter foreign cloisters in Continental Europe. By the end of the sixteenth century, the sizeable expatriate English Catholic community in France and the southern Netherlands, which had already established colleges and seminaries for men, supported the foundation of religious institutes for their female kin. The first such establishment was the Benedictine abbey in Brussels, begun in 1598 by Lady Mary Percy and seven companions. During the following twenty-five years, other monastic orders, including the Poor Clares (discussed in an earlier chapter by Natasha Korda), Augustinians, Carmelites, and Third Order Regular Franciscans, were revived. The houses' popularity, combined with difficult economic and political circumstances locally and back in England, led to several filiations from the original foundations (Walker 2003, 13–19).[1] Thus, by 1700, twenty-two cloisters were in existence, and their inhabitants continued their original purpose of intercessory prayer for the conversion of their homeland.

The Cambrai convent was founded in 1623 by Helen (Dame Gertrude) More, the great-great-granddaughter of Sir Thomas More, and eight other English gentlewomen, including Catherine Gascoigne, the abbess at the centre of the 1655 furore.[2] Unlike the majority of English cloisters, Cambrai was affiliated with the English Benedictine congregation, which meant that the nuns were subject to its superior (termed the president) rather than to the local bishop. The founders had chosen Benedictine jurisdiction to avoid some of the spiritual and administrative conflicts which had beset earlier foundations, most notably the Benedictine abbey in Brussels, where the nuns and their abbess were divided over the issue of spiritual direction (Walker 2003, 70–2, 139–42; Guilday 1914, 257–64). Gertrude More and her companions were eager to be trained in Benedictine spirituality rather than pursue the more commonly practised Jesuit meditation. The novices accordingly petitioned Rudisind Barlow, the president of the English Benedictine congregation at the time, for someone who could train them in Benedictine contemplative prayer. They were sent Augustine Baker.

Baker's nine years at Cambrai grounded a particular brand of mysticism there, which the nuns maintained beyond his departure in 1633 and his death eight years later. Rather than impose a specific meditational regime upon the entire community, the monk encouraged individuals to seek the devotional path which best suited their ability and temperament. Seeking appropriate spiritual writings to assist the nuns, Baker turned to the works of the great late-medieval mystics, which he translated into English. In addition, he composed several pious treatises, advice books, and prayer manuals to advance the women's religious quest. In so doing, he modified established spiritual courses in accordance with his observation of the nuns' experiences. Together Baker and the Cambrai sisters fostered an alternative spirituality which was based firmly in the English medieval mystical tradition and the *devotio moderna* of the Low Countries (Lunn 1975, 268; Spearritt 1974, 294–300; Knowles 1927, 178–87).

It was Baker's noninterventionist approach to spiritual direction, the very element the nuns found most liberating, which was questioned by his detractors. The problem was that Baker was advocating it at a time when the Catholic Church recommended greater clerical regulation of spirituality, particularly for women. It was for this reason that Jesuit devotion was so popular. Ignatius Loyola's original liberal schema had been modified by his followers into a more mechanical piety, centred upon good works, attendance at the sacraments, frequent confession, and set meditations. Moreover, it was accompanied by regular clerical monitoring to ensure the orthodoxy of the person undertaking it. Inevitably some clerics became disturbed by Augustine Baker's influence on the Cambrai nuns. At a time when strict ecclesiastical control of personal spirituality was the norm, he was encouraging women to assert their spiritual independence. Accounts of Gertrude More's death from smallpox in 1633 would have fuelled rather than quelled suspicions. The night before she died, More was asked if she would like to speak with a priest, but she reportedly declined, saying 'give [Baker] thanks a thousand times, who had brought her to such a pass that she could confidently go out of this life without speaking to any man' (Weld-Blundell 1910–11, 1: 271).

In fact, shortly before Gertrude More's illness and death, Baker had been removed from Cambrai because of a dispute within the cloister over his spiritual direction. The majority of the nuns were his disciples, but a small number preferred the set meditations and devotions advocated by Fr Francis Hull, the official Benedictine chaplain of the house. Tension between Hull and Baker led to open conflict. Hull accused the mystic of preaching anti-authoritarian doctrines, and the charge brought Baker before the General Chapter of the English Benedictine congregation (McCann and Connolly 1933, 138–40). Both Gertrude More and Catherine Gascoigne, who had been elected the convent's first abbess in 1629, wrote eloquent defences in support of Baker for the chapter. Abbess Gascoigne's submission, comprising an account of her spiritual journey in which she contradicted Hull's accusation, declared 'this plaine and simplie [sic] exercise of the will taught us by father baker, tends to no other thing (so farre as I understand it) then this, to bring the soule to a totall subjection to God, and to others for God and according to his will' (Baker MS 33, f. 343). Baker's clerical peers agreed with her assessment and his writings were deemed orthodox. However, despite being cleared of heretical leanings, the monk was removed from the Cambrai monastery to St Gregory's College in Douai. From Douai he was sent on the English mission in 1638. He died in London in 1641 (Low 1970, 47–50).

The spirituality fostered at Cambrai by Baker survived his departure and death. The nuns continued to practise it and they actively disseminated its principles beyond their convent's walls. The meditation method it propounded came to be identified positively with the cloister, and the nuns acquired a reputation for intense piety. Therefore, they were alarmed when, in 1655, Claude White, the president of the English Benedictine congregation, demanded that Abbess Catherine Gascoigne relinquish the original Baker treatises. White argued that Baker's writings contained 'poysonous, pernicious and diabolicall doctrine' and therefore asked to be given the manuscripts in order to expunge them of all erroneous teaching (Rawlinson MS A.36, f. 45). During a visit in his capacity as their clerical overseer, White apparently terrified many of the nuns by threatening them with dire consequences if they refused to submit to his wishes. He told them that to persist in their opposition was 'absolut disobedience.' When Abbess Gascoigne staunchly maintained her position, he announced that she was 'in a damnable way running to perdition' (Rawlinson MS A.36, ff. 45, 49). Thus, the implication was that although heretical in themselves, the writings of Baker also subverted ecclesiastical authority by encouraging the nuns to assert their independence in matters beyond the purely spiritual realm.

Ultimately, the abbess was able to resist White's efforts to acquire the manuscripts, and his death a few months later silenced her opponents. However, it did not completely lay to rest questions about the orthodoxy of Baker's methods. On the eve of her death in 1676, Catherine Gascoigne remained worried that the events of 1655 might well be repeated, and she voiced these fears to Fr Benedict Stapleton, who was the congregation's president at the time. Stapleton did not take her concerns lightly and he recommended:

> The only expedient I can thinke of at present for their preservation is that in case it shall please god to call you out of this world that you recommend those bookes to some faithfull and intelligent person of the howse and I doe earnestly require the Ladie Abbesse to put them into such hands as you shall desire that they may be preserved entire and without any alteration. (ADN, 20 H 10, f. 505)

Thus, by 1676, the ownership issue had been resolved in the convent's favour. Stapleton evidently held Catherine Gascoigne and her successor as abbess, Catherine (Dame Maura) Hall, responsible for the manuscripts' safekeeping.[3] However, in 1655 the right of the nuns to protect Baker's writings was far from clear.

Spiritual Property: The Manuscripts and the 'Cambrai School'

The ownership of the Baker manuscripts and the spirituality they conveyed are a complex issue. In the early seventeenth century there were no copyright laws which might have established Augustine Baker as their originator and thus attributed to him (and his estate) rights over the ideas and words they contained. In any case, Baker's writings were not entirely original. They comprised his collation of translated material from the late medieval mystics. So the first problem to resolve is the extent to which Baker owned the content of his manuscripts. Laura Rosenthal's study of *King Lear* as literary property offers a point of analogy. Dramatic texts often retold old stories and borrowed elements from earlier versions, which were part of the public domain. Even after Shakespeare there were further adaptations of the stories he had dramatized, like Lear. Yet while Shakespeare used previous works as the basis for his own plays without attribution, he also 'improved' them by adding new aspects. Revisions were commonplace in the theatre and none of Shakespeare's contemporaries would have deemed his use of others' work and changes to the story line problematic (Rosenthal 1995, 323–7). Spiritual writings were similarly eclectic. Religious authors drew upon existing methodologies and images to outline their recommended path to divine union. As devotional books were often guides to achieve spiritual satisfaction, it was natural that they would suggest tried and successful measures. Just as no one 'owned' the Lear story, similarly no one 'owned' pious reflections.

However, there was a tradition of attribution in the genre of devotional writing. Although authors, like Baker, cited the ideas and even words of their sources, they generally acknowledged their author. There was an important reason for this practice. The writers needed to establish the orthodoxy of their doctrine, so it was essential to ground it firmly within the existing canon. As I have explained, Baker based his method upon the writings of the late medieval mystics, including Blosius, John Ruysbroeck, John Tauler, Walter Hilton, and Henry Suso. Thus, although the Cambrai nuns spoke of 'Fr Baker's way' and promoted the methodology as his creation, Baker acknowledged a debt to his spiritual forebears. His friend and biographer Leander Prichard noted his great respect for them, writing 'and very glad was he to find in them things confirming his doctrin and practise' (McCann and Connolly 1933, 123). Catherine (Dame Christina) Brent, Abbess Gascoigne's assistant during the 1655 crisis and later abbess herself, also attested to the 'Authors both auncieuncient [i.e., ancient] and moderne, whom he followed, and with whom he concurred' (ADN, 20 H 10, f. 902).

Yet, like Shakespeare, Baker moved beyond his sources and modified existing spiritual practices. He had developed his meditation regime via a personal experience of spiritual desolation. Equating monasticism with contemplation and mysticism, he had attempted mental prayer (as opposed to vocal prayer) when a novice but failed because of inadequate guidance. For several years he endeavoured to discover the secret to successful meditation, and in the process, he turned to the 'true spirituall and mistick authers' (McCann and Connolly 1933, 101). Thus, his writings comprised a blend of both his reading and his experience, and it was the latter that constituted his originality. Nevertheless, there was another element to Baker's genius. He also relied upon his friends for references they had uncovered in their own reading, for their ideas and suggestions, and for their critical evaluation of his ideas and writings (McCann and Connolly 1933, 122–3).

After Augustine Baker had left Cambrai and was living at Douai Abbey, he intimated to Leander Prichard the importance of his friends' contributions. Prichard had discerned a difference in the treatises written during his nine years with the nuns and the works produced in the masculine environment of Douai, noting 'those of Cambray (for the most part) were institutions or canons of a contemplative life.' The Douai material was more casuistic and historical in nature, and Prichard reported 'I have heard him say, when he at Doway perused some of his Cambray works, that if he were then to writ or give such instructions or canons of contemplation, he could not possibly do it' (McCann and Connolly 1933, 122). Thus, Baker himself acknowledged that Cambrai advanced his spiritual method. He had been sent there to teach the new nuns Benedictine spirituality, so his advice and writings were governed by the religious women's needs. He had established his technique for meditation prior to arriving at the convent, but he had not learned how to impart it to others. Initially several nuns, including Gertrude More, found his approach difficult to comprehend. Gradually both Baker and the nuns came to terms with each other's position, and they forged a working relationship which enabled individual nuns to discover the devotions which best suited their circumstances. The key to Baker's approach was his refusal to be intrusive, which necessitated the nuns' active participation in the process. Thus, Baker's method was not solely his creation. It was the product of collaboration with the nuns.

Gertrude More's discovery of the most appropriate meditation technique for her serves as an example of this joint creation. After some sessions with Baker, she began to experience some success in prayer, but she continued to be troubled regularly by distractions and feelings of spiritual aridity. Baker simply encouraged her to persevere, even when she felt most desolate, but she found little solace in his words. More eventually discovered the solution to her problems in a Latin treatise, and asked Baker to translate it for her. He wrote of the incident, 'I gave her the passage in English, and she took it and made great use of the doctrine, continuing her prayer notwithstanding all her frequent desolations' (Weld-Blundell 1910–11, 1: 30). In this interaction between the monk and the nun, More identified the words of comfort which enabled her to progress spiritually, and Baker noted them. In the process he too gained an insight into which advice might assist someone suffering More's condition.

Thus, the nuns could claim partial ownership of Baker's technique because of their participation in its development and consolidation. Yet, although they were co-authors of the method, what rights did they have to the actual manuscripts which explicated it? In a recent analysis of correspondence as property, Dena Goodman has discussed letters as jointly owned by the writer and the addressee. A letter is composed with an 'audience' in mind, and it is not complete until it has been read by its intended recipient (Goodman 1995, 345–50). Although spiritual writings and letters, such as those discussed by Jennifer Summit in the introductory chapter to this section, appear to constitute very different literary forms, there are similarities which imply the nuns' joint ownership of Baker's manuscripts. Baker wrote specifically for the convent, which was in effect his 'addressee.' Fr Serenus Cressy, Baker's friend and editor of the first published edition of his work, noted that the monk committed his instructions to paper only at the insistence of the nuns (Salvin and Cressy 1933, 125). Moreover, Baker left the documents in the nuns' hands when he departed Cambrai, suggesting that they were intended for use by the convent. So it seems that the religious community could claim title to the spirituality which they had co-created, and to the manuscripts which contained its tenets.

However, this is a modern interpretation which is alien to the nuns' conception of their spiritual property. Not unsurprisingly they viewed it in distinctly monastic terms. Like the community's other assets, Baker's doctrine and the papers upon which it was written were communally owned. The convent's constitutions, which adapted the Benedictine rule for use in the house, stated 'All the bookes must belong to the common librarie, and ... have written on them the name of the Monasterie, and be common to all indifferentlie' (ADN, 20 H 1, f. 32). The nuns understood this decree to extend not only to the books but also to any document entering the cloister. As I mentioned earlier, private letters were forbidden. They were only acceptable if their contents were spiritually edifying and could be shared. Individual devotional writings were viewed in the same way. So personal correspondence about religious matters and pious recollections were often collated for communal use. Cambrai's weighty manuscript tome of 908 pages, now held by the Archives Départementales du Nord at Lille, comprises letters, spiritual advice, extracts from favoured religious authors, and texts of speeches copied by one of the cloister's indefatigable writers, Barbara Constable (ADN, 20 H 10). Although many of the individual items in this collection were written with a particular nun in mind, they ultimately became common property. In addition to the monastic precept of all goods held in common, those of a devotional nature had to be circulated to assist others along their path to God. Therefore there was a missionary imperative implicit in ownership of spiritual property.

Upon quitting Cambrai, Baker left the nuns the duty of disseminating his writings to others. They were largely responsible for copying the Baker manuscripts for their own use and for distribution among other Benedictine houses (e.g., ADN, 20 H 39/3–4; Baker MS 26; Gillow MS 68812). The late 1640s witnessed a vast increase in copying to supply Cambrai's proposed daughter-house in Paris (founded in 1650) with a complete set of his works. The nuns also continued his practice of collating the wisdom of other spiritual authorities in prayer manuals and advice books, and these digests were similarly passed between the cloisters (e.g., ADN, 20 H 10, 20 H 33/ 'Thau,' 20 H 39/3; Baker MS 33, ff. 281–90, 290–328; Gillow MS Baker 4, f. 152). The spirituality was even promoted beyond the Benedictine order. In the mid-1630s the nuns corresponded with the English Carmelites at Antwerp and sent them many copies of Baker's books (McCann and Connolly 1933, 139).

Baker had also endorsed his disciples as competent teachers of his method. After his departure, he refused Abbess Gascoigne's request for visits to instruct the novices, claiming that the nuns were 'sufficiently entered and founded in their spirituall course ... to undertake the office of teaching the younger [nuns]' (McCann and Connolly 1933, 139). Even clergy outside the Benedictine order recognized the women's capacity for spiritual tutelage and noted the benefits it might bring to other monastic establishments. In 1642, Catherine Gascoigne, Bridget More, and Anne (Dame Clementina) Cary were sent by the archbishop of Cambrai to reform the local Benedictine monastery of St Lazare. Catherine Gascoigne conducted the restoration of regular discipline there as the house's temporary superior. She instructed the nuns in

Baker's method and compiled a collection of his writings for their use (ADN, 20 H 10, f. 905). Her success led to accolades from the archbishop and other local worthies, who 'affirmed they had never met a person of greater light and experience than she had in the conduct of souls' (*In a Great Tradition* 1956, 21). Thus, Baker's former pupils became 'missionaries' and passed on their knowledge to others.

However, the nuns did not promote a static spiritual method which rested solely upon Baker's texts. They too wrote devotional works which aimed to explicate their prayer regime and the struggle to discern and preserve it. Spiritual diaries and devotional treatises were written for private and collective edification and circulated among members of the Cambrai and Paris cloisters (e.g., Hazlemere MS 1886). The devotions of Margaret Gascoigne, Abbess Gascoigne's younger sister, supplemented by Baker's evaluation of her spiritual progress, provided her sisters with evidence that perseverance in the face of desolation ultimately paid spiritual dividends (Gillow MS Baker 4, ff. 55–152). Such compositions reflect the convent's ongoing adaptation of Baker's ideology to suit evolving personal and communal needs. Yet while these texts were compiled principally for their own consumption, Cambrai's spirituality was disseminated beyond an exclusively female monastic readership. Barbara Constable, responsible for many copies of Baker's works, wrote pious treatises for her family in England and advice manuals for the clergy (Gillow 1913, 10–12; Downside MS 552/82145). Her 'Advises for Confessors and Spiritual Directors,' completed in 1650, was grounded in the cloister's experience of inadequate religious guidance (Downside MS 629/82146, ff. ix–xiii, 378–91). The publication in 1658 of Gertrude More's pious reflections, titled *The Spiritual Exercises*, conveyed the spirituality to an even wider audience. Fr Serenus Cressy acknowledged More's vital contribution to the spiritual welfare of both her sisters and diverse others, writing:

> She proved, as it were, a Domestick Mistresse after her Death, to All the present, and Succeeding souls in That Convent. Yea, Many others, of divers Conditions, have not only Received much Edification, but Great Profit, by the sight of the said Writings, in being drawn and Encouraged by them, to Give themselves very seriously to prayer; as her Example and Counsell, when Living did worke the like Effects in Many. (BM, MS 1755, f. 182)

Therefore, as Cressy suggests, beyond the simple preservation and dissemination of Baker's teaching, the nuns stamped it with their own mark. Although the convent persistently referred to it as 'Fr Baker's Way,' in the eyes of others it became increasingly identified as the 'Cambrai School.'

In 1655, despite widespread recognition that the 'Cambrai School' was grounded in the collaborative efforts of both Baker and the nuns, and that it comprised not only the monk's texts but also the women's writings, Claude White opted for a narrow definition of ownership which centred upon the autograph manuscripts. He demanded the convent relinquish Baker's documents so that the 'poysonous, pernicious and diabolicall doctrine' they contained could be censored (Rawlinson MS A.36, f. 45). Thus, he implied that Baker's words, written in his own hand, were at fault, and their elimination would cleanse the spirituality of any dangerous tendencies. White made no allusion to the cloister's partial ownership of these offensive passages, nor did he propose to censor any of the nuns' writings which were based upon them. Indeed, he explicitly denied that the manuscripts were the religious women's intellectual property. According to Catherine Gascoigne, he declared 'that he meant not to alienat anything from our convent but to purge the bookes that we might not feed upon poisnous doctrine' (Rawlinson MS A.36, f. 49). Obviously White had to acknowledge the cloister's custodianship of Baker's manuscripts, but he was unwilling to attribute any errors in the treatises to the nuns. Thus, he seemingly denied that the manuscripts were communal property.

The Benedictine president's reason for distancing Baker's doctrine from the convent was obvious. He wanted to brand part of the monk's ideology as heretical. Given the nuns' reputation for piety, it would have been unwise to implicate them in such damaging allegations. The cloister's supporters, like the admiring archbishop of Cambrai, would have denied the charge and, in any case, as the nuns' clerical superior White could not afford to endanger their livelihood. However, in spite of his efforts to distance the convent from his accusations against Baker, few accepted his limited definition of ownership, least of all Catherine Gascoigne. The abbess knew that the documents were not just paper, ink, and Baker's words. They stood for everything she and her nuns believed in and had profited from spiritually. Expunge the so-called erroneous words, and the integrity of their devotional method would be undermined. Moreover, despite White's assertions to the contrary, the nuns' part in creating the spirituality, their role in its dissemination, and their own writings would be called into question. The convent was in grave danger of being labelled heretical. Seeking the assistance of Fr

Anselm Crowder, her agent in England, Gascoigne wrote, 'this it seemes to me will be so great a prejudice to the bookes, and so great an injury to all such of the Congregation that do esteeme them, that I cannot in conscience give my consent to put them into his hands.' She continued,

> I humbly beseech you therfore to looke upon this affaire, not as a thing only concerning our house, but the whole Congregation, which indeed is interested in it, both in respect of the Bookes, and the proceedings of our Very Reverend Father President against us, upon such grounds, which may be the case of any other house of the Congregation upon every difference betwixt the President and the superior of it, to the prejudice of their spirituall and temporall good, and the unmeasurable disturbance of their peace so much desired and regarded by all. (Rawlinson MS A.36, f. 50)

The abbess's appeal for assistance from the monks, and her warning that White might threaten other houses if allowed to get away with his attack on the nuns, was grounded in her monastic conception of ownership. She argued that Baker's manuscripts and the 'Cambrai School' did not belong to the nuns alone; they were the property of the entire English Benedictine congregation.

Reputation and Property

Given Cambrai's relationship with Augustine Baker and his teaching, Claude White would surely have understood his actions' negative repercussions for the convent's reputation and economic security. Therefore the question remains as to why White was intent on censoring the manuscripts. The existing historiography is partisan, written by Catholic (often Benedictine) historians. They have located the president's actions within political tensions among the English Benedictines. Baker had been controversial during his lifetime. He had reportedly offended the former president, Rudisind Barlow, by penning an unflattering portrait of him, and it has been suggested that Barlow was behind White's actions (*In a Great Tradition* 1956, 23–4; Lunn 1975, 272–3). This is one explanation for the extraordinary events which took place at Cambrai in 1655, but I think the answer lies more in the complexities of the ownership issue, in particular, the far-reaching definition of communal ownership articulated by Catherine Gascoigne. White feared for the congregation's reputation and the negative impact on its resources triggered by continued murmuring about Baker's orthodoxy.

As I discussed in the first section, Baker's laissez-faire approach to spirituality ran against the prevailing tide of tight regulation and rigidly prescribed devotional regimes. It had been questioned in 1633 when he was still at Cambrai, and a group of learned clerics had examined his treatises and exonerated both Baker and the nuns. Yet in the post-Reformation Catholic Church there were constant fears about potential heresy, especially when it came to houses of religious women. So doubts about the wisdom contained in Baker's teaching resurfaced periodically. Moreover, the nuns were promoting the 'Cambrai School,' and perhaps even working towards the canonization of their former spiritual guide, for they referred to him as the 'Venerable Augustine Baker,' as if the canonization process was under way (*In a Great Tradition* 1956, 24). In her version of the controversy, written around twenty years after the event, Christina Brent, one of Catherine Gascoigne's staunchest supporters, acknowledged the nuns had created a perception that Baker had advanced a completely new spirituality, which with the benefit of hindsight she admitted was a mistake (ADN, 20 H 10, ff. 901–2). In the reforming Catholic Church new and liberal doctrines were not looked upon kindly; nor were those who practised them. Therefore, despite Claude White's efforts to pinpoint ownership of the 'Cambrai School' to Baker alone, in reality he understood that teachings created and promoted by Benedictines implied communal ownership. Doubts regarding the orthodoxy of the spirituality ultimately damaged the reputation of the entire English Benedictine congregation. Thus, White's actions can be interpreted as an attempt to disown Baker by questioning his ideology and endeavouring to expunge the dubious elements of his teaching.

Claude White's concern that the English Benedictines might be damaged by Baker's unorthodox approach to spiritual direction was particularly poignant in 1655 because at the time Serenus Cressy was compiling an edition of Baker's writings, published in 1657 as *Sancta Sophia*. Whereas previously the doctrine, available only in manuscript copies, circulated within the relatively closed circles of the Benedictine and other English religious orders, it would soon reach a much wider readership. The eighteenth-century French lawyer Michel de Servan observed the impact of printing on intellectual property:

> The thoughts of a man are surely the most incontestable of properties; but before the invention of printing, it was the least solid: a mouse could nibble away in a week thirty years of reflections. Since [the invention of] printing, on the contrary, ideas are the most durable property; not a building on

earth is more imperishable than a good work, and the most fertile soil will be buried beneath the sand before a good work is buried in oblivion. (Goodman 1995, 350)

Servan encapsulates White's fears well. Should Baker's orthodoxy be questioned after publication of *Sancta Sophia*, the congregation could not easily disown it. Cressy's complicity by editing the treatises further identified Baker's doctrine as the intellectual property of the English Benedictines.

Claude White had not been the first to fear that questions surrounding Baker's orthodoxy might damage the reputation of the monastic order. Christina Brent explained how, after the first challenge to Baker's teaching in 1633, the monks were reluctant to advertise the affair:

The Reverend Fathers of our Generall chap[ter] being verie carefull of the good and peace of our house and the honour of our Congre[gation] thought fitte at the verie first to stifle any report or opinion of any errour that might be thought to have been introduced or tolerated. (ADN, 20 H 10, ff. 903–4)

They had organized an exhaustive examination of all Baker's writings by several learned religious scholars which exonerated him entirely. But Brent revealed that rather than publicize their findings, the monks stifled discussion because they felt that too much publicity would damage the reputation of the order further. She disagreed with their handling of the affair, declaring the decision 'more contributed to the increase of the mistake or ignorance in the matter then in any sort diminish[ed] it' (ADN, 20 H 10, f. 905).

However, the impact of the 1655 controversy on Cambrai's livelihood confirmed the wisdom of the 1633 investigators. As I noted earlier, any hint of scandal in a religious house would deter parents from sending their daughters to its novitiate and school. It also discouraged patrons from bestowing alms. In 1655, the Benedictine convent was already in some financial difficulty. In addition to pecuniary problems caused by the English civil war and interregnum, which had seen most of their income from England cease, the convent's assets had been poorly managed by its male Benedictine administrators. Fr Anselm Crowder, their recently appointed procurator, angrily denounced the mismanagement of his predecessors and told Abbess Gascoigne that the congregation should compensate the nuns (Rawlinson MS A.36, f. 89). Thus, in 1655, the convent could ill afford the bad press it would receive in the months to come. The dispute with Claude White not only severely damaged the house's good name, it proved detrimental to its economic survival.

The president was well aware of the nuns' financial predicament. Yet, contrary to his efforts to quarantine the convent from the taint of heresy, White pressured the abbess to acquiesce to his demands by directly threatening their income. Three novices were due to make their final vows in 1655. Anselm Crowder was in the final stages of securing their dowries (to be paid upon their religious profession), which would provide approximately £1,000 (Rawlinson MS A.36, f. 89).[4] Amidst the furore of White's visit to the convent during which he railed at the nuns for not obeying his wishes, the abbess attempted to obtain his permission for the novices to profess. This could not occur without his approval, which normally would be given after he had interviewed the women. The president resorted to blackmail, saying 'he would not see or speake with them [i.e., the novices], before he had satisfaction in what he desired' (Rawlinson MS A.36, f. 49). Monks who supported the abbess were aghast at his tactics. Fr Augustine Conyers noted that the convent might well have to give in because of 'the difficulties you are in for the non profession of your Prentices' (Rawlinson MS A.36, f. 85). Indeed, once the novices learned that they had become pawns in the battle, rumours spread that they were not prepared to remain at Cambrai (Rawlinson MS A.36, ff. 50, 53, 89). Notwithstanding their initial determination to quit the troubled house, all three women ultimately chose to remain, so their portions were not lost (Rawlinson MS A.36, ff. 50, 73, 79). However, although the immediate threat to their livelihood had been averted, the dissension did have long-term negative consequences.

Since its inception in 1623 the convent had attracted a steady stream of recruits. Although the civil war had resulted in diminished numbers of novices, most years had provided one or two new entrants. In the aftermath of the White affair, the popularity of the house plummeted. Apart from the abbess's niece, Frances Gascoigne, who entered in July 1655, there were no further candidates for the choir until 1660, when three women joined, of whom only one persevered. Then there was another lull until 1666, after which recruitment patterns became more regular (Gillow 1913, 49). The 1650s saw increased numbers at the other religious houses, so Cambrai's poor standing points clearly to diminished confidence in the community's reputation.

In conclusion, the altercation over the Baker manuscripts highlights the complex relationship between intellectual property, reputation, and financial security in a seventeenth-century English convent. The composition of Baker's spiritual treatises alone reveals the difficulty in attributing authorship in specific documents. These documents' dissemination and development in the nuns' hands raise further issues about the ownership of the spirituality they contained. It had originated with Baker but, by the 1650s, it was identified increasingly with Cambrai. Perceptions of the convent's ownership proved a double-edged sword for the religious women. On the one hand, the 'Cambrai School' endowed them with a reputation for sanctity which garnered respect and new recruits in the 1630s and 1640s, despite ongoing financial difficulties. On the other, it focused the attention of those who disliked the independence so characteristic of its spirituality squarely upon the cloister. Abbess Catherine Gascoigne's determination to uphold the integrity of the 'Cambrai School' brought severe economic hardship upon the house. Yet, ultimately, the abbess secured a legacy for the Benedictines which is not shared by any other post-Reformation English order. At a time when all other English communities practised derivatives of Jesuit and Teresian spirituality, the Benedictines owned a unique form in the 'Cambrai School.' And despite the abbess's insistence that it was the common property of the entire English Benedictine congregation, her contemporaries and subsequent scholars have acknowledged the nuns' indisputable ownership.

Notes

1 There were other orders also. The Bridgettines of Syon Abbey had survived the Dissolution to settle in Lisbon in 1594. The Canonesses of the Holy Sepulchre began a cloister in Liège in 1642. A filiation of Third Order Regular Franciscans to Paris in 1658 changed their rule to that of the order of the Immaculate Conception. And in 1661 a Dominican convent was set up in Vilvorde (later transferring to Antwerp). For a full account of the initial foundations and their filiations, see chapter 1 of Walker (2003).

2 'Helen' was her baptismal name and she became 'Dame Gertrude' upon her religious profession. I will provide both names upon initial mention, and thereafter use the name by which the nun is commonly known – in this case, Gertrude More.

3 Catherine Gascoigne had retired as abbess in 1673 and had been replaced by Maura Hall.

4 I do not have exact dowry figures for all three novices. Margaret Smith's

portion had been negotiated at £300. Clare and Ursula Radcliffe would have received roughly the same amount. The average dowry for Benedictines was usually £300 to £350.

Works Cited

Archives Départementales du Nord, Lille (ADN).

Baker MSS. Downside Abbey Library and Archives, nr. Bath.

Bibliothèque Mazarine, Paris (BM).

Downside MSS. Downside Abbey Library and Archives, nr. Bath.

Gillow, J., ed. 1913. Records of the Abbey of Our Lady of Consolation at Cambrai, 1620–1793. In *Miscellanea VIII*. Catholic Record Society, vol. 13. London: Catholic Record Society.

Gillow MSS. Downside Abbey Library and Archives, nr. Bath.

Goodman, D. 1995. Epistolary Property: Michel de Servan and the Plight of Letters on the Eve of the French Revolution. In *Early Modern Conceptions of Property*, ed. J. Brewer and S. Staves, 339–64. London and New York: Routledge.

Guilday, P. 1914. *The English Catholic Refugees on the Continent, 1558–1795*. London: Longmans, Green and Co.

Hazlemere MSS. Downside Abbey Library and Archives, nr. Bath.

Hirschon, R. 1984. Introduction to *Women and Property – Women as Property*, ed. R. Hirschon, 1–22. London and Canberra: Croom Helm.

In a Great Tradition: Tribute to Dame Laurentia McLaughlan Abbess of Stanbrook by the Benedictines of Stanbrook. 1956. London: John Murray.

Knowles, D. 1927. *The English Mystics*. London: Burns, Oates and Washbourne.

Low, A. 1970. *Augustine Baker*. New York: Twayne.

Lowie, R.H. 1929. *Primitive Society*. London: George Routledge & Sons.

Lunn, D. 1975. Augustine Baker (1575–1641) and the English Mystical Tradition. *Journal of Ecclesiastical History* 26: 267–77.

McCann, J., and H. Connolly, eds. 1933. *Memorials of Father Augustine Baker and Other Documents Relating to the English Benedictines*. Catholic Record Society, vol. 33. London: Catholic Record Society.

Rawlinson MSS. Bodleian Library, Oxford.

Rosenthal, Laura J. 1995. (Re) Writing Lear: Literary Property and Dramatic Authorship. In *Early Modern Conceptions of Property*, ed. J. Brewer and S. Staves, 323–38. London and New York: Routledge.

Salvin, P., and S. Cressy. 1933. *The Life of Father Augustine Baker, OSB (1575–1641)*, ed. Justin McCann. London: Burns, Oates and Washbourne.

Spearritt, P. 1974. The Survival of Medieval Spirituality among the Exiled English Black Monks. *American Benedictine Review* 25: 287–316.

Walker, C. 1999. Combining Martha and Mary: Gender and Work in Seventeenth-Century English Cloisters. *Sixteenth Century Journal* 30: 397–418.

– 2003. *Gender and Politics in Early Modern Europe: English Convents in France and the Low Countries*. Basingstoke and New York: Palgrave.

Weld-Blundell, B., ed. 1910–11. *The Inner Life and Writings of Dame Gertrude More*. 2 vols. London: Burns and Oates.

12

The Titular Claims of Female Surnames in Eighteenth-Century Fiction

ELEANOR F. SHEVLIN

'Titles like *Tom Jones* and *Clarissa*,' Paul Hunter once declared, 'tell us nothing at all about the social, economic, political, religious, or philosophical commitments in these novels' (1979, 71).[1] Such textual titles, however, reveal more than Hunter's remark would have us believe: at the very least, these and similar titles of eighteenth-century novels encapsulate the social and economic connections among gender, marriage, and property. If we heed their various enunciations, *Tom Jones*, *Clarissa*, and the host of similar titular names labelling eighteenth-century novels attend directly to property relationships. Indeed, the absence of surnames in the titles of novels named after their heroines as opposed to the almost certain inclusion of surnames in the titles of those named after their heroes can only be adequately explained in terms of eighteenth-century social and economic mores.

Names, and naming as a practice, possess undeniable power through their close links to matters of property. 'What is at stake in the naming process,' as Michael Ragussis has asserted, 'is no less than an act of possession' (1986, 7). While the naming of a text involves the registering of ownership claims over that text, novels named for their heroes or heroines produce a special subset of claims and expectations generated by the personal name appearing in the title. Names occupied a central place of importance not only in eighteenth-century philosophical, scientific, and intellectual thought but also in everyday life (Ragussis 1986, 4–9).[2] In terms of their cultural significance, personal names became increasingly important as signs of the personal property one has in one's self,[3] and this growing importance often conflicted with the traditional importance of names as signs of status and markers of landed property.

Fittingly, the adoption of hereditary surnames in England came about, in part, through an act of possession – the conquest of England by the Normans. The Norman legal system and its concomitant methods of maintaining records made it a necessity for the English to adopt surnames (Barton 1990, 42; Bowman 1931, 5–7). The practice took solid hold initially among the aristocracy, those feudal lords and knights owning and identified with forms of real property, the legal term for land and other immovable property. Not surprisingly, surnames associated with lands, buildings, and estates were the first type of hereditary surnames to be adopted; 'local names,' as these surnames derived from place names are termed, also constitute the largest class of last names. In addition, three other types of surnames exist, derived respectively from patronymic or familial relationships (calling this category 'patronymic' obscures those names passed on through maternal lines), occupations or offices held, and nicknames (Bowman 1931, 10–11; Reaney 1958, xii). With time the practice of having a 'gentilitous appellation' became more and more established (Bowman 1931, 8), though the rate at which diverse social ranks and geographic regions adopted surnames varied. As might be expected given the links between surnames and property ownership, those individuals occupying the lower ranks of society, especially those in rural areas, were the last to adopt the use of surnames.

Surnames held special relevance to issues of gender and the transfer of property. Like property in the eighteenth century, surnames were also not as stable as society pretended and desired them to be. After the Restoration the process of substituting one's surname for another, typically done in order to facilitate the familial inheriting and transfer of property, grew rapidly in popularity. In fact, roughly one-fourth of all private Acts of Parliament at mid-century concerned name changes, and this number only partially represents the amount of surname substitution occurring at this time since petitioning the monarch offered an alternative, less costly, and more efficient route of changing one's surname (Gibson 1992, 17–18).[4] As William Gibson has discussed, the scant study of this practice has focused on its significance to primogeniture among the peerage while ignoring the popularity of this practice among untitled landed classes and even clergyman (1992, 171). Like other aspects of property, the ability to change one's surname was a peculiarly English phenomenon; such changes on the Continent not only were highly illegal but also carried harsh penalties.

That the sociohistorical, cultural connotations of actual names crossed over into the fictional realm is evident in the interest displayed in the names of fictional characters during the eighteenth century. By mid-century, for example, eighteenth-century theatre audiences were not only desirous of learning the names of the actors and the actresses in advance, but they also wished to learn the full names of the characters well before the performance (Barton 1990, 175). In *The Names of Comedy* Anne Barton asserts that Restoration dramatists went to great lengths to avoid giving their heroines surnames in order to distinguish these young women from all the other characters in their comedies (1990, 179). Although Barton is speaking about character names, her comments are pertinent to personal names occurring in textual titles and the ability of these names to reflect contemporary social relations and attitudes. Barton historicizes this practice in terms of Restoration comedy's characteristic stance towards marriage as an unhappy state and growing old as an awkward, difficult process (1990, 179). The heroine's lack of a sur-name – which in Restoration comedy emphasized the self-possession and spirit of the young female protagonist actively pursuing the rake (1990, 178–9) – carries very different connotations for mid-eighteenth-century novels. Speaking about names, titles, and novels in the long eighteenth century, Ian Watt observed that 'the use of a single Christian name for women, but of a full name for men, is part of a tacit discrimination between the sexes which is traditional in the novel and which is reflected in the traditional novel-title' (1949, 331). He explains that the hero's full name in the title bespeaks his status as a 'complete social being combin-ing both public and private functions,' while the heroine's lack of a surname in titles highlights her social instability and incompleteness as well as her dependence on 'male generosity' to anchor her socially and make her whole (1949, 331–2).

Watt's description alludes to the ways these eponymous titles evoke key aspects of the gendered tensions between real and personal property in eighteenth-century England. If of legal age, a woman's acquisition of a surname through marriage typically coincided with the loss of the prop-erty she legally had in her self; if under twenty-one years, this acquisition usually meant that the property her father had in her person was now transferred to her husband. And depending upon the status of the parties involved, the taking and bestowing of a surname in wedlock went hand in hand with the acquiring, securing, and transferring of landed property and the rights attached to that land. Yet while Watt's observa-tions about the gendered significance of surnames provides a useful start for decoding the ideologies of property relations that eponymous titles embody, his seemingly clear-cut breakdown of these titles based on gender furnishes a partial and ultimately skewed picture of actual practices.

What Watt deems the 'traditional novel-title' is indeed the title of tradition, but it is hardly the title of eighteenth-century convention. Instead, the examples Watt cites are all titles of novels belonging to what has become the eighteenth-century literary canon. Although surnames always appear in the titles of eighteenth-century novels named for their heroes, the eponymous heroine without a surname is by no means the norm. For all the mid-eighteenth-century novels bearing only the Christian name of their heroines – *Pamela, Clarissa, Amelia, Lydia, Henrietta, Sophia,* and *Evelina* provide ready examples – an even greater number include the heroine's surname. *Betsy Thoughtless, Lady Julia Mandeville, Emily Montague, Sukey Shandy,* and *Sidney Bidulph* rank among the most familiar today, but many other instances exist. Between the years 1740 and 1769, 126 titles containing the Christian name of their work's heroine were published; of these, seventy-four – almost 59 per cent – also gave the heroine a surname in the title.[5] If we omit the frequent number of reprints of *Clarissa, Pamela, Roxana,* and *Moll Flanders* issued during these years (in order not to tip the scales unfairly in the other direction), the percentage of heroines with surnames increases to over 66 per cent, or two-thirds of the total number.

This high incidence of titles bearing both the Christian name and surname of the female protagonist advises that titular claims of female incompleteness and instability are not standard. At the same time, such a high occurrence begs the question of what is being contested or perhaps even claimed. Examining the titles featuring fully named heroines alongside the works these titles label reveals no single, simple answer. For one, a potential dilemma surrounds the inclusion of a female character's surname in the titles of eighteenth-century realistic fiction. If the heroine's marriage concludes the novel, as characterizes the ending of many of these works, then supplying her married surname in the title would seem to risk disclosing the work's outcome and diminishing the narrative suspense related to discovering whom and if the heroine will marry. Even in cases not involving a 'marriage plot,' the decision to include or exclude a titular surname can have ramifications for giving away too much, too soon.

Likewise, the use of the heroine's maiden name carries its own connotative difficulties. In some cases, the titular heroine whose surname is ostensibly the name she has received at birth engages in behaviour typically deemed nonvirtuous – whether that behaviour takes the form of sexual promiscuity, acquiring financial independence, exhibiting emotional and/or social independence, or a combination of these actions. Consider *The History of Miss Betsy Thoughtless* or even the pre-1740s example, *The Fortunes and Misfortunes of the Famous Moll Flanders* (as an alias, Moll's name rightfully occupies another category, but it nevertheless has some relevance here). In other cases, the titular use of a heroine's maiden name bespeaks ensuing tragedy. In *Memoirs of Miss Sidney Bidulph*, for instance, the presence of a surname signals the ultimately tragic fate stemming from a woman's status as an object of exchange in this society. Similarly, although Samuel Richardson's main title for his 1748–9 masterpiece was simply '*Clarissa*,' contemporary and even later readers often referred to the work as *Clarissa Harlowe*. This addition of a titular surname marks not only the respectful distance these readers placed between themselves and Clarissa but also the tragic position she occupies as a pawn of family ambitions and jealousies.

The claims extended by mid-eighteenth-century titles containing fully named heroines are not limited to suggestions of nonvirtuous behaviour or tragic conclusions. In fact the very presence of surnames contributes to titular enunciations of changing social conditions. For centuries baptismal names held more weight than surnames in many circles. As the jurist Sir Edward Coke noted, 'special heed [must] be taken to the name of baptism, for that a man cannot have two names of baptism as he may have divers surnames' (Withycombe 1977, xxi). The habit of adopting and discarding surnames without legal recourse was still viewed as custom in some quarters as late as the early decades of the eighteenth century. In the 1730 case of *Barlow v. Bateman*, Sir Joseph Jekyll declares 'I am satisfied the usage of passing Acts of Parliament for the taking upon one a surname is but modern, and that anyone may take upon him a surname, and as many surnames as he pleases, without an Act of Parliament' (Withycombe 1977, xxi).[6] Yet surnames from the sixteenth century on had nonetheless assumed an increasing importance for the entire population, with more and more of the middling sorts and, eventually, the lower ranks adopting last names. By the second half of the eighteenth century and on, even those owning little or no property were expected to use surnames. The Marriage Act of 1753, in fact, made the recording of both Christian names and surnames a legal requirement for obtaining a marriage licence.

An awareness of surname substitution as a material, sociohistorical practice in the eighteenth century enhances our understanding of the expectations engendered by titular surnames in at least two ways. First, such an awareness draws attention to the complicated ways in which contemporary readers may have viewed titular surnames as harbingers of plot developments and unreliable signs of identity. The very process of surname substitution undertook to establish a sociocultural fiction of an uninterrupted line of descent within a family; the substituted surname could not be considered a false name without disrupting the fiction of a continuous family line. Second, Gibson has argued that surname substitution not only served the desires of individual families for dynastic continuity but also fulfilled social and communal needs for a sense of stability and coherence. Demographic crises in the long eighteenth century exacerbated these needs and help account for the era's increased use of surname substitutions.[7] Against the backdrop of disruptions brought on by fluctuations in population (especially a decrease in the number of males), the enclosure movement, and the trend towards market-driven agriculture, surname substitution can be viewed as 'a public attempt to revive confidence [political and economic] within the community' through a reassertion of the 'inseparability of land and name' (Gibson 1992, 26, 24). This attention to the social and communal functions of surnames lends added weight to the important cultural enunciations that titular surnames articulate. The remainder of this chapter will examine two noncanonical novels whose titles contain the full names of their heroines: *The History of Betty Barnes* (1753) and *Memoirs of a Magdalen; Or, The History of Louisa Mildmay* (1767). Their examination will illustrate the interpenetrations that occurred between the law (especially the laws governing property rights) and novels in the eighteenth century. What this investigation will also demonstrate is the instrumental role that class issues played in portraying and shaping relationships between gender and property in these works.

Deceptively simple, the title *The History of Betty Barnes*[8] creates a web of social and economic associations. By the middle of the century, 'Betty,' a diminutive form of 'Elizabeth,' had lost any fashionable aura it once enjoyed and instead had become a name frequently used generically for chambermaids and serving women (Withycombe 1977, 100). The association with servitude evoked by 'Betty' suggests that the novel's heroine will occupy the lower rungs of the social ladder, and this suggestion is intensified by the evocations generated by the surname. Early English surnames were commonly adopted from the names of places and buildings (Barton 1990, 42). For many eighteenth-century readers, the surname 'Barnes,' meaning 'residence near or employment at the barns,' would link the titular heroine to a building used to store grain or house animals (Reaney 1958, 22) – an association quickly confirmed at the start of the novel, when readers learn that Betty's surname 'allud[es]' to the place of her birth' ([1753] 1974, 1: 10). For those readers well acquainted with the more minute details of Henry Fielding's *The History of Tom Jones* (1749), the name might recall the surname of Molly Seagrim's first paramour, Will Barnes, who fathered her illegitimate child she tries to stave off on the unsuspecting Tom: 'This Will Barnes was a country gallant, and had acquired as many trophies of this kind as had any ensign or attorney's clerk in the country ... He had, indeed, reduced several women to a state of utter profligacy' ([1749] 1985, 220).

Like most novel titles with surnamed heroines in the eighteenth century, the personal female name in this title does not stand alone but is preceded by a keyword – in this case, 'history.' As a titular lead in the eighteenth century, 'history' would have evoked a range of narrative practices from ones built on causality, observation, and experience to those offering moral instruction and improved understanding. These associations, in turn, offset the notions of disorder, unruliness, and, given the gender of this work's protagonist, sexual licentiousness that 'Betty Barnes' conjures up as a signifier for the lower ranks of society. For some readers, the tempering effects of 'history' might also awaken cultural memories of a more socially elevated sense of 'Barnes.'[9] Although obscure among the great British family names remembered today, 'Barnes' (as opposed to 'Barns') was the name of a noble Suffolk family whose coat of arms featured bears symbolic of the perfect teacher (Arthur [1857] 1969, 63; Hassall 1967, 147). This resonance of 'Barnes' when coupled with the keyword 'history' may well have yielded expectations of a narrative aimed at edifying its readers.

Many of these titular intimations come to pass as the narrative unfolds. As with many novels titularly styled a 'history,' *Betty Barnes* employs a third-person narrator given to offering broad commentary and directive remarks about society drawn from the incidents that make up the protagonist's journey through life. The opening of the novel sets the stage for the mapping of identity, marked by one's name, within the larger context of social issues and attitudes. Its first sentence informs readers that its 'heroine has neither birth nor titles to render her illustrious' ([1753] 1974, I: [1]), but readers soon discover that Betty's situation is far more impoverished than these deficiencies would imply. The chapter's headnote has already alerted readers to the import of her situation and to the narrator's ensuing satirical handling of those who see poverty as a crime: 'The high misdemeanor of being poor. The compassion of parish officers, and charity of a fine lady' ([1753] 1974, 1: [1]). In describing the events that lead up to Betty's essentially orphaned condition, the narrator treats unfeeling attitudes towards poverty in terms of the law, not only metaphorically through the use of legal language ('misdemeanor' and 'crime' to denote impoverishment) but also materially by reference to the laws governing the poor and settlement. In desperation, Betty's father had left his pregnant wife to seek the family's financial salvation at sea. The wife, now alone and far advanced with child, is forced by hardhearted parish officers from the village where the family resides. Since the family has lived in this parish for less than a year, it is thus not entitled to parish aid; legally Betty's mother is compelled to travel to the parish of her husband's birth for support.[10] Before reaching this parish, she goes into labour but is turned away at house after house until servants of a wealthy squire finally allow her refuge in their master's barn. The mother dies soon after giving birth to Betty, her death occasioned in part by being turned out yet again, this time by the squire's wife. Betty, in turn, is placed in the care of the parish nurse and acquires the stigma of being a charity case and a parish bastard. As local authorities had traditionally done in naming foundlings (Bardsley 1880, 233), the parish officials adopt the name of the exact site where Betty was born as her surname.

Betty having been born in a barn, her status as a propertyless and socially disenfranchised person is underlined in the first few pages of the novel. The cycle of unfeeling treatment interspersed with the occasional compassionate gesture towards the poor and those who have suffered financial decline that surrounded Betty's birth is repeated throughout the novel. Yet while the work often draws attention to the lack of rights the poor possess and the inability of this group, especially among impoverished females, to claim what rights they do have, in the end it does not recommend a dismantling or even restructuring of property relations. Rather the novel delineates the responsibilities and appropriate behaviours tied to various stations in life as it reinforces the gendered nature of property. At the same time, its frequent critiques of the law suggest that these prescribed responsibilities and behaviours are especially needed in order to compensate for the official law's shortcomings in regulating society.

In the second chapter, for instance, Betty, now five years old, is struck by Lady Benson's coach and is brought to the Benson estate to tend to her injuries. When a servant concludes that Betty is 'some parish bas-

tard' and recommends that she be turned out rather than remain while
her injuries heal ([1753] 1974, 1: 12–13), Lady Benson severely chastises
the maid ([1753] 1974, 1: 13). Not only does Lady Benson refuse to see
poverty as a crime, but she also makes clear that refusal to care for those
less fortunate constitutes a serious offence equal to or greater than other
crimes. Offering a moral universe outside the institutional parameters of
law, Lady Benson characterizes the measures the law has instituted for
the upbringing of the poor as ineffective when she explains her reasons
for allowing Betty to remain in her house: 'to keep her in the family, and
to give her an education that would enable her to get her living without
being a vagabond, or at best a meer drudge, which *must have been the case,
if she had been suffered to return to her nurse, and continued at the expence of the
parish*' ([1753] 1974, 1: 14; my emphasis). Her reasoning is based on a
belief that the parish care of impoverished, orphaned, and illegitimate
children under the poor laws inevitably produces 'vagabonds' and 'mere
drudges.' Private care of these unfortunate children through the offices
of well-to-do individuals, in contrast, is represented as enabling the
young charges to maintain themselves upon reaching adulthood. Betty's
work history as a young woman attests to the soundness of Lady Benson's
belief and the education Betty received from Lady Benson's house-
keeper, Mrs Evans. Supporting herself in London at times as a lady's
maid and at others as a companion, Betty executes her duties to much
satisfaction, proves herself virtuous, and never cheats her mistresses.

Throughout the novel Betty's name and its transformations mark her
social identity. As the narrative advances, the narrator frequently refers
to the heroine by her full name rather than just her first name. This
atypical habit (most narrators of eighteenth-century novels use just the
Christian names of their protagonists) serves as a constant reminder of
the humble circumstances of Betty's birth and her ensuing low social
status. Betty, however, needs no reminding, for the shame associated with
her surname clearly haunts her. While Betty is in the care and service of
Lady Benson's household, the lady's serving maid uses Betty's presumed
illegitimacy to scorn and insult her. Betty believes that she is truly a
bastard until Joseph, the squire's servant who had provided Betty's
mother with succour in her final hours, finally fulfils his promise to
watch over Betty and visits her at Lady Benson's. So firmly has Betty
believed her birth to be infamous that she replies to Joseph's query
about any news or discovery of her father with sheer confusion and
despair: 'How is it possible, that I should know any thing of my father,
when I don't so much as know my own name; but am called by one that is

always bringing to my mind the unlikelihood there is that I should ever know him?' ([1753] 1974, 1: 57). Learning from Joseph that her parents were married and that poverty had caused their unwanted separation, Betty exclaims, 'Oh that I could but see and know my father! then I should be no more wretched; for I think I could work, or even beg and be happy, if I had but somebody to own and shield me from the shame of hearing myself called a bastard' ([1753] 1974, 1: 59). Shortly after this encounter, persecution, in part based on her name and questionable status, by a jealous servant forces Betty to flee the safety of Lady Benson's estate for London. There she hopes to find Mrs Evans, Benson's house-keeper, who had gone to London for an extended visit, but she fails and must make her way alone. The anonymity of London alleviates her problems with the associations her surname generated among the gossip of a country village and its extended neighbouring estates. Still referred to as 'Betty Barnes,' our heroine possesses a name that marks her iden-tity as a country person alone and friendless in an urban world.

Betty's desire to know her father is realized much later in the novel after she has proven her ability to maintain herself in the world by honest labour. When Betty and her father are reunited, the narrator stresses that this reunion occasions the restoration of her true paternal surname: 'In the mean time our fair one, who we shall no longer call Betty Barnes, *as she had an undoubted right to the name of her father*' ([1753] 1974, 2: 112; my emphasis). That her father has physically surfaced puts to rest any questions about the legitimacy of Betty's birth; her right to her father's name is 'undoubted.' Twelve pages later the narrator again mentions the restoration of her rightful surname, and this time he also revises the terms of the relationship that he and the readers have with Betty: 'Betty, who for the future we shall call Miss Hammond, as about that time she was called by the name of her father' ([1753] 1974, 2: 124). Up until now, the title 'Miss' had never preceded Betty's name, nor had her last name ever appeared without her Christian name. The announcement that 'for the future we shall call [Betty] Miss Hammond' replaces a stance of familiarity towards Betty with an attitude of respectful distance. The omission of the first name is in keeping with the change that her father's return has wrought in her life. This change, though, has less to do with acquiring fortune and social status (beyond the very important removal of the stigma of illegitimacy) and more to do with the notion of paternal control reinforced by the adoption of her father's surname. Financially, her father's means are slender but adequate 'to afford her all decent necessaries' ([1753] 1974, 2: 110); socially, having been 'always kept at a distance from genteel life,' he is ill at ease with 'the company of the gay and grand' ([1753] 1974, 2: 113).

Yet Betty – or 'Miss Hammond' as she is invariably called for the next hundred pages or so – is now under the control and protection of a father. For someone who has had to make her way in the world, this discovery requires more adjustments than simply becoming accustomed to being known as 'Miss Hammond.' Having received a small inheritance from her old friend Joseph, Betty Barnes had 'resolved to go no more to service' now that she possessed the means to support herself as an independent woman, but the discovery of her father makes her independent no more. Shortly before she moves in with her father, she gives Joseph's sister Katherine[11] 'thirty pounds, lest the authority and care of her father, should take it out of her hands' ([1753] 1974, 2: 111). The timing of this gesture demonstrates her acute awareness that while she may now have a rightful name, the acquisition of a paternal name brings with it the potential loss of control over her own actions and desires. The precaution Betty takes proves unnecessary since her father does not reign over her. Nonetheless, he does interfere with her lover's visits, especially since the young man's grandfather may well oppose the match. The formality and distance that the appellation 'Miss Hammond' engenders function well in representing Betty's new position as a daughter under the protection and watchful eye of her father.

As the novel draws to a close, Betty acquires yet another name, that of Mrs Marshall. Mr Marshall, the young officer whom she met on her initial trip to London and with whom an immediate, mutual attraction arose, turns out to be the son of Lady Benson's housekeeper, Mrs Evans. Mrs Evans had always been fond of Betty and welcomes the match. Though Mrs Evans hailed from a good family, circumstances brought on by her marrying her father's clerk against the wishes of her parents had afforded her a life of limited expectations, hardships, and disappointments. Once a schoolmate of Lady Benson, Mrs Evans, like Betty, had been the beneficiary of Lady Benson's compassion and had gratefully accepted the post of being her housekeeper. By the time of Betty's marriage to her son, Mrs Evans had reconciled with her father. In turn her son, Betty's husband, had gained the favour of his grandfather and is now heir to his estate. Although her marriage represents an extreme shift in Betty's social position, the novel does not offer, as a critic for the *Monthly Review* claims, another *Pamela* without its merit (1752, 470). Rather than depict the rewards of preserving the most valued form of a woman's personal property, her body, against repeated attacks aimed at violation, *The History of Betty Barnes* charts the progress of a self-sufficient woman who exists in the grey borders between the labouring poor and the world of the lady's companion, at once a servant but not a domestic drudge. The progression of Betty Barnes from a girl born in a barn to the young Mrs Marshall, benefactor of the 'poor, the industrious poor' ([1753] 1974, 2: 297), is a story not of preservation but of the disappearance of the property she had in her self, ironically, through the acquisition of legitimacy.

Compared with the initial claims extended by *The History of Betty Barnes,* those advanced by the title *Memoirs of a Magdalen* (1767)[12] deliver explicit expectations of tragedy and sexual lapses. Since this main title lacks a personal name, its placement in the female-surname category may seem inappropriate. *Memoirs of a Magdalen,* however, bears a subtitle, *The History of Louisa Mildmay,* that does conform to the pattern being examined. Given the potential that surnamed-heroine titles as a class have for anticipating tragic ends and nonvirtuous behaviour, the occurrence of this subtitle alongside a main title that explicitly forecasts calamity and ruin warrants *Memoirs of a Magdalen*'s inclusion in this discussion. In addition, *The History of Louisa Mildmay* is almost certainly the title that Hugh Kelly, the novel's author, claimed for the work since it, and not *Memoirs of a Magdalen,* appears as the head and running title.[13] That the subtitle most likely represents the author's original choice further recommends including the work.

Commercial reasons partially explain why Kelly's novel entered the marketplace with *Memoirs of a Magdalen* as its lead title. A title promising the memoirs of a reformed prostitute would lay claim to readers beyond those drawn primarily to novels. Potential overlaps among audiences notwithstanding, using 'magdalen' as a titular word increased the possibility of attracting readers seeking titillation and voyeuristic thrills (a third edition of Cleland's *Memoirs of a Woman of Pleasure* had appeared in 1766). Its connotations also spoke to a readership drawn to charitable endeavours and morally edifying tales, for the word 'magdalen' carried timely philanthropic associations. In 1758 a group of reformers, headed by a wealthy merchant, had founded the Magdalen House to provide compassionate assistance for repentant prostitutes. In 1765, a year or so before Kelly's novel first received press, Queen Charlotte bestowed her royal patronage on this institution, which had already garnered 'much interest on the part of the "polite" classes' (Langford 1989, 144–5). By the time the novel was published, the polite classes had been exposed to a rich market of print materials tied to this charity institution: sermons preached at meetings of the Magdalen House governors; tunes and hymns used at the Magdalen Chapel; fictionalized histories of the penitents purportedly narrated by themselves; annual reports that included the House's rules, lists of subscribers, and advice given to the magdalens; and treatises sold specifically for the benefit of the House.[14] As their imprints indicate, some of these works were sold in Bath as well as London, a testimony to the appeal that the Magdalen House had among the fashionable. These commercial reasons coincide with textual justifications for this title: the novel's heroine, Louisa Mildmay, deems herself a magdalen of sorts, and at one point in the work, she takes refuge at the Magdalen House. Reflecting market savvy, the use of 'magdalen' in the lead title succeeds in balancing commercial aims and textual claims.

Although *Memoirs of a Magdalen* as a title effectively fulfils the mandate to 'reconcile *Book* and *Title*, and make 'em kin to one another' (Dunton 1691, 2: 2), its claims best anticipate the text when they are combined with the claims extended by the subtitle. While subtitles typically gloss their main titles, the reverse is at work here.[15] The use of *Memoirs of a Magdalen* as the lead title unquestionably colours perceptions of the subtitle, *The History of Louisa Mildmay*. The syntactic parallel between 'Magdalen' and 'Louisa Mildmay' results in a sullying of the heroine's reputation before a page of the novel proper is turned. Taken together, the main title and subtitle embody the prevalent ideology surrounding female virtue and property relations professed (but not necessarily always practised) by the middling and upper ranks of eighteenth-century society; an unmarried woman who has willingly lost her virginity is no longer marriageable, as David Lemmings explains in an earlier chapter in this book. Such behaviour signals an unmistakably immoral, deeply flawed character that would make the woman unwelcome in polite circles. The novel proper, in turn, embraces these claims, only to interrogate them relentlessly.

Given the novel's arguments about female behaviour and property relations, the success of this now virtually forgotten work is striking. Besides London and Dublin editions in 1767, *Memoirs* was issued at least four more times by the end of 1795.[16] The favourable assessment that the *Critical Review* gave the novel prior to its full-fledged marketplace debut undoubtedly contributed to the work's success: 'Tho' the subject of the volumes before us is common to the last degree, yet the story is affecting, and the characters are supported with more spirit and propriety, than we have found in any novels we have lately reviewed' (1766, 373).[17] 'Common to the last degree' as the subject of a fallen woman may be in eighteenth-century novels, what is uncommon about *Memoirs of a Magdalen* is its treatment of Louisa Mildmay and her 'fall.' The novel, as Susan Staves has noted, 'is something of a problem on the subject since the Magdalen in question is seduced by her fiancé after the marriage settlements have been arranged and only four days before the wedding ceremony' (1980–1, 112). But its problematic nature extends beyond simply the timing of the transgression or the parties involved.

Louisa Mildmay, the novel's heroine, hails from a family 'not more ancient than respectable' whose 'ancestors on her father's side [include] the great Sir Philip Sidney' ([1767] 1974, 1: 9) and whose present family enjoys 'the reputation of a considerable house' ([1767] 1974, 1: 88–9). For the elder Mildmay and his son, Colonel Mildmay, the reputation of the family name defines their identity, and they both view Louisa primarily through her connections to real property and family honour. When Louisa and her fiancé, Sir Robert Harold, consummate their relationship before their wedding, the male Mildmays view the couple's transgression as a blow to the family's good name. Sir Robert takes a similar stance towards Louisa in regard to himself and her family, noting that prior to that evening he had viewed Louisa 'as a lady, whose reputation was immediately connected to my own – I saw her, besides, the only daughter of an honourable family, which it would be unpardonable to disgrace' ([1767] 1974, 1: 41). Their reactions to the event – Robert, who had forsworn his libertine ways to marry her, is now repulsed by Louisa; her father turns her out of the house when she confesses her conduct; and her brother upon discovering the news brands her 'an infamous strumpet' who has dishonoured the family ([1767] 1974, 1: 114) – are typical of the treatment that eighteenth-century novels accord single women who voluntarily yield to their desires and those of their partners. Yet this epistolary novel rejects these attitudes and instead argues forcefully for Louisa's ultimate virtue and the irrationality of the stance taken by her fiancé, father, and brother.

The Mildmay men's condemnation of Lousia lends an ironic cast to the meanings of the surname 'Mildmay' as does their approach to protecting and advancing the family reputation. 'Mildmay' means 'gentle maid[en]' (Reaney 1958, 221; Hassall 1967, 108) or, even more apropos to the plot, 'soft or tender judge' (from a combination of the Saxon words 'mild' and 'dema'), and its history claims that the surname was given to its original bearer because of 'his tempering the severity of the law with mercy' (Arthur [1857] 1969, 200). Neither the father's nor son's reaction to Louisa's behaviour, however, exhibits any hint of benevolent judgment. Not only are they unable to forgive Louisa for succumbing to passion, but they remain at odds with her for almost the novel's entirety. Obsessed with upholding and increasing the honour of the family name, the father is equally willing to sacrifice his son's happiness to indulge his ambition for the Mildmay line ([1767] 1974, 2: 38). As the elder Mildmay explains, 'My house ... is a very antient one; there have been more than two peerages in it; and I have myself some expectations of a title ... I should be very sorry to oppose [my son's] inclinations ... but you know the raising of one's family is a very essential point' ([1767] 1974, 2: 37). When it is suggested that 'it might be difficult to make [the son] sacrifice the interest of his heart even to gratify the laudable ambition of his father,' Mildmay retorts that he knows 'how to punish his obstinacy when I come to dispose of my fortune' ([1767] 1974, 2: 38).

Although the Mildmay men act as the antithesis of a 'soft or tender judge,' the role is taken up by other characters. Of all the novel's correspondents, Lady Haversham (Sir Robert's sister) and Charles Melmoth (Sir Robert's friend) display the most good sense, experience, heart, maturity, and moral integrity, and consequently their opinions carry the most weight. Far from condemning Louisa, their letters exonerate her. In a letter that the *Critical Review* recommends as 'a masterpiece of affectionate and sentimental reasoning' (1766, 374), Lady Haversham, Louisa's strongest defender, declares, 'In whatsoever light I view her conduct, I see a woman of exalted principle' ([1767] 1974, 1: 83) and 'I place no inconsiderable share of her ruin down to the account of her virtue' ([1767] 1974, 1: 91–2). Similarly, Melmoth berates Robert for rejecting Louisa: 'this unaccountable delicacy of yours in breaking off with a lady merely because she has given you the most convincing proof of her affection, is what, in my opinion favors more of romance than of real understanding' ([1767] 1974, 1: 78). The practical, rational judgments proffered by Lady Haversham, Melmoth, and Louisa's friend, Miss Beauclerk, throughout the novel work to indict the Mildmay men and Sir Robert for misplaced pride and skewed values. Casting the men and their logic in an absurd light,[18] these judgments implicitly question the exclusive privileging of family status over personal worth as they critique the treatment of women as forms of property among those belonging to the upper ranks.

Treatments of marriage and sexual relations as socially and legally constructed property transactions permeate the early pages of the *Memoirs*. When Sir Robert initially contemplates marriage, he does so as, essentially, a form of property insurance: 'it is high time ... to think of getting sons and daughters for myself, instead of wasting my time to increase the families of other people' ([1767] 1974, 1: 31). His desire to beget direct heirs who will inherit his real property and ensure that his name will endure after his death is complemented by his desire to find a wife 'whose mind has been improved in some proportion with her person' ([1767] 1974, 1: 10). His criteria here suggest that he aspires to a spouse who would function not merely as a biological means of preserving his property holdings but also as an intellectual and emotional companion. Sir Robert's core view of women, however, is highly coloured by notions of property and sexual exchange. Tired of gratifying 'the licentious disposition' of female suitors 'who are more despicable in [his] opinion, and less attached to [his] person, than many of the mercenary poor creatures, whom [he] can purchase for a couple guineas' ([1767] 1974, 1: 31–2), he claims to desire a relationship based on love rather than commercially driven exchanges of sex for status, money, or sport. Yet as much as he may have first regarded Louisa 'in quite a different light from any of those women with whom [he] had formerly trifled' ([1767] 1974, 1: 41), once she succumbs to desire, he can see her only in terms of marketplace values and the risk she poses if she were to become a direct extension of his personal property by bearing his surname and heirs. That both Robert and Louisa employ diction evocative of a legal proceeding in discussing their lapse is equally telling. Robert, for example, confesses that he was astonished to discover his culpability in the evening's events upon '*review[ing] the state of the case*' ([1767] 1974, 1: 102; my emphasis). Speaking about the effects of the 'recent unhappy transaction' between them, Louisa admonishes Sir Robert for making professions that are 'idle things when contradicted *by the incontestible* [sic] *evidence of facts*' ([1767] 1974, 1: 71; my emphasis). Such recourse to legal language indicates their keen, mutual awareness of the very real legal and social implications surrounding their behaviour.

In many ways the *Memoirs* is about sorting through the two conflicting views of Louisa: a magdalen, as her male relatives and revolted lover regard her, or the ever-virtuous Louisa Mildmay, the 'gentle maiden' whose lapse is not only forgiven but even construed as a sign of her virtue by her most ardent champion. Like the actual Magdalen House, the *Memoirs* resolves its conflicts by a remaking of sexual and social mores within the framework of identity, property, and gender. Yet the novel's project of reformation differs conceptually in significant ways from that of the charity house. In a recent analysis of the Magdalen House as an institution that exemplifies the 'gendered geographies of modern subjectivity,' Miles Ogborn illustrates the ways in which this charity house's project undertook 'the remaking of the individual through a reordering of space' (1998, 43, 58). In the eyes of its founders, the ordered, functional spaces of the Magdalen House promoted self-reflection, which led to self-regulation, enabling the penitent to control her sexual and material appetite. This victory of reason over passion, in turn, transformed the magdalen into a rational, accountable subject (Ogborn 1998, 66–72).

While the *Memoirs* also seeks the remaking of selves and a victory of reason over passion, it reverses the gender dynamics at work in the Magdalen project and other contemporary constructions of the fallen woman. In the novel it is Robert who is transformed through self-reflection and the Mildmay men who are taught to curb their passion over injured family honour and adopt a rational stance towards the couple's transgression. As for its 'magdalen,' the novel presents Louisa as a woman who possesses a self that requires no remaking, who accepts blame for her role in the transgression, and who esteems herself too much to marry a man whose professions of respect now transparently mark his disdain for her. In short, unlike Watt's heroines who lack surnames, Louisa Mildmay rejects dependence on 'male generosity' to anchor her socially and make her whole.

In keeping with the *Memoirs*'s gender reversals, the novel employs geographies that invert the logic of the Magdalen project's use of space. Unlike the spaces of modernity that Ogborn sees informing the Magdalen project – the disordered urban space in which the corrupt self emerges and the 'disciplinary institution's solitary cell' that remakes this self (1998, 73) – the *Memoirs* situates both the problem and its resolution within the space of aristocratic tradition, the patriarchal estate. That Louisa and Sir Robert's transgression occurs in the Mildmay family home arguably signals the violation of this space, but it soon becomes evident that this space also signifies the disordered priorities of the aristocratically oriented, male value system. In the Magdalen House project the institution inculcates family values by reordering the self; in the *Memoirs* it is the family itself as an institution that needs restructuring. The elder Mildmay rules supreme over the house and its inhabitants, with family interest subsuming individual will. That he and his son eventually adopt a more reasonable, forgiving position towards the couple is effected not by solitary contemplation but by Melmoth and Lady Haversham's visit to the Mildmay estate ([1767] 1974, 2: 23–32).

While a complete transformation of the elder Mildmay is not accomplished – he still retains an overreaching sense of family pride and ambition – the remaking of Sir Robert is more successful. Like the magdalens, Robert engages in self-reflection, but his reflections are prompted not by solitude but by the letters he exchanges with his sister and Melmoth. Admonishing him for recoiling from Louisa, Melmoth declares that his sentiments 'may perhaps make [Robert] the hero of a very pretty novel; but must in actual life, expose you to the unremitting ridicule of every body' ([1767] 1974, 1: 78). Although Melmoth's letter never mentions any specific work, let alone a specific character, Robert nevertheless takes Melmoth's remarks about novels as references to Lovelace in Richardson's *Clarissa*. Robert's subsequent musings demonstrate how fictions – both literary and those inherent in maintaining various social conventions – pervade his thinking. His partial relinquishing of these fictions – especially those involving overly idealized constructions of women – form part of the larger case the *Memoirs* makes for Louisa's ultimate virtue.

As the novel progresses, explicit and implicit references to *Clarissa* intermittently crop up, encouraging readers to draw comparisons with Richardson's work. For example, writing to Miss Beauclerk about the trials she has undergone, Louisa recounts that she was 'reading Clarissa Harlowe; and had just got into that passage where the vile Lovelace attempts the sanctity of her chamber at midnight, in the house of that detestable monster Sinclair' when she 'felt an instinctive kind of terror' ([1767] 1974, 2: 83–4). Her apprehension, brought on by 'above all, the subject which [she] had been just reading,' turns out to be justified ([1767] 1974, 2: 84); she is kidnapped and imprisoned by the rake Sir Harry, who is aided by Mrs Darnel, the false family friend with whom Louisa stays after being banished by her father. That these events recall Lovelace and Mrs Sinclair spurs the identification of Louisa with Richardson's heroine, heightening reader sympathy and admiration for her. Louisa's use of Clarissa's full name is especially evocative, for the harlot-versus-hallowed connotations of 'Harlowe' parallel the conflicts surrounding Louisa's identity as magdalen or Mildmay.

The novel's numerous cases of surname changes strike an added blow to the value of fixed identity derived from real property. In some cases, the surname alterations stem from legal stipulations; at other times a need for anonymity drives the change. For example, Melmoth's surname is not his by birth, but one he assumed after a friend left him 'no less than eighty thousand pounds to take the name of Melmoth' ([1767] 1974, 2: 143). His wife – who is known for most of the novel as 'Mrs Beauclerk' and whom Melmoth thought had died while he was in the

Indies – adopted 'Beauclerk' as a surname to avoid discovery when she fled to London, seeking refuge from her father-in-law's incessant, violent advances ([1767] 1974, 2: 148). Mrs Dobson, the woman who harbours and nurses Louisa upon her escape from Sir Harry, was at one time 'Mrs Jenkins' ([1767] 1974, 2: 134, 148), though her surname alteration occurs through the familiar channels of a first husband's death followed by remarriage. That only those characters who are reliable and virtuous undergo surname changes reinforces the novel's contention that selfhood manifests itself through one's personal traits rather than one's line of descent.

Louisa Mildmay remains Louisa Mildmay for much of the novel. Only when she enters the Magdalen House does she cease being 'her self,' adopting the name 'Charlotte Windham.' Writing from the charity house, she confesses that she assumed the name 'in the *unsettled state of my mind*, to prevent her family from receiving any farther disgrace' ([1767] 1974, 2: 115; my emphasis). Earlier in the letter she notes that her 'numberless distresses' of late, coupled with an overwhelming sense of responsibility for all her misfortunes, had left her mind 'totally unhinged' ([1767] 1974, 2: 111) and adds 'if my imagination had not been disturbed, I had never dreamt of entering a place, particularly dedicated to public penitence of prostitution' ([1767] 1974, 2: 114). Unlike her character elsewhere in the novel, Louisa's presentation here mirrors the representations of the penitent women in the Magdalen House literature. And, indeed, she rhetorically asks how she is any 'better than the unhappy poor creatures, whom the pinching hand of necessity, or the poignant stings of remorse, have brought to the same salutary, yet humiliating habitation' ([1767] 1974, 2: 114). Still, her letter, tinged with allusions to class – 'poor creatures,' her admittance to the house, 'with some essential deviations, from the customary mode of accepting Penitents' ([1767] 1974, 2: 112) – tempers the sameness being claimed as do the events that ensue. Upon being reunited with her family, 'in less than two hours [into the reunion], Miss Mildmay, at the desire of her parents, consented to overlook [Robert's] behaviour' and agreed to marry him ([1767] 1974, 2: 140). On the one hand the mention of consent points to a recognition of Louisa's individual will and the marriage as a final testament to her virtue. On the other hand, their marriage signals a return to the status quo, for her exoneration necessitates her being accepted as a Mildmay, a 'gentle maiden' judged worthy enough to marry Sir Robert. Never referred to as Mrs or Lady Harold, Louisa retains her titular identity even at the end: 'Bob is married to Miss Mildmay' ([1767] 1974, 2: 131).

The *Memoirs*'s conclusion, while indicative of the novel's status as ultimately a sentimental work, demonstrates not a resolution of female
identity but instead its complex, problematic nature.

Social, economic, and moral tensions are if anything more readily
announced in novels containing female surnames than those that give
only the Christian names of their heroines. Besides notions of virtuous
versus nonvirtuous behaviour, these titles invoke the relationship of
property to issues of parental control, preservation of a family line, and
symbolic social and economic power. In the plots of novels whose titles
bear only the Christian names of their heroines, it is typically the heroine
who undergoes a struggle for identity and a secure social and economic
position in society. Specifically, in novels such as Richardson's *Pamela*
(1740), Shebbeare's *Lydia* (1755), Lennox's *Henrietta* (1758) and her
Sophia (1762), and Burney's *Evelina* (1778), the heroines all marry propertied men who are socially and financially well established and who
often possess a title as well. A list of these heroines' partners reveals,
respectively, a country squire, an earl, a marquis, a baronet, and a lord.
In contrast, novels whose titles contain the full name of their heroines
from the mid-century on often feature not only heroines who suffer
hardship and uncertainty but also heroes who must struggle and endure
great trials to achieve financial security and a place among the propertied. Their achievements, in turn, enable them to marry and/or maintain the heroine.[19] The *Adventures of Sylvia Hughes* (1761) offers an
immediate example of the struggling male protagonist, while Sir Robert's
battles with his conscience in the *Memoirs* demonstrate that even a male
love interest possessing a title is not exempt from experiencing personal
conflict in these works.

The possible reasons why these latter, often noncanonical, novels
bearing female-surname titles have receded into the background are
complex and not easily reducible to a single explanation. Perhaps the
significance of the sociohistorical, cultural, and economic concerns these
novels addressed became too nuanced with time, obscuring for subsequent readers the pertinence and fascination these narratives initially
held. Perhaps these works' representations of identity and social relations, their overt preoccupation with property concerns, and their plot-
ting of gender and class relations made them seem too absurd, contrived,
or flimsy to later eyes. Rather than any one explanation, this chapter has
offered a sampling of what these titles can tell us about the works they
label. As I have argued, reading eponymous titles of eighteenth-century
novels as encoded signs of social and economic values affords insights

not only about shifting conceptions of selfhood within familial structures in the eighteenth century but also about the ramifications of individuality within the era's broader framework of gender, class, and property relations. These insights, in turn, demonstrate the complexities of individual identity and teach us that attempts at understanding their intricacies within the context of eighteenth-century notions of property and law must entail considerations of class as well as gender. Marking the points of intersection between gender, class, and property, these titles graph the shifting, contested nature of identity as plotted by eighteenth-century novels.

Notes

1 Elsewhere in the essay, Hunter displays sensitivity to the tales that titles tell. He discusses the number of contemporary readers who referred to *Tom Jones* as 'The Foundling,' the frequency with which this title alteration was written simply 'F——G,' and the anxieties about legitimacy, paternity, and rights to property via inheritance that such a renaming, generally registered as unprintable in full, discloses (1979, 71).

2 Ragussis (1986, 4–9) provides a cogent summary of English Enlightenment attitudes towards names and naming.

3 See Dickenson (1997, chap. 4) for an analysis of this concept. For the ways in which Enlightenment feminists applied Locke's writings on personhood, see Ready (2002).

4 I am indebted to Gibson (1992) for the particulars related to surname substitution.

5 I have begun with the year 1740 because titles bearing everyday names were atypical in the earlier decades of the century. Figures for the 1740s have been taken from Beasley (1972). Using Beasley's descriptions of each work, I have excluded from my count those titles of texts appearing to be crime reports, morality pamphlets, and the like. Figures for the 1750s and 1760s have been taken from Raven (1987), although I have ignored titles under 'Miscellanies' because they label short fictional pieces. My count includes only titles featuring a single protagonist, overlooking those that feature multiple heroines or a heroine and hero. My figures do not reflect the five titles appearing between 1757 and 1761 that offered only a few letters of a surname and used dashes to represent the letters omitted.

6 The House of Lords, maintaining that name changes required parliamen-

tary action, subsequently reversed Jekyll's decision: 'the individual ought to have inherited by birth, or have obtained an authority for using the name' (Baring-Gould [1910] 1969, 396).

7 This demographic crisis was occasioned by a dramatic rise in the number of fathers who died without leaving a son to succeed them, and, as Brian McCrea notes, 'greatly complicated "the descent of property and seats from generation to generation"' (1998, 16). For a broad examination of the early British novel through the lens of the demographic crisis of 1650–1740, see McCrea (1998).

8 Although this novel has been attributed to Sarah Fielding, by Halkett (1926–[1962]), the attribution seems erroneous based on stylistic and thematic grounds. Moreover, the entry for Sarah Fielding in Todd (1987, 125–6) makes no mention of this work. The narrator of *Betty Barnes* refers to his fellow novelists as males on several occasions.

9 In fact, for some readers, the surname 'Barnes' may have actually suggested well-to-do connections since the Domesday Book records 'Barne' as an ancient byname for aristocratic men (Reaney 1958, 22).

10 *The Law of Settlement and Removal* (1662) instituted a national poor law that was administered locally. Each person in England had only one place – that is, parish – of legal settlement. Essentially a property right, a settlement could be secured by a various means: '(a) birth in a parish if a bastard, (b) having a father settled there, (c) marrying a husband there, (d) being hired as a covenant servant there for a year, (e) being apprenticed there, or (f) renting a house there.' A person in need of relief had only 'the right to relief in that parish and no other' (Porter 1986, 143).

11 Significantly, Katherine, who was lured into prostitution but had long rejected and repented her grave lapse, is always called only by her first name, sometimes preceded by 'Mrs.' The use of first names alone was usually reserved for situations in which an intimacy existed between the parties or for servants whose surnames were of little importance. In the nineteenth century, however, it became common to refer to one's female domestics by their last names.

12 The title page is dated 1767, but the novel was undoubtedly available near the end of the previous year because it was reviewed in the November 1766 issue of the *Critical Review*. See Bataille (2000, 29) and Raven (1987, 262, entries 1017 and 1111) for additional assessments of the novel's initial appearance.

13 As Ronald McKerrow has noted, 'we may probably infer that this heading [head titles] preserves the name that the author originally intended'

([1928] 1962, 91). Even though titles were increasingly coming under the control of the authors, many title pages were still the province of the printer/bookseller. For a detailed discussion, see Shevlin (1999).

14 A search of the *ESTC* database turns up thirty works, published between 1758 and 1767, whose titles contain the word 'magdalen.' Twenty-one of these works are related to the Magdalen House; the other nine works include three editions of Kelly's novels, a piece about a schooner christened 'Magdalen,' a legal case, and sermons preached at various churches named St Mary Magdalen.

15 *Pamela; Or, Virtue Rewarded* (1740) offers an example of the 'standard' formula.

16 The British Library has copies of both the first and 'second' (reissue with new title pages) London editions printed by W. Griffin, 1767(BL Shelfmark 1264.eee.15 and BL Shelfmark C. 135.e.21). The *ESTC* indicates that a 'third edition' was published for T. Lowndes in 1776. Another edition was issued with engravings as part of Harrison's *The Novelist's Magazine* (vol. 7) in 1782 (BL Shelfmark 1207.c.8.3.), and Harrison and Co. issued it again, according to the *ESTC*, in 1784 and 1792. Cooke also issued the novel in 1795 (BL Shelfmark 12612.de.26 and BL Shelfmark 1485.a.18). A French version, *Les égaremens réparés, ou histoire de Miss Louise Mildmay*, appeared in 1773 (BL Shelfmark 1568/6958), and another French translation bearing the title *Les Dangers d'un Tête-à-tête* was published in 1800 by an A. Colleville (BL Shelfmark ch.800/230).

17 The review does criticize two of the novel's subplots for smacking too much of typical contrivances novelists resort to, and it also regrets the hasty conclusion. Nonetheless, it devotes two and half pages to the novel, with close to a page and a half offering positive remarks. At the very onset, the reviewer also reminds readers of 'the strict impartiality with which we treat publications of this kind, however they may be recommended by the lively chit-chat of modern novel-writing' (1766, 373), and these remarks, regardless of their merit, would seem to reinforce rhetorically the encouraging words given in the review about Kelly's novel.

18 Robert Bataille has claimed that Kelly was aiming for a comedy rather than tragedy in his first and only novel (2000, 35). The novel's comic effects derive overwhelmingly from jabs at the male Mildmays' and Sir Robert's nonsensical creed of honour, reputation, and breeding. Typical of the novel's deflation of such priorities is the Irish servant's comic commiseration with the Mildmay men: 'The honour of a good family is a very nice affair; I am come of as good a family myself as any in Ireland, and know how to feel for such a misfortune as has happened to my masters' ([1767]

1974, 2: 4). While lightheartedly trading on class and ethnic prejudices, the alignment of the Mildmay men's views with those of their servant acts to undermine them.

19 Fielding's *Amelia* (1751) offers an obvious exception. Unlike many plots, *Amelia* deals with the life of its heroine after marriage, and Captain Booth, her husband, is beset by financial woes for most of the novel.

Works Cited

Arthur, William. [1857] 1969. *An Etymological Dictionary of Family and Christian Names*. Detroit: Gale Research.

Bardsley, Charles. 1880. *Curiosities of Puritan Nomenclature*. New York: R. Worthington.

Baring-Gould, S. [1910] 1969. *Family Names and Their Story*. Detroit: Gale Research.

Barton, Anne. 1990. *The Names of Comedy*. Toronto: University of Toronto Press.

Bataille, Robert R. 2000. *The Writing Life of Hugh Kelly: Politics, Journalism and Theatre in Late-Eighteenth-Century London*. Carbondale and Edwardsville: Southern Illinois University Press.

Beasley, Jerry C. 1972. *A Check List of Prose Fiction Published in England, 1740–1749*. Charlottesville: University Press of Virginia.

Bowman, William Dodgson. 1931. *The Story of Surnames*. New York: Alfred Knopf.

Critical Review. 1766. 22 (Nov.): 373–5.

Dickenson, Donna. 1997. *Property, Women and Politics: Subjects or Objects?* New Brunswick, NJ: Rutgers University Press.

Dunton, John. 1691. *A Voyage Round the World*. 3 vols. London: Printed for Richard Newcome.

Fielding, Henry. [1749] 1985. *The History of Tom Jones*, ed. R.P.C. Mutter. London and New York: Penguin.

Gibson, William T. 1992. 'Withered Branches and Weighty Symbols': Surname Substitution in England 1660–1880. *British Journal of Eighteenth-Century Studies* 15.1: 17–33.

Halkett, Samuel. 1926–[1962]. *Dictionary of Anonymous and Pseudonymous English Literature*. Edinburgh: Oliver and Boyd.

Hassall, W.O. 1967. *History through Surnames*. Oxford: Pergamon Press.

The History of Betty Barnes. [1753] 1974. 2 vols. in 1. New York and London: Garland Publishing.

Hunter, J. Paul. 1979. Biography and the Novel. *Modern Language Studies* 9.3: 68–84.

[Kelly, Hugh]. [1767] 1974. *Memoirs of a Magdalen: or, The History of Louisa Mildmay.* 2 vols. in 1. New York and London: Garland Publishing.

Langford, Paul. 1989. *A Polite and Commercial People: England 1727–1783.* Oxford: Clarendon Press.

McCrea, Brian. 1998. *Impotent Fathers: Patriarchy and Demographic Crisis in the Eighteenth-Century Novel.* Newark: University of Delaware Press.

McKerrow, Ronald B. [1928] 1962. *An Introduction to Bibliography for Literary Students.* Oxford: Oxford University Press.

Monthly Review. 1752. 7 (Dec.): 470.

Ogborn, Miles. 1998. *Spaces of Modernity: London's Geographies 1680–1780.* London: The Guilford Press.

Porter, Roy. 1986. *English Society in the Eighteenth Century.* Harmondsworth: Penguin.

Ragussis, Michael. 1986. *The Act of Naming: The Family Plot in Fiction.* New York and London: Oxford University Press.

Raven, James. 1987. *British Fiction: 1750–1770. A Chronological Check-List of Prose Fiction Printed in Britain and Ireland.* Newark: University of Delaware.

Ready, Kathryn. 2002. Damaris Cudworth Masham, Catherine Trotter Cockburn, and the Feminist Legacy of Locke's Theory of Personal Identity. *Eighteenth-Century Studies* 35.4: 563–76.

Reaney, P.H. 1958. *A Dictionary of British Surnames.* London: Routledge and Kegan Paul.

Shevlin, Eleanor. 1999. 'To Reconcile *Book* and *Title,* and Make 'em Kin to One Another': The Evolution of the Title's Contractual Functions. *Book History* 2: 42–77.

Staves, Susan. 1980–1. British Seduced Maidens. *Eighteenth-Century Studies* 14.2: 109–34.

Todd, Janet, ed. 1987. *A Dictionary of British and American Women Writers 1660–1800.* Totowa, NJ: Rowman and Littlefield.

Watt, Ian. 1949. The Naming of Characters in Defoe, Richardson and Fielding. *Review of English Studies* 25: 322–38.

Withycombe, E.G. 1977. *The Oxford Dictionary of English Christian Names.* 3rd ed. Oxford: Clarendon Press.

13

Early Modern (Aristocratic) Women and Textual Property

PAUL SALZMAN

I went not out of the house nor out of my chamber today. (Anne Clifford 1990, frequent entry in the 1676 diary)

It is most certain, That those that perform Public Actions, expose themselves to Public Censures; and so do Writers, live they never so privately and retir'd, as soon as they commit their Works to the Press. (Margaret Cavendish 1668, Preface to *Plays, Never before Printed*)

This chapter explores some issues surrounding the ownership of, and investment in, a selection of texts by early modern women. In particular I want to explore connections between the way certain early modern aristocratic women allowed their texts to circulate while maintaining a particular kind of possession of them, and the possession and recirculation of them after they were first written. I examine Anne Clifford and Margaret Cavendish as examples of early modern women who wrote in very different ways and in different genres but who were particularly concerned with the reception of their writing and the way that reception might be controlled. Clifford seems to fit the model of the early modern woman writer outside of any public sphere, who wrote for herself alone and who would never have dreamed of publication as an option, while Cavendish saw herself as fitting the category of 'writer' and not only published her work but distributed it to the centres of learning from which she craved recognition. However, I will argue that both women had a strong sense of audience and that Clifford, while not searching for a wholly public audience, was indeed writing for a set of readers. The later history of both women's writing allows the ongoing intersection between their carefully 'targeted' texts and their readers to be traced through to the twenty-first century.[1]

Anne Clifford is now canonized as an example of an early modern woman who held out against the pressures placed upon her by her first husband, Richard Sackville, Earl of Dorset, and pretty well every other powerful man in her society up to and including the king, to relinquish her hereditary rights to estates and the baronies of Clifford, Vesci, and Veteripont in Westmorland – as explained in an earlier chapter by Mary Chan and Nancy E. Wright in this book (cf. Acheson 1995, 2). Mary Ellen Lamb has offered an important account of Clifford as a reader who uses her library and her portrait (the famous triptych composed around 1646 and reproduced in many modern accounts of Clifford) to support, in Lamb's telling phrase, her 'creation of herself as an heir' (Lamb 1992, 366). But it is in her writing that Clifford supports most substantially her claim to her estates and titles, and she does this by reaching out to an audience who will, in the fullness of time, see the enduring validity of her actions. This is particularly apparent when she turns from the detailed diaries that so entrance modern scholars (myself included) to the summaries of years and collections of family material made up into the *Great Books of the Clifford Family*. These are, as described clearly by Katherine Acheson, *presentation* copies of family material, surviving in three copies prepared by scribes and corrected by Clifford herself. It seems that there were in fact originally four copies of the *Great Books*, deposited at Skipton, Appleby Castle, Hothfield, and London (see Acheson 1995, 15). In other words, once Clifford did indeed inherit and move to Westmorland, her writing shifted from the more contemplative and, to at least some extent, more private diary form towards a form of family chronicle that would preserve for the future the detailed material that was the essence of Clifford's identity as inheritrix. I do not want to push this apparent dichotomy too far, because it seems to me that the diaries are also a form of testimony which looks outwards to those who will, in retrospect, see how Clifford withstood her ordeal.

Given that my interest is in the transmission of this material, it might be worth setting out exactly what Clifford wrote, as well as how it was later reproduced. We have individual diaries for the years 1616, 1617, 1619, and 1676; these are, on the whole, daily entries which detail events that occurred involving Clifford herself and her immediate family. These entries then have later marginal comments that tend to concern retrospective, personal material, but also more public events, such as changes in position at court. These diaries may well have been written throughout Clifford's life as the basis for the more elaborately worked-up chronicles of individual years. These chronicles survive for 1603 and for the years from 1650 to 1675, and are summaries of often no more than two or three pages, though some are longer. The chronicles are contained within the third volume of the *Great Books*, along with more extensive genealogical material. Clifford also wrote a narrative autobiographical account of her life from conception to 1650 (see Acheson 1995, 14–16).

In her useful general account of Clifford as a 'subversive' re-writer of patriarchy, Barbara Lewalski stresses the diaries as a key to Clifford's representation of a 'self in process' (1994, 150). But this is perhaps an overemphasis on Clifford's writing as self-directed; the diaries themselves are, it seems to me, her writing in process, as she moved towards the *Great Books*, which would be her most elaborate testimony to those who succeeded her and, given the number of copies made, to an even wider audience that would be told the story of the Clifford and Russell families and of Anne Clifford's ultimate right to inherit the family estates and titles. We have learned, most notably from Arthur Marotti and Harold Love, that the dichotomy between the 'private' world of manuscript writing and the 'public' world of print is misleading, given that manuscript writing was in itself a form of publication (see Love 1993; Marotti 1995). If we only looked at her diaries, Clifford might seem to fall into the still remaining category of 'private' women's writing, but the *Great Books* offer a clear (and self-confident) defiance of attempts to silence her and to keep her 'private' in the same way that Dorset kept confining her to Knole – a defiance as adamant as her defiance of King James when he attempted to persuade her to sign away her rights.[2]

As described in Richard Spence's recent biography of Clifford, the *Great Books* are presented as a public record with the clear implication of a wide readership (1997, chap. 9). The title page, as reproduced by Spence, is set out with great care and looks similar to the title page of a printed book or a manuscript intended for circulation (Spence 1997, 161).[3] It is worth reproducing some of the details here, given that the title page indicates to the reader right from the start that Clifford is testifying to her hereditary rights. It begins on the pious note that is repeated throughout Clifford's writing, most especially in the diary of her last months, where references to Job and the Psalms in particular are often placed at the end of paragraphs:

Through the mercies of the holy trinity: / God the Father, creator of the world/God the Sonn, Christ Jesus Redeemer of the world/God the Holie Ghost, sanctifier and preserver of the world/Doth proceed all blessings, both temporall and eternall.

Under this is an elaborate interwoven rule, followed by (in capitals):

This is the first booke of the recordes concerning the two noble families of the Cliffords. which weare [sic] Lords Cliffods [sic] of Clifford Castle in Herefordshire, and of the Veteriponts, who were lords Barons and high shreifs of Westmerland Which booke was compiled Anno 1649 by the care & industrie of the Lady Ann Clifford, Countess of Dorsett, Pembroke & Montgomery, Daughter and sole heire of Georg Clifford late Earl of Cumberland, which lady by birthright from her father and his auncestors is Barones Clifford of Westmerland, and Vescy, and High Shreives of that county and Lady of the Honor of Skipton in Craven being lineally descended from both those noble familyes.

The first two volumes contain the elaborate and scholarly genealogical records which Clifford had compiled in order to trace back her family descent in complete detail; much of this work was done by an antiquarian. As is the case with all Clifford's writing, retrospective annotation occurs throughout the *Great Books.* The scribal work was corrected and annotated in Clifford's own hand, although when scribes prepared a third copy they transcribed her instructions rather than making the corrections. The third volume moves from past family history to Anne Clifford's own lifetime and contains summaries of each year from 1650 to 1675. I want to argue that this volume, along with the other two, is more than just a genealogical memorial for a readership confined to the family. The endless descriptions of visits by children, grandchildren, and relatives are all in the third person, so that the records are not, as they might be, addressed to any family member who stood to inherit (for example, Anne's eldest daughter Margaret, who was next in line). Reading rather like a public statement, the detailed descriptions of Clifford's sleeping quarters in each of her five castles respectively function as a reiterated claim of ownership. This seems further emphasized by the repeated citing of how each person encountered relates to Clifford; thus we hear always that someone is a grandchild, and no one is ever really referred to by name alone. This creates the impression that the reader being addressed is someone outside the family, although one might also speculate that, given the record of constant family deaths, Clifford wanted to hand on a total family record to whichever more distant relative might inherit. Indeed, Clifford made elaborate arrangements to divide her estate between her eldest daughter Margaret and Alethea, the only surviving child of her younger daughter Isabella. Clifford's writings are all part of her attempt, not just to assert her own rights over her inheritance but to influence those who came after her both within and outside of her family. The writings are a means of control and they imply both the preservation of the Clifford inheritance and the preservation of Anne Clifford's key role in the transmission of that inheritance. (Spence notes that one copy of the *Great Books* was kept in Lincoln's Inn for use by Clifford's legal adviser, Matthew Hale, and they were used by her grandson Thomas Earl of Thanet in his claim for the title of Lord Clifford [1997, 171, 249].)

The title page of Clifford's *Great Books* bears an interesting resemblance to the title page of Mary Wroth's romance *Urania*, which was published in 1621. We cannot know for certain whether Wroth herself was responsible for the title page, but it indicates how her textual authority, her right to publish, so to speak, was derived from her family position as Sir Philip Sidney's niece, and therefore, from a literary point of view, she was, like Clifford, an inheritrix. Thus the *Urania* title page reads:

> The Countess of Montgomeries Urania. Written by the right honorable the Lady Mary Wroath. Daughter to the right Noble Robert Earle of Leicester. And Neece to the ever famous, and renowned Sr Philip Sidney knight. And to the most excelent Lady Mary Countesse of Pembroke late deceased.

Now of course the story of Wroth's venture into print is very different from the story of Clifford's 'publications' because Wroth had to retreat under the scandal that arose from her depiction of notorious stories from the Jacobean court, notably one that recounted the marriage of James Hay to Lord Denny's daughter, thereby arousing Denny's ire (see Roberts 1977; Salzman 1978). Wroth's problems arose in part because, as Wendy Wall has pointed out so cogently in her study of the interrelationship between early modern publication and issues of gender and identity, Wroth's venture into print was especially transgressive given that 'her public texts did not work within sanctioned and decorous paradigms' (1993, 338). Clifford knew Wroth and has an intriguing reference in her 1617 diary to Wroth, 'who told me a good deal of news from beyond sea' (19 August 1617, Acheson 1995, 91). And Clifford's own relationship to the Sidney family was cemented when she became the second wife of Philip Herbert, Earl of Pembroke, Mary Sidney's nephew. While Clifford's writing cannot in any way be compared to the literary output of Wroth, her manuscript production was still a form of publication which was intended to circulate, albeit within carefully constrained limits. Those limits were achieved initially by the control Clifford had over the circulation of her manuscripts. But the manuscripts were also clearly intended to have an ever-increasing readership, and their later transmission shows just how far that readership reached: an outcome completely in accord with Clifford's efforts to memorialize herself and her inheritance.

The transmission of the 1616–19 diary is perhaps the most interesting example of this memorializing. The diary has attracted modern scholars because of its intimacy and its glimpses of what Lewalski has described as 'the relation between authoring a text and authoring a self' (1994, 142). But the self in question is a particularly layered one and the diary is more of a palimpsest than a simple daily narrative. Thus the day-by-day entries are accompanied by marginal comments that offer a retrospective account of events from Clifford's own life or from the wider world of, especially, court affairs. This creates something of the same effect as the restrospective yearly accounts in the third volume of the *Great Books*. The 1616–19 diary records Clifford's resistance to the pressure placed upon her to relinquish her claims to her estates and also features her daughter Margaret, usually referred to as 'the child.' Dorset even used Margaret in an attempt to blackmail Clifford into acquiescing to his demands, at various stages removing the child from her mother. Clifford initially wanted to divide her estate between her two daughters, Margaret and Isabella, and, following Isabella's death in 1661, between Margaret and Isabella's surviving daughter, Alethea. The most intriguing aspect of the transmission of the 1616–19 diary is that the original has disappeared.[4]

This diary, which is so interested in the relationship between mothers and daughters and in inheritance through the female line, was copied in the eighteenth century by Margaret Bentinck, the Duchess of Portland (see the detailed discussion in Acheson 1995, 17–29). Clifford's daughter Margaret married John Tufton; their son Thomas, who ended up as Clifford's only surviving heir, married Catherine Cavendish, daughter of Henry Cavendish, the Duke of Newcastle (the son of William Cavendish and step-son of Margaret Cavendish). Catherine's sister Margaret's daughter, Henrietta Cavendish Holles, married Edward Harley, second Duke of Oxford, a great collector of manuscripts (see *DNB*). Their daughter was Margaret Bentinck, and she therefore probably had access to Clifford's diaries through the family connection, though they may also have been part of her father's manuscript collection. The bulk of the Harley manuscripts were sold in 1751. In 1737 a scribal copy of Clifford's autobiographical account of her own life as well as her family history was made by Henry Fisher and was part of the Harley manuscript collection; Margaret Bentinck had a copy of this made for her and it forms part of what are now the Portland Papers in the collection of the Marquess of Bath at Longleat (see Acheson 1995, 22; Spence 1997, 174–5).[5] Margaret Bentinck herself, rather than a scribe, copied the 1616–19 diary. It is this copy of the diary that has only recently come to light and been edited by Katherine Acheson. One might see the copying as an act of homage by Margaret to Anne Clifford – Margaret herself was a great manuscript collector and compiler.

The second scribal copy of the 1616–19 diary is linked to the descendants of Edward Sackville, the brother of Clifford's first husband, Richard Sackville, Earl of Dorset. By the mid-nineteenth century, Elizabeth Sackville and her husband George West were in residence at Knole, the Dorset family house that features so prominently in Clifford's diary. Acheson has tentatively identified Elizabeth Sackville's hand as one of two in the transcript of the diary now known as the Knole diary (Acheson 1995, 18). This copy, according to Acheson's collation, was transcribed from Bentinck's transcription (now known as the Portland diary), although there is no external evidence indicating exactly why, or indeed where, such a transcription from the Portland manuscript took place. Once again, it is significant that the line of manuscript descent is through another woman attracted to Clifford's diary. Elizabeth Sackville was Vita Sackville-West's grandmother. In 1923 Vita Sackville-West published an edition of the diary, the manuscript at Knole by then seeming to be the unique copy.

Sackville-West's view of Anne Clifford is complex. Her edition of the diary is, to some extent, a twentieth-century version of the eighteenth- and nineteenth-century transcriptions, but moving from family homage to public homage. In some ways the public transmission of Clifford undertaken by Sackville-West is a belated version of the public memorials undertaken by Clifford herself in terms of monuments, paintings, almshouses, memorial columns, and restored castles (for the memorials see Spence 1997, chap. 10). Sackville-West aptly summed up Clifford's memorializing impulses in her family history *Knole and the Sackvilles*: 'Her past was ever present to her' (Sackville-West 1958, 82). Sackville-West's edition of the diary carries forward that very aspect of Clifford's writing, presenting, at a distance of three hundred years, Clifford's account of her stand for her inheritance to the public. (It is ironic that, while *Knole and the Sackvilles* had fourteen editions by 1984, Sackville-West's edition of the diary was never reprinted.)

The 1616–19 diary (which is accompanied in all transcriptions by a retrospective summary account of 1603) models Clifford's resistance to attempts to rob her of her inheritance for a particular audience. I would like to speculate that that audience includes Margaret Sackville, the daughter who features in the diary as a small child, and then the audience of 'daughters' stretches through a further three centuries, from Margaret Bentinck to Elizabeth Sackville to Vita Sackville-West. The *Great Books* posit a wider audience still, and during the eighteenth and ninteenth centuries, while the 1616–19 diary was transmitted within branches of the family, what we might call the Anne Clifford legend was perpetuated more widely. For example, in 1795 William Seward tells Clifford's story and reproduces the 1603 summary in *Anecdotes of Some Distinguished Persons Chiefly of the Present and the Two Preceding Centuries*, putting her in varied but usually distinguished company, which would undoubtedly have appealed to her (1795, 302–17). Spence notes the influence of the *Great Books* and other manuscript material on regional historians in the late eighteenth and early nineteenth centuries, such as Nicholson and Burn's *History and Antiquities of the Counties of Westmorland and Cumberland* and T.D. Whitaker's *History and Antiquities of the Deanery of Craven* (1997, 250). The idea of Clifford as an unusual and notable figure is then taken up in such works as Hartley Coleridge's *Lives of Northern Worthies* (1852), which draws upon Whitaker, rather than the diaries, and offers a paean to Clifford as an exemplary woman who 'happily combined the graces and charities of the high-born woman with the sterner qualifications of a ruler' (Coleridge 1852, 7). The sense of Clifford as belonging to regional and family history continued into the twentieth century, as the biographical compilation by George Williamson, published in a limited edition in Kendal in 1922, testifies, as do the family connections (however distant) of those who followed, including D.J.H. Clifford, who edited the diaries in 1990, and Hugh Clifford, who published a family history (Williamson 1922; Clifford 1990; Clifford 1987). At present, Clifford's audience is split between academics and students who now have wide access to the 1616–19 diary and readers attracted to biographical information about such an arresting figure (see, for example, Holmes 1973). Only with wider transmission of the *Great Books* will Clifford's construction of herself as a particular kind of writer reach an audience outside the family.

As I noted at the beginning of this essay, at first glance Margaret Cavendish seems a complete contrast to Anne Clifford. Cavendish saw herself as an author and published a large number of volumes in a variety of literary, scientific, and philosophical genres. However, in venturing into print, Cavendish clearly turned to a series of strategies that reflect her anxiety about her role. The dizzying switch between bravado and modesty that is so characteristic of Cavendish's discussions of her own writing and ventures into print has often been remarked upon by modern critics (see, for example, Bowerbank 1984; Price 1996). Cavendish was quite clearly conscious of the reaction that Mary Wroth received when she ventured into print.[6] She therefore set out to control the reception of her work in a variety of ways, most noticeably in the way she manipulated the reader's first experience of one of her books. Like Clifford and Wroth, Cavendish's title pages are designed to call attention to her status, and therefore they offer an initial buffer against criticism by stressing Cavendish's rank and family (attained through her marriage to William Cavendish, Duke of Newcastle). For example, *Poems and Fancies*, which was Cavendish's first published work, along with *Philosophical Fancies*, in 1653, is on the title page declared to be written by 'the Right Honourable the Lady Margaret Marchioness of Newcastle.' This volume also begins with one of the three engraved frontispieces that Cavendish attached to many of her volumes. James Fitzmaurice, who has written at length on the prefaces and on the prefatory material, notes that these engravings enable Cavendish to shift her self-representation between the solitary and melancholy writer (which is the frontispiece in most copies of *Poems and Fancies*) and the figure with a laurel wreath sitting next to her husband at a crowded family table (the frontispiece commonly attached to copies of *Nature's Pictures Drawn by Fancy's Pencil to the Life* [1656/1671]) (Fitzmaurice 1990; Fitzmaurice 1997). *Poems and Fancies* then has a dedication 'To Sir Charles Cavendish, my noble brother-in-law,' which again offers a degree of family protection for the writer. A general preface to 'all noble and worthy ladies' is followed by one specifically to Cavendish's maid and close friend Elizabeth Topp, with a reply from Topp herself. In other volumes, Cavendish relies upon a series of prefaces and introductory poems to and by her husband to reinforce the 'legitimacy' of her ventures.

Most relevant to my argument is the beginning of a poem which prefaces *Poems and Fancies*:

Condemne me not for making such a coyle
About my Book, alas it is my Childe.
Just like a Bird, when her Young are in Nest,
Goes in, and out, and hops and takes no Rest;
But when their Young are fledg'd, their heads out peep,
Lord what a chirping does the Old one keep.
So I, for feare my Strengthlesse Childe should fall
Against a doore, or stoole, aloud I call,
Bid have a care of such a dangerous place:
Thus write I much, to hinder all disgrace. (Cavendish 1653b, A4v)

While Cavendish describes her book as a child, I think that she also signals an attachment that leads her to treat each individual copy of her book as a child. This is evidenced by the way she hand-corrected individual copies and by the way she presented individual copies to colleges at Oxford and Cambridge and elsewhere. Here there is perhaps a parallel with the surviving copies of Aemilia Lanyer's *Salve Deus Rex Judaeorum* (1611), in which various combinations of the ten dedications exist, indicating that each copy may well have had a specific reader in mind (see Lanyer 1993). Cavendish makes a link between the way that a printed book may seem less personal than a manuscript publication and the investment in the individual copy that is, on the surface at least, more evident in the production of manuscripts.

Just as Clifford oversaw the individual copies of the *Great Books* and annotated them herself, so Cavendish focused on individual copies of a number of her books. In his study of these hand corrections, James Fitzmaurice speculates that Cavendish concentrated on the volumes that meant the most to her: he compares the corrected and annotated *Sociable Letters* with the uncorrected *Philosophical Letters*, which was published in the same year (1664) (Fitzmaurice 1991). The proliferation of prefaces, the presentation of individual copies to worthy recipients, the hand correction and annotation, and the heavy revision evident in new editions of certain volumes, notably *Poems and Fancies*, which was reprinted in 1664 and 1668 with a bewildering number of variants, all point to constant attempts by Cavendish to monitor and control her audience. It is perhaps worth noting that this possession of the individual printed book is also evident in the prophetical writings of Eleanor Davies/Douglas, who often made hand corrections and insertions. As an aristocratic woman writing prophecy, Davies was very different from nonaristocratic women, who seem to have viewed their prophetic visions as embodied within themselves, rather than in a text, so that they might have their work written out by someone else (as in the case of Anna Trapnel), or at least be more willing to relinquish possession of the written text.[7]

While Clifford looked to her daughters for the perpetuation of her heritage and her writing, Cavendish, who only had step-daughters (themselves authors of a comic play which contains a satirical picture of their future step-mother as the vain Lady Tranquillity), had to embody a readership within her writing (see Cavendish and Brackley 1996). The Cavendish and Clifford families actually intertwined when, in 1684, Clifford's grandson, Thomas Tufton, married Catherine, the fourth daughter of Henry Cavendish, who was Margaret's only surviving step-son and who succeeded William as Duke of Newcastle. Cavendish's writing, however, had a quite different history from Clifford's. By the nineteenth century, Cavendish was seen as an eccentric figure whose work was scarcely read. When Cavendish did receive some praise, it was as a curiosity, the best example being Charles Lamb's aside: 'a dear favourite of mine, of the last century but one – the thrice noble, chaste, and virtuous, – but again somewhat fantastical, and original-brain'd, generous Margaret Newcastle' (Lamb 1987, 87).[8]

During much of the twentieth century, the perception of Cavendish as an eccentric figure overshadowed the serious analysis of her writing. While this situation has now changed and Cavendish has attracted a reasonable amount of sophisticated criticism, her actual texts have suffered an unfortunate, albeit understandable, mutilation. Wrenched away from the careful protection of prefaces, frontispieces, annotation, and emendation, certain favoured literary texts have been edited and reproduced outside of their correct contexts. This is most notably the case with the utopian narrative 'The Blazing World,' twice edited (by myself and by Kate Lilley) as a free-standing text, rather than attached to *Observations Upon Experimental Philosophy* (1666) (see Salzman 1991; Lilley 1994).[9] Only *Sociable Letters* has appeared in its entirety as a full scholarly edition (Cavendish 1997). This has had the result that, for all the efforts of scholars, modern readers of Cavendish find that her texts are owned, and their responses to them directed, by her editors, rather than by Cavendish herself. Of course, if Cavendish's main aim was fame, she might not be so concerned about the mode of transmission three centuries after she wrote, so long as she has readers.

Taken together, Clifford and Cavendish offer telling examples of how early modern aristocratic women might tackle the issue of how their potential readership could be controlled, of how their texts could remain in their possession even as they went into circulation. There are undoubtedly large differences between the manuscript writing of Clifford and the printed texts of Cavendish, but both envisage the individual text as a means of presenting to a reader an exemplary instance of the writer's self. Even as they handed their writing over to a reader, both women endeavoured to keep a firm grip upon the reading process itself.

Notes

1 My starting point for this argument is Margaret Ezell's clear exposition of the significance of manuscript circulation for early modern women's writing (see in particular Ezell 1987, chap. 3).

2 Clifford's account of this incident is in the entry for 18 January 1617. My notion of Clifford's sense of audience is related to some recent work on Clifford, notably Suzuki (2001) and a forthcoming essay by Susan Wiseman, 'Knowing Her Place: Anne Clifford and the Politics of Retreat' (I am grateful to Susan Wiseman for allowing me to read her essay on Clifford).

3 Beal (1998, 15–19) notes that manuscripts usually omit the details provided by a printed book's title page.

4 George Williamson believes that the original was destroyed by Clifford's grandson and heir Thomas Tufton (1922, 322). There was a considerable amount of recopying of Clifford's writing in the early eighteenth century, although this would not necessarily entail the destruction of the original manuscripts. Katherine Acheson notes that Clifford herself clearly wanted the diaries preserved given their 'daily importance' for her own sense of her self (1998, 45).

5 The Fisher scribal copy is now British Library MS Harley 6177.

6 Cavendish quotes from Denny's vituperative poem, which attacks Wroth for publishing *Urania*, in these lines from the preface to *Sociable Letters* (1664): 'It may be said to me, as one said to a Lady, *Work Lady*, Work let writing Books alone, for surely Wiser Women n'er writ one' (1997, b).

7 For examples of Davies's/Douglas's work, see copies of *The Benediction* (1651) and *Revelations: The Everlasting Gospel* (1649) in the Cambridge University Library, British Library, and Bodleian Library. Anna Trapnel's *The Cry of a Stone* (1664) and *Strange and Wonderful News from White Hall* (1654) are both testimonies to her words and deeds written by others, though Trapnel herself wrote *Report and Plea* (1654).

8 Her biography of William and her autobiographical writing did have some nineteenth-century admirers: see especially Cavendish (1872).

9 See also the individual play texts edited by Jennifer Rowsell, taken from Cavendish's collections: *The Convent of Pleasure* (1995) and *The Sociable Companions* (1996).

Works Cited

Acheson, Katherine O. 1995. *The Diary of Anne Clifford 1616–1619.* New York: Garland.

– 1998. The Modernity of the Early Modern: The Example of Anne Clifford. In *Discontinuities: New Essays on Renaissance Literature and Criticism,* ed. Viviana Comensoli and Paul Stevens, 27–51. Toronto: University of Toronto Press.

Beal, Peter. 1998. *In Praise of Scribes.* Oxford: Clarendon Press.

Bowerbank, Sylvia. 1984. The Spider's Delight: Margaret Cavendish and the Female Imagination. *English Literary Renaissance* 14: 392–408.

Cavendish, Jane, and Elizabeth Brackley. 1996. The Concealed Fancies. In *Renaissance Drama by Women,* ed. S.P. Ceresano and Marion Wynne Davies, 127–54. London: Routledge.

Cavendish, Margaret. 1653a. *Philosophical Fancies.* London: n.p.

– 1653b. *Poems and Fancies.* London: T.R. for Martin and Allestrye.

– 1656. *Natures Pictures.* London: Martin and Allestrye.

– 1668. *Plays, Never before Printed.* London: A. Maxwell.

– 1872. *Lives of William Cavendish Duke of Newcastle and of His Wife Margaret Duchess of Newcastle,* ed. Mark Antony Lower. London: John Russell Smith.

– 1995. *The Convent of Pleasure,* ed. Jennifer Rowsell. Oxford: Seventeenth Century Press.

– 1996. *The Sociable Companions,* ed. Jennifer Rowsell. Oxford: Seventeenth Century Press.

– 1997. *Sociable Letters,* ed. James Fitzmaurice. New York: Garland.

Clifford, Lady Anne. n.d. *Great Books of the Clifford Family.* Hothfield Papers, Cumbria Record Office (WD/Hoth/10).

– 1990. *The Diaries of Lady Anne Clifford.* Ed. D.J.H. Clifford. Stroud: Alan Sutton.

Clifford, Hugh. 1987. *The House of Clifford.* Chichester: Phillimore.

Coleridge, Hartley. 1852. *Lives of Northern Worthies,* ed. Derwent Coleridge. Vol. 2. London: Edward Moxon.

Dictionary of National Biography. 1917. Vol. 8. Oxford: Oxford University Press.

Ezell, Margaret. 1987. *The Patriarch's Wife: Literary Evidence and the History of the Family.* Chapel Hill: University of North Carolina Press.

Fitzmaurice, James. 1990. Fancy and the Family: Self-Characterizations of Margaret Cavendish. *Huntington Library Quarterly* 53: 198–201.

– 1991. Margaret Cavendish on Her Own Writing: Evidence from Revision and Handmade Correction. *Papers, Bibliographical Society of America* 85: 297–308.

– 1997. Front Matter and the Physical Make-up of Natures Pictures. *Women's Writing* 4: 353–67.

Holmes, Martin. 1973. *Proud Northern Lady.* Chichester: Phillimore.

Lamb, Charles. 1987. Mackery End, in Hertfordshire. In *Elia*, ed. Jonathan Bate. Oxford: World's Classics.

Lamb, Mary Ellen. 1992. The Agency of the Split Subject: Lady Anne Clifford and the Uses of Reading. *English Literary Renaissance* 22: 347–68.

Lanyer, Aemilia. 1993. *Salve Deus Rex Judaeorum*, ed. Susanne Woods. New York: Oxford University Press.

Lewalski, Barbara. 1994. *Writing Women in Jacobean England.* Cambridge, MA: Harvard University Press.

Lilley, Kate. 1994. *The Blazing World and Other Writings.* Harmondsworth: Penguin.

Love, Harold. 1993. *Scribal Publication in Seventeenth Century England.* Oxford: Clarendon Press.

Marotti, Arthur. 1995. *Manuscript, Print and the English Renaissance Lyric.* Ithaca: Cornell University Press.

Nicholson, J., and R. Burn. 1777. *The History and Antiquities of the Counties of Westmorland and Cumberland.* London: Strachan and Cadell.

Price, Bronwen. 1996. Feminine Modes of Knowing and Scientific Enquiry: Margaret Cavendish's Poetry as Case Study. In *Women and Literature in Britain 1500–1700*, ed. Helen Wilcox, 117–39. Cambridge: Cambridge University Press.

Roberts, Josephine. 1977. An Unpublished Literary Quarrel Concerning the Suppression of Mary Wroth's *Urania*. *Notes & Queries* 222: 532–5.

Sackville-West, Vita. 1958. *Knole and the Sackvilles.* Rev. ed. Tonbridge: Ernest Benn.

Salzman, Paul. 1978. Contemporary References in Mary Wroth's *Urania*. *Review of English Studies* 24: 178–81.

– 1991. *An Anthology of Seventeenth-Century Fiction.* Oxford: World's Classics.

Seward, William. 1795. *Anecdotes of Some Distinguished Persons Chiefly of the Present and Two Preceding Centuries.* Vol. 4. London: T. Cadell.

Spence, Richard T. 1997. *Lady Anne Clifford: Countess of Pembroke, Dorset and Montgomery (1590–1676).* Stroud: Sutton.

Suzuki, Mihoko. 2001. Anne Clifford and the Gendering of History. *Clio* 30: 195–229.

Wall, Wendy. 1993. *The Imprint of Gender: Authorship and Publication in the English Renaissance.* Ithaca: Cornell University Press.

Whitaker, T.D. 1805. *The History and Antiquities of the Deanery of Craven in the County of York.* London.

Williamson, George. 1922. *Lady Anne Clifford.* Kendal: Titus Wilson and Son.

Afterword

MARGRETA DE GRAZIA

Had the property laws of early modern England applied in Eden, Eve would not have fared well. In a system that privileges first-born males, to be born second and female was doubly bad luck. Nor did the fall help matters. Both Eve and Adam were penalized with the pains and sorrows of labour, she in childbirth and he in the fields. But Eve was given an additional punishment: she was made subject to Adam – 'he shall rule over thee' (Genesis 3: 16). This penalty put her in the same category as the other creatures over which Adam had been given 'dominion': fish, fowl, cattle, and every creeping thing (Genesis 1: 26). And the Ten Commandments kept woman in that category by including her among the possessions a man must not covet in his neighbour, along with house, servants, ass, ox, and 'any thing that is thy neighbour's' (Exodus 21: 17). Falling more in the category of property than proprietor, women throughout Scripture tend to be excluded from the contests over birthright, inheritance, and dominion. Or if they do participate, they do so indirectly, even deviously. Only through deceit does Rebekah succeed in transferring the birthright from the son her husband intends to the one she favours. She covers the smooth-skinned Jacob with hairy goatskins so that his blind father, when he reaches out to confer his blessing, will mistake him for his hirsute son Esau.

In early modern England, a wife's status was not so different from Eve's. Indeed, the common law might be said to have upheld the Edenic sentence. As Eve was put under Adam's rule by God's penalty, so the wife (feme) was put under the regulation of the husband (baron) by the common law doctrine of coverture. By the law of coverture, a wife was denied access to property: she could not own it (even property she held before marriage), acquire it (through legacies or gifts), or alienate it (by will or gift). In the eyes of the law, her inability to own property accorded with her loss of personal identity. Blackstone makes her legal status quite plain, 'the very being or legal existence of the woman is suspended during the marriage, or at least incorporated and consolidated into that of the husband: under whose wing, protection, and *cover*, she performs everything' (1979, 1: 430). The identity she brought to the marriage is subsumed by that of her husband, just as her surname is surrendered to his. The relation is, as Blackstone maintains, protective: coverture puts her under the husband's wing, shielding her from want, danger, and injury. But the relation is also regulative: she is under his rod as well as wing, and subject to his discipline and correction.

In short, the wife is at the husband's disposal, like the rest of his property. While the wedding vow requires that each take the other 'to have and to hold,' it is only the bride who is 'given away' and 'received.' And it is only she who is physically subjugated in the sexual act, which finalizes the marriage. It appears that coverture was first used in medieval law–French to refer to the baron's sexual 'covering' of the feme's body: his 'topping' or 'mounting' her.[1] The covering of a piece of land by setting a roof over it was a form of enclosure signalling occupation. (Similarly the covering of a servant in the cloth of livery signified that he was his lord's man.)[2] In the rich metaphorics used to designate the sexual act, women and territory were virtually interchangeable. Both could be acquired by conquest, by contract, by purchase, by occupation or tenancy. Once acquired or 'possessed,' both could be 'used,' 'enjoyed,' and made fruitful by the owner. A man who had sex with another man's wife encroached on his territory, ignoring the boundary separating his property from the other's, the *meum* from the *tuum*, as if there were 'No borne 'twixt his and mine' (*The Winter's Tale* 1974, 2.3.196). There was need, too, to identify woman with property more mobile than land. In order to suggest both her value and her alienability, woman was compared to a precious object, which, unlike land, could be removed. Both rape and adultery were represented as acts of theft against the husband. Though rape originally referred to the seizure of goods including women, it came increasingly to designate the violation of one kind of 'good': a woman's sexual part. Even if a wife gave herself willingly to another man, her act constituted robbery: adultery took from the husband what properly belonged to him. Of course, it was not the removal of the wife herself which offended. Rather it was the 'taking' of that one part: hence the notorious chastity belt, which kept that part, like a jewel, under lock and key. But the wife needed to be kept chaste in word as well as deed. It might be said that a whole court system – the ecclesiastical or 'bawdy' courts – evolved to protect that particular possession from libel or defamation. Woman's chastity was not only a coveted property in itself; as Samuel Johnson wryly maintained, it was the basis of the entire property system: 'all property depends upon it' (Boswell 1980, 537, 702). Patrilineal inheritance depended upon the guarantee of pure lineage. And as Engels (1978, 745) brilliantly noted, the flip side of priceless chastity was sex for a price. Prostitution was the commercial counterpart to monogamous possession – the property that served as mainstay of social order could like any commodity circulate in exchange for cash.

A law debarring a woman from owning, inheriting, and purchasing property deprived her of the status of personhood. Without property, persons tend to slide into the category of nonpersons. This is King Lear's great insight at the point when he himself is being stripped of his possessions: persons (of whatever rank) need belongings (of whatever value) in order to be human, 'our basest beggars / Are in the poorest thing superfluous' (*King Lear* 1974, 2.4.259–60; see also de Grazia 1997, 17–42). By this rationale, it is not speech or reason which distinguishes man from beast but the possession of some thing; without it, 'Man's life's as cheap as beast's' (*King Lear* 1974, 2.4.262). That indispensable thing reemerges in Blackstone as an 'inherent right' to private property, one of 'the three great and primary rights' (1979, 1: 136) along with the right to life and liberty guaranteed to all Englishmen.[3] And yet in 1769, the term Englishmen was decidedly gendered. No such right could inhere in a feme covert, for she was a person *in her husband* rather than *in her own right*. Women appear to be similarly excluded from the founding assumption of Locke's treatise on property, 'Every man has property in his own person' (1952, 17). If a woman is not owner of herself, she cannot by Locke's logic be entitled to what she produces. While the man who performs Adam's labour of tilling is entitled to what he tills, the woman who suffers Eve's labour of childbirth has no special right to what she bears. It is to God's 'workmanship' rather than to the mother's labour that children are attributed (Locke 1952, 32). By Locke's logic, a woman under coverture who labours at her needlework or at her writing could not lay claim to the results, at least not when – during the period of her greatest productivity – she remained under the conjugal wing and rod of her husband.

One could continue to identify the ways in which the property laws of early modern England were disabling to women. Many of the essays in this volume have focused not on the limitations imposed by the letter of the law but instead on women's roles within property relationships. Christine Churches reveals that not all regions of England conformed to common law practices: in the seaport of Whitehaven, a form of customary tenure enabled married women to retain property they inherited and daughters to inherit rather than sons. David Lemmings discusses the ready and affordable access common women had to the ecclesiastical courts, where they defended their reputations and their attendant material assets. Claire Walker describes how communal ownership in a convent extended beyond material goods to the spiritual rules of the order (and the manuscripts in which they were inscribed). As we are reminded by Natasha Korda, convents as well as monasteries were dissolved in England during the Reformation; no longer sharing in the benefits of a marriage to Christ, the sisters were reduced to 'singlewomen' without place or position. Several of the essays look to ways in which women resisted or circumvented the biases of the unwritten common law through various forms of writing: from Elizabeth Cary's petitions to the king (Introduction), to Anne Clifford's diaries recording the genealogy on which she based her entitlement (Chan and Wright, Salzman), to spiritual testaments that bequeathed ethical and religious wisdom in lieu of material goods (Davis), to collections of letters by women which foreground the extensive lateral relations of surrogacy and service in the patrilineal household (Summit), to a fictionalized memoir of a prostitute who ends up obtaining vast estate by capitalizing on her sole inheritance of 'a very Small Spot' (Rosenthal).

Many of the volume's essays illustrate the need to expand our understanding of gender in the early modern property regime beyond the workings of the common law. It is tempting to see the counter-examples to coverture as anticipating a modern and more liberal dispensation. And indeed it does at times appear as if women had found ways to obtain agency in property matters before the law conferred it on them legally. Such a view, however, risks losing sight of what may be the more valuable contribution of these essays: their demonstration of how women were able to participate in property relationships before they enjoyed the full right to private property.

But did men enjoy such a right? That is, did the baron have the power to retain and dispose his property as he wished, 'in total exclusion of the

right of any other individual in the universe' (Blackstone 1979, 2: 2)?
After all, he was bound by coverture to maintain his wife, under all
conditions short of criminal offence. Elizabeth Cary, in insisting that her
husband suitably maintain her – even in her state of estrangement – was
demanding no more than was her due. By the same law of coverture, a
husband was liable for the debts his wife incurred (both before and
during the marriage) as well as for the children she bore, even if begot-
ten by another man.[4] Nor did his obligations end at death: the husband
was bound by common law to leave to his widow a dower of one-third of
his freehold lands. Does this not suggest that the 'very being' of the
baron was consolidated in the feme, as hers in him? Bound by his wife's
actions, needs, and desires, he could hardly be said to have been the
autonomous person in his own right assumed by theories of liberal
individualism.

So both husband and wife were constrained by coverture, but only if
we think of them as two individuals with vying claims. It may be helpful
instead to see them as 'individual' in the etymological but now obsolete
sense Milton intends when Adam welcomes Eve as his 'individual solace
dear' (*Paradise Lost* 1957, 4.486); made of his flesh and his bone, she
cannot be divided (*in*, non + *dividuus*, divisible) from him.[5] The common law aspired to a similar conjugal 'individuality' when it forbade a
man from giving his wife gifts on the grounds that it would presuppose
'her separate existence.' For the same reason, neither could bear witness
against the other lest they bear witness against themselves. A wife could,
however, represent her husband legally and sue on his behalf, for that
implied no separation from the husband. Thus wives who sued for the
return of their husband's sequestered or confiscated property during
the interregnum were authorized by coverture; there are numerous
cases on record of female litigants entreating in place of their absent or
deceased husbands (Churches); and wives not uncommonly served as
executors of their wills. As these substitutions indicate, the collapsing of
the feme covert into the *baron de covert* constitutes a 'union of person,'
which, like an artificial person, is recognized by the law. Like an artificial
person (a joint-stock company, for example), this 'union of persons' was
formed in order to outlast its individual members and achieve a 'perpetual succession' or 'a kind of legal immortality' (Blackstone 1979, 1:
433). So, too, was the couple conjoined by coverture. Neither was to
benefit as individual: both benefited insofar as their common interest
lay in the consolidation and perpetuation of their household made up
of persons (family, servants, retainers), things (houses, land, movables,

heirlooms), and traditions (a religion, aesthetic, ethos, genealogy). Coverture did not incorporate two Lockean individuals, each of whom could be 'seen essentially as the proprietor of his own person or capacities, owing nothing to society for them' (Locke 1952, 17). For neither is self-owned, and both feel a duty which may be inseparable from a desire to preserve and reproduce through the generations the social nexus that is their household (Murray).

This is not to endorse Blackstone's outrageous conclusion to his discussion of coverture: 'So great a favourite is the female sex of the laws of England.' There can be no denying that woman is subordinate in this 'union of person' (1979, 1: 430). As the saying goes, 'Man and wife are one, and man is the one.'[6] All the same, it is important to acknowledge that the law's unevenness existed within a shared structure designed to collapse his and hers (or, more realistically, hers *into* his) to the end of reproducing in perpetuity a nexus of relations between persons and things. The law of coverture may be important precisely because the persons it brings into 'union' cannot be understood as individuals. Even Anne Clifford, who flouts all expectation that her property (or what *she* determines is her property) would be dissolved into her husband's, was not out for herself. Her possessiveness could hardly be less individualistic: for thirty-eight years she clung to her entitlement not in her own name but in that of her heritage, what she termed the 'Inheritance of my forefathers' (Chan and Wright). Indeed, she defended her claim with an appeal not to a personal inherent right, but to the more ancient entitlement of common law, held since time immemorial. Her determination not to part with her ancestral estate draws us back to the etymology of *individual*, providing what may be our boldest historical example of the inalienability of person from property, of the indivisibility of baron and baronry.

The period designation 'early modern' tends to suggest a special rapport with the modern, as if its 'then' were the onset of our 'now.' We are inclined, therefore, to look back to it for signs of an emergent modernity: for ways in which women, despite the law's curtailments, began to exercise self-determining agency. They, too, can then be imagined as following the progressive trajectory toward possessive individualism, though several steps behind. Their activity thus loses its specificity when streamlined into the dominant historical narrative. It is as if we wanted all roads to lead to private property. A hierarchical system like coverture may be uneven (hierarchies always are), but how equitable are the exclusions of private property? Upon second look, the majority of property relationships singled out by this volume are collective or collaborative: the goods held in common by the convent (Walker and Korda), the letters tracing communal circuits of influence (Summit), the defence of reputation in the name of communal and social concerns (Lemmings), the grounding of title in an ancestral nexus (Buck), and the incorporation of wife into husband as one legal entity (Afterword). All these examples suggest that private property, held individually to the exclusion of others, may be more the anomaly than the rule.

After all, the primary form of property in this period – land – could not be owned absolutely. The distinguishing feature of land in England was that it was in theory *owned* by the monarch and only *held* – by descent, transfer, or purchase – by his subjects. Landlords were legally only holders or tenants of the land, and they in turn portioned it out to still others who had the right to live on it and work it. Nor does the proprietorship of land end here. For a number of rights were held in common – to pasturage (grazing of cattle), piscary (catching of fish), turbary (digging for metals or peat), and estovers (cutting wood). From what kind of property, then, does exclusivity derive?

The essays in this volume chart out new courses of inquiry and open up vast areas of research, demonstrating how much there is to be understood about the gendering of property relations in the early modern period. Common law coverture, a system we might have assumed as transparent as primogeniture itself, turns out to have been astonishingly complex and variable, depending on region, time period, circumstance, as well as individual agency. And as these essays establish, there is no understanding of a property regime unless women's positions and relations to it are factored in, as they both confirm and resist those presently familiar to us.

Notes

1 See Pollock and Maitland (1923, 2: 407, n. 1). Compare Shakespeare's use of the term in *Othello:* 'You'll have your daughter cover'd with a Barbary horse' (1974, 1.1.111). In Elegy 19, 'To His Mistris Going to Bed,' Donne puns on the sexual and legal sense of coverture in laying claim to his mistress, 'What needs thou more covering than a man?' (1965, line 48). He puns, too, on entitlement through its semantic opposite, *discovery*, the imperialist claim over native occupancy (see Cheyfitz 1997, 49).

2 On the importance of livery as a form of corporate or household identification, see Jones and Stallybrass (2000, esp. 17–21, 273–7).

3 On the switch from the right to the 'pursuit of property' to the right to the 'pursuit of happiness' in the American Declaration of Independence, see Fliegelman (1993).

4 Bastardy laws are explained in *Lex Spuriorum* (Brydall 1703): 'If a man be within the 4 Seas and his wife hath a child, it is presumed the child is of the husband and against this presupposition [the court] will admit no proof.'

5 See Williams's entry on *individual* (1976, 133–6) and Stallybrass's elaboration (1992, 593–610).

6 The precedent for the effacement of the wife's surname in the husband's is in Genesis: 'Male and female created he them; and blessed them, *and called their name Adam*, in the day where they were created' (5: 2; emphasis added).

Works Cited

Blackstone, William. [1765–9] 1979. *Commentaries on the Laws of England*, ed. A.W.B. Simpson. 4 vols. Facsimile ed. Chicago: University of Chicago Press.

Boswell, James. 1980. *Life of Johnson*, ed. R.W. Chapman and J.D. Fleeman. Oxford: Oxford University Press.

Brydall, John. 1703. *Lex Spuriorum: or, the law relating to bastardy*. London.

Cheyfitz, Eric. 1997. *The Poetics of Imperialism*. Philadelphia: University of Philadelphia Press.

de Grazia, Margreta. 1997. *King Lear* as Period Piece: The Ideology of Superfluous Things. In *Subject and Object in Renaissance Culture*, ed. Margreta de Grazia, Maureen Quilligan, and Peter Stallybrass, 17–42. Cambridge: Cambridge University Press.

Donne, John. 1965. Elegy 19: To His Mistris Going to Bed. In *The Elegies and the Songs and Sonnets*, ed. Helen Gardner, 14–16. Oxford: Clarendon Press.

Engels, Friedrich. 1978. The Origins of the Family, Private Property, and the State. In *The Marx-Engels Reader*, ed. Robert C. Tucker, 734–59. 2nd ed. New York and London: W.W. Norton.

Fliegelman, Jay. 1993. *Declaring Independence: Jefferson, Natural Language, and the Culture of Performance*. Stanford: Stanford University Press.

Jones, Ann Rosalind, and Peter Stallybrass. 2000. *Renaissance Clothing and the Material of Memory*. Cambridge: Cambridge University Press.

Locke, John. 1952. *The Second Treatise of Government*, ed. Thomas P. Peardon. Indianapolis: Bobbs-Merrill.

Milton, John. 1957. *Paradise Lost*. In *John Milton: Complete Poems and Major Prose*, ed. Merritt Y. Hughes, 173–469. Indianapolis: The Odyssey Press.

Pollock, Frederick, and Frederic William Maitland. 1923. *The History of English*

Law before the Time of Edward I. 2nd ed. 2 vols. Cambridge: Cambridge University Press.

Shakespeare, William. 1974. *King Lear, Othello, The Winter's Tale.* In *The Riverside Shakespeare,* ed. G. Blakemore Evans, 1249–1305, 1198–1248, 1564–1605. Boston: Houghton Mifflin.

Stallybrass, Peter. 1992. Shakespeare, the Individual, and the Text. In *Cultural Studies,* ed. Lawrence Grossberg, Cary Nelson, and Paula A. Treichler, 593–610. New York and London: Routledge.

Williams, Raymond. 1976. *Keywords: A Survey of Culture and Society.* London: Croom Helm.

Contributors

A.R. Buck teaches in the Division of Law at Macquarie University, Australia, where he also edits the *Australian Journal of Legal History*. He is the co-editor (with John McLaren and Nancy Wright) of *Land and Freedom: Law, Property Rights and the British Diaspora* (2001).

Mary Chan is Professor Emeritus in the School of English at the University of New South Wales, Australia. She is the author of *Life into Story: The Courtship of Elizabeth Wiseman* (1998) and editor of several of the writings of Roger North, including *Life of the Lord Keeper North* (1995).

Christine Churches was formerly a Research Fellow in History at the University of Adelaide, Australia. She has published essays on litigation in early modern England, most recently in Wilfrid Prest and Sharon Roach Anleu (eds), *Litigation Past and Present* (2003), and is currently writing a monograph on the experience of going to law in early modern England.

Lloyd Davis is a Reader in English at the University of Queensland, Australia. He has published on early modern and nineteenth-century literature, and is the author of *Guise and Disguise: Rhetoric and Characterization in the English Renaissance* (1993), and the editor of *Sexuality and Gender in the English Renaissance* (1998) and *Shakespeare Matters: History, Teaching, Performance* (2003).

Margaret Ferguson is Professor of English at the University of California, Davis. She has taught at Yale, Columbia, and the University of Colorado and has recently published *Dido's Daughters: Literacy, Gender, and Empire in Early Modern England and France* (2003).

Margreta de Grazia is Clara M. Clendenen Term Professor of English at the University of Pennsylvania. She is the author of *Shakespeare Verbatim* (1991) and co-editor (with Maureen Quilligan and Peter Stallybrass) of *Subject and Object in Renaissance Culture* (1996), and (with Stanley Wells) *The Cambridge Companion to Shakespeare* (2001), and is presently completing a book entitled *Hamlet as Anachronism.*

Natasha Korda is an Associate Professor of English at Wesleyan University. She is the author of *Shakespeare's Domestic Economies: Gender and Property in Early Modern England* (2002) and co-editor (with Jonathan Gil Harris) of *Staged Properties in Early Modern English Drama* (2002).

David Lemmings is an Associate Professor of History in the School of Liberal Arts at The University of Newcastle, Australia. He is the author of *Gentlemen and Barristers: The Inns of Court and the English Bar* (1990) and *Professors of Law: Barristers and English Legal Culture in the Eighteenth Century* (2000).

Mary Murray is Senior Lecturer in Sociology at Massey University, New Zealand. Her main research and teaching interests are in the areas of death and dying, society and emotion, and animals and society. Her publications include *The Law of the Father* (1995).

Patricia Parker is Watkins University Professor of English and Comparative Literature at Stanford University. Her most recent work includes *Women, 'Race,' and Writing in the Early Modern Period,* co-edited with Margo Hendricks, and *Shakespeare from the Margins.* She is currently at work on a new Arden edition of *A Midsummer Night's Dream,* a Norton Critical Edition of *Much Ado about Nothing,* and books on gender, religion, and race in early modern England.

Laura J. Rosenthal is Associate Professor of English at the University of Maryland, College Park. She is the author of *Playwrights and Plagiarists in Early Modern England* (1996) and co-editor (with Mita Choudhury) of *Monstrous Dreams of Reason: Body, Self and Other in the Enlightenment* (2002), and is completing a manuscript on prostitution in eighteenth-century British literature and culture.

Paul Salzman is a Reader in English at La Trobe University, Australia. The editor of a number of anthologies of early modern writing, he has recently published *Literary Culture in Jacobean England: Reading 1621* (2003).

Eleanor F. Shevlin, Assistant Professor of English at West Chester University, Pennsylvania, has published essays on the title as textual practice, cartography and postcolonial fiction, and the relationship between law, property, and the eighteenth-century novel. She is currently working on a print-culture account of the making of the English novel.

Jennifer Summit is an Associate Professor in the English Department at Stanford University. She is the author of *Lost Property: The Woman Writer and English Literary History, 1375–1589* (2000) and articles on women and writing in late medieval and early modern England.

Claire Walker lectures in early modern European History in the School of Liberal Arts at the University of Newcastle, Australia. She is the author of *Gender and Politics in Early Modern Europe: English Convents in France and the Low Countries* (2003), as well as several articles on women religious in the seventeenth century.

Nancy E. Wright is the Director of the Centre for the Interdisciplinary Study of Property Rights at the University of Newcastle, Australia. She is the co-editor (with A.R. Buck and John McLaren) of *Despotic Dominion: Property Rights in British Settler Societies* (2004).

Index